Chinese Religion
Publications in Western Languages
1981 through 1990

About the Compiler

LAURENCE G. THOMPSON, emeritus professor of East Asian Languages and Cultures at the University of Southern California, was a founding member of the Society for the Study of Chinese Religions and its president for nine years. Besides having published many articles on Chinese religion, he is the author of *Chinese Religion: An Introduction* (fourth edition 1989) and *The Chinese Way in Religion* (1973). He is also compiler and editor of the previous two editions of this bibliography.

About the Editor

Gary Seaman is associate professor of anthropology at the University of Southern California. He is translator and commentator of *Journey to the North: pei-yu-chi*. He is presently editing Thompson's six volume translation of Wu Yao-yü's study of the three traditions in Chinese religion, *San-chiao Li-ts'e*. He has also edited several volumes of scholarly works on central and east Asian cultures published by Ethnographics Press.

Association for Asian Studies Monograph No. 47
Rhoads Murphey, Editor

Chinese Religion
Publications in Western Languages
1981 through 1990

Compiled by
Laurence G. Thompson

Edited by
Gary Seaman

Published by
The Association for Asian Studies

Produced for the Association for Asian Studies by
Ethnographics Press
Center for Visual Anthropology
University of Southern California
Los Angeles, CA

Published by the Association for Asian Studies
1 Lane Hall, University of Michigan, Ann Arbor, Michigan 48109

Printed in the U.S.A.

Library of Congress Cataloging-in-Publication Data
Thompson, Laurence G.
    Chinese Religion : publications in Western languages, 1981 through
1990 / compiled by Laurence G. Thompson ; edited by Gary Seaman.
        p. cm. — (Association for Asian Studies monographs ; no. 47)
    A supplementary volume to Chinese religion in Western languages.
    "Produced for the Association for Asian Studies by Ethnographics
Press, Center for Visual Anthropology, University of Southern
California, Los Angeles, CA."
    Includes indexes.
    ISBN 0-924304-13-8 $32.00

    1. China—Religion—Bibliography.   I. Seaman, Gary, 1942-
II. Thompson, Laurence G. Chinese religion in Western languages.
III. Title.   IV. Series: Monographs of the Association for Asian
Studies ; no. 47.

Z7757.C6T556 1993   93-3757
016.2'00951—dc20   CIP

The publication of this volume has been financed from a revolving fund, supported in part by the Luce
Foundation. A full listing of the Association for Asian Studies Monograph Series appears at the end of this
volume.

This volume like its two predecessors is dedicated to my friend

Fred Streng

with respect and appreciation

Foreword

The evolution, rationale, and limitations of this bibliography are explained in the Foreword to the 1985 edition, *Chinese Religion in Western Languages,* which covers publications in the field through 1980. At the time that version was compiled, I certainly had no intention of continuing such work, especially with retirement from teaching coming up in the immediate future. That this supplementary volume has nevertheless been compiled is the fault of several friends and colleagues, who pressed the view that it was somehow my duty to carry on. Karmic justice has brought about that the principal advocate of this thesis has in turn become entangled in the web. I refer to Gary Seaman, who became responsible for editing and producing the book. Without his indispensable cooperation, it is very doubtful that this catalogue would actually have appeared.

I shall not rehearse what was set out in the above-mentioned Foreword of 1985, but merely explain here just what the supplementary volume intends to accomplish: (1) We have attempted to bring together all publications in English, French and German on Chinese religion from 1981 through 1990. (2) We have made extensive corrections and updated many items from the earlier edition. (3) We have added some new categories, and rearranged others, to accord with developments in the field. In certain cases, as for example the Ch'an category or the new Tun-huang categories, we have for the convenience of the user included all the relevant items from the earlier edition, as well as the new items from 1981 through 1990. It will be noted that the Index of the earlier version is included here, along with Index of the present volume. In that regard, it is quite unexpected to find that there are well over 1200 *new* names in the scholarship of just this recent decade.

The march of progress has included among its victims many diacritical marks that we originally intended to use, particularly in the section on Buddhism. It proved just too expensive and time consuming to accommodate these in the word processing program that nowadays replaces printing of the old type. For this we beg the indulgence of Buddhist scholars (as well as those who miss the macrons in some Japanese names). The same practical consideration led us to abandon use of boldface type in the text, and we hope this will not inconvenience the user.

Finally, I want to stress that the obligations and gratitude expressed to many persons in earlier Acknowledgments have in no way diminished, and are here reaffirmed. In the composition of this volume, Mae Horie did the corrections and created the indexes: her assistance was invaluable. I would also like to thank Deborah Williams and Michael Mascha for their help.

Laurence G. Thompson
University of Southern California, emeritus

Table of Contents

Part One
Bibliography, General Treatments
and Other Overall Categories

Part Two
Chinese Religion Exclusive of Buddhism

Part Three
Chinese Buddhism

Part Four
Indices

Abbreviations

A. GENERAL

abbrev/abbreviated
abrmt/abridgement
abstr/abstract
acc/ according
add/additional, additions
ann/année(s)
annot/annotated, annotations
anthol/anthology
app/appendix(es)
arch/architecture, architectural
art/article(s)
assoc/association

bd/band
betw/between
bibliog/bibliography
bk/book
b-&-w/black and white
budd/Buddhist, Buddhism

cat/catalogue
c/century, centuries
chap/chapter(s)
char/characters
chin/China, Chinese, chinois
chron/chronology
col/column(s), color
collab/collaboration, collaborator
comm/commentary
comp/compiled, compiler(s)
corr/corrected, corrigenda

d/date(d)
dept/department
descr/description
diagr/diagram(s)
dir/direction
dyn/dynasty, dynasties

ed/edited, edition, editor(s)
engl/English, England
enl/enlarged
esp/especially
extr/extract(ed)

fasc/fascicule(s)
fig/figure(s)
fr/from

gloss/glossary
govt/government

heraus/herausgegeben
HK/Hong Kong

illus/illustration(s) illustrated
incl/includes, including, included
indiv/individual
inscr/inscription
intl/international
intro/introduction

jap/Japan(csc)
lit/literature
lith/lithographs

mél/mélanges
MIT/Massachusetts Institute of Technology

natl/national
no/number(s)
n.d./no date
n.p./no place
n.s./new series
NY/New York

offpr/offprint
orig/original(ly)

p/page(s)
pl/plate(s)
pop/popular
pref/preface
proc/proceedings
pseud/pseudonym
pt/part(s)
publ/publication, published, publisher

ref/references
reimp/reimpression
relig/religion/religious

repr/reprint(ed)
republ/republished
rev/review(ed), revised

s/seite
sec/section(s)
sel/selected
sep/separate(ly)
ser/series
sér/série
soc/society/social
subj/subject
summ/summary
suppl/supplement

t/tome
trad/traduit
trans/transactions
tsl/translated, translation, translator

übers/übersetzt
univ/university
unk/unknown

vol/volume(s)

Abbreviations

B. Publications

A

AA---Artibus asiae

AAA---Archives of asian art

AAAG---Association of american geographers. Annals.

A&T---Art & thought, issued in honour of dr. ananda k. coomaraswamy on the occasion of his 70th birthday. London (1947)

AArch---Art and archaeology

AB---Art bulletin

AC---Aspects de la chine. Paris, musée guimet (1959)

ACASA---Archives of the chinese art society of america

ACF---Annuaire du collège de france

ACP---Annales de chimie et de physique

ACQ---Asian culture quarterly

AC:SEC---David T. Roy & Tsuen-hsuin Tsien (ed) Ancient china: studies in early civilization. Chin univ hk (1978)

ACSS---Annual of the china society, singapore

ActaA---Acta asiatica

AdSin---Adversaria sinica

AEO---Annales de l'extrême-orient

AGP---Archives of general psychiatry

AIPHO---Annuaire de l'institut de philologie et d'histoire orientale

AJCM---American journal of chinese medicine

AJT---The asia journal of theology. Singapore

AL---Annali lateranensi

AM---Asia major

AmEth---American ethnologist.

AMG---Annales du musée guimet

AMH---Annals of medical history

AMHAV---Asia major, hirth anniversary volume (introductory vol of this journal, pref by ed Bruno Schindler d Oct 1922)

AMS---Charles Leslie (ed) Asian medical systems. Univ calif (1976)

AMZ---Allgemeine missions-zeitschrift

ANA---Art news annual

Ancestors---William H. Newell (ed)Ancestors. The hague (1976)

AnHaf---Leif Littrup (ed) Analecta hafniensia: 25 years of east asian studies in copenhagen, London (1988)

AnnEPHE---Annuaire, école pratique des hautes études

AnthroTS---E M. Ahern & Hill Gates (ed) The anthropology of taiwanese society. Stanford univ. (1981)

AO---Acta orientalia (Copenhagen)

AofA---Arts of asia

AP---Aryan path

APC---Annales de philosophie chrétienne

APQCSA---Asian & pacific quarterly of cultural and social affairs

AQ---Art quarterly

AQR---Asiatic quarterly review

AR---Asiatic review

AR-HR---Harry Partin (comp) Asian religions-history of religions: 1974 proceedings; preprinted papers for the section on asian religions-history of religions, annual meeting of american academy of religion. Florida state univ (1974)

ArsO---Ars orientalis. The arts of islam and the east

ARW---Archiv für religionswissenschaft

ArchOr---Archiv orientální

ArtsAs---Arts asiatiques

AS---Asiatische studien; études asiatiques

ASAB---Annales de la société royale d'archaeologie, bruxelles

AsArt---Asian art. Oxford univ in assoc with arthur m. sackler gallery, smithsonian institution

ASBIE---Academia sinica, bulletin of the institute of ethnology (Taipei)

ASBIHP---Academia sinica, bulletin of the institute of history and philology (Taipei)

AsFS---Asian folklore studies

Asiatica---Asiatica; festschrift friedrich weller zum 80. geburstag überreicht. Leipzig (1954)

Asien---Lydia Brüll & Ulrich Kemper (ed) Asien: Tradition und fortschritt. Festschrift für horst hammitzsch zu seinem 60.geburstag. Wiesbaden (1971)

ASONT---Marjorie Topley (ed) Aspects of social organization in the new territories, hong kong. HK (1965)

ASR---Archives de sociologie des religions

ASSR---Archives de sciences sociales des religions

AsSur---Asian survey

ATOW---Wilhelm Bitter (heraus) Abendländische therapie und östliche weisheit; ein tagungstericht. Stuttgart (1967)

ATS---Asian thought & society: an international review

AUFS---American universities field staff

AV---Archiv für völkerkunde

AWGN---Akademie der wissenschaft in göttingen, philologisch-historischeklasse, nachrichten

B

BAAFC---Bulletin de l'association amicale franco-chinoise

BAF---Bulletin asie-française

BAIC---Bulletin of the art institute of chicago

B&J---Harish Chandra Das et al (ed) Buddhism and jainism. Cuttack, orissa (1976)

BAV---Boas anniversary volume; anthropological papers written in honor of franz boas . . .NY (1906)

BCAR---B.C. asian review

BCL---D. R. Bhandarker et al (ed) B.c. law volume. Calcutta, pt 1(1945) pt 2 (1946)

BCMA---Bulletin of the cleveland museum of art

BCS---Buddhist-christian studies

BCUP---Bulletin of the catholic univer-sity of peking

BDIA---Bulletin of the denver institute of arts

BDetIA---Bulletin of the detroit insti-tute of arts

BEA---Bulletin of eastern art

BEFEO---Bulletin de l'école française d'extrême-orient

BetSA ---Alain Forest, Eiichi Kato & Léon Vandermersch (dir) Bouddhismes et sociétés asiatiques; clergés, sociétés et pouvoirs. Paris & tokyo-sophia univ-(1990).

BFoggMA---Bulletin of the fogg museum of art

BGCSE---John Carman & Mark Juergensmeyer (ed supervisors) A bibliographic guide to the comparative study of ethics. Cambridge univ (1991)

BHerm---Donald S. Lopez jr (ed) Buddhist hermeneutics. Univ hawaii (1988)

BHM---Bulletin of the history of medicine

BIHM---Bulletin of the institute of the history of medicine

BJP---British journal of psychiatry

BJS---British journal of sociology. London. 1-(1950)

BlM---Blackwood's magazine

BM---Burlington magazine

BMFA---Bulletin of the museum of fine arts (Boston)

BMFEA---Bulletin of the museum of far eastern antiquities (Stockholm)

BMFJ---Bulletin de la maison franco-japonaise

BMMA---Bulletin of the metropolitan museum of art (NY)

BMQ---British museum quarterly

BMSAP---Bulletin et mémoires de la société d'anthropologie de paris

BOR---Babylonian and oriental record

BROMA---Bulletin of the royal ontario museum of archaeology

BSAB---Bulletin de la société royale belge d'anthropologie, bruxelles

BSEIS---Bulletin de la société d'études indochinoises de saigon

BSOAS---Bulletin of the school of oriental and african studies (Univ london)

BSR---Buddhist studies review

BSYS---Bulletin of sung and yuan studies. Through 13 (1977) titled Sung studies newsletter.

BT&AC---Leslie S. Kawamura & Keith Scott (ed) Buddhist thought and asian civilization: essays in honour of herbert v. guenther on his sixtieth birthday. Emeryville, calif (1977)

BTLVK---Bijdragen tot de taal-, land- en volkskunde

BTS—I---Michael Saso & David W. Chappell (ed) Buddhist and taoist studies-l. Univ hawaii (1977)

BTTSoc---Buddhist text translation society, affiliate of sino-american buddhist association, san francisco

BUA---Bulletin de l'université l'aurore (Shanghai)

BuddIcon---Buddhist iconography. New delhi (1989)

BuddSt---Buddhist studies

BVAMG---Bibliothèque de vulgarisation des annales du musée guimet

C

CAAP---Ro Bong Rin (ed) Christian alternatives to ancestor practices. Taichung (1985)

CalR---Calcutta review

C&C---James D. Whitehead, Yu-ming Shaw & Norman J. Girardot (ed) China and christianity. Historical and future encounters. Notre dame univ (1979)

C&EO---Robin W. Lovin & Frank E. Reynolds (ed) Cosmogony and ethical order. Univ chicago (1985)

CB---Current background (U.S. consulate general, HK)

CBA---Robert E. Buswell jr (ed) Chinese buddhist apocrypha. Univ hawaii (1990)

CBS---William P. Lebra (ed) Culture-bound syndromes, ethnopsychiatry, and alternate therapies. Univ hawaii (1976)

CBWK---Chinesische blätter für wissenschaft und kunst

CbyM---Timothy Richard. Conversion by the million in china. Shanghai, vol 1 (1907)

CC---Chinese culture (Taipei)

CCHC---Michael Loewe. Crisis and conflict in han china. London (1974)

CCJ---Chung chi journal

CCS---Collectanea commisionis synodalis.Peking (1935)

CCY---China christian yearbook

CD---B. C. Henry. The cross and the dragon.NY (1885)

CDA---Chinesisch-deutsch almanach

CE---Eugene N. Anderson jr & Marja L.Anderson. Mountains and water: essays on the cultural ecology of south coastal china. Taipei (1973)

CEA---Cahiers d'extrême-asie

CEB---Paul Demiéville. Choix d'études bouddhiques (1929-1970) Leiden (1973)

CEC---Cahiers d'études chinoises

CEd---Chinese education

CES---Paul Demiéville. Choix d'études sinologiques (1921-1970) Leiden (1973)

CETH 1---Michel Soymié (dir) Contributions aux études sur touen-houang, vol 1. Paris (1979)

CETH 3---Michel Soymié (dir) Contributions aux études sur touen-houang, vol 3. Paris (1984)

CF---Ching feng

CFL&SC---David C. Buxbaum (ed) Chinese family law and social change. Univ washington(1978)

CFQ---California folklore quarterly

CFRB---Hsieh Jih-chang & Chuang Ying-chang (ed) The chinese family and its ritual behavior. Taipei (1985) Institute of ethnology, academia sinica.

CFRSM---John R. Clammer (ed) Studies in chinese folk religion in singapore and malaysia. Singapore univ, dept of sociology (aug 1983)

CHAS---Arthur Kleinman et al (ed) Culture and healing in asian societies. Cambridge, mass (1978)

ChBudd---W. Pachow. Chinese buddhism: aspects of interaction and reinterpretation.Washington d.c. (1980)

CHC---Cambridge history of china. Cambridge univ, multi-vol.

CH&NC---Chan, Wing-tsit (ed) Chu hsi and neo-confucianism. Univ hawaii (1986)

ChFor---China forum

ChLit---Chinese Literature: essays. articles, reviews. Madison, wis

CHM---Cahiers d'histoire mondiale

CH:NS---Chan Wing-tsit. Chu hsi: new studies. Univ hawaii (1989)

ChPen---The chinese pen. Taipei.

ChrCent---Christian century

ChRec---Chinese recorder

ChRep---Chinese repository

ChRev---China review

ChSci---Chinese science

CIHR---Congrès internationale d'histoire des religions

CINS---Charles LeBlanc & Susan Blader (ed) Chinese ideas about nature and society: studies in honour of derk bodde. Univ HK (1987)

CISE---Congrès internationale des sciences ethnographiques, session de 1878

CJ---China journal

CL---Chinese Literature. Peking

CLG---Chinese law and government

CLIC---G. William Skinner (ed) The city in late imperial china. Stanford univ (1977)

CM---Charles A. Moore (ed) The chinese mind.Univ hawaii (1967)

CM&P---Culture, medicine, and psychiatry

CMBA---China Missionary; later China missionary bulletin; later Mission bulletin, later Asia

CME&W---Comparative medicine east and west

CMG---Conférences faites au musée guimet

CMH---China mission hand-book

CMI---Church missionary intelligencer

CMJ---Chinese medical journal

CN---China notes

CNA---China news analysis

CP---Arthur F. Wright and Denis Twitchett (ed) Confucian personalities. Stanford univ(1962)

CPOL---Congrès provinciale des orientalistes, lyon (1878)

CQ---China quarterly

CR---Contemporary review

CRAIBL---Comptes rendus de l'académie des inscriptions et belles-lettres

CRJ---Contemporary religions in japan

CRecon---China reconstructs

CRWMS---W. Moese, G. Reinknecht & E Schmitz-Seisser. Chinese regionalism in west-malaysia and singapore. Hamburg, MDGNVO 77 (1979)

CSA---Chinese sociology and anthropology

CSH---Chinese studies in history. Journal of translations.

CSM---Chinese students' monthly

CSP---Chinese studies in philosophy. Journal of translations.

CSPSR---Chinese social and political science review

CSSH---Comparative studies in society and history

CSWT---Ch'ing-shih wen-t'i. With 6.1 (june 1985) title changes to Late imperial china, abbrev LIC.

CTA---Nancy Shatzman Steinhardt (ed) Chinese traditional architecture. NY (1984)

CTI---John K. Fairbank (ed) Chinese thought and institutions. Univ chicago (1957)

CToday---T. T. Lew et al. China today through chinese eyes. NY, lst ser (n.d.—1922) 2nd ser, london (1926)

CW---Catholic world

CWayRel---Laurence G. Thompson (ed) The chinese way in religion. Encino and belmont, calif. (1973)

CWR---China weekly review

CYT---E T. Williams. China yesterday and today. NY(1923 et seq; 4th ed (1928)

D

D&A---Dialogue and alliance

DBT---Roy C. Amore (ed) Developments in buddhist thought: canadian contributions to buddhist studies. Wilfrid laurier univ (1979)

DeathRit---James L. Watson & Evelyn S. Rawski (ed) Death ritual in late imperial and modern china. Univ calif (1988)

Deviance ---Amy A. Wilson, Sidney L. Greenblatt & Richard R. Wilson (ed) Deviance and social control in chinese society. NY (1977)

DR---J. M. Reid (ed) Doomed religions: a series of essays on great religions of the world. NY and cincinnati (1884)

DV---Justus Doolittle (ed) Vocabulary and handbook of the chinese language. Foochow (1872) 2 vol

E

EA---East of asia

EAC-2---Wolfram Eberhard, K. Gawlikowski & C. A. Seyschab (ed) East asian civilization, no. 2: nation and mythology. Federal republic of germany [verlag simon & magiera] (1983)

EAJT---East asia journal of theology

EarlyCC---Chang Kwang-chih. Early chinese civilization. Harvard univ (1976)

EArt---Eastern art

EB---Eastern Buddhist

EBio---Encyclopedia of bioethics. Georgetown univ (1978)

EC---Early china

ECA---Noel Barnard (ed) Early chinese art and its possible influence in the pacific basin. "Authorized taiwan edition" (1974) Orig publ (1972) repudiated by ed.

ECC---Derk Bodde. Essays on chinese civilization. Ed & intro Charles Le Blanc & Dorothy Borei

Ec&Emp---Gary Seaman (ed) Ecology and empire: nomads in the cultural evolution of the old world. Los Angeles, Univ southern calif, center for visual anthropology (1989)

EH---Eastern horizon

EJ---Eranos jahrbuch

ELC---Edwin Joshua Dukes. Everyday life in china. London (1885)

EM---Encyclopédie moderne

EMM---Evangelisches missions-magazin

EMO---M. M. Davy (dir) Encyclopédie des mystiques orientales. ?Paris (1975)

EncyA---Encyclopedia americana

EncyB---Encyclopaedia britannica

EncyP:HR---Encylopédie de la pléiade. Histoire des religions. Paris (1976)

EncyRel---The encyclopedia of religion. Mircea Eliade (ed in chief) NY & london (1987) 16 vol

EncyUniv---Encyclopaedia universalis. Paris. Ed of (1990)

EncyWA---Encyclopaedia of world art. NY (1959-68)

EncyWF---The encyclopedia of world faiths. NY & oxford (1987)

E0E0---Extrême-orient extrême occident; cahier de recherches comparatives

EORL---Études d'orientalisme, publiées par le musée guimet à la mémoire de raymond linossier.

EP---Essays in philosophy of the university of chicago. Univ chicago (1929)

ER---Études religieuses

ERTh---Evangelical review of theology.

ESC---Études sociologiques sur la chine. Collected papers of Marcel Granet. Préface Louis Gerner, intro R. A. Stein. Paris (1953)

ESCBP---Eugene N. Anderson jr.

Essays on south china's boat people. Taipei (1972)

ESCH---Donald D. Leslie, Colin Mackerras & Wang Gung-wu (ed) Essays on the sources for chinese history. Australian natl univ (1973) univ south carolina (1975)

EsurR ---Essais sur rituel. II. Coloque du centenaire de la section des sciences religieuses de l'école pratique des hautes études. Anne-marie Blondeau et Kristopher Schipper (dir) Louvain-Paris (1990)

ET---Expository times

EtCh---Etudes chinoises. Paris. 1- (1983)

EtSong---Francoise Aubin (ed) Etudes song; in memoriam étienne balazs. Sér 1, Histoire et institutions, no. 2 (1971) no. 3 (1976) Sér 2, Civilisation, no. 1 (1973)

EtTrad---Etudes traditionnelles. Paris.

Etudes---Études des pères de la compagnie de jésus

EUF---Encyclopaedia universalis france. Paris (1968)

EW---Eastern world

EWCR---East-west center review

ExHum---Agehananda Bharati (ed) The realm of the extra-human: agents and audience. The hague (1976)

EZT---Essays on the history of buddhism presented to professor zenryu tsukamoto. Kyoto university (1961)

E&W---East and west

F

FA---France-asie

FA:BPB---René de Berval (ed) Présence du bouddhisme (FA 16,1959)

FC---G. Kemp. The face of china. NY (1909)

FCR---Free china review

FE---Far east

FEER---Far eastern economic review

FEQ---Far eastern quarterly

FestColpe---Christoph Elsas & Hans G. Kippenburg et al (heraus) Loyalitätskonflikte in der religionsgeschichte: festschrift für carsten colpe. Würzburg (1990)

FF---Fortschungen und fortschritte

FKCS---Maurice Freedman (ed) Family and kinship in chinese society. Stanford univ(1970)

FLJ---Folk-lore journal

FMB---Field museum bulletin

FO---Ferne osten

FRWVSP---Folk religion and the worldview in the southwestern pacific. Tokyo (1968)

FS---Folklore studies

FT---Holmes Welch & Anna Seidel (ed) Facets of taoism. Essays in chinese religion. Yale univ (1979)

FukienD&D---Edward B. Vermeer (ed) Development and decline of fukien province in the 17th and 18th centuries. Leiden (1990)

FW/CG---Hans Waldenfels & Thomas Immoos (heraus) Fernöstliche weisheit und christlicher glaube. Festgabe für heinrich dumoulin s.j. zur vollendung des 80. lebensjahres. Mainz (1985)

G

G&R---Caroline Walker Bynum et al (ed) Gender and religion: on the complexity of symbols. Boston (1986)

GBA---Gazette des beaux-arts

GC---Genevieve Wimsatt. A griffin in china. NY & london (1927)

GCR---Sebastian A. Matczak (ed) God in contemporary thought; a philosophical perspective. NY etc (1977)

GE---La grande encyclopédie

GM---Geographical magazine

Goddesses---Larry W. Hurtado (ed) Goddesses in religions and modern debate. Univ manitoba (1990)

H

H&SC---Tu Wei-ming. Humanity and self-cultivation: essays in confucian thought. Berkeley, calif (1979)

HCP-HR---Henri-Charles Puech (ed) Histoire des religions. T 1, Les religions antique... Paris (1970)

HERE---James Hastings (ed) Encyclopaedia of religion and ethics. 13 vol (1908-26)

HET---Graham Parkes (ed) Heidegger and eastern thought. Univ hawaii (1987)

HFHD---Homer H. Dubs (tsl) The history of the former han dynasty by pan ku. Baltimore. 3 vol: (1938, 1944, 1955)

HHM---Hommage à henri maspero. Paris (1984)

HHYC:CS---Han-hsüeh yen-chiu; chinese studies. Taipei.

HJ---Hibbert journal

HJAS---Harvard journal of asiatic studies

HKS---Symposium on historical, archaeological and linguistic studies on southern china, south east asia and the hong kong region. HK (1967)

HLC---Isaac Taylor Headland. Home life in china. NY (1914)

HM---Histoire de la médecine

HMRC---Henri Maspero. Les religions chinoises. Mélanges posthumes sur les religions et l'histoire de la chine, t 1. Paris (1950)

HPEW---S. Radhakrishnan (ed) History of philosophy, eastern and western. London (1952)

HR---History of religions

HRAF---Human relations area files

HR&WR---Leroy S. Rouner (ed) Human rights and the world's religions. Univ notre dame (1988)

HTR---Harvard theological review

HZ---Hansei zasshi

I

IA---Indian antiquary

I&B---Indianisme et bouddhisme. Mélanges offerts à mgr e. lamotte. Louvain- la-neuve (1980)

IAC---Indo-asian culture

IAE---Internationales archiv für ethnographie

IAF---Internationales asien forum

I&C---Sarvapelli Radhakrishnan. India and china. Lectures delivered in china may 1944. Bombay, 3rd ed (1954)

I&S---Issues and studies

IAQR---Imperial and asiatic quarterly review

IBFQ---International buddhist forum quarterly

ICG---Indo-chinese gleaner

ICO---International congress of orientalists

ICHR---International congress for the history of religions

ICR---International congress of religions

ICTCL---William H. Nienhauser jr et al (ed) The indiana companion to traditional chinese literature. Indiana univ (1986)

IHQ---Indian historical quarterly

IJSP---International journal of social psychiatry

Incontro---Lionello Lanciotti (ed) Incontro di religioni in asia tra il III e il X secolo d.c. Firenze (1984)

India---India antiqua. A volume of oriental studies presented to jean philippe vogel. Leiden (1947)

IntC---Mrs Archibald Little. Intimate china. London (n. d.—ca. 1900)

IPQ---International philosophical quarterly

IQB---Iqbal, later Iqbal review

IRM---International review of missions

ISCI---International symposium on chinese-western cultural interchange in commemoration of the 400th anniversary of the arrival of matteo ricci, s.j. in china. Fu-jen univ (1983)

J

JA---Journal asiatique

JAAR---Journal of the american academy of religion

JAAS---Journal of asian and african studies

JAC---Journal of asian culture

JAFL---Journal of american folk-lore

JAH---Journal of asian history

JAK---Jahrbuch der asiatischen kunst

JAOS---Journal of the american oriental society

JAS---Journal of asian studies

JBBRAS---Journal of the bombay branch, royal asiatic society

JCE---Journal of chemical engineering

JCS---Journal of the china society, taipei

JCLTA---Journal of the chinese language teachers association

JCP---Journal of chinese philosophy

JCStudies---Journal of chinese studies.

JCUHK---Journal of the chinese university of hong kong

JD---Journal of dharma

JEAC---Journal of esthetics and art criticism

JHI---Journal of the history of ideas

JHKBRAS---Journal of the hong kong branch, royal asiatic society

JHMAS---Journal of the history of medicine and allied sciences

JHP---Journal of humanistic psychology

JIA---Journal of the indian archipelago

JIABS---Journal of the international association of buddhist studies

JIBS---Journal of indian and buddhist studies: Indogaku bukkyogaku kenkyu

JIC---Journal of intercultural studies

JICS---Journal of the institute of chinese studies of the chinese university of hong kong. Replaced by JICS:CUHK

JICS:CUHK---Journal of the institute of chinese studies, chinese university of hong kong.

JISOA---Journal of the indian society of oriental art

JJRS---Japanese journal of religious studies. Tokyo.

JMBRAS---Journal of the malayan branch, royal asiatic society

JMGS---Journal of the manchester geographical society

JMP---Journal of medicine and philosophy.

JNCBRAS---Journal of the north china branch, royal asiatic society

JOR---Journal of oriental research (Madras)

JOS---Journal of oriental studies (Univ HK)

JOSA---Journal of the oriental society of australia

JPOS---Journal of the peking oriental society

JPTS---Journal of the pali text society

JQ---Japan quarterly

JR---Journal of religion

JRAS---Journal of the royal asiatic society

JRASB---Journal of the royal asiatic society of bengal

JRE---Journal of religious ethics

JRH---Journal of religious history

JRLB---John rylands library, bulletin

JRS---Journal of ritual studies. Univ Pittsburgh

JSBRAS---Journal of the straits branch, royal asiatic society

JSEAS---Journal of southeast asian studies

JSMVL---Jahrbuch der stadtliches museums für völkerkunde zu leipzig

JSR:HS---Japan science review: humanistic studies

JSR:LPH---Japan science review: literature, philosophy and history

JSS---Journal of social science, national taiwan university college of law

JSiamSoc---Journal of the siam society. Bangkok. 1- (1904)

JSSR---Journal for the scientific study of religion

JTP---Journal of transpersonal psychology

JWCBorderResS---Journal of the west china border research society

K

KDBR---Kansai daigaku bunka ronshu

KdeO---Kunst des orients

KGUAS---Kwansei gakuin university annual studies

KT:OS---Keleti Tanu/manyok. Oriental studies

L

L&S---John McGowan. Lights and shadows of chinese life. Shanghai (1909)

LD---Light of dharma

LIC---Late imperial china. New title superseding CSWT with 6.1 (june 1985)

LL&R---Sarah Allan & Alvin P. Cohen (ed) Legend, lore, and religion in china: essays in honor of wolfram eberhard on his seventieth birthday. San francisco (1979)

LO---M. Kern (ed) Das licht des ostens. Stuttgart (1922)

LSS---W. L. Idema (ed) Leyden studies in sinology (1981)

LTY:SP---Liu Ts'un-yan. Selected papers from the hall of harmonious wind. Leiden (1976)

M

MA---William Watson (ed) Mahayanist art after a.d.900 . . .

MAI---Mémoires de littérature tirés des registres de l'académie des inscriptions

MAIBL---Mémoires de l'académie des inscriptions et belles-lettres

M&HS---Eric J. Sharpe & John R. Hinnels (ed) Man and his salvation: studies in memory of s. f. g. brandon. Manchester univ (1973)

M&M---Phyllis Granoff & Shinohara Koichi (ed) Monks and magicians: religious biographies in asia. Oakville, calif (1988)

MB---Maha bodhi

MBM---Minoru Kiyota (ed) Mahayana buddhist meditation: theory and practice. Univ hawaii (1978)

MC---Missions catholiques

MCAM---Mémoires couronnés et autre mémoires, académie royale de belgique

MCB---Mélanges chinois et bouddhiques

MCC---Arthur Kleinman et al (ed) Medicine in chinese cultures: comparative studies of health care in chinese and other societies. Washington d.c. US dept of HEW (1975)

MCLC---Mémoires concernant l'histoire, les sciences, les arts, les moeurs, les usages etc des chinois, par les missionaires de pékin

MCSJ---Mémoires du comité sinico-japonais

MDGNVO---Mitteilungen der deutschen gesellschaft für natur- und völkerkunde ostasiens. Tokyo

MEO---Message d'extrême-orient

MetC---Mythes et croyances du monde entier, t.4. Paris (1985)

MexICHS---30th international congress of human sciences in asia and north africa (formerly ICO) El colegio de méxico. Proceedings (1976) See vol 2, china

MIHEC---Mélanges, paris universitaire institut des hautes études chinoises

MingSt---Ming studies

MIOF---Mitteilungen, deutsche (preussische) akademie der wissenschaften zu berlin (institut für orientforschung)

MIWR---Charles Wei-hsun Fu & Gerhard Spiegler (ed) Movements and issues in world religions, vol 1: Religion, ideology, and politics. NY etc (1987)

MJ---Museum journal

MLA---Magazin für die literatur des auslandes

MMDFL---Hugo Kuhn and Kurt Schier (ed) Märchen, mythos, dichtung: festschrift, Zum 90. geburtstag friedrich von der leyens...München (1963)

MN---Monumenta nipponica

ModCh---Modern china. Beverly hills, Calif. 1.- (1975)

MRT---Steven T. Katz (ed) Mysticism and religious traditions. Oxford univ (1983)

MRW---Missionary review of the world

MS---Monumenta serica

MS/CA---Actes du XXIXe ICO, sec organisée par Michel Soymié: chine ancienne (pre-modem china) Paris (1977)

MSGFOK---Mitteilungen der schweitzerischen gesellschaft der freunde ostasiatische kultur

MSL---Mémorial sylvain lévi. Paris (1937)

MSOS---Mitteilungen des seminars für orientalische sprachen

MSPD---Mélanges de sinologie offerts à monsieur paul demiéville. Paris. T 1 (1966) t 2 (1974)

MSVC---Wolfram Eberhard. Moral and social values of the chinese: collected essays. Taipei (1971)

MW---Middle way

MWSt---Wolfgang Schluchter (heraus) Max webers studie über konfuzianismus und taoismus; interpretation und kritik. Frankfurt am main (1983)

N

NABCC---Arthur Kleinman & T. -Y. Lin (ed) Normal and abnormal behavior in chinese culture. Dordrecht (1980)

Nachr-DGNVO---Nachrichten der deutschen gesellschaft für natur- und völkerkunde ostasiens, hamburg

NC---Nineteenth century

NC&O---Arthur E. Moule. New china and old. London (n.d.—ca.1900)

NC:CR---Michael Chu (ed) The new china: a catholic response. NY (1977)

NCE---New catholic encyclopedia. Catholic univ of america (1967, 1988)

NCEduc---Chaffee, John W. & William Theodore deBary (ed) Neo-confucian education: the formative stage. Univ calif (1989)

NCELYY---Frederick Wakeman, jr (ed) 'Nothing concealed': essays in honor of liu yü-yün. Taipei (1970)

NCET---Soymié, Michel (dir) Nouvelles contributions aux études de touan-houang. Genève (1981) This is in fact CETH vol 2.

NCH---North china herald

NCR---New china review

NEAJT---Northeast asia journal of theology

NGM---National geographic magazine

NH---Natural history

NLIP---Natural law institute proceedings (Univ notre dame)

NO---New Orient

NPBR---Anthony K. Warder (ed) New paths in buddhist research. Durham, north carolina (1985)

NPMB---National palace museum bulletin (Taipei)

NQ---Notes and queries on china and japan

NR---Nouvelle revue

NRJ---National reconstruction journal

NZM---Neue zeitschrift für missionswissenschaft

O

OA---Oriental art

OC---Open court

OE---Oriens extremus

OL---Orientalische literaturzeitung

OLIC---Liu Kwang-ching (ed) Orthodoxy in late imperial china. Univ calif (1990)

OM---Overland monthly

OR---Ostasiatische rundschau

OSCEP---Val Dastur Cursetji Pavri (ed) Oriental studies in honor of cursetji evachji pavri. London (1933)

OstL---Ostasiatische lloyd (shanghai)

OZ---Ostasiatische zeitschift

P

PA---Pacific affairs

PAAAS---Proceeding of the american academy of arts and sciences

PC---People's china

PCCS---David K. Jordan & Marc J. Swartz (ed) Personality and the cultural construction of society. Univ alabama (1990)

PCEW---Charles A. Moore (ed) Philosophy and culture east and west. Univ hawaii (1962)

PCIEEO---Première congrès internationale d'études d'extrême-orient, hanoi (1902)

PEW---Philosophy east and west

PFEH---Australian natl univ, papers in far eastern history

PFV---Paranavitana felicitation volume on art and architecture presented to senarat paranavitana. Colombo (1966)

PIAHA---Proceedings of the 2nd biennial conference, international association of historians of asia. Taipei (1963)

PIAJ---Proceedings of the imperial academy of japan

PJGG---Philosophisches jahrbuch der görres-gesellschaft

PM&MD---Soymié, Michel (ed) Les peintures murales et les manuscrits de dunhuang. Paris (1984)

PMB---Philadelphia museum bulletin

PMK---Pearls of the middle kingdom. A selection of articles from the national palace museum monthly of chinese art. Taipei (1984)

PMSS---Jean Chesneaux (ed) Popular movements and secret societies in china 1840-1950. Stanford univ (1972)

PopCult---David Johnson, Andrew J. Nathan & Evelyn S. Rawski (ed) Popular culture in late imperial china: diversity and integration. Univ. calif (1985)

PR---Peking review

PrAnthro---Practical anthropology

ProcC&S---Proceedings of the first international symposium on church and state in china: past and present. Taipei (1987)

ProcICS---Proceedings of the first international conference on sinology, academia sinica, taipei, 1980. Taipei (1981)

PRPCC---Clarence B. Day. Popular religion in pre-communist china. San francisco (1975)

PRS---Lewis Lancaster (ed) Prajnaparamita and related systems. Studies in honor of edward conze. Berkeley, calif (1977)

PS---Popular science monthly

Psychologia---Psychologia; international journal of psychology in the orient

P-S---Carolyn T. Brown (ed) Psycho-sinology. The universe of dreams in chinese culture. Lanham, md (1988)

PT---People's tribune

PTP---Phi theta papers

PW---Pacific world

Q

QE---The quest for eternity. Los angeles county museum of art, & san francisco, chronicle books (1987)

QJCA---Quarterly journal of current acquisitions, u.s. library of congress

QNCCR---Quarterly notes on christianity and chinese religion (HK)

R

RA---Revue archéologique

RAA---Revue des arts asiatiques

R&Rev---Guenter Lewy. Religion and revolution. Oxford univ (1974)

RC---Relations de chine (Kiangnan)

RCCS---Albert R. O'Hara. Research on changes of chinese society. Taipei (1971)

RCDA---Religion in communist dominated areas

RCHK---James Hayes. The rural communities of hong kong; studies and themes. Oxford univ (1983)

RCL---Religion in communist lands.

RDC---Rodney L. Taylor. The religious dimensions of confucianism. SUNY (1990)

RDChArch---Recent discoveries in chinese archaeology. Beijing (1984)

RDH---Revue des droits de l'homme

RDM---Revue de deux mondes

RDR---Ryukoku daigaku ronshu, the journal of ryukoku univ

RE---Revue d'ethnologie

RECEL---Les rapports entre la chine et l'europe des lumières; actes due IIe colloque international de sinology, 16-18 sept. 1977, chantilly. paris (1980)

RechScRelig---Recherches de sciences religieuse

RelEd---Religious education

Religion---Religion. A journal of religion and religions

Renditions---Renditions. A chinese-english translation magazine

REO---Revue de l'extrême-orient

RFEA---George A. Vos & Takao Sofue (ed) Religion and the family in east asia. Univ calif (1986)

RGI---Revue géographique internationale

RH---Religious humanism

RHR---Revue de l'histoire des religions

RIC---Revue indochinoise

RIID---Charles Wei-hsun Fu & Gerhard Spiegler (ed) Religious issues and inter-religious dialogues. An analysis and sourcebook of developments since 1945. NY etc (1989)

RMHA-PU---Record of the museum of historic art, princeton univ

RMM---Revue de métaphysique et de morale

ROA---Revue de l'orient et de l'algérie

RofR---Review of religion

RO/OR---David Johnson (ed) Ritual opera, operatic ritual. "Mu-lien rescues his mother" in chinese popular culture. Univ calif institute of east asian studies (1989)

RPO-A---Gert Naundorf et al (ed) Religion und philosophie in ost-asien. Festschrift für hans steininger. Würzburg (1985)

RR---Revue des religions

RRCS---Arthur P. Wolf (ed) Religion and ritual in chinese society. Stanford univ (1974)

RRR---Janos M. Bak & Gerhard Benecke (ed) Religion and rural revolt. Manchester univ (1984)

RS---Religious studies

RS&P---Richard H. Cox (ed) Religious systems and psychotherapy. Springfield, ill (1973)

RSJ---Religious studies in japan. Tokyo (1959)

RSO---Revista degli studia orientali

RSR---Religious studies review

RSW---Religious systems of the world. London and NY (1889 et seq)

RTrad---Religion traditions

R-WAW---Rheinisch-Westfälische akademie der wissenschaften

S

SA---Robert K. Sakai (ed) Studies on asia 1963. Univ nebraska (1963)

S&G---Peter N. Gregory (ed) Sudden and gradual: approaches to enlightenment in chinese thought. Honolulu (1987)

SAR---Sino-american relations

SarGaz---Sarawak gazette. Kuching.

SAWW---Sitzungsberichte der . . . akademie der wissenschaften in wien (phil.-hist. klasse)

SCEAR---Studies in central and east asian religions

SCHY---Robert M. Gimello & Peter N. Gregory (ed) Studies in ch'an and hua-yen. Honolulu (1983)

SCFRE---Wolfram Eberhard. Studies in chinese folklore and related essays. Indiana univ (1970)

SCMM---Survey of china mainland magazines (U.S. consulate general, HK)

SCMP---Survey of the china mainland press

SCP---Stories from china's past: han dynasty pictorial tomb reliefs and archaeological objects from sichuan province, people's republic of china. San francisco (1987)

SCR---Studies in comparative religion

SCT---Arthur F. Wright (ed) Studies in chinese thought. Univ chicago (1953)

SEAJSocSci---Southeast asia journal of social science. Singapore.

SEAJT---South east asia journal of theology

SES---Senri ethnological studies

SF---Uno Seiichi et al (ed) Studies on oriental culture. A collection of articles in commemoration of the seventieth birthday of dr. yoshijiro suzuki. Tokyo (1942) All art in jap except for 2

SG---S. F. G. Brandon (ed) The saviour god: comparative studies in the concept of salvation. Manchester univ(1963)

SHB---A. K. Narain (ed) Studies in the history of buddhism. Delhi (1980)

SICS---Sidney L. Greenblatt, Ridchard W. Wilson & Amy Auerbach Wilson (ed) Social interaction in chinese society, NY(1982)

SIEW---Charles A. Moore (ed) with assistance of Aldyth V. Morris. The status of the individual in east and west. Univ hawaii (1968)

SIJ---Sino-indian journal

SinSon---Sinica sonderausgabe (1934)

SIS---Sino-indian studies

SJ---Silliman journal

SJFAW---Sino-japonica; festschrift andré wedemeyer zum 80. geburstag. Leipzig (1956)

SJV---Silver jubilee volume, kyoto university; jimbun kagaku kenkyu-sho (1954)

SLC---Justus Doolittle. Social life of the chinese. NY, 2 vol (1865), repr Singapore (1986)

SM---Studia missionalia

SOERF---Maurice Freedman (ed) Social organization. Essays presented to raymond firth. London (1967)

SpF---James Bogan & Fred Goss (ed) Sparks of fire: blake in a new age. Richmond calif (1982)

SPRCM---Selections from peoples republic of china magazines

SR/DP---D. Klimburg Salter (ed) The silk route and the diamond path: esoteric buddhist art on the trans-himalaya trade routes. UCLA art council catalog (1982)

SR/SR---Sciences religieux/studies in religion

SS---Studia serica

SSBKD---Søren Egerod (ed) Studia serica bernhard karlgren dedicata. Copenhagen (1959)

SSCRB---Society for the study of chinese religions, bulletin

SSM---Social science and medicine

SSM/FHF---Wolfgang Bauer (ed)

Studia sino-mongolica: festschrift für herbert franke.Wiesbaden (1979)

SSMT---William Theodore deBary (ed) Self and society in ming thought. Columbia univ (1970)

SSP---Schafer sinological papers

StAs---Laurence G. Thompson (ed) Studia asiatica. Essays in felicitation of the seventy-fifth anniversary of professor ch'en shou-yi. San Francisco (1975)

STR&MT---Tsao Pen-yeh & Daniel P. L. Law (ed) Studies of taoist rituals and music of today. Chin univ HK (1989)

Stupa---Anna Libera Dallapiccola & Stephanie Zingel-Avé Lallemant (ed) The stupa—its religious, historical and architectural significance. Wiesbaden (1980)

SW---W. S. McCullough (ed) The seed of wisdom: essays in honor of t.j. meek. Univ toronto (1964)

SWJA---Southwestern journal of anthropology

Synthesis---Synthesis; the undergraduate journal in the history and philosophy of science

SyY:T&W---Ssu yü yen: Thought & word

T

TAC---Susan Bush & Christian Murck (ed) Theories of the arts in china. Princeton univ (1983)

T&L---W. L. Idema & E. Zürcher (ed) Thought and law in qin and han china: studies dedicated to anthony hulsewé on the occasion of his eightieth birthday. Leiden (1990)

T&T---Frank E. Reynolds & Theodore M. Ludwig (ed) Transitions and transformations in the history of religions. Essays in honor of joseph m. kitagawa. Leiden (1980)

T&TStudies---Michel Strickmann (ed) Tantric and buddhist studies in honour of r. a. stein. vol 1 (= MCB 20) Bruxelles (1981) vol 2 (=MCB 21) Bruxelles (1983) vol 3 (=MCB 22) Bruxelles (1985).

TaoRes---Taoist resources

TASJ---Transactions of the asiatic society of japan

TBMRD---Toyo bunko, memoirs of the research department

TC---James T.C. Liu and Wei-ming Tu (ed) Traditional china. Englewood cliffs, n.j. (1970)

TCGB--Taiwan church growth bulletin.

Tch'an---Tch'an (zen) Textes chinois fondamentaux, témoignages japonais, expériences vécues contemporaines.Hermés 7. Paris (1970)

TdelaR---Le temps de la réflexion

TheE&TheW---The east and the west. A quarterly review for the study of missions

THM--- T'ien hsia monthly

TibJ---The tibet journal

TibRev---Tibetan review

TICHK---Marjorie Topley (ed) Some traditional chinese ideas and conceptions in HK social life today. Hong kong (1967)

TJ---Tsinghua journal of chinese studies

TJR---Tenri journal of religion

TJT---Taiwan journal of theology

TLLP---Vatro Murvar (ed) Theory of liberty, legitimacy and power. London, boston etc (1985)

TM---A travers le monde

TMLT---Livia Kohn (ed) in cooperation

with Yoshinobu Sakade. Taoist meditation and longevity techniques. Univ michigan (1989)

TOCS---Transactions of the oriental ceramic society

TP---T'oung pao

TPJS---Transactions and proceedings of the japan society

TPZB---Toshihiko Izutsu. Toward a philosophy of zen buddhism. (1977)

TR---Tamkang review

TradMed---Peter N. Gregory (ed) Traditions of meditation in chinese buddhism. Honolulu (1986)

TransKBRAS---Korea branch, royal asiatic society, transactions

TRC---Akizuki Kan'ei (ed) Dokyo to shukyo bunka. Tokyo (1987) Engl title, Taoism and religious culture.

TS---T'ang studies

TT:RCT---Julian F. Pas (ed) The turning of the tide: religion in china today. HKBRAS/Oxford univ (1990)

TTV---Mark C. Thelin (ed) Two taiwanese villages. An interdisciplinary study conducted by faculty and students of tunghai university. N.p. ?Tunghai univ; acc to Preface publ in (1976)

TUAS---Toyo university asian studies

U

UPUMB---University of pennsylvania museum bulletin

USJPRS---U. S. joint publications service

UW---Nancy A. Falk & Rita M. Gross (ed) Unspoken words. Women's religious life in non-western cultures. San francisco etc (1980)

V

VBA---Visva-bharati annals

VBQ---Visva-bharati quarterly

VBS---Vajra bodhi sea

VC---Jonathan Lipman & Stevan Harrell (ed) Violence in china. SUNY (1990)

VFCC---William Parish & Martin King Whyte. Village and family in contemporary china. Univ chicago (1978)

W

Waifs & strays---Frederic H. Balfour. Waifs and strays from the far east, being a series of disconnected essays on matters relating to china. Shanghai (1877)

WBKKGA---Wiener beiträge zur kunst- und kulturgeschichte asiens

WCS---Margery Wolf & Roxanne Witke (ed) Women in chinese society. Stanford univ (1975)

Wen-lin---Tse-tsung Chow (ed) Wen-lin; studies in the chinese humanities. Univ wisc (1968)

WGM---C. Müller (ed) Wege der götter und menschen; religionen im traditionellen china. Berlin (1989) Exhibition catalog.

WinC---Constance F. Gordon-Cumming. Wanderings in china. Edinburgh & london, 2 vol (1886)

WMM---Wesleyan methodist magazine

WPDMD---Ram Jee Singh (ed) World perspectives in philosophy, religion and culture: essays presented to professor dhirenda mohan datta. Patna (1968)

WPR---John Henry Barrows (ed) The world's parliament of religions. Chicago (1893) 2 vol.

WWR---Arvind Sharma (ed) Women in world religions. SUNY (1987)

WZKM---Wiener zeitschrift für die kunde die morgenlandes

Y

Yana---Yana. Zeitschrift für buddhismus und religiöse kultur auf buddhistischen grundlage

YE---Young east

YT---Hok-lam Chan & W. Theodore deBary (ed) Yüan thought. Chinese thought and religion under the mongols. Columbia univ (1982)

Z

Z&H---Harold Heifetz (comp) Zen and hasidism. Wheaton, ill (1978)

ZBK---Zeitschrift bildende kunst

ZCE---R. C. Zaehner (ed) Concise encyclopaedia of living faiths. London (1959)

ZCJEAA---H. Brinker, R. P. Kramer & C. Ouwehand (ed) Zen in china, japan, east asian art. Berne etc (1985)

ZDMG---Zeitschrift der deutschen morgenländischen gesellschaft

ZE---Zeitschrift für ethnologie

ZMK---Zeitschrift für missionskunde

ZMR---Zeitschrift für missionswissenschaft und religionswissenschaft

ZRGG---Zeitschrift für religious- und geistes-geschichte

Part One

Bibliography,
General Treatments
and
Other Overall Categories

I.1 Bibliography

N.B. This category does not incorporate relevant items previously listed in 1985 bibliography.

Asian religious studies information. Institute for advanced studies of world religions, SUNY, stony brook; no 1 (jan 1987) no 2 (july 1987) no 3 (jan 1988) no 4 (july 1988)

Aubin, Francoise. Religions et philosophies de la chine. A propos de quelques travaux récents. l'Année sociologique, 3rd sér, 32 (1982) 273-284 Rev art.

Baldrian-Hussein, Farzeen & Anna Seidel. Max Kaltenmark: a bibliography. CEA 4 (1988) 1-17.

Bokenkamp, Stephen. Taoist literature, part I: through the t'ang dynasty. In ICTCL (1986) 138-152. Incl canonical texts and other materials.

Boltz, Judith Magee. Taoist literature, part II: five dynasties to the ming. In ICTCL (1986) 152-174. Incl canonical and other materials.

Born, Gerald M. (comp) Chinese jade: an anno-tated bibliography. Chicago (1982) 431 p, title index, index.

Brown, Iem. Religions of the chinese in indonesia. In Leo Suryadinata (ed) The ethnic chinese in the ASEAN states: bibliographical essays. Singapore (1989) 97-118.

Catalogue des manuscrits chinois de touen-houan. Fonds pelliot chinois de la bibliothèque nationale, vol III, no 3001-3500. Paris (1983) xx + 482 p. Sec 1, Bouddhisme; sec 2, Taoïsme; sec 3, Textes divers; sec 4, Particularités diverses.

Cheng, Peter. China. Oxford & santa barbara (1983) 89-102. Vol 35 of world bibliographical series. See sec, Religion and philosophy.

Cheng, Peter. Current books on china 1983-1988; an annotated bibliography. NY & london (1990) See sec, Religion and philosophy, 57-71.

Cleary, Christopher. Ancient chinese ethics. Sec 3 in BGCSE (1991) 102-124.

Cohen, Alvin P. Western language publications on chinese religions, 1981-1987. In TT:RCT (1989) 313-345.

Complete and current listing of publications on taoism by selected scholars. TaoRes 1.2 (winter 1989) 114-125. Scholars on this list incl jan yün-hua, livia kohn (née knaul) daniel l. overmyer, isabelle robinet, tao-chung (ted) yao, jae-seo chung.

Conze, Edward. Ed & rev by Lewis Lancaster. Buddhist scriptures: a bibliography. NY & london (1982) xiv + 161 p, comparative catalog, indices.

Dragan, Raymond. Ways to the way: a review of bibliographies on taoism. TaoRes 1.2 (winter 1989) 21-27.

Durt, Hubert. Recent japanese publications on chinese and japanese religions. CEA 2 (1986) 271-287.

Exner, Walter. Asien-bibliographie. Bad Wildungen.

Gardner, James L. Zen buddhism: a classified bibliography of western-language publications through 1990. Salt lake city (1991) 412 p, author & subj indexes.

Grönbold, Günter. Der buddhistische kanon; eine bibliographie. Wiesbaden (1984) 70 p, index. See 23-26; 30-31; sekundär literatur, 45-62 passim. Romanized entries.

Ho, David Yau-fai, John A. Spinks & Cecilia Siu-hing Yeung (ed) Chinese patterns of behavior: a sourcebook of psychological and psychiatric stud-ies. NY etc (1989) 401 p, subj index. See index, particularly 496. Covers lit thru 1986.

Honey, David B. & Stephen R. Bokenkamp. An annotated bibliography of the works of Edward H. Schafer. PTP 16 (1984) 8-30.

Howard, Diane. A survey of some western works on chinese buddhism from the han to the sui dynasty written since 1960. Newsletter for research in chinese studies (Han-hsüeh yen-chiu t'ung-hsün) 6.1, no 21 (mar 1987) 8-14.

Jacobs, J. Bruce, Jean Hagger & Anne Sedgley (comp) Taiwan: a comprehensive bibliography of english-language publications. LaTrobe univ & columbia univ (1984) For relig see esp 7, Society, and 8, Culture.

Kleeman, Terry F. Taoist ethics. Sec 5 in BGCSE (1991) 162-194.

Lee, Wei-chin. Taiwan. Oxford & santa barbara (1990) See sec, Religion, 34-41. Vol 113 of World bibliographical series.

Martin, Helmut & P. Günther. Deutsche fernostbibliographie. German far east bibliography. Munich (1982) 87; 75 p.

Mitros, Joseph F. Religions; a select, classified bibliography. NY etc (1973) See chap 11, Religions of china, 139-152.

Na, Tsung-shun. Chinese studies in english: a selected bibliography of books. N.p. [American institute of chinese studies] (1991) See sec 2, Philosophy and religion, 38-49.

Newsletter 1. International research institute for zen buddhism, hanazono college, kyoto (june 1990)

Nieh, Yu-hsi. Bibliography of chinese studies 1982: selected articles on china in chinese, english and german. Berlin (1982) 78 p.

Notes toward a comprehensive bibliography and directory: taoist resources. TaoRes 1.1 (autumn 1988) 56-61.

Pas, Julian. A select bibliography on taoism. Institute for advanced studies of world religions, SUNY, stony brook (1988) 52 p.

Pfandt, Peter. Mahayana texts translated into western languages; a bibliographical guide. Köln (1983) 167 p; rev ed with supplement (1986) 208p.

Religion index one: periodicals. From vol 1 (1953) to vol 12 (1977-78) titled Index to religious periodical literature. Annual in two parts. American theological library assoc, chicago, then evanston, ill. (1953) continuing.

Religion index two: multi-volume works. First vol (covering 1960-1969) titled Religion index two: festschriften. American theological library assoc, evanston, ill. Annual. (1960) continuing.

Religious studies review. A quarterly review of publications in the field of religion and related disciplines. Council on the study of religion. (1974) continuing. Each issue rev a few books on chin relig.

Religious and inspirational books and serials in print 1987. R. R. Bowker Co. NY & london (1987) 1 vol, quadruple col. See various relevant indexes.

Religious books 1876-1982. Subject index, author index, title index. R. R. Bowker Co. NY & london (1983) 4 vol in quadruple col. See esp vol 1, 912-914.

Reynolds, Frank E, John Holt & John Strong (ed) Guide to Buddhist religion. Boston (1981) See Contents passim for relevant topics.

Scott, Ian. (comp) Hongkong. Oxford & santa barbara (1990) See sec, Religion, 75-79.

Seidel, Anna. Chronicle of taoist studies in the west 1950-1990. CEA 5 (1989-1990) 223-347. The whole art is bibliog in nature, with lengthy bibliog of material discussed.

Selover, Thomas W. Neo-confucian religious ethics. Sec 6 in BGCSE (1991) 195-227.

Tanaka, Kenneth K. Bibliography of english-language works on pure land buddhism: primarily 1983-1989. PW n.s. 5 (fall 1989) 85-99. Classified by topic.

Tanis, Norman, David L. Perkins & Justine Pinto. China in books: a basic bibliography in western languages. Greenwich, conn (1979) See Religion and philosophy, 200-216; also Social life and customs, 217-225.

Teng, Ssu-yü. (comp) Protest and crime in china: a bibliography of secret societies, popular uprisings, peasant rebellions. NY & london (1981) See Part A, works in "occidental languages" 1-147.

Thilo, Thomas. Katalog chinesischer buddhistischer textfragmente. Band 2: schriften zur geschichte und kultur des alten orients. Berlin (1985) 1-94, 52 pl.

Thompson, Laurence G. Chinese religion in western languages; a comprehensive and classified bibliography of publications in english, french, and german through 1980. Univ arizona (1985) xlix + 302 double-col p, genl abbrev, abbrev of publ, index of authors, editors, translators, photographers, illustrators.

Tokuno, Kyoko. Chinese buddhist ethics. Sec 4 in BGCSE (1991) 125-161.

Walf, Knut. (comp) Westliche taoismus-bibliographie (WTB): Western bibliography of taoism. Essen (1986) 101 p. Excludes serial art.

Yu, David C. With contributions by Laurence G. Thompson. Guide to chinese religion. Boston (1985) xxviii + 200 p, author/title index, subj index.

I.2 General Treatments

Aubin, Francoise. Religions et croyances de la chine et de la haute asie. ASSR 62.2 (1989) 175-189.

Berthrong, John. Sages and immortals: chinese religions. In Eerdman's handbook to the world's religions, grand rapids, mich (1982) 245-254, illus.

Bloomfield, Frena. The book of chinese beliefs. NY (1983) 230 p. Miscellany of relig subj in popular journalistic style.

Bush, Richard C. et al. The religious world: communities of faith. NY & london (1982) See Religion in china, 172-196.

Carmody, Denise Lardner. Shamans, prophets, and sages: an introduction to world religions. Belmont, calif (1985) See chap 13, Chinese religion, 142-155; app 7, Chinese religion, 273-284.

Carmody, Denise L. & John T. Carmody. Eastern ways to the center. An introduction to asian religions. Belmont, calif (1981 & 1983) See chap 3, Chinese relig, 118-158, notes, bibliog, gloss, indexes, illus.

Carmody, Denise Lardner & John Carmody. The great questions. NY (1983)

Carmody, Denise Lardner & John Carmody. The story of the world religions. Mt view, calif (1988) See chap 12 & 13, 369-433.

Chao, Paul. The chinese natural religion: confucianism and taoism. Asian studies, univ of philippines, 20 (1982) 45-57. Same title in CC 24.1 (mar 1983) 1-14.

Cheng, Te-k'un. The world of the chinese—a struggle for human unity. Chin univ of HK (1980) See passim, esp chap 9, Confucian humanism—struggle for religious unity, 113-125; chap 10, contact with india—sinification of buddhism, 127-139; chap 11, Neo-confucianism—search for sagehood, 141-154. Parts repr in SAR 9.1-9.3 (1983)

Chidester, David. Patterns of transcendence; religion, death & dying. Belmont, calif (1990) See Chinese harmony, 114-124.

Chih, Andrew. Chinese humanism. A religion beyond religion. Fu jen catholic univ (1981) 548 p, notes, sources & bibliog, index.

Chih, Andrew. Nature and the natural in asian thinking: classical asian religions—a response to the paper. EAJT 1.1 (1983) 60-62.

Ching, Julia. The challenge of chinese religion. In Hans Küng & Jürgen Moltmann (ed) Christianity & world religions, edinburgh (1986) 84-89.

Ching, Julia. China's "three religions" In Leonard Swidler & Paul Mojzes (ed) Attitudes of religions & ideologies toward the outsider: the other, lewiston NY (1990) 125-134.

Chiu, Milton M. The tao of chinese religion. Lanham, md (1984) 432 p, notes, engl language bibliog, index.

Edsman, Carl-Martin. Die hauptreligionen des heutigen asiens. Tübingen (1971) See Chinas religionen, 23-38; 116-136.

Fellows, Ward J. Religions east and west. NY etc (1979) See chap 5, Confucianism, 199-241; chap 6, Taoism, 243-269.

Geden, Alfred S. Studies in the religions of the east. London (1913) See Confucianism, 618-660; Taoism, 661-674.

Hook, Brian (genl ed) The cambridge encyclopedia of china. Cambridge univ (1982) See Beliefs, customs and folklore, 304-311; Philosophy and religion, 312-325, by various contributors.

Huard, Pierre & Ming Wong. Chine d'hier et d'aujourd'hui. Paris (1960) See Chap 11, La pensée, le comportement, la philosophie et les religions des chinois, 162-177; profusely illus.

Kiernan, V. G. The great asiatic religions and their social functions. Journal of contemporary asia, stockholm, 13.2 (1983) 229-235.

King, Paul. Weighed in china's balance. London (1928) 238 p, index. See passim.

Kitagawa, Joseph. The quest for human unity; a religious history. Minneapolis (1990) 289 p, notes, bibliog, index. See passim.

Kitagawa, Joseph. Some reflections on chinese religion. CF 29.2/3 (sept 1986) 145-152. Same title in Inter-religious newsletter 9 (spring 1986) 17-23.

Küng, Hans & Julia Ching. Christianity and chinese religions. NY (1989) 309p, basic lit, indexes. See passim for chin relig. Engl tsl of Christentum und chinesische religion, münchen (1988)

Ladstätter, Otto. China und japan; die kulturen ostasiens. Wien & heidelberg (1983) See Die einführung des buddhismus in china, 85-98; die taoistische volksreligion, 99-106.

Lagerwey, Jean. (sic) La cosmologie ancienne de la chine, 56-66, Le confucianisme, 97-110, Le bouddhisme, 111-128. Chap in Francois Châtelet (ed) Histoire des idéologies, t.1, paris (1978)

Lai, Whalen. Religious pluralism in china: the history and the dynamics. CF 27.1 (mar 1984) 1-8.

Larre, Claude. Les chinois. Paris (1981) See Part I, Racines, 17-126, passim.

Lee, Peter K. H. A brief presentation of chinese religion: an exercise in communication. CF 25.2 (june 1982) 79-91. From a talk to art soc at chin univ of HK.

Li, Yih-yuan. In search of harmony and equilibrium—notes on basic principles of chinese religious belief and practice. D&A 4.2 (summer 1990) 15-30. On explicating a "system" in chin relig.

Loewe, Michael. The pride that was china. London & NY (1990) See chap 6, Beliefs, hopes and fears, 79-97; chap 14, Tombs and their treasures, 209-222.

Ludwig, Theodore M. The sacred paths. Understanding the religions of the world. NY & london (1989) See part 4, Religions of china and japan, 377-461.

Martinson, Paul V. A theology of world religions. Interpreting god, self, and world in semitic, indian, and chinese thought. Minneapolis (1987) See passim.

McAffee, Ward. A history of the world's great religions. Lanham, md (1983) See chap 3, sec 5, China's religious heritage, 120-127.

McFarlane, Stuart. Chinese religions. In John R. Hinnells (ed) The penguin dictionary of religions. London; U.S. title: The facts on file dictionary of religions. (1984) See Synoptic index, X, 451, for entries.

Miller, Alan L. Religions of china. In Niels C. Nielsen et al (ed) Religions of the world, NY, 2nd ed (1988) See chap 12 thru 14, 262-315.

Morgan, Kenneth W. Reaching for the moon; on asian religious paths. Chambersburg, pa (1990) 207 p, notes. See passim.

Müller, Claudius and Shunchi Wu (heraus) Wege der götter und menschen: religion im traditionellen china. Berlin (1989)

Noss, David S. & John B. Noss. A history of the world's religions. NY & london, 8th ed. (1990) See Part 3, Religions of east asia, chap 9 and 10.

Overmyer, Daniel L. Chinese religion: an overview. EncyRel 3 (1987) 257a-289a.

Overmyer, Daniel L. Religions of china. San francisco etc (1986) xii + 125 p, chronol, map, notes, gloss, sel reading list, illus photos.

Parrinder, Geoffrey. World religions from ancient history to the present. NY & bicester, engl (1983) See chap 17, China, 304-352. New version of 1971 publ; title in england, Man and his gods; U.S. title, Religions of the world.

Rausch, David A. & Carl H. Voss. World religions: our quest for meaning. Minneapolis (1989) See 5, Confucianism and taoism, 83-100.

Ronan, Colin A. The shorter science & civilisation in china. An abridgement of Joseph Needham's original text. Cambridge univ (1978) See vol 1, which incl material from Needham's vol 1 and 2; for relevant items, see Contents.

Ruland, Vernon. Eight sacred horizons. NY & london (1985) See 2, Chinese-japanese tao, 25-50; further reading.

Saso, Michael. Blue dragon white tiger. Taoist rites of passage. Washington, d.c. (1990) xii + 219 p, fig. Despite subtitle, this is a general treatment of chin relig.

Saso, Michael. Chinese religions. In John R. Hinnells (ed) A handbook of living religions, middlesex, engl & NY (1984) 344-364, bibliog.

Schwarz, Henry G. Some random thoughts on religion and religous policy in china. Asia univ, asia research institute bulletin (a-ji-a daigaku a-ji-a kenkyu-so kiyo) 7 (1980) 1-39.

Sharma, Arvind. The harmonization of the 'three teachings' in chinese culture. VBQ 47.3/4 (nov 1981-apr 1982) 228-235.

Smart, Ninian. The world's religions. Englewood cliffs, n.j. (1989) See China, 103-128.

Smart, Ninian & Richard D. Hecht (ed) Sacred texts of the world. A universal anthology. NY (1982) See Buddhism, 231-275; Taoism, 291-304; Confucianism, 305-318.

Smith, Richard J. China's cultural heritage. The ch'ing dynasty, 1644-1912. Boulder, colorado & london (1983) See chap 7, Religion, 124-155.

Spector, Stanley. A question of balance (a study of chinese religions) In Students' guide to the long search: a study of religions, a project of miami-dade community college; dubuque, iowa (1978) 97-112.

Steininger, Hans. Konfuzianismus, taoismus, naturreligion. In China: colloquim-verlag otto h. hess, berlin (1980) 88-97.

Stilson, Max. Leading religions of the world. Grand rapids, michigan (1964) See 4, Confucianism, 39-44; 5, Taoism, 47-52. "The study of religions is interesting and will readily prove the superiority of Christianity over the other religions of the world"

Tan, Yun-shan. Chinese religion. In Shree Amiya Kumer Mazumder & Swami Prajnanananda (ed) The bases of indian culture, calcutta (1971) 363-370.

Thompson, Henry O. World religions in war and peace. Jefferson, n.c. & london (1988) See 8, Taoism, 106-113; 9, Confucianism, 114-126.

Thompson, Laurence G. Chinese religion; an introduction. Belmont, calif. 4th ed (1988) xxi + 184 p, table of chin relig hist, time line of chin relig hist, 3 app, notes, gloss, sel readings, index.

Thompson, Laurence G. The scrutable chinese religion. In C&C (1979) 36-61.

Tucker, Mary Evelyn. China, religion in. NCE 18 (suppl 1987-1988) 88b-92b.

Verellen, Franciscus. Histoire des religions de la chine ancienne et moderne. ACF 95 (1986-87) 115-120.

Weber-Schäfer, Peter. Die religionen chinas. In Verlag Ploetz (heraus) China, freiburg & würzburg (1981) 158-172.

Weller, Robert P. Unities and diversities in chinese religion. Univ washington (1987) 215 p, app on geomancy, char list, notes, ref, index.

Wieger, Leon. Tsl and ed by Derek Bryce. Philosophy and religion in china. Felonfach, lkampeter, dyfed (1988) 178 p. "Selected edited translations from 'Histoire des croyances et des opinions philosophiques en chine,' hsien-hsien, 1917" q.v.

Wolcott, Leonard & Carolyn. Religions around the world. Nashville & NY (1967) See chap 5, Chinese religions, 71-88. Juvenile level.

I.3 Religion and Gender

N.B. In this new category all relevant items from 1985 bibliography have also been incorporated.

Ahern, Emily M. The power and pollution of chinese women. In WCS (1975) 193-214.

Anderson, Mary K. Kuan yin: goddess of mercy. Echo 3.9 (oct 1973) 28-32, 55-56, col photos.

Aufhauser, Johannes B. Avalokitsesvara—kuan-yin (kwannon)—maria. OR 10.13 (1929) 366-367.

Barnes, Nancy Schuster. Striking a balance: women and images of women in early chinese buddhism. In Yvonne Yazbeck Haddad & Ellison Banks Findly (ed) Women, religion, and social change, SUNY (1985) 87-112.

Berthier, Brigitte. La dame-du-bord-de-l'eau: la femininité à travers un culte de la religion populaire chinoise. Nanterre (1988) 300 p, illus, photos, notes, bibliog.

Berthier, Brigitte. Le miroir brisé ou le taoïste et son ombre. l'Homme 19.3/4 (juil-déc 1979) 205-222. Re taoism and femininity.

Black, Alison H. Gender and cosmology in chinese correlative thinking. In G&R (1986) chap 7, 166-195.

Blofeld, John. Compassion yoga: the mystical cult of kuan yin. Alternative title: Bodhisattva of compassion; the mystical tradition of kuan yin. London & boulder, colo (1977 and 1978) 158 p, app, gloss, illus.

Borel, Henri. Tsl fr dutch by Alfred Reuss. Kwan yin, die göttin der gnade. (1912) 72 p.

Buck, Samuel (pseud) Why chinese women worship kuan yin. Orient 2.8 (1952) 18-20, 22.

Buddhist monasteries of taiwan. I. Kuan-yin hill and lin-yün buddhist temple; II. Yuan tung shih, a nunnery. New force 2.4 (feb 1951) 20-25, illus photos.

Cahill, Suzanne. Performers and female taoist adepts: hsi wang mu as the patron deity of women in medieval china. JAOS 106.1 (jan-mar 1986) 155-168.

Cahill, Suzanne. Practice makes perfect: paths to transcendence for women in medieval china. TaoRes 2.2 (nov 1990) 23-42.

Cahill, Suzanne. Sex and the supernatural in medieval china: cantos on the transcendent who presides over the river. JAOS 105.2 (1985) 197-220.

Cahill, Suzanne. A white clouds appointment with the queen mother of the west. JCR 16 (1988) 43-53.

8

Carmody, Denise Lardner. Women and world religions. Nashville (1979) See chap 3, East asian religions. 2nd ed (1989) see chap 5, Chinese women, 93-114.

Carmody, Denise Lardner. Taoist reflections on feminism. Religion in life 46.1 (summer 1977) 234-244.

Cass, Victoria B. Female healers in the ming and the lodge of ritual and ceremony. JAOS 106.1 (jan-mar 1986) 233-240.

Cernada, E. C. and G. Cernada. Ethical judgments about induced abortion. ASBIE 41 (spring 1976) 47-59.

Cernada, George P. Basic beliefs about a new human life and ethical judgment: family planning field workers in taiwan. Univ mass area studies programs occ papers ser no 5 (1979) 46 p.

Chamberlayne, John H. The development of kuan yin, chinese goddess of mercy. Numen 9 (1962) 45-62.

Chan, Alan K. L. Goddesses in chinese religions. In Goddesses (1990) 9-81. Focuses particularly on taoist female deities.

Chan, Stephen Chingku. The return of the ghost woman: a critical reading of three sung hua-pen stories. ACQ 15.3 (autumn 1987) 47-72.

Chen, Ellen Marie. Tao as the great mother and the influence of motherly love in the shaping of chinese philosophy. HR 14.1 (aug 1974) 51-64.

Chen, Ying-chieh. She calls the winds and cures the sick. FCR 22.6 (june 1972) 19-22, illus photos. Re matsu.

Cleary, Thomas (ed & tsl) Immortal sisters. Secrets of taoist women. Boston & london (1989) 96 p. Re six chin women, 4th-12th c.

Cohn, W. Ein chinesisches kuanyin-bild. Berliner museum 49 (1928) 70-74.

Collins, Valerie. Pilgrimage to peikang. Echo 1.5 (may 1971) 27-32, illus. Pilgrimage to matsu shrine.

Crane, L. Honoring the goddess of mercy; pootoo, the island sanctuary of kuan yin. Travel 56 (mar 1931) 22-26.

Day, Clarence B. Kuan-yin: goddess of mercy. CJ 10 (1929) 288-295. Repr in PRPCC (1975)

Despeux, Catherine. Immortelles de la chine ancienne; taoïsme et alchimie féminine. Paris (1990) 371 p.

Despeux, Catherine. l'Ordination des femmes taoïstes sous le tang. EtCh 5.1-2 (printemps-automne 1986) 53-100.

Dudbridge, Glen. The goddess hua-yüeh san niang and the cantonese ballad ch'ien-hsiang t'ai-tzu. HHYC:CS 8.1, vol 2 (june 1990) 627-646. From medieval cult to contemporary ballad text.

Dudbridge, Glen. The legend of miao-shan. London (1978) 128 p, app, works cited, index. See rev by Anna Seidel in JAS 38.4 (aug 1979) 770f.

Eastman, A. C. A chinese fresco of kuan yin. BDetIA 9 (apr 1928) 81-83.

Eitel, E. J. A buddhist purgatory for women. NQ 2 (1868) 66-68, 82-85.

Erkes, Eduard. Der primat des weibes im alten china. Sinica 10 (1935) 166-176.

Erkes, E. Zum problem der weiblichen kuanyin. AA 9 (1946) 316-320, illus.

Fielde, Adele M. Pagoda shadows. Boston (1890) See chap 13, The stone princess and her train, 102-107 (re matsu)

Fisher, Tom. The peikang pai pai. Echo 3.3 (mar 1973) 21-25, illus col photos. Re matsu festival.

Fracasso, Riccardo. Holy mothers of ancient china: a new approach to the hsi-wang- mu problem. TP 74.1-3 (1988) 1-46.

Frodsham, J. D. (tsl) Goddesses, ghosts and demons: the collected poems of li he (790-816) San francisco (1983) lx + 290 p, bibliog, index. Rev ed of The poems of li ho, oxford univ (1970)

Fu, Tien-chun. The sculptured maidens of the tsin temple. CL 4 (apr 1962) 92-98.

Fuchs, Walter. Der wille der kwan-yin. Eine chinesische legende. Zürich & stuttgart (1955) 46 p, pl.

Goddess of mercy. Orientations 1.12 (dec 1970) 46, 1 illus. Re kuan yin.

Goodrich, G. Nuns of north china. Asia 37 (1937) 90-93.

Grant, Beata. The spiritual saga of woman huang: from pollution to purification. In RO/RO (1989) 224-311. Re "one of the many story cycles that... make up the rich complexity of the chinese popular narrative tradition"

Gulik, R. H. van. Indian and chinese sexual mysticism. App 1 in author's Sexual life in ancient china, leiden (1961) 339-359.

Gundert, Wilhelm (tsl) Die nonne liu bei we-schan; das 24. kapitel des bi-yän-lu, eingeleitet, übersetzt und erläutert. In Asiatica (1954) 184-197.

Gutzlaff, Charles. Temple of teen how [t'ien hou] at meichow. ChRep 2 (1834) 563-565.

Hart, H. H. Kuan yin, the goddess of mercy. AP 11 (1940) 527-529.

Hase, P. H. Cheung shan kou tsz (chiang shan ku ssu), an old buddhist nunnery in the new territories, and its place in local society. JHKBRAS 29 (1989) 121-157.

Hawkins, R. B. A statue of kuan-yin: a problem in sung sculpture. RMHA-PU 12 (1953) 1-36, illus.

Hsu, Vivian. Monks and nuns as comic figures in yüan drama. Dodder 2 (jan 1970) 10-12.

Hummel, Siegbert. Guan-yin in der unterwelt. Sinologica 2 (1950) 291-293. Descr of a scroll.

Irwin, Lee. Divinity and salvation: the great goddesses of china. AsFS 49.1 (1990) 53-68.

Iwai, Hirosato. The buddhist priest and the ceremony of attaining womanhood during the yüan dynasty. TBMRD 7 (1935) 105-161.

Johnson, Elizabeth L. Grieving for the dead, grieving for the living: funeral laments of hakka women. In DeathRit (1988) 135-163.

Kajiyama, Yuichi. Women in buddhism. EB n.s.15.1 (spring 1982) 53-70. Historically and acc to budd texts.

Karutz, Richard. Maria im fernen osten; das problem der kuan yin. Leipzig (1925) 99 p, illus.

Kelleher, Theresa. Confucianism. In WWR (1987) 135-159.

Kendall, Laurel. Korean shamanism: women's rites and a chinese comparison. In RFEA (1986) 57-73.

Kim, Sung-hae. Confucian understanding of woman: cultivation of self through learning. Pastoral theology (july 1986) 61-73.

Kinsley, David R. The goddesses' mirror; visions of the divine from east and west. SUNY (1989) See chap 2, Kuan-yin, the chinese goddess of mercy, 25-57.

Koerber, Hans Nordewin von. Kuan yin, the buddhist madonna. Theosophical forum 19 (1941) 6-16.

Kroll, Paul W. Notes on three taoist figures of the t'ang dynasty. SSCRB 9 (1981) 19-41. Re Szuma ch'eng-chen, refined mistress chia, and the lady of the highest prime.

Lacouperie, Terrien de. The silk goddess of china and her legend. BOR 4.12 and 5.1 (1890 and 1891) 270-290; 5-10.

Larsen, Jeanne. Women of religion in t'ang poetry: toward a new pedagogy of reading traditional genres. JCLTA 22.3 (oct 1987) 1-25.

Lee, Lily Hsiao Hung. The emergence of buddhist nuns in china and its social ramifications. JOSA 18-19 (1986-87) 82-100.

10

Leuridan, Thre. Sur une statuette chinoise du musée de roubaix, la déese pou-ssa. Mémoires de la société d'emulation de roubaix 15.

Levering, Miriam L. The dragon girl and the abbess of mo-shan: gender and status in the ch'an buddhist tradition. JIABS 4.2 (1982) 19-35.

Levering, Miriam Scripture and its reception: a buddhist case. Chap 3 in author-edited Rethinking scripture, SUNY (1989) 58-101.

Lévi, J. Connais le masculin, garde le féminin. Stratégies du yin et du yang. Le sexe des nombres. Genre humain, paris (1984) no 10, le masculin 75-89.

Li, Jung-hsi (tsl) Engl text rev by Christopher Cullen. Biographies of buddhist nuns: pao-chang's pi-ch'iu-ni chuan. Osaka (1981) 144 p, index. See rev art by Kathryn Tsai in CEA 1 (1985) 87-101. Text is early 6th c comp.

Li, Wai-yee. Dream visions of transcendence in chinese literature and painting. AsArt 3.4 (fall 1990) 53-78. Taoism and immortality.

Linck, Gundula. Frau und familie in china. München (1988)

Little, Mrs Archibald. Buddhist monasteries; a chinese (buddhist nuns') ordination. Chap 17-18 in author's IntC (ca.1900) 227-250.

Liu, Mau-tsai. Der niang-niang kult in der mandschurei. OE 19.1/2 (dec 1972) 109-119.

Loewe, Michael. Ways to paradise. The chinese quest for immortality. London (1979) 270 p, illus, app, notes. Based on han dyn silk painting, TLV bronze mirrors, and representations of hsi wang mu.

Martin, Emily. Gender and ideological differences in representations of life and death. In DeathRit (1988) 164-179.

McNair, Amy. On the date of the shengmudian sculptures at jenci. AA 49.3/4 (1988/89) 238-253, 10 fig. Hall of the sage mother, chin-tz'u, shanxi.

Sculptures supposedly represent yi jiang, wife of king wu of chou.

Nagel, August. Die sieben schwestern. OstL 25.46 (17 nov 1911) 425-426.

Needham, Joseph. Femininity in chinese thought and christian theology. CF 23.2 (1980) 57-70.

Ng, Yong-sang. Lung mu, the dragon mother. The story of the west river's own guardian angel. CJ 21.1 (july 1936) 18-20.

Paper, Jordan. The persistence of female deities in patriarchal china. Journal of feminist studies in religion 6 (spring 1990) 25-40.

Parkin, Harry. Confucian thoughts on women. CN 22.2/3 (spring-summer 1984) 294-298. "Confucian underpinnings" of traditional society.

Parrinder, Geoffrey. Sex in the world's religions. Oxford univ (1980) See chap 5, Chinese yin and yang, 77-102.

Paul, Diana. Empress wu and the historians: a tyrant and a saint of classical china. In VW (1980) 191-206.

Paul, Diana. Kuan-yin: savior and savioress in chinese pure land buddhism. Chap 12 in Carl Olson (ed) The book of the goddess past and present, NY (1983) 161-175.

Paul, Diana. Portraits of the feminine: buddhist and confucian historical perspectives. In SHB (1980) 209-221.

Paul, Diana Y. With contributions by Frances Wilson. Women in buddhism. Images of the feminine in the mahayana tradition. Berkeley, calif (1979) 333 p, gloss, bibliog, index. Tsl mostly fr chin texts.

Peri, N. & H. Maspero. Le monastère de la kouan-yin que ne vent pas s'en aller. BEFEO 9 (1909) 797-807. Re P'u-t'o shan.

Pohlman, W. J. (tsl) Translation of a buddhist print descriptive of the one thousand hands, one thousand eyes, the all-prevalent and most merciful to-lo-ni (goddess of mercy) ChRep 15 (1846) 351-354.

Pruitt, Ida. Old madame yin. A memoir of peking life, 1926-1938. Stanford univ (1979) See chap 13 for description of woman's burial clothes.

Reed, Barbara. Taoism. In WWR (1987) 161-181.

Robinet, Isabelle. Sexualité et taoïsme. In M. Bernos (ed) Sexualité et religions, paris (1988) 50-71.

Rosner, Erhard. Frauen als anführerinnen chinesischer sekten. In RPO-A (1985) 239-246. Re women in ch'ing sectarianism.

Rousselle, E. Der kult der buddhistischen madonna kuan-yin. NachrDGNVO 68 (1944) 17-23.

S[huck] J. L. (tsl) Sketch of kwanyin, the chinese goddess of mercy. Translated from the sow shin ke [sou shen chi] ChRep 10 (1841) 185-191.

S[huck] J. L. (tsl) Sketch of teën fe [t'ien fei] or matsoo po, the goddess of chinese seamen. Translated from the sow shin ke [sou shen chi] ChRep 10 (1841) 84-87.

Sangren, P. Steven. Female gender in chinese religious symbols: kuan yin, matsu, and the "eternal mother" Signs 9 (1983) 4-25.

Sangren, P. Steven. History and the rhetoric of legitimacy: the matsu cult of taiwan. CSSH 30 (oct 1988) 674-697.

Schipper, K. M. Le pays du milieu et la fin du monde. Axes. Recherches pour un dialogue entre christianisme et religions, paris (1978) 32-42. Re a messianic sect of the middle ages based on cult of hsi wang mu.

Schlegel, G. Ma-tsu-po . . . koan-yin with the horsehead. TP 5 (1898) 402-406.

Schuster, Nancy. Changing the female body: wise women and the bodhisattva career in some maharatnakuta sutras. JIABS 4.1 (1981) 24-69.

Schuster, Nancy. Yoga-master dharmamitra and clerical misogyny in fifth century china. TibJ (1984) 33-46.

Seaman, Gary. The sexual politics of karmic retribution. In AnthroTS (1981) 381-396.

Sowerby, A. de C. S. Legendary figures in chinese art. Kuan yin, the goddess of mercy. CJ 14.1 (jan 1931) 4, frontispiece, illus.

Stein, Rolf A. Avalokitesvara/kouan-yin, un exemple de transformation d'un dieu en déesse. CEA 2 (1986) 17-80. Engl summ 78-80.

Stein, Rolf A. Grottes-matrices et lieux saints de la déesse en asie orientale. Paris (1988) 83 p, 21 pl, liste des ouvrages cités. See passim.

Stiassny, M. Einiges zur 'buddhistischen madonna' JAK 1 (1924) 112-119. Re kuan-yin. Same title in Cicerone 15 (1923) 1011-1020.

Stockard, Janice E. Daughters of the canton delta; marriage patterns and economic strategies in south china, 1860-1930. Stanford univ (1989) See chap 5, Arranging a spirit marriage, 90-101.

Sung, Lung-fei. Two examples of the pilgrimage activities in taiwan. ASBIE 31 (1971) engl summ 129-133, 20 pl. Re pilgimages to matsu temples.

Sung, Shi. Tsl by Earl Wieman. On the road to peikang. Echo 3.3 (mar 1973) 26-33, 55-56, col photos. Re matsu.

Suzuki, D. T. The kuan-yin cult in china. EB 6 (1935) 339-353.

Takakusu, Junjiro. Kwan-yin. In HERE 7.

Tay, C. N. Kuan-yin, the cult of half asia. HR 16.2 (nov 1976) 147-177.

Thireau, Isabelle. Les femmes chinoises et l'essor de la religion populaire. In M. Clévenot (ed) l'Etat des religions dans le monde, paris (1987) 570-572.

Thompson, Laurence G. The cult of matsu. In author's CWayRel (1973) 196-201.

Thompson, Laurence G. Popular and classical modes of ritual in a taiwanese temple. SSCRB 9 (1981) 106-122. Matsu is the deity of this temple.

Ting, Nai-t'ung. The holy man and the snake-woman. Fabula 8.3 (1966) 145-191. The "king and the lamia" tale in comparative study (in china it is the story of white snake)

Tirone, Gail (text) & Lin Bor-liang (photos) A gathering of deities occasions folk celebrations. FCR 36.7 (july 1986) 36-41. Re Peikang matsu festival 27 apr 1986.

Topley, Marjorie. Chinese women's vegetarian houses in singapore. JMBRAS 27.1 (may 1954) 51-67.

Tsai, Kathryn. The chinese buddhist monastic order for women: the first two centuries. In Richard W. Guisso & Stanley Johannesen (ed) Women in china, youngstown NY (1981) 1-20. Same title in Historical reflections;Reflexions historiques 8.3 (fall 1981) 1-20.

Tsu, Y. Y. (tsl) A diary of a buddhist nun. JR 7.5/6 (oct 1927) 612-618. Tsl fr Hai ch'ao yin 3.11/12 (feb 1923) repr in CWayRel (1973) 120-124.

Tucci, G. Buddhist notes. MCB 9 (1948-51) 173-220. Re evolution of kuan-yin in art and texts.

Waley, Arthur D. Hymns to kuan-yin. BSOAS 1 (1920) 145-146.

Waltner, Ann. T'ang-yang-tzu and wang shih-chen: visionary and bureaucrat in the late ming. LIC 8.1 (june 1987) 105-133. T'ang is female visionary worshiped in cult; wang is prominent literatus.

Wang, Wen-hsing. Tsl by Chen Chu-yun. The day of the sea-goddess. ChPen (spring 1986) 70-90. Fictional re-creation of matsu festival in taiwanese fishing harbor.

Watson, James L. Standardizing the gods: the promotion of t'ien hou ("empress of heaven") along the south china coast, 960-1960. In PopCult (1985) 292-324.

Wiethoff, Bodo. Der staatliche ma-tsu kult. ZDMG 116.2 (1966) 311-357.

Williams, E. T. The worship of lei tsu, patron saint of silk workers. JNCBRAS 66 (1935) 1-14.

Wolf, Margery. The woman who didn't become a shaman. AmEth 17.3 (aug 1990) 419-430. Taiwan case.

Wright, Arthur F. Biography of the nun an-ling-shou. HJAS 15 (1952) 192-196.

Wu, Linda. Home, grand auntie, let's go home! Echo 4.4 (apr 1974) 19-38, 56, illus. Re pilgrimage to matsu shrine in peikang.

Wu, Ping-chung. Matsu, goddess of the sea. Echo 1.1 (jan 1971) 12-17, illus.

Yeh, Sui Yen. Ma chu—the goddess of sailors. ACSS (1964-67) 35-38, 2 photos.

Yü, Chün-fang. Feminine images of kuan-yin in post-t'ang china. JCR 18 (1990) 61-89, illus.

I.4 Religion and Music

N.B. In this new category all relevant items from 1985 bibliography have also been incorporated.

Blacking, John. Problems in the documentation and analysis of ritual. In STR&MT (1989) 10-14.

Boltz, Judith Magee. Neumatic notation in the taoist canon and performance practice today. In STR&MT (1989) 88-109.

Chamberlain, Ida Hoyt. 'Magic writing' from ear to the east series. China monthly 2 (nov 1941) 9-12, 17-21. Account of recording music of tao-te ching as chanted by priests.

Chou, Ta-fu. Three buddhist hymns. SIS 1 (1944) 85-98.

Dean, Kenneth. Taoism in southern fujian: field notes, fall, 1985. In STR&MT (1989) 74-87.

Demiéville, Paul. Mission paul pelliot. Documents conservés à la bibliothèque nationale. II. Airs de touen-houang (touen-houang k'iu) Textes à chanter des VIIIe—Xe siècles. Manuscrits reproduits en facsimilé. avec une introduction en chinois par Jao Tsung-yi. Adaptes en francais avec la traduction de quelques textes d'air, par p. demiéville. Paris (1971) 370 p, 58 p.

Demiéville, Paul. Notes on buddhist hymnology in the far east. In Buddhist studies in honour of walpola rahula, london & sri lanka (1980) 44-61.

DeWoskin, Kenneth J. Music and entertainment themes in the han funerary sculptures. Orientations 18.4 (apr 1987) 34-40.

Fritzen, Joachim. Das schlagzeug in der buddhistischen liturgischen musik chinas. OE 22.2 (dec 1975) 169-182, illus musical examples.

Jan, Yün-hua. The bridge between man and cosmos: the philosophical foundation of music in the t'ai p'ing ching. In STR&MT (1989) 15-27.

Johnson, David. Actions speak louder than words: the cultural significance of chinese ritual opera. In RO/OR (1989) 1-45.

Kagan, Alan L. Eight immortals' longevity blessings: symbolic and ritual perspectives of the music. In STR&MT (1989) 121-135.

Kohl, Louis von. Die grundlagen des altchinesischen staates und die bedeutung der riten und der musik. Baessler-archiv 17.2 (1934) 55-98.

Lagerwey, John. The fachang ritual in northern taiwan. In STR&MT (1989) 66-73.

Lagerwey, John. Rapport sur une conférence taoïste, tenue à hong kong en décembre 1985. CEA 2 (1986) 185-190. On taoist ritual and music. See papers sep listed in this bibliog fr STR&MT (1989)

Lü, Ch'ui-k'uan. Enquete préliminaire sur la musique taoïste de taiwan. Sommaire en francais par j. l. [john lagerwey] CEA 4 (1988) 112-126.

Liu, Chun-jo. Five major chant types of the buddhist service, gong-tian. Chinoperl 8 (1978) 130-160, app, transcriptions, musical scores.

Lu, Ping-chuan & Tsao Pen-yeh. The ritual music of taoist "chiao"—studies made in lin-cheung and p'eng-hu. Proc 31st ICHS, Tokyo, vol 2 (1984) 656-658. Abstr.

Mollard, Sidney G. jr. Confucius and music. EWCR 3.3 (feb 1967) 31-39.

Pas, Julian. Rituals of cancellation of evil (hsiao-chai) In STR&MT (1989) 28-35.

Perris, Arnold. Feeding the hungry ghosts: some observations on buddhist music and buddhism from both sides of the taiwan strait. Ethnomusicology 30.3 (1968) 428-448.

Provine, Robert C. The sacrifice to confucius in korea and its music. TKBRAS 50 (1975) 43-69, illus.

Saso, Michael. The structure of taoist liturgy in taiwan. In STR&MT (1989) 36-65.

Saso, Michael. Introduction. In STR&MT (1989) 5-9.

Schafer, Edward H. The dance of the purple culmen. TS 5 (1987) 45-68. Re taoist temples, music and dances of the 8th c in ch'angan.

Schafer, Edward H. Two taoist bagatelles. SSCRB 9 (1981) 1-18. 1. Re yin-transmitting lithophones 2. the mutations of mercurial maid.

Schipper, Kristofer M. A study of buxu: taoist liturgical hymn and dance. In STR&MT (1989) 110-120.

Su, Ying-hui. The dancing guidebook of tunhuang. APQCSA 12.1 (spring 1980) 47-49. A text fr 2 mss.

Tsao, Pen-yeh. Variation technique in the formal structure of music of taoist jiao-shi in hong kong. JHKBRAS 23 (1983) 172-181.

14

Tsao, Pen-yeh and Daniel P. L. Law (ed) Studies of taoist rituals and music of today. HK: Chinese univ of HK (1989) 1985 conference; engl language papers sep listed in this bibliog; abbrev STR&MT.

Tsui, Bartholomew. Taoist ritual books of the new territories. In STR&MT (1989) 136-143.

Waley, Arthur D. Hymns to kuan-yin. BSOAS 1 (1920) 145-146.

Wieger, Léon (tsl) Hymnes chinoises. RechScRelig 1 (1910) 359-372. Examples through the ages.

Wong, Isabel. Music and religion in china, korea, and tibet. EncyRel 10 (1987) 195a-203a.

I.5 The Study of Chinese Religion

N.B. In this revised category all relevant items from 1985 bibliography have also been incorporated.

Bagchi, P. C. Buddhist studies in japan and the taisho edition of the chinese tripitaka. New asia 1.1 (1939) 16-20.

Baldrian-Hussein, Farzeen & Anna Seidel. Max Kaltenmark: a bibliography. CEA 4 (1988) 1-17.

Bareau, André. Necrologie: Etienne Lamotte (1903-1983) TP 69.1-3 (1983) i-ii.

Barrett, T. H. Change and progress in understanding chinese religion. Numen 29.2 (dec 1982) 239-249.

Barrett, T. H. The study of chinese eschatology. Modern asian studies 17.2 (apr 1983) 333-352. Rev art on a no of recent books.

Barrett, T. H. Taoism: history of study. EncyRel 14 (1987) 329b-332b.

Bechert, Heinz. Etienne Lamotte (1903-1983) JIABS 8 (1985) 151-156.

Bell, Catherine. Religion and chinese culture: toward an assessment of "popular religion" HR 29.1 (aug 1989) 35-57. Rev art on several recent books.

Berthrong, John. Trends in the interpretation of confucian religiosity. CF 32.4 (1989) 224-244. Incl lengthy bibliog.

Birnbaum, Norman. Max Weber. EncyRel 15 1987) 364b-367a.

Campany, Robert F. "Survival" as an interpretive strategy: a sino-western comparative case study. Method & theory in the study of religion 2.1 (spring 1990) 2-26.

Cohen, Alvin P. In memoriam Wolfram Eberhard, 1909-1989. JCR 18 (1990) 177-185. Same title in AsFS 49.1 (1990) 125-133; CAJ 34.3-4 (1990) 177-186.

DeMarco, Michael A. Taoism in new china-hands. CC 30.3 (sept 1989) 41-49. Re expansion of taoist studies in the west.

Dhavamony, Mariasusai. Chinese religion in the phenomenology of religion. In ISCI (1983) 214-230.

Durt, Hubert. Etienne Lamotte. EncyRel 8 (1987) 437a-b.

Durt, Hubert. In memoriam Paul Demiéville (1895-1979) Numen 27 (june 1980) 1-9.

Eliasberg, Danielle. Maspero: l'histoire de la religion populaire chinoise. In HHM (1984) 55-59.

Feuchtwang, Stephen. The study of chinese popular religion. Revue européene des sciences sociales 27 (1989) 84ff.

Flinn, Frank K. Weber and the study of religion in china. D&A 4.2 (1990) 71-89.

Fujieda, Akira. Recent trends of dunhuang and turfan studies. Proc 31st ICHS, Tokyo, vol 2 (1984) 1000-1002. Abstr.

Gao, Wangzhi. On chen yuan's contributions to the study of the history of religions. In McGill univ, Re-examination of china's religious legacy: a chinese perspective (1982) 13-34. Mimeo fr 1980 conference paper.

Garrett, William R. The confucian conundrum in "the religions of china" D&A 4.2 (summer 1990) 90-107. Re max weber's work.

Gernet, Jacques. Notice sur la vie et les travaux de Paul Demiéville. CRAIBL (juil-oct 1986) 595-607.

Gernet, Jacques. La vie et l'oeuvre d'Henri Maspero. In HHM (1984) 15-24.

Girardot, N. J. Chinese religion: history of study. EncyRel 3 (1987) 312a-323a.

Girardot, N. J. Granet, Marcel. EncyRel 6 (1987) 94a-95b.

Hendrischke, Barbara. Chinese research into daoism after the cultural revolution. AS 34 (1984) 25-42.

Henricks, Robert G. Demiéville, Paul. EncyRel 4 (1987) 278b-279b.

Henricks, Robert G. Groot, J. J. M. de. EncyRel 6 (1987) 134b-135b.

Howard, Diane. A survey of some western works on chinese buddhism from the han to the sui written since 1960. Newsletter for research in chinese studies; Han-hsüeh yen-chiu t'ung-hsün 6.1 (mar 1987) 8-14.

Hwang, Philip H. Fingarette's interpretation of confucius' view of ritual. D&A 4.1 (spring 1990) 96-104.

Jackson, David. A group of young tun-huang scholars in the kyoto-osaka area. CEA 3 (1987) 143-145.

Jan, Yün-hua. Recent chinese research publications on religious studies. In TT:RCT (1989) 25-42.

Jan, Yün-hua. The religious situation and the studies of buddhism and taoism in china: an incomplete and imbalanced picture. JCR 12 (1984) 37-64.

Jochim, Christian. "Great" and "little," "grid" and "group": defining the poles of the elite-popular continuum in chinese religion. JCR 16 (1988) 18-42.

Jong, J. W. de. Lamotte and the doctrine of non-self. CEA 3 (1987) 151-153.

Jong, J. W. de. A brief history of buddhist studies in europe and america. EB n.s.7.1; 7.2 (may and oct 1974) 55-106; 49-82. See esp, chap 4, Future perspectives, 70-82, re tsl of chin budd texts.

Jong, J. W. de. Recent buddhist studies in europe and america, 1973-1983. EB n.s. 17.1 (spring 1984) 79-107.

Kaltenmark, Max. Henri Maspero et les études taoïstes. In HHM (1984) 45-48.

Kaltenmark, Max. Das tao-tsang project. ZDMG Supplementa 7 (1989) 443-446.

Knaul, Livia. The habit of perfection—a summary of fukunaga mitsuji's studies on the chuang tzu tradition. CEA 1 (1985) 71-84. Fukunaga looks at chuang tzu as philos of relig.

Lagerwey, John. Rapport sur une conférence taoïste, tenue à hong kong en décembre 1985. CEA 2 (1986) 185-190. On taoist ritual and music. Engl language papers sep listed in this bibliog in STR&MT (1989)

Lancaster, Lewis R. Buddhist studies. EncyRel 2 (1987) 554b-560b.

Lauridsen, Kirsten Ronbol. Long live confucius: some remarks on creel, confucius, and humanistic values. In AnHaf (1988) 78-81.

Leung, Man Kam. Chinese language publications in chinese religions, 1977-1987. In TT:RCT (1989) 346-373. A list in chin, with no comm.

16

Leung, Man Kam. The relations between religion and peasant rebellions: a review of the interpretations by chinese historians. In TT:RCT (1989) 43-50.

Magnin, Paul. l'Apport de Maspero à l'histoire du bouddhisme chinois. In HHM (1984) 49-53.

Martin, Mary Lou & Donald MacInnis. Values & religion in china today: a teaching workbook and lesson series. Maryknoll NY (1985) 135 p, guide to resources. High school level.

Martinson, Paul V. The chin p'ing mei as wisdom literature: a methodological essay. MingSt 5 (1977) 44-56. On utilizing novels as source for relig studies.

Mayeda, Egaku. Japanese studies on the schools of the chinese agamas. In Heinz Bechert (heraus) Zur schulzugehövigkeit von werken der hinayana-literatur, göttingen (1985) 94-103.

McRae, John R. et al. The historical legacy of religion in china. Report on a workshop held at harvard university. JCR 17 (1989) 61-116.

Nadeau, Randall Religious studies in taiwan: a review article BCAR 2 (1988) 56-65.

Paper, Jordan. "Religion" and chinese culture: a fundamental definition and suggested approach. In Michael Pye & Peter McKenzie (ed) History of religions, leicester (?1989).

Parkin, Harry. Postscript: chinese religious studies today. In CFRSM (1983) 161-174.

Pocock, J. G. A. Gibbon and the idol fo: chinese and christian history in the enlightenment. In David S. Katz & Jonathan I. Israel (ed) Sceptics, millenarians and jews, leiden (1990) 15-34.

Ren, Jiyu. T'ang yung-t'ung. EncyRel 14 (1987) 269b-270a.

Schafer sinological papers. CEA 1 and 2 (1985 and 1986) 103-104; 269-270. Notices by A.S. (Anna Seidel) and A.S. & L.K. (Livia Knaul?)

Schmidt-Glintzer, Helwig. Eine methodische überlegungen zur religionsgeschichte chinas. ZDMG Supplementa 3.2 (1977) 1322-1332.

Seidel, Anna. Chronicle of taoist studies in the west 1950-1990. CEA 5 (1989-1990) 223-347. Detailed discussion followed by extensive bibliog.

Seidel, Anna. Maspero, Henri. EncyRel 9 (1987) 277a-278a.

Seiwert, Hubert et al. The institutional context of the history of religions in china. In Michael Pye (ed) Marburg revisited; institutions & strategies in the study of religion, Marburg (1989) 127-141. Report of IAHR working group, june 1988.

Seiwert, Hubert. Loyalitäts- und orientierungs konflikte in der religionsforschung: religionstheorie in china 1979-1988. In FestColpe (1990) 162-175.

Shih, Kuang-ch'ing. Achievements in china's tun-huang studies. AofA 19.1 (jan-feb 1989) 158-159. Re new discoveries and studies.

Soymié, Michel. Paul Demiéville (1894-1979) JA 268.1-2 (1980) 1-10.

Stein, Rolf. Necrologie: Étienne Lamotte. TP 69.1-3 (1983) 138-140.

Swanson, Paul L. T'ien-t'ai studies in japan. CEA 2 (1986) 219-232.

Tanaka, Ryosho. A historical outline of japanese research on the chinese chan writings from dunhuang. SCEAR 1 (1989) 141-170.

Tang, Yi-jieh. A perspective on the meaning of comparative philosophy and comparative religious studies: the case of the introduction of indian buddhism into china. CSP 15.2 (winter 1983-84) 39-106.

Tang, Yi-jieh. The significance of comparative philosophy and comparative religion: a view from the introduction of indian buddhism into china. CSP 18.4 (summer 1987) 3-63.

Taylor, Rodney L. The study of confucianism as a religious tradition: notes on some recent publications. JCR 18 (1990) 143-159. Rev art on a no of works.

Thompson, Laurence G. In memoriam Holmes Welch (1921-1981) SSCRB (1981) 126-128.

Werblowsky, R. J. Z. l'Image occidentale de la religion chinois de leibniz à de groot. Diogène 133 (1986) 113-121. Engl version has same pagination.

Yampolsky, Philip. New japanese studies in early ch'an history. In ECCT (1983) 1-11.

Yü, David C. Religious studies in china at crossroads. JCR 18 (1990) 167-172.

Yu, David C. Present-day taoist studies. RSR 3.4 (oct 1977) 220-239.

I.6 Collective Works in Multiple Categories

Bodde, Derk. Ed and intro by Charles le Blanc & Dorothy Borel. Essays on chinese civilization. Princeton univ (1981) Repr of many scholarly papers, incl a no on chin relig, listed sep in this bibliog; abbrev ECC.

Buswell, Robert E. jr. Chinese buddhist apocrypha. Univ hawaii (1990) 342 p, genl index, index of texts. Indiv art sep listed in this bibliog; abbrev CBA.

Chan, Wing-tsit. Chu hsi: new studies. Univ hawaii (1989) Incl 5 relevant chap sep listed in this bibliog; abbrev CH:NS.

Chappell, David W. (ed) Buddhist & taoist studies II: Buddhist and taoist practice in medieval chinese society. Univ hawaii (1987) 222 p, gloss, contributors, index. Indiv art sep listed in this bibliog; abbrev BTS-II.

Coward, Harold, Eva Dargyayl & Ronald Neufelt (ed) Readings in eastern religions. Wilfrid laurier univ (1988) See 5, Early chinese thought; 6,

Confucian thought; 7, Taoist thought; 8, Mao Tse-tung, 247-305. All are taken fr standard engl tsl.

Crim, Keith (genl ed) Abindon dictionary of living religions. Nashville (1981) See passim.

Dialogue and alliance 4.2 (summer 1990) Special issue consisting of papers fr conference held in may 1989, on Religion in china, past and present. Indiv papers sep listed in this bibliog; abbrev D&A.

Demiéville, Paul. Choix d'études bouddhiques (1929-1970) Leiden (1973) xli + 497 p, bibliog of author, 1920-1971 comp by Gisèle de Jong. Repr in 1 vol of 13 art and 4 rev; each repr sep listed in this bibliog; abbrev CEB.

Demiéville, Paul. Choix d'etudes sinologiques (1921-1970) Leiden (1973) xli + 633 p, bibliog of author 1920-1971 comp by Gisèle de Jong. Repr in 1 vol of many art relating to relig among other subj; each relevant repr sep listed in this bibliog; abbrev CES.

Du bon usage des dieux en chine. l'Homme 27 (no 101) (janv-mars 1987) Cover -title for this issue.

Ebrey, Patricia. Chinese civilization & society. A source book. NY (1981) 429 p, pronunciation guide guide, ref matter, chronol of chin history, intro, map, gloss, further reading, orig sources, index. 89 sel. For relig see passim, titles of selections and index.

Eliade, Mircea (ed in chief). The encyclopedia of religion. NY, 16 vol (1987) Art sep listed in this bibliog; abbrev EncyRel.

Wolf, Arthur P (ed). Religion and ritual in chinese society. Stanford univ (1974) xii + 377 p. Indiv art sep listed in this bibliog; abbrev RRCS.

Part Two

Chinese Religion
Exclusive of Buddhism

II.1 Terminology

Benedict, P. K. The gods of sino-tibetan. AO 51 (1990) 161-172. Relig elements in names of sino-tibetan gods, revealing aspects of ancient chin relig.

Chan, Wing-tsit. Chu hsi on t'ien. Chap 12 in author's CH:NS (1989) 184-196.

Dehergne, Joseph. Un problème ardu: le nom de dieu en chinois. In Appréciation par l'europe de la tradition chinoise: à partir du xviie siècle: actes du iiie colloque international de sinologie. Paris (1983) 13-46.

Hummel, Siegbert. Tao und nü-kua. AS 43.1 (1989) 28-33. Paleographical study.

Kaltenmark, Max. King yu pa-king [ching yü pa-ching] In Fukui Kojun festschrift, Toya bunka ronshu, tokyo (1969) 1147-1154. Re important term in mao shan taoist texts.

Nikkilä, Pertti. Early confucianism and inherited thought in the light of some key terms of the confucian analects. I. The terms in shuching and shihching. Helsinki, studia orientalia vol 53 (1982) 275 p, primary sources, literature, abbrev, index.

Schafer, Edward H. The grand aurora. Chinese science 6 (1983) 21-32. Term used in taoist cosmological speculation.

Yang, En Cheng. The idea tien-ming in the book of historical documents. CF 29.4 (dec 1986) 207-220.

Yeo, Khiok-Khng. Amos (4:4-5) and confucius: the will (ming) of god (thien) AJT 4.2 (oct 1990) 472-488.

II.2 Archeology and Antiquity

Aho, James A. Religious mythology and the art of war. Comparative religious symbolisms of military violence. Westport, conn (1981). See chap 6, The gentleman warrior: ritual warfare in ancient china, 101-126.

Allan, Sarah. Drought, human sacrifice and the mandate of heaven in a lost text from the shang shu. BSOAS 47.3 (1984) 523-539.

Allan, Sarah. The heir and the sage; dynastic legend in early china. Taipei (1981) 165 p, index.

Allan, Sarah. Yao and Shun. EncyRel 15 (1987) 502a-502b.

Allan, Sarah. Sons of suns: myth and totemism in early china. BSOAS 44.2 (1981) 290-326.

Benedict, P. K. The gods of sino-tibetan. AO 51 (1990) 161-172. Relig elements in names of sino-tibetan gods, revealing aspects of ancient chin relig.

Berger, Patricia. An ideology of one: the offering shrine of wu liang. EC 15 (1990) 223-235. Rev art on Wu Hung, The wu liang shrine: the ideology of early chinese pictorial art (1989) q.v.

Bielenstein, Hans. Han portents and prognostications. BMFEA 56 (1984) 97-112.

Bulling, A. Guttkind. A late shang place of sacrifice and its historical significance. Expedition 19.4 (1977) 1-11, illus.

Bulling, Anneliese Guttkind. Rites mentioned in han tomb inscriptions and the funerary art of han and pre-han periods. Proc31stICHS, Tokyo, vol 2 (1984) 929. Abstr.

Chan, Alan K. L. Goddesses in chinese religions. In Goddesses (1990) 9-81. Focuses particularly on taoist female deities.

Chang, Cheng-lang. Tsl by H. Huber, R. Yates, et al. An interpretation of the divinatory inscriptions on early chou bronzes. EC 6 (1980-81) 80-96.

Chang, Kwang-chih. Art, myth and ritual: the path to political authority in ancient china. Harvard univ (1983) 160 p, 38 photos, 24 line drawings. See chap 3, Shamanism and politics, 44-55; chap 4, Art as the path to authority, 56-80. Chap 4 is

20

slightly rev version of art on The animal in shang and chou art, HJAS 41 (dec 1981)

Chang, K. C. An essay on cong [ts'ung] Orientations 20.6 (june 1989) 37-43, illus. Ancient jade tube, supposedly of relig significance.

Chang, K. C. The "meaning" of shang bronze art AsArt 3.2 (spring 1990) 9-17.

Chard, Robert. Magicians as artisans: a han usage of the word kung. PTP 16 (1984) 61-81.

Cheng, Anne. De la place de l'homme dans l'universe: la conception de la triade ciel-terre-homme a la fin de l'antiquité chinoise. EOEO 3 (1983) 11-22.

Cheng, Te-k'un. Ch'in-han mortuary architecture. JICS:CUHK 11 (1980) 193-269, illus.

Childs-Johnson, Elizabeth. The shang bird: intermediary to the supernatural. Orientations 20.11 (nov 1989) 53-61, illus.

Chow, Tse-tsung. Ancient chinese wu shamanism and its relationship to sacrifices, history, dance-music, and poetry. TJ n.s. 13.1/2 (dec 1981) engl summ 23-25.

Cooper, Eugene. The potlatch in ancient china: parallels in the sociopolitical structure of the ancient chinese and the american indians of the northwest coast. HR 22.2 (1982) 103-128.

Croissant, Doris. Grabkult und jenseitsvorstellung in der han-zeit. In WGM (1989) 115-121.

Doty, Darrel. Why did the ancient chinese not develop a creator god? TR 20.3 (spring 1990) 317-331.

Eliade, Mircea. Tsl by Willard R. Trask. A history of religious ideas. Vol. 2: From gautama buddha to the triumph of christianity. Univ chicago (1982) See chap 16: The religions of ancient china, 3-43; also see bibliog note, 419-433.

Eno, Robert. Was there a high god ti in shang religion? EC 15 (1990) 1-26.

Fu, Pei-jung. On religious ideas of the pre-chou china. CC 26 (1985) 23-39.

Glum, Peter. Rain magic at anyang? Speculations about two ritual bronzes of the shang dynasty filled with revolving dragons. BMFEA 54 (1982) 241-265.

Harper, Donald. A chinese demonography of the third century b.c. HJAS 45 (1985) 459-498.

Ho, Chuan-kun. Burial patterns of prehistoric taiwan (part I) JICS 19 (1988) 433-468.

James, Jean M. The dating of the left wu family offering shrine. OA n.s. 31.1 (spring 1985) 34-41. Re Wu liang tz'u.

Jao, Tsung-i. Le canon des rites et quelques théories majeures du ritualisme suivant le commentaire de zuo des annales des printemps et automnes. In EsurR (1990) 27-44.

Kalinowski, Marc. Les traités de shuihudi et l'hémérologie chinois à la fin des royaumes-combattants. TP 72.4-5 (1986) 175-228. From tomb excavation at shuihudi in hupei.

Keightley, David N. Late shang divination: the magico-religious legacy. In Henry Rosemont (ed) Explorations in early chinese cosmology, chico, calif (1984) 11-34.

Keightley, David N. Shang divination and metaphysics. PEW 38.4 (1988) 367-397.

Kohl, Louis von. Die grundlagen des altchinesischen staates und die bedeutung der riten und der musik. Baessler-archiv 17.2 (1934) 55-98.

Kudo, Motoo. Tsl by P. A. Herbert. The ch'in bamboo strip book of divination (jih-shu) and ch'in legalism. ActaA 58 (mar 1990) 24-37.

Kurihara, Keisuke. On the yin-ssu in ancient china. MexICHS 2: China (1976) 3-7. Re ancient sacrifice.

Lai, Whalen. Looking for mr ho po: unmasking the river god of ancient china. HR 29 (may 1990)

335-350, illustrations.

Larre, Claude & Elisabeth Rochat de la Vallé. La bannière funéraire de mawangdui. Paris (1985)

Levi, Jean. Les fonctionnaires divins; politique, despotisme et mystique en chine ancienne. ?Paris (1989) See esp Troisième partie, Bureaucratie et transcendance, 203-269 and notes.

Levi, Jean. Identité et bureaucratie divines en chine ancienne. RHR 225.4 (1988) 447-465.

Levi, Jean. Le silence du rîte. TdelaR 6 (1985) 75-80. Education, incl relig aspects, in ancient china.

Loewe, Michael. The almanacs (jih-shu) from shui-hu-ti: a preliminary survey. AM 3rd ser 1.2 (1988) 1-27. Texts fr recent excavations in hupei.

Loewe, Michael. The oracles of the clouds and the winds. BSOAS 51.3 (1988) 500-520.

Major, John S. New light on the dark warrior. JCR 13/14 (1985/86) 65-86.

Makeham, John. Ming-chiao in the eastern han: filial piety, reputation, and office. HHYC:CS 8.2 (dec 1990) 79-107.

Mathieu, Rémi. Etude sur la mythologie et l'ethnologie de la chine ancienne. T.1, Traduction annotée du shanhai jing. T.2, Index du shanhai jing. Paris (1983) cxvi + 1223 p.

Mathieu, Rémi. Le lièvre de la lune dans l'antiquité chinoise. RHR 207.4 (1990) 339-365.

Mathieu, Rémi. Le songe de zhao jianzi. Etude sur les rêves d'ascension céleste et les rêves d'esprits dans la chine ancienne. AS 37 (1983) 120-138.

Munsterberg, Hugo. Symbolism in ancient chinese art. NY (1985) ca. 250 p, ca. 100 pl, bibliog, index. Re ornamentation of shang bronzes.

Naundorf, Gert. Raumsvorstellungen in den chiao-opfern bis zur han-zeit. In RPO-A (1985) 323-330.

Paper, Jordan. The feng in protohistoric chinese religion. HR 25.3 (feb 1986) 213-235, illus.

Poo, Mu-chou. Ideas concerning death and burial in pre-han and han china. AM 3rd ser 2 (1990) 25-62.

Powers, Martin J. Hybrid omens and public issues in early imperial china. BMFEA 55 (1983) 1-56. Re offering shrines of wu clan, dated 147-167. "Hybrid" refers to "confucian" and taoist inspirations.

Powers, Martin J. A late western han tomb near yangzhou and related problems. OA n.s. 29.3 (autumn 1983) 275-290.

Qui, Xigui. Tsl by K. Fowler. On the burning of human victims and the fashioning of clay dragons in order to seek rain as seen in the shang dynasty oracle-bone inscriptions. EC 9-10 (1983-85) 290-306.

Riegel, Jeffrey K. Early chinese target magic. JCR 10 (1982) 1-18.

Riegel, Jeffrey. Kou-mang and ju-shou. CEA 5 (1989-90) 55-83. Re a pair of warring states deities of life and death.

Roth, Harold. Fang-shih. EncyRel 5 (1987) 282b-284a.

Roth, Harold. Huang-lao chün. EncyRel 6 (1987) 483b-484b.

Roth, Harold. Liu an. EncyRel 9 (1987) 1a-2b.

Schipper, Kristofer M. Comment on créé un lieu-saint local: à propos de Danses et légendes de la chine ancienne. EtCh 4.2 (automne 1985) 41-61.

Schwartz, Benjamin I. The world of thought in ancient china. Harvard univ (1985) 490 p, notes, sel bibliog, gloss, index. See passim.

Seidel, Anna. Traces of han religion in funeral texts found in tombs. In TRC (1987) 23-57.

Seiwert, Hubert Michael. Orakelwesen und zukunft deutung in chinesischen altertum. Bonn (1979) 352 s, tabellen, anmerkungen,

22

literaturverzeichnis.

Seiwert, Hubert. Mythologie in chinesischen altertum. ZMR 62 (july 1978) 203-208.

Shih, Joseph. Revelation in chinese religion. SM 20 (1971) 237-266.

Silberman, Jerome. Mawangdui, excavated materials, and transmitted texts: a cautionary note. EC 8 (1982-83) 79-92. Mostly re interpretations of the T-shaped banner.

Sjöholm, Gunnar. The boundaries between religion and culture with reference to the interpretation of ancient chinese religion. CF 13.4 (1970) 5-20.

Teng, Ssu-yü. Orthodoxy and heterodoxy in ancient chinese patterns of thought. ASBIHP 55.3 (sept 1984) 339-414. From oracle bones to tung chung-shu.

Thote, Alain. Une tombe princière chinoise du ve siècle avant notre ère. CRAIBL (avr-juin 1986) 393-413. Re tomb no 1 at leigudun of marquis yi of tseng.

Touponce, William F. The wei tzu document of the shu ching: a sacrificial crisis in confucian thought. TR 13.2 (winter 1982) 185-202.

Vandermeersch, M. L. Religions de la chine. ACF 88 (1979-80) 137-142. 1. Etude des traditions chinoises de l'époque archaïque et naissance de confucianisme. 2. Inscriptions oraculaires de l'époque yin. 3. Inscriptions sur bronze.

Vervoorn, Aat. Men of the cliffs and caves; the development of the chinese eremitic tradition to the end of the han dynasty. HK (1990) 368 p.

Vervoorn, Aat. The origins of chinese eremitism. JICS:CUHK 15 (1984) 249-295.

Wu, Hung. Myths and legends in han funerary art: their pictorial structure and symbolic meanings as reflected in carvings on sichuan sarcophagi. In SCP (1987) 72-81.

Wu, Hung. The wu liang shrine: the ideology of

early chinese pictorial art. Stanford univ (1989) xiv + 412 p, photos, rubbings, drawings.

Yang, Hsi-chang. The shang dynasty cemetery system. In K. C. Chang (ed) Studies of shang archaeology, yale univ (1986) 49-63.

Yeung, Arnold Mik. Nature and the natural in asian thinking: classical asian religions. EAJT 1.1 (1983) 45-59.

Zhang, Yachu & Liu Yu. Tsl by Edward Shaughnessy. Some observations about milfoil-divination based on shang and zhou bagua numerical symbols. EC 7 (1981-82) 46-55.

Zheng, Chan-tal. Les structures totémiques de la religion chinoise primitive. RHR 203.2 (avr-juin 1986) 115-129.

II.3 Mythology

Allan, Sarah. The myth of the xia dynasty. JRAS (1984, no 2) 242-256. The hsia as a mythical construct of the shang.

Allan, Sarah. Sons of suns: myth and totemism in early china. BSOAS 44.2 (1981) 290-326.

Allen, Joseph Roe iii. The myth studies of wen i-to: a question of methodology. TR 13 (1982) 137-160.

Boltz, William G. Kung kung and the flood: reverse euhemerism in the yao tien. TP 67.3-5 (1981) 141-153.

Bonnefoy, Yves (comp) Engl version prepared under direction of Wendy Doniger (tsl not named) Mythologies. Paris (orig french version) Univ chicago (engl version) (1981 & 1991) See vol 2, East asia and inner asia, 1007-1037 in engl version.

Cahill, Suzanne. Beside the turquoise pond: the shrine of the queen mother of the west in medieval chinese poetry and religious practice. JCR 12 (1984) 19-32.

Cahill, Suzanne. Performers and female taoist adepts: hsi wang mu as the patron deity of women in medieval china. JAOS 106.1 (jan-mar 1986) 155-168.

Cahill, Suzanne. Reflections of a metal mother: tu kuang-t'ing's biography of hsi wang mu. JCR 13/14 (1985-86) 127-142.

Cahill, Suzanne. A white clouds appointment with the queen mother of the west. JCR 16 (1988) 43-53.

Cavendish, Richard (ed in chief) Man, myth and magic. NY etc (1983) See Index, under China. 11 vol encyclopedia, profusely illus.

Chan, Alan K. L. Goddesses in chinese religions. In Goddesses (1990) 9-81. Focuses particularly on taoist female deities.

Chao, Denise. The ox and the mulberry in chinese belief: the myth of the cowherd and the weaving girl. Folklore 26.5 (may 1985) 81-86.

Cheng, Hsiao-chieh, Hui-chen Pai Cheng & Kenneth Lawrence Theru (tsl) Shan hai ching. Legendary geography and wonders of ancient china. Taipei (1985) 426 p, app, bibliog, map. Commentary by Kuo P'o, chin dyn; explanatory notes by Hao Yi-hsing, ch'ing dyn.

Ching, Julia. The ancient sages (sheng): their identity and their place in chinese intellectual history. OE 30 (1983-86) 1-18.

Christie, Anthony. China. Chap 5 in Richard Cavendish (ed) Mythology; an illustrated encyclopedia. London (1980) 58-73.

Christie, Anthony. Chinese mythology. Feltham, middlesex, engl (1968) 141 p, illus. Repr NY (1985)

Diény, Jean-Pierre. Mythologie et sinologie. EtCh 9.1 (1990) 129-150.

Fracasso, Riccardo. Holy mothers of ancient china: a new approach to the hsi-wang-mu problem. TP 74.1-3 (1988) 1-46.

Fracasso, Riccardo. Teratoscopy or divination by monsters: being a study of the wu-tsang shan-

ching. HHY:CS 1.2 (dec 1983) 657-700. Text is first five books of shan hai ching.

Girardot, Norman J. Chinese religion: mythic themes. EncyRel 3 (1987) 296b-305a.

Girardot, N. J. & John S. Major. Introduction to symposium issue: myth and symbol in chinese tradition. JCR 13/14 (1985/86) 1-14.

Hong, Liu. Myths of the creation of mankind in chinese mythology and the myths of nugua, the accepted creator of mankind. JAC 7 (1983) 121-158.

Hsu, C. Y. The queen mother of the west: historical or legendary? ACQ; pt I, 16.2; pt II, 16.3 (summer-autumn 1988) 29-42; 49-65.

Hu, Shiguang (tsl) The tale of nezha—three chapters from the "canonization of the gods." CL (july 1983) 71-113.

Hummel, Siegbert. Tao und nü-kua. AS 43.1 (1989) 28-33. Paleographical study.

Jabouille, M. P. Le phénix fabuleux de la chine et le falcon ocellé. Bulletin des amis du vieux hué 16.4 (oct-déc 1929)

Jan, Yün-hua. The change of images: the yellow emperor in ancient chinese literature. JOS 19.2 (1981) 117-137.

Javary, G. Hou ji, prince millet, l'agriculteur divin: interpretation du mythe chinois par le r. p. joachim bouvet, s.j. Introduction et traduction du latin. NZM 39.1-39.2 (1983) 107-119; 16-41.

Kaltenmark, Max. Grottes et labyrinthes en chine ancienne. In Yves Bonnefoy (ed) Dictionnaire des mythologies, paris (1981) 140a-141b.

Kuhn, Dieter. Tracing a chinese legend: in search of the identity of the "first sericulturist" TP 70.4-5 (1984) 214-245.

Lai, Whalen. Icons and iconoclasm: the earth diver hsi in taoistic recall. TaoRes 1.2 (winter 1989) 28-36.

Lai, Whalen. Symbolism of evil in china: the k'ung-chia myth analyzed. HR 23.4 (1984) 316-343.

LeBlanc, Charles. A re-examination of the myth of huang-ti. JCR 13/14 (1985/86) 45-64.

Lee, Peter K. H. Theology and myth: a reflection on the lady flying to the moon and the archer shooting down nine suns. EAJT 3.2 (1985) 228-242. Same title in CF 28.1 (mar 1985) 8-29.

Lemoine, Jacques. Mythes d'origine, mythes d'identification. l'Homme 27, no 101 (janv-mars 1984) 58-85.

Loewe, Michael. Hsi wang mu. EncyRel 6 (1987) 479b-480b.

Major, John S. New light on the dark warrior. JCR 13/14 (1985/86) 65-86.

Mathieu, Rémi. Anthologie des mythes et légendes de la chine ancienne. Paris (1989) 262 p.

Mathieu, Rémi. Le corbeau dans la mythologie de l'ancienne chine. RHR 201.3 (1984) 281-309.

Mathieu, Rémi. Etude sur la mythologie et l'ethnologie de la chine ancienne.T. 1, Traduction annotée du shanhai jing. T. 2, Index du shanhai jing. Paris (1983) cxvi + 1223 p.

Mathieu, Rémi. Images de l'imaginaire dans la mythologie chinoise ancienne: des mythes solaires. EOEO 7 (1985) 83-92.

Mathieu, Rémi. Le lièvre de la lune dans l'antiquité chinoise. RHR 207.4 (oct-déc 1990) 339-365.

Mathieu, Rémi. La patte de l'ours. l'Homme 24.1 (janv-mars 1984) 5-42. Bear paws and symbolic thinking in china and northeast asia.

Mitarai, Masaru. Tsl by Ilsa Lenz & Derek Herforth. On the legends of the yellow sovereign. EAC-2 (1983) 67-96.

Paper, Jordan. The feng in protohistoric chinese religion. HR 25.3 (feb 1986) 213-235, illus .

The quest for eternity. Chinese ceramic sculptures from the people's republic of china. Los angeles county museum of art (1987) xiv + 161 p, chronol, map of china, gloss, char list, suggested reading, profusely illus. Exhibition catalog, incl 5 essays sep listed in this bibliog. Abbrev QE.

Riegel, Jeffrey. Kou-mang and ju-shou. CEA 5 (1989-90) 55-83. Re a pair of warring states deities of life and death.

Schiffeler, John W. Chinese folk medicine: a study of the shan hai ching. AJCM 12.1-4 (1984) 2-31.

Seidel, Anna. Yü. EncyRel 15 (1987) 540b-541a.

Seiwert, Hubert. Mythologie im chinesischen altertum. ZMR 62.3 (juli 1978) 203-208. Rev art on W. Münke, Die klassische chinesische mythologie, q.v.

Sievers, Armin. Mythography versus history: the wuji case. EAC-2 (1983) 38-66. Wuji are fantastic humanoids such as appear in shan hai ching.

Teiser, S. F. Engulfing the bounds of order: the myth of the great flood in mencius. JCR 13/14 (1985/86) 15-44.

Topley, Marjorie. China. In Man, myth and magic: the illustrated encyclopedia of mythology, religion and the unknown. NY etc (1985) 456-464, profusely illus.

Walls, Jan & Yvonne (ed and tsl) Classical chinese myths. HK (1984) 134 p, illus.

Werner, E. T. C. Myths and legends of china. London (1922) 454 p, gloss, illus, index. Repr singapore (1986)

Whittaker, Clio, "contributing ed" An introduction to oriental mythology. London (1989) See Chinese mythology, 13-49.

Wu, Hung. Myths and legends in han funerary art: their pictorial structure and symbolic meanings as reflected in carvings on sichuan sarcophagi. In SCP (1987) 72-81.

Wu, Hung. Xiwangmu, the queen mother of the west. Orientations 18.4 (apr 1987) 24-33. Mostly concerned with sculptural evidences.

Yü, David C. The creation myth and its symbolism in classical taoism. PEW 31.4 (oct 1981) 479-500.

Yü, David C. The creation myth of chaos in the daoist canon. JOS 24.1 (1986) 1-20.

Zhao, Qiguang. Chinese mythology in the context of hydraulic society. AsFS 48.2 (1989) 231-246.

Zheng, Chantal. Mythes et croyances du monde chinois primitif. Paris (1989) 156 p, chronol, notes, bibliog, index, maps.

Yang, Xin, Li Yihua & Xu Naixiang. The art of the dragon. Peking (1988) 216 p, 192 pl & illus, bibliog. Items fr palace museum, peking.

II.4 Art and Symbol

Ancient chinese woodblock new year prints. Peking (1985) 184 p.

Andrews, Julia F. (tsl) Catalogue of the exhibition, by lei congyun, lu shaochen, shi yazhu, & wei yongye. Translated and with additions by Julia F. Andrews. In QE (1987) 95-154.

Andrews, Julia F. Chickens and dogs in the clouds: self-cultivation and transcendence in the painting of cui zizhong [ts'ui tzu-chung] (1597-1644) PTP 16 (1984) 31-60, illus.

Barmé, Geremie. Yin guangzhong and the gods of cathay. CL (autumn 1985) 207-215, preceded by 12 col photos of yin's earthenware masks.

Bartholomew, Teresa Tse. Pious hopes carved on chinese beads—a discussion of rebuses and legends in chinese art. Orientations 19.8 (aug 1988) 23-30.

Berger, Patricia. An ideology of one: the offering shrine of wu liang. EC 15 (1990) 223-235. Rev art on Wu Hung: The wu liang shrine ... q.v.

Berger, Patricia. Purity and pollution in han art. AAA 36 (1983) 40-58. Re ritual, myth, exorcism in stone pictures of han.

Berliner, Nancy. Monsters and myths. AsArt 3.2 (spring 1990) 43-62. Re folk art and relig.

Bulling, Anneliese Guttkind. Rites mentioned in han tomb inscriptions and the funerary art of han and pre-han periods. Proc31stICHS, Tokyo, vol 2 (1984) 929. Abstr.

Cammann, Schuyler. The eight trigrams: variants and their uses. HR 29 (may 1990) 301-317, illus.

Cammann, Schuyler. A ming dynasty pantheon painting. ACASA 18 (1964) 38-46.

Cammann, Schuyler. The origin of the trigram circles in ancient china. BMFEA 62 (1990) 185-205.

Cammann, Schuyler. Some early chinese symbols of duality. HR 24.2 (feb 1985) 215-254, fig.

Cammann, Schuyler. Symbolic expressions of yin-yang philosophy. In CINS (1987) 101-116.

Chang, I-chu. Woodcarvers, gods, and profits. FCR 38.11 (nov 1988) 54-63. Carving of relig and secular themes by chiu hua-hai et al in sanyi, miaoli, taiwan.

Chang, Kwang-chih. Art, myth, and ritual: the path to political authority in ancient china. Harvard univ (1983) 160 p, 38 photos, 24 line drawings. See chap 3, Shamanism and politics, 44-55; chap 4, Art as the path to authority, 56-80, earlier publ in slightly different version as The animal in shang and chou bronze art, HJAS 41 (1981) 527-554.

Chang, K. C. The "meaning" of shang bronze art. AsArt 3.2 (spring 1990) 9-17.

Chang, Lin-sheng. Tsl and adapted by Claudia B. Jones. The dragon motif in cloisonné examples. NPMB 11.4 (sept-oct 1976) 1-17.

Chen, Yuyin. Chen hongshou's "zhong kui" CL (autumn 1985) 216-218, 1 pl. Re a painting by chen hongshou (1598-1652)

Chi Jo-hsi. Tsl by Andrew Morton. Designs symbolizing lucky meanings. In PMK (1984) 128-133, illus col reproductions.

Childs-Johnson, Elizabeth. The shang bird: intermediary to the supernatural. Orientations 20.11 (nov 1989) 53-61, illus.

Chinese paper cutting patterns of gods and buddhas (shen fo chien chih) Taipei (1983) 112 p.

Ching, Julia. The mirror symbol revisited: confucian and taoist mysticism. In MRT (1983) 226-246.

Ching, Julia. The symbolism of the great ultimate "(t'ai-chi)": myth, religion and philosophy. MexICHS 2: China (1976) 64-91.

Cohen, Alvin P. Symbolic amulets and jewelry in chinese popular culture. In TT:RCT (1989) 102-157, copiously illus with b-&-w photos.

Croissant, Doris. Der unsterbliche leib: ahneneffigies und reliquienporträt in der porträtplastic chinas und japans. In M. Kraatz et al (ed) Das bildnis in der kunst des orients, Stuttgart (1990) 235-260.

Deeley, Eileen. Early chinese symbolism. Sawaddi (jan-feb 1982) 8-13, 38.

Delahaye, Hubert. Les antécédents magiques des statues chinoises. Revue d'esthétique n.s. 2 (1983) 45-53.

Delahaye, Hubert. Les premières peintures de paysages en chine: aspects religieux. Paris (1981) 139 p, illus, bibliog.

Delahaye, Hubert. Le yun taishan revisite: une grande première dans l'histoire de l'art du paysage chinois. ArtsAs 37 (1982) 38-43. Re cosmic landscape symbolism.

DeMarco, Michael A. Mirror symbolism: a chinese bronze art. CC 25.4 (dec 1984) 57-63.

Diény, Jean-Pierre. Le fenghuang et le phénix. CEA 5 (1989-90) 1-13.

Diény, Jean-Pierre. Pour un lexique de l'imagination littéraire en chine. Le symbolisme du soleil. BEFEO 69 (1981) 119-152.

Diény, Jean-Pierre. Le symbolisme du dragon dans la chine antique. Paris (1987) xxi + 277 p.

Doeringer, Franklin M. The gate in the circle: a paradigmatic symbol in early chinese cosmology. PEW 32.3 (july 1982) 309-324.

Dragon tales. A collection of chinese stories. Beijing (1988) 232 p, illus sketches. Various comp and tsl into engl.

Eberhard, Wolfram. Tsl of engl version by G. L. Campbell. Lexikon chinesischer symbole. Engl title: A dictionary of chinese symbols. French title: Dictionnaire des symboles chinois. Cologne; Paris; London (1983; 1984; 1986) 332 double-col p in engl version, illus, bibliog.

Ebert, Jorinde, Barbara M. Kaulbach & Martin Kraatz (ed) Religiöse malerei aus taiwan. Köln (1981) Catalog of exhibition, oct-nov 1980, marburg univ.

Fontein, Jon. Inscriptions on taoist statues. ProcICS (1981) Art hist vol, 95-100, fig.

Girardot, N. J. & John S. Major. Introduction to symposium issue: myth and symbol in chinese tradition. JCR 13/14 (1985/86) 1-14.

Glum, Peter. Rain magic at anyang? Speculations about two ritual bronze vessels of the shang dynasty filled with revolving dragons. BMFEA 54 (1982) 241-272.

Gray, Basil. A great taoist painting. OA 11 (1965) 85-94, illus. On yen pien hsiang—"metamorphoses of heavenly beings" Repr in author's collection, Studies in chinese and islamic art, vol 1, london (1985) 132-150.

Guan, Tianxiang. Mural paintings discovered in a sui tomb. CL (jan 1982) 124-128.

Hargett, James M. Playing second fiddle: the luan-bird in early and medieval chinese literature. TP 75.4-5 (1989) 235-262.

He, Zhenghuang. Tang tomb murals. CL (apr 1983) 111-115.

James, Jean M. Bridges and cavalcades in eastern han funerary art. OA 28.2 (summer 1982) 165-171.

James, Jean M. The role of nanyang in han funerary iconography. OA n.s. 36.4 (winter 1990/91) 222-232.

Juliano, Annette L. Teng-hsien: an important six dynasties tomb. AA suppl (1980) 84 p, gloss, bibliog, 149 pl.

Kalinowski, Marc. Remarques sur les miroirs TLV dans leur rapport avec les tables liu-jen. Numen 29.1 (1982) 114-122. Re Michael Loewe's Ways to paradise q.v.

Kaltenmark, Maxime & Michel Soymié. Symbolisme traditionel et religions populaires. In EncyUniv 5 (1990) 621b-625b.

Karetzky, Patricia Eichenbaum. The engraved designs on the late sixth century sarcophagus of li ho. AA 47.2 (1986) 81-106, 14 fig. Taoist cosmological themes.

Karetzky, Patricia Eichenbaum. A scene of the taoist afterlife in a sixth century sarcophagus discovered in loyang. AA 44.1 (1983) 5-20.

Kuei, Liang. Tsl by Claudia B. Jones. The dragon motif in blue-and-white porcelain. NPMB 11.2 (may-june 1976) 1-13.

Kuwayama, George. The sculptural development of ceramic funerary figures in china. In QE (1987) 63-93, illus, notes.

Lai, Whalen. Symbolism of evil in china: the k'ung-chih myth analyzed. HR 23.4 (1984) 316-343.

Laufer, Berthold. Jade. A study in chinese archaeology and religion. Chicago (1912) 370 p, illus. Repr south pasadena, calif (1946) repr NY (1974) repr NY (1989) with new subtitle: Its history and symbolism in china.

Ledderose, Lothar. The earthly paradise: religious elements in chinese landscape art. In TAC (1983) 165-183, illus.

Ledderose, Lothar. A king of hell. In Suzuki kei sensei kanreki kinen: chugoku kaiga shi ronshu, tokyo (1981) 33-42.

Ledderose, Lothar. Kings of hell. ProcICS (1981) Art hist vol, 191-196.

Lei, Congyun. Catalogue of the exhibition, by lei conyun . . . In QE (1987) 95-154.

Leu, Chien-ai. Photos by Chung Yung-ho. Temple roof art. FCR 40.11 (nov 1990) 34-45, col photos. Re ornamentation of temple roofs in chien nien technique.

Liang, Ssu-ch'eng. Ed by Wilma Fairbank. A pictorial history of chinese architecture. MIT (1984) xxv + 201 p, profusely illus, dynastic chart, gloss technical terms, guide to pronunciation, sel bibliog, index. See passim.

Little, Stephen. The demon queller and the art of qiu ying (ch'iu ying) AA 46.1/2 (1985) 8-80, 62 fig.

Little, Stephen. Realm of the immortals. Daoism in the arts of china. Cleveland art museum in conjunction with indiana univ (1988) 67p, intro, col pl, catalog, chronol, gloss, bibliog, index.

Liu, Laurence G. Chinese architecture. NY (1989) 297 p, notes, gloss, bibliog, index, profusely illus. See passim, esp Chap 4, Religious buildings, 55-160; Chap 7, Funeral and ceremonial buildings, 219-246.

Lu, Shaochen. Catalogue of the exhibition by . . . lu shaochen . . . In QE (1987) 95-154.

Luo, Feng. Lacquer painting on a northern wei coffin. Orientations 21.7 (july 1990) 18-29, illus.

M. K. [Max Kaltenmark] & M. S. [Michel Soymié] Symbolisme traditionelle et religions populaires. EUF 4 (1968) Chine, sec 5, 362a-365c. Same title in EncyUniv 5 (1990) 621b-625b.

28

Mahdihassan, S. Symbols designed by european alchemists incorporating elements of chinese origin. AJCM 15.1-2 (1987) 3-12.

Mahdihassan, S. T'ao-t'ieh, a motif of chinese funerary art as the iconographic counterpart of cinnabar, an alchemical drug. AJCM 10.1-4 (1982) 5-13.

Major, John S. New light on the dark warrior. JCR 13/14 (1985/86) 65-86.

Markbreiter, Stephen. Fukienese wood carvings; a survival in taiwan. AofA 19.3 (may-june 1989) 97-104. Mostly relig carvings.

McNair, Amy. On the date of the shengmudian sculptures at jenci. AA 49.3/4 (1988/89) 238-253, 10 fig. Hall of the sage mother, chin-tz'u, shanxi. Sculptures supposedly represent yi jiang, wife of king wu of chou.

Meyer, Jeffrey F. Traditional peking: the architecture of conditional power. In Bardwell Smith & Holly Baker Reynolds (ed) The city as a sacred center, leiden etc (1987) 113-133.

Mindich, Jeffrey H. Painting eyes on the dragon. FCR 40.11 (nov 1990) 30-33, col photos. Re carvings in tainan confucian temple.

Mindich, Jeffrey H. A paragon for all generations. FCR 40.11 (nov 1990) 22-29, col photos Re history and present aspect of tainan's confucian temple.

Mindich, Jeffrey H. Restored grandeur. FCR 40.11 (nov 1990) 4-21, col photos. Re restoration of tainan confucian temple.

Moes, Robert (comp) Auspicious spirits: korean folk paintings and related objects. Washington d.c. (1983) 200 p, intro, sel bibliog, topical index, profusely illus. Altho korean in subj matter, much of the material relates to china.

Moss, Paul. Between heaven and earth. Secular and divine figural images in chinese paintings and objects. London (1988) no pagination; 66 col illus of paintings and objects, with comments; char

index, bibliog, map of chiangnan region.

Munakata, Kiyohiko. Concepts of lei and kan-lei in early chinese art theory. In TAC (1983) 105-131.

Munsterberg, Hugo. Symbolism in ancient chinese art. NY (1985) ca. 250 p, ca. 100 pl, bibliog, index. Re ornamentation of shang bronzes.

Paper, Jordan. The feng in protohistoric chinese religion. HR 25.3 (feb 1986) 213-235.

Paper, Jordan. Religion and art in contemporary china. JCR 15 (1987) 51-60, illus.

Paper, Jordan. Riding on a white cloud: aesthetics as religion in china. Religion 15 (1985) 3-27. Humanities in traditional china and their relig aspects.

Pearls of the middle kingdom. A selection of articles from the national palace museum monthly of chinese art. Taipei. National palace museum (1984) Art sep listed in this bibliog. Abbrev PMK.

Pederson, Bent Lerbaek. Qing dynasty statues of the three gods of happiness. Helsinki/studia orientalia 64 (1988) 367-372.

People's daily press (ed) The dragon. ?Peking (1988) 155p, 169 col pl.

Petit, Karl. Talismans monetiformes de chine et du japon - coin-shaped charms of china and japan. Paris (1981) 184 p.

Petit, Karl. La monde des symboles dans l'art de la chine. Bruxelles (1982) 153 p.

Powers, Martin J. An archaic bas-relief and the chinese moral cosmos in the first century a.d. ArsO 12 (1981) 25-40, 17 fig.

Prest, John. Gardens. EncyRel 5 (1987) See sec, The east, 488a-489a.

Rawson, Jessica. Chinese ornament: the lotus and the dragon. British museum (1984) See rev by Margaret Medley in Orientations 16.5 (may 1985) 52-56.

Rawson, Jessica. The lotus and dragon sources of chinese ornament. Orientations 15.11 (1984) 22-36.

Reiter, Florian. The visible divinity. The sacred icon in religious taoism. NachrDGNVO 144 (1989) 51-70.

Ross, Daniel G. Chinese and western religious symbols as used in taiwan: a sociological study. Fu jen univ (1980) 226 p.

Sangren, P. Steven. Female gender in chinese religious symbols: kuan yin, matsu, and the "eternal mother" Signs 9 (1983) 4-25.

Shaw, Miranda. Buddhist and taoist influences on chinese landscape painting. JHI 49 (apr-june 1988) 183-206.

Shen, Shan-hong. The principle of tao as the foundation of chinese art. American asian review, jamaica NY, 2.4 (winter 1984) 24-69.

Shi, Yazhu. Catalogue of the exhibition, by ... shi yazhu ... In QE (1987) 95-154.

Silberman, Jerome. Mawangdui, excavated materials, and transmitted texts: a cautionary note. EC 8 (1982-83) 79-92. Mostly reinterpretations of the T-shaped banner.

Stein, Rolf A. Le monde en petit. Paris (1987) 345 p, char list, notes, illus. 3 up-dated art: Jardins en miniature d'extrême-orient; l'Habitation, aspects réels; Le monde et l'architecture dans la pensée religieuse. Engl tsl by Phyllis Brooks sep listed.

Stein, Rolf A. Tsl by Phyllis Brooks. Intro by Edward H. Schafer. The world in miniature. Container gardens and dwellings in far eastern religious thought. Stanford univ (1990) 396 p, profusely illus, notes, bibliog of secondary sources, sel char list, index. 3 up-dated art; for french orig see under Stein, Le monde en petit (1987)

Steinhardt, Nancy Shatzman. Altar to heaven complex. In CTA (1984) 139-149, illus.

Steinhardt, Nancy Shatzman (ed) Chinese traditional architecture. NY (1984) Relevant essays sep listed in this bibliog. Abbrev CTA.

Steinhardt, Nancy Shatzman. The han ritual hall. In CTA (1984) 69-77, illus.

Steinhardt, Nancy Shatzman. Kong family mansion. In CTA (1984) 151-157, illus.

Steinhardt, Nancy Shatzman. The mingtang of wang mang. Orientations 15.11 (nov 1984) 42-48.

Steinhardt, Nancy Shatzman. Temple: Confucian temple compounds. EncyRel 14 (1987) 38lb-383a.

Steinhardt, Nancy Shatzman. Yuan period tombs and their decoration: cases at chifeng. OA n.s. 36.4 (winter 1990-91) 198-221. Chifeng county is in present inner mongolian "autonomous region"

Steinhardt, Nancy Shatzman. Zhu haogu reconsidered: a new date for the ROM [royal ontario museum] painting and the southern shanxi buddhist-daoist style. AA 48.1/2 (1987) 5-20, illus. See W. C. White, Chinese temple frescoes (1940)

Suo, Yü-ming. Tsl by Sung Yu & Ronald Dickson. The dragon motif in lacquerware with a note on its occurrence in the collection of the national palace museum. NPMB 14.1 (mar-apr 1979) 1-14.

T'an, I-ling. Tsl by Andrew Morton. Flower-symbolism in chinese paintings. In PMK (1984) 98-109, illus.

Ten kings of hades. The vidor collection. Taipei. National museum of history (1984) 80 p, 66 pl. Preface by Ho Hao-tien and Intro by Paul Vidor (Wei Po-ju) Evolution of traditional chin views of nether world. Bi-lingual text.

Thorp, Robert L. The qin and han imperial tombs and the development of mortuary architecture. In QE (1987) 17-37, illus, notes.

Thorp, Robert (ed) Son of heaven: imperial arts of china. Seattle (1988) Exhibition catalog. See esp 1, The altar; 3, The temple; 5, The tomb. Profusely illus, maps, suggested readings.

Till, Barry & Paula Swart. Funerary sculptures of the northern sung dynasty. In RDChArch (1984) 81-89.

Ts'ai Yüan-p'ei. Tsl by Douglas Lancashire. Aesthetics as a substitute for religion. In CERF (1981) 240-251.

Volker, T. The animal in far eastern art and especially in the art of the japanese netsuke. With reference to chinese origins, traditions, legends and art. Leiden (1950; repr with corrections 1975) 190 p, 19 pl.

Vollmer, J. E. Five colours of the universe—symbolism in clothes and fabrics of the ch'ing dynasty (1644-1911) Edmonton art gallery (1980) 72 p.

Wang Jiashu. Tsl by Mei Zhong. Mystical ancestors—the art of phoenix and dragon designs. CL (winter 1989) 87-90.

Wang, Chongren. Stone sculpture of the han and tang tombs. In RDChArch (1984) 27-30.

Wang, Emily. New year prints. FCR 35.3 (mar 1985) 42-53, many col illus.

Wang, Renbo. Tsl by Julia F. Andrews. General comments on chinese funerary sculpture. In QE (1987) 39-61, illus, notes.

Wei, Yongye. Catalogue of the exhibition, by . . . wei yongye . . . In QE (1987) 95-154.

Werblowsky, R. J. Zwi. On mortuary symbolism and a chinese hell-picture. In J. H. Kamstra et al (ed) Funerary symbols and religion, kempen, netherlands (1988) 154-164.

Williams, Marjorie. Dragons, porcelains and demons: cultural exchange between china and persia. Orientations 17.8 (aug 1986) 22-32. Deals with chin artworks.

Wilson, J. K. Powerful form and potent symbol: the dragon in asia. BCMA 77 (oct 1990) 286-323.

Wu, Hung. From temple to tomb: ancient chinese art and religion in transition. EC 13 (1988) 78-115. The "revolution" within ancestral cult.

Wu, Hung. Myths and legends in han funerary art: their pictorial structure and symbolic meanings as reflected in carvings on sichuan sarcophagi. In SCP (1987) 72-81.

Wu, Hung. The wu liang shrine: the ideology of early chinese pictorial art. Stanford univ (1989) xiv + 412 p, illus photos, rubbings, drawings.

Yüan, Te-hsing. A discussion of the dragon motif in the decoration of a kuei. NPMB 13.2 (may-june 1978) 1-14.

Yüan, Te-hsing. Tsl by Andrew Morton. The pairing of the dragon and the phoenix. In PMK (1984) 34-39, illus col reproductions.

II.5 Religion and History

Aubert-Chen, R.-y. C. Han yü and the confucianists' anti-buddhism in t'ang china. CC 29.1 (1988) 75-92.

Bays, Daniel H. Christianity and chinese sects: religious tracts in the late nineteenth century. In Suzanne Wilson Barnett & John King Fairbank (ed) Christianity in china: early protestant missionary writings, harvard univ (1985) 121-134.

Ch'en, Ch'i-yün. Confucian, legalist, and taoist thought in later han. In CHC vol 1: The ch'in & han empires, 221 b.c.-a.d.220 (1986) Sec 15, 766-807.

Cheng, Te-k'un. Sketches of a trip of archaeological investigation in hopei, honan and shantung. Orig publ in Supplement of Yenching journal of chinese studies; repr in author's Studies in chinese archaeology, chin univ HK (1933 and 1982) (1982: p 95-118) Incl brief descr of many ancient sites important in relig history.

Cheung, Frederick Hok-Ming. The political role of religion in medieval empires. ACQ 13.3 (autumn 1985) 35-53. Brief analysis of "christianity in norman england (1066-1154)" and "taoism and buddhism in t'ang china (618-906)"

Cheung, Frederick Hok-Ming. Religion and politics in early t'ang china: taoism and buddhism in the reigns of kao-tsu and t'ai-tsung. JICS:CUHK 18 (1987) 265-276.

Ching, Julia. The ancient sages (sheng): their identity and their place in chinese intellectual history. OE 30 (1983-86) 1-18.

Dehergne, Joseph. l'Exposé des jésuites de pékin sur le culte des ancêtres présenté à l'empereur k'anghi en novembre 1700. In RECEL (1980) 185-229.

Demiéville, Paul. Philosophy and religion from han to sui. In CHC vol 1: The ch'in & han empires, 221 b.c.-a.d.220 (1986) Sec 16, 808-872.

DeWoskin, Kenneth J. (tsl) Doctors, diviners, and magicians of ancient china: biographies of fang-shih. Columbia univ (1983) 224 p, intro, notes, bibliog, index. Tsl fr Hist of later han, Records of the 3 kingdoms, and Hist of chin.

DeWoskin, Kenneth J. A source guide to the lives and techniques of han and six dynasties fang-shih. SSCRB 9 (1981) 79-105.

Dubs, Homer H. The custom of mourning to the third year. Chap 11, app 1 in HFHD vol 3 (1955) 40-42.

Dubs, Homer H. The sacred field. Chap 4, app 2 in HFHD vol 1 (1938) 281-283. Re field personally plowed by emperor to open agricultural season.

Dubs, Homer H. The victory of han confucianism. JAOS 58 (1938) 435-449. Same title in author's HFHD vol 2 (1944) chap 9, app 2, 341-353.

Edkins, Joseph. The early spread of religious ideas especially in the far east. Oxford (1893) 144 p. Repr london (1983)

Elvin, Mark. Was there a transcendental breakthrough in china? In S. Eisenstadt (ed) Origins and diversity of axial age civilizations, SUNY (1986) 325-359.

Forte, Antonino. Mingtang and buddhist utopias in the history of the astronomical clock; the tower, statue and armillary sphere constructed by empress wu. Rome & paris (1988) 333 p, app, bibliog, genl index, illus. Inter-connections of history, science and relig.

Franz, Rainer von. Die unbearbeiteten peking-inschriften der franke-lauferschen sammlung. Wiesbaden (1984) 259 p, photo-pl. Contains info re "official" relig history, fr Peking temples.

Gernet, Jacques. La vie quotidienne en chine à la veille de l'invasion mongole 1250-1276. Paris (1959) Engl tsl by H. M. Wright, Daily life in china on the eve of the mongol invasion 1250-1276, london (1962) See chap 5, The seasons and the universe: The seasons and days of the year—festivals—religion, 179-218. The 3rd sec of this chap repr in TC (1970) 161-179.

Hansen, Valerie. Changing gods in medieval china, 1127-1276. Princeton univ (1990) 256 p, 3 app, gloss, bibliog, index to temple inscriptions, genl index.

Hartmann, Karl. Atlas-tafel-werk zur geschichte der weltreligionen. Bd I: Die geschichte der fernöstlichen religionen. Stuttgart (1987) See 5 teil: Chinas geschichte und religionswelt, 81-114. Maps and charts, index.

Ho, Yün-yi. Ideological implications of major sacrifices in early ming. MingSt 6 (spring 1978) 55-73.

Ho, Yün-yi. The ministry of rites and suburban sacrifices in early ming. Taipei (preface 1980) 327 p, 9 app, illus, notes, bibliog.

Ho, Yün-yi. Revitalization of the cult of heaven: ceremonial politics in the early ming. National chengchi univ journal 42 (dec 1980) 17-30.

Holzman, Donald. The cold food festival in early medieval china. HJAS 46.1 (june 1986) 51-80.

32

Hong, Jun. A survey of the various religious sects during the yuan dynasty. In Sidney Shapiro (tsl and ed) Jews in old china: studies by chinese scholars, NY (1984) 3-6.

Jagchid, Sechin. Chinese buddhism and taoism during the mongolian rule of china. Mongolian studies 6 (1980) 61-98.

Jagchid, Sechin. The mongol khans and chinese buddhism and taoism. JIABS 2.1 (1979) 7-28.

Johnson, David. The city-god cults of t'ang and sung china. HJAS 45.2 (dec 1985) 363-457.

Jung, Sheng, Lung Sheng-yün & Ho Ling-hsiu. Tentative views on relation between peasant wars and religion in china. SCMP no 2370 (2 nov 1966) 7-16.

Kelley, David E. Temples and tribute fleets: the luo sect and boatmen's associations in the eighteenth century. ModCh 8.3 (july 1982) 361-391.

Kramers, Robert P. The development of the confucian schools. In CHC vol 1: The ch'in and han empires, 221 b.c.-a.d.220 (1986) Sec 14, 747-765.

Kuhn, Philip A. Soulstealers. The chinese sorcery scare of 1768. Harvard univ (1990) 299 p, notes, bibliog, maps, illus, index.

Lai, Whalen. Religious pluralism in china: the history and dynamics. CF 27.1 (mar 1984) 1-18.

Langlois, John D. jr & Sun K'o-k'uan. Three teachings syncretism and the thought of ming t'ai-tsu. HJAS 43.1 (june 1983) 97-139.

Leung, Man Kam. The relation between religion and peasant rebellions: a review of the interpretations by chinese historians. In TT:RCT (1989) 43-50.

Li, Thomas Shiyu and Susan Naquin. The baoming temple: religion and the throne in ming and qing china. HJAS 48.1 (june 1988) 131-188. Re a "small buddhist nunnery" near peking, and white lotus sectarianism.

Lin, Kai-shyh. The eternal mother and the heavenly father: two deities of rebellion in late imperial china. ASBIE 69 (1990) 161-180. White lotus and taiping myths.

Lipman, Jonathan N. & Stevan Harrell (ed) Violence in china. SUNY (1990) Pertinent essays sep listed in this bibliog; abbrev VC.

Liu, James T. C. The sung emperors and the ming-t'ang or hall of enlightenment. In EtSong sér 2.1 (1973) 45-58.

Liu, Kwang-ching (ed) Orthodoxy in late imperial china. Univ california (1990) Relevant art sep listed in this bibliog; abbrev OLIC.

Liu, Ts'un-yan & Judith Berling. The "three teachings" in the mongol-yüan period. In YT (1982) 479-512, notes, gloss.

Loewe, Michael. Chinese ideas of life and death. Faith, myth and reason in the han period (202 b.c.-a.d.220) London (1982) 226 p, refs and notes for further reading, gloss, table, index.

Loewe, Michael. Imperial china's reactions to the catholic missions. Numen 35.2 (dec 1988) 179-212.

Loewe, Michael. The religious and intellectual background. In CHC vol 1: The ch'in and han empires, 221 b.c.-a.d.220. (1986) Sec 12, 649-725.

McMullen, David. Bureaucrats and cosmology: the ritual code of t'ang china. In D. Cannadine & S. Price (ed) Rituals of royalty, cambridge univ (1987) 181-236.

McMullen, D. L. A note on the feng ritual of 742 in response to professor elling eide. TS 2 (winter 1984) 37-40.

Moran, Craig. CF 29.4 (dec 1986) 221-229. Rev art on Susan Naquin, Millenarian rebellion in china (1976) q.v.

Naquin, Susan. Connections between rebellions: sect family networks in qing china. ModCh 8.3 (july 1982) 337-360.

Naquin, Susan. Millenarian rebellion in china. The eight trigrams uprising of 1813. Yale univ (1976) 384 p, maps, 3 app, notes, sel bibliog, gloss-index. See rev by Timothy Jensen in HR 18.1 (aug 1978) 98-105; by Craig Moran in CF 29.4 (dec 1986) 221-229.

Naquin, Susan. Shantung rebellion. The wang lun uprising of 1774. Yale univ (1981) 228 p, app, notes, gloss, bibliog, index. Re white lotus sects in ch'ing society.

Naquin, Susan. The transmission of white lotus sectarianism in late imperial china. In PopCult (1985) 255-291.

Noguchi, Tetsuro. Revolts and religious sects in chiang-hsi in the end of the 19th century. Proc31stICHS, Tokyo, vol 2 (1984) 878-879. Abstr.

Overmyer, Daniel L. The white cloud sect in sung and yüan china. HJAS 42 (1982) 615-642.

Perry, Elizabeth J. Taipings and triads: the role of religion in inter-rebel relations. In RRR (1984) 342-353.

Perry, Elizabeth J. Worshipers and warriors: white lotus influence on the nian rebellion. ModCh 2.1 (jan 1976) 4-22.

Ren, Jiyu. The trend of confluence of the three religions after t'ang and sui. Proc31stICHS, Tokyo, vol 1 (1984) 251. Abstr.

Ricci, Matteo. Tsl by Douglas Lancashire & Hu Kuo-chen. The true meaning of the lord of heaven (t'ien-chu shih-i) Taipei (1985) xiv + 485 p. Chin-engl text, ed by J. Malatesta.

Rosner, Erhard. Frauen als anführerinnen chinesischer sekten. In RPO-A (1985) 239-246. Re women in ch'ing sectarianism.

Sawatzky, Sheldon. State-church conflict in taiwan: its historical roots and contemporary manifestations. Missiology 9 (1981) 449-463. Some historical, non-christian ref.

Schafer, Edward H. The empire of min. Rutland, vt & tokyo (1954) See chap 6, Religion, 90-109.

Schipper, K. M. Millenarismes et messianismes dans la chine ancienne. In Understanding modern china; proceedings of the 26th conference of chinese studies, european association of chinese studies, rome (1979) 31-49.

Schmidt-Glintzer, Helwig. Die manipulation von omina und ihre beurteilung bei hofe. Die beispiel der himmelsbriefe wang ch'in-jo (962-1025) unter chen-tsung tregierte 998-1023. AS 35.1 (1981) 1-14.

Seaman, Gary. The divine authorship of pei-yu chi [journey to the north] JAS 45.3 (may 1986) 483-497.

Seaman, Gary. The emperor of the dark heavens and the han river gateway into china. In Ec&Emp (1989) 165-177.

Seiwert, Hubert. Religion und kulturelle integration in china. Die sinisierung fujians und die integration der chinesischen nationalkultur. Saeculum 38.2/3 (1987) 225-265.

Shek, Richard. Chinese millenarian movements. EncyRel 9 (1987) 532b-536b.

Shek, Richard. The practices and aspirations of ming-qing sectarians. Proc31st ICHS, Tokyo, vol 2 (1984) 877-878. Abstr.

Shek, Richard. Sectarian eschatology and violence. In VC (1990) 87-114.

Smith, D. Howard. Conflicting ideas of salvation in a.d. fifth century china. In M&HS (1973) 291-303.

Smolin, Georij Jakovlevic. La révolte de la société secrète du mi-le-chiao conduite par wang tsê (1047-1048) EtSong sér 1 no 2 (1971) 143-170.

Sun, K'o-k'uan. Yü chi and southern taoism during the yüan period. In John D. Langlois, jr (ed) China under mongol rule, princeton univ (1981) 212-253.

34

Taylor, Romeyn. An imperial endorsement of syncretism: ming t'ai-tsu's essay on the three teachings. Translation and commentary. MingSt 16 (spring 1983) 31-38.

Taylor, Romeyn. Ming t'ai tsu and the gods of the walls and moats. MingSt 4 (spring 1977) 31-49.

Taylor, Romeyn. Official and popular religion and the political organization of chinese society in the ming. In OLIC (1990) 126-157.

Vandermeersch, Léon. Aspects rituels de la popularization du confucianisme sous les han. In T&L (1990) 89-107.

Vandermeersch, Léon. Le confucianisme à l'époque des han postérieurs. AnnEPHE 94 (1985-86) 161-171.

Vandermeersch, Léon. Bouddhisme et pouvoir dans la chine confucianiste. In BetSA (1990) 31-39.

Vandermeersch, Léon. l'Eclipse du confucianisme sous les dynasties du nord et du sud de la chine désunifiée. AnnEPHE 96 (1987-88) 93-99.

Vandermeersch, Léon. Le confucianisme des "trois-royaumes" aux "jin occidentaux." Pénétration de l'influence taoïste. AnnEPHE 95 (1986-87) 121-126.

Verellen, Franciscus. Histoire des religions de la chine ancienne et médiévale. AnnEPHE 95 (1986-87) 115-120.

Verellen, Franciscus. Liturgy and sovereignty: the role of taoist ritual in the foundation of the shu kingdom (907-925) AM 3rd ser 2.1 (1989) 59-78.

Waltner, Ann. T'ang-yang-tzu and wang shih-chen: visionary and bureaucrat in the late ming. LIC 8.1 (june 1987) 105-133. T'ang is female visionary worshiped in cult; wang is prominent literatus.

Wechsler, Howard J. Offerings of jade and silk. Ritual and symbol in the legitimation of the t'ang

dynasty. Yale univ (1985) xi + 313 p, notes, sel bibliog, gloss-index.

Weng, T'ung-wen. Identity of wan yun lung, founder of t'ien-ti hui. Proc31stICHS, Tokyo, vol 2 (1984) 880-881. Abstr.

Young, John D. Confucianism and christianity. The first encounter. Univ HK (1983) 182 p, notes, gloss, bibliog, index.

Zdún, Genowefa. Matériaux pour l'étude de la culture chinoise du moyen age: le lo-yang k'ie-lan ki. Warszawa (1982) 160 p, 10 fig, 2 folding plans, bibliog, index.

Zhu, Weizhang. Tsl by Ruth Hayhoe. Coming out of the middle ages. Armonk NY & london (1990) See 2, The drama of "god-making" 360 years ago, 57-62. Mostly about wei zhongxian (1568-1627) encouraging his own divinization during his lifetime.

II.6 Religious Thought

Ames, Roger T. The common ground of self-cultivation in classical taoism and confucianism. TJ 17.1-2 (dec 1985) 65-97.

Bauer, Wolfgang. Das "allein" als eine metapher das "ich" In FW/CG (1985) 177-195.

Bellasen, Jérôme. A propos d'une vision du monde, ou un jardin sans jardinier. EOEO 6 (1985) 103-108. Theme of this issue: "Une civilisation sans théologie?"

Black, Alison H. Gender and cosmology in chinese correlative thinking. Chap 7 in G&R (1986) 166-195

Ch'en Ch'i-yün. Confucian, legalist, and taoist thought in later han. In CHC vol1, The ch'in and han empires, 221 b.c.-a.d.220. (1986) Sec 15, 766-807.

Ch'ien, Edward T. The conception of language and the use of paradox in buddhism and taoism. JCP 11 (dec 1984) 375-399.

Chan, Wing-tsit. Chinese religion: religious and philosophical texts. EncyRel 3 (1987) 305a-312a.

Chan, Wing-tsit. Chu hsi on t'ien. Chap 12 in author's CH:NS (1989) 184-196.

Chang, Aloysius. The concept of the tao. In GCR (1977) 80-95.

Chao Tzu-ch'en. Tsl by Douglas Lancashire. On creation. In CERF (1981) 167-196.

Chao, Paul. Discourse on the main stream chinese ideas of ultimate reality and meaning. Ultimate reality & meaning 3.1 [assen, netherlands]. (1980) 3-22.

Chao, Tze-chiang (tsl) A chinese garden of serenity. Epigrams from the ming dynasty 'discourse on vegetable roots' Mount vernon NY (1959) 60 p. Eclectic views by Hung Tzu-ch'eng.

Cheng, Anne. De la place de l'homme dans l'universe: la conception de la triade ciel-terre-homme à la fin de l'antiquité chinoise. EOEO 3 (1983) 11-22.

Chou, Chao-ming. Death, funerals and sacrifices in wang ch'ung's philosophy. TR 17.2 (winter 1986) 175-195.

Chryssides, George D. God and the tao. RS 19.1 (mar 1983) 1-11.

Copleston, Frederick. Religion and the one; philosophers east and west. NY (1982) See chap 3, The one in taoism and buddhism, 40-67.

Decaux, Jacques. The way of the kuan yintse. CC 23.3 (sept 1982) 67-87.

Dien, Albert E. Chinese beliefs in the afterworld. In QE (1987) 1-15.

Doeringer, Franklin M. A paradigmatic symbol in early chinese cosmology. PEW 32.3 (july 1982) 309-324. What author calls the "cosmic gate"

Doty, Darrel. Why did the ancient chinese not develop a creator-god? TR 20.3 (spring 1990) 317-331.

Durrant, Stephen W. Moism. EncyRel 10 (1987) 25a-27b.

Elvin, Mark. Was there a transcendental breakthrough in china? In S. Eisenstadt (ed) Origins & diversity of axial age civilizations, SUNY (1986) 325-359.

Forte, Antonino. Mingtang and buddhist utopias in the history of astronomical clock; the tower, statue and armillary sphere constructed by empress wu. Rome & paris (1988) 333 p, app, bibliog, genl index, illus. Inter-connections of history, science, and relig.

Fung, Hu-hsiang. Chinese philosophical foundations for interreligious dialogue. D&A 3.1 (spring 1989) 45-50.

Gernet, Jacques. Sur le corps et l'esprit chez les chinois. In Poikilia; études offerts à jean-pierre vernant (1987) 369-377. Incl tsl of fan chen's essay, shen mieh lun.

Goodrich, Anne Swann. Chinese hells. The peking temple of eighteen hells & chinese conceptions of hell. St augustin, germany (1981) 167 p, app, bibliog, index, 32 pl.

Gregory, Peter N. (rapporteur) The sudden/gradual polarity: a recurrent theme in chinese thought. JCP 9.4 (dec 1982) 471-486. Report of a conference held in may 1981.

Grimm, Tilemann. Der edle und der weise im nicht-theistischen raum chinas. In Heinrich von Stietencron (heraus) Theologen und theologien in verschiedenen kulturkreisen, düsseldorf (1986) 147-163.

Hang, Thaddäus T.C. Von himmlischen mandat zum fatum—aspekte der chinesischen religiosität. In Wolfgang L. Gambocz (ed) Philosophy of religion: proceedings of the 8th international wittgenstein symposium, vienna (1984) 202-204.

Henderson, John B. The development and decline of chinese cosmology. Columbia univ (1984) 331 p, notes, 3 gloss, sel bibliog, index, illus.

36

Hu, Shih. Tsl by Douglas Lancashire. Immortality—my religion. In CERF (1981) 252-267.

Jan, Yün-hua. The bridge between man and cosmos: the philosophical foundation of music in the t'ai p'ing china. In STR&MT (1989) 15-27.

Jullien, Francois. La conception du monde naturel, en chine et en occident, selon tang junyi. EOEO 3 (1983) 117-125.

Jullien, Francois. Procès ou création. Une introduction à la pensée des lettrés chinois. Paris (1989). Relig thought esp that of wang fu-chih (1619-92)

Keightley, David N. Shang divination and metaphysics. PEW 38.4 (1988) 367-397.

Kim, Yung Sik. Kuei-shen in terms of chi: chu hsi's discussion of kuei-shen. TJ 17.1-2 (dec 1985) 149-163.

Knaul, Livia. Chuang tzu and the chinese ancestry of ch'an. JCP 13 (1986 411-428.

Knaul, Livia. The habit of perfection—a summary of fukunaga mitsuji's studies on the chuang tzu tradition. CEA 1 (1985) 71-84. Fukunaga looks at chuang tzu as philosophy of relig.

Kwee, Swan-Liat. Dualism and wholeness in a chinese perspective. ZMR 66.2 (apr 1982) 118-134.

Lai, Whalen. Beyond the debate on 'the immortality of the soul': recovering an essay by shen yueh. JOS 19.2 (1981) 138-157.

Larre, Claude. The meaning of transcendence in chinese thought. Concilium 126 (1979) 42-51.

Levi, Jean. Les fonctions religieuses de la bureaucratie céleste. l'Homme 27, no 101 (janv-mars 1987) 35-57.

Liu, Ming-wood. Fan chen's treatise on the destructibility of the spirit and its buddhist critics. PEW 35.4 (oct 1987) 402-428.

Liu, Shu-hsien. Toward a new relation between humanity and nature: reconstructing "t'ien-jen ho-i" Zygon 24.4 (1989) 57-68. Relig and ecology.

Loewe, Michael. Chinese ideas of life and death. Faith, myth and reason in the han period (202 b.c.-a.d.220) London (1982) 226 p, ref, notes for further reading, gloss, table, index.

Long, J. Bruce. Cosmic law. EncyRel 4 (1987) 90a-91b.

Mahdihassan, S. Indian and chinese cosmologies reconsidered. AJCM 13.1-4 (1985) 5-12.

Mahdihassan, S. Venus, the goddess of fertility, numerologically 15 in babylon and the origin of the chinese system of designs, called pa-kua. AJCM 15.3-4 (1987) 89-97.

Major, John S. Ch'i. EncyRel 3 (1987) 238a-239a.

Major, John S. The five phases, magic squares and schematic cosmography. In Henry Rosemont (ed) Thematic studies; JAAR 50 (1984) 133-166.

Major, John S. Shang-ti. EncyRel 13 (1987) 223a-224a.

Major, John S. Yin-yang wu-hsing. EncyRel 15 (1987) 515a-516b.

McMorran, Ian. Wang Fu-chih. EncyRel 15 (1987) 333a-334a.

Meglio, Jean-Francois di. La nature comme "destin émanant du ciel" d'après mou zongsan. EOEO 3 (1983) 126-134.

Mei, Y. P. Hsün-tzu. EncyRel 6 (1987) 482b-483b.

Mei, Y. P. Lü Pu-wei. EncyRel 9 (1987) 54a-54b.

Mei, Y. P. Mo-tzu. EncyRel 10 (1987) 129b-130b.

Needham, Joseph. Gunpowder as the fourth power, east & west. Univ HK (1985) See 4, Rocks, religion and meteorology, 34-40; illus, chin char, bibliog.

Needham, Joseph. Tao: illuminations and corrections of the way. Theology [london] 81 (july 1978) 244-252.

Neville, Robert C. The tao and the daimon. SUNY (1982) See chap 7, The notion of creation in chinese thought, 131-145; chap 8, Process and the neo-confucian cosmos, 147-170; chap 9, Buddhism and process philosophy, 171-192; chap 10, The daimon and the tao of faith, 193-215; chap 11, The daimon and the tao of practice, 217-234.

Parkes, Graham (ed) Heidegger and eastern thought. Univ hawaii (1987) Indiv art sep listed in this bibliog; abbrev HET.

Pas, Julian. Yin-yang polarity: a binocular vision of the world. ATS 8 (nov 1983) 188-201.

Peerenboom, Randall P. Han dynasty cosmology: the emergence of naturalism. ACQ 16.1 (spring 1988) 13-40.

Peerenboom, R.P. Naturalism and immortality in the han: the antecedents of religious taoism. CC 29.3 (sept 1988) 31-53.

Powers, Martin J. An archaic bas-relief and the chinese moral cosmos in the first century a.d. ArsO 12 (1981) 25-40, 17 fig.

Raguin, Yves. l'Eschatologie dans le monde chinois. SM 32 (1983) 181-194.

Raguin, Yves E. In der chinesischen tradition spricht der himmel nicht. Missions jahrbuch der schweiz (1984) 105-106.

Ries, Julien. Tsl fr french by David M. Weeks. Immortality. EncyRel 7 (1987) See sec, Religions of china, 130b-131b.

Robinet, Isabelle. La notion de hsing dans le taoïsme et son rapport avec celle du confucianisme. JAOS 106.1 (jan-mar 1986) 183-196.

Robinet, Isabelle. l'Unité complexe et la pensée chinoise. In Encyclopédie philosophique universelle, paris, t 1 (1989) 1595-1599.

Robinet, Isabelle. l'Unité transcendante des trois enseignements selon les taoïstes des song et des yuan. In RPO-A (1985) 103-125.

Robinet, Isabelle. Wang Pi. EncyRel 15 (1987) 334a-335a.

Roetz, Heiner. Mensch und natur im alten china. Frankfurt am main etc (1984) 423 p.

Roth, Harold D. Liu An. EncyRel 9 (1987) 1a-2b.

Roth, Harold D. Shen and consciousness in the huai-nan tzu. Proc 31st ICHS, Tokyo, vol 1 (1984) 257-258. Abstr.

Ru, Xin. The unity of man in ancient chinese philosophy. Diogenes 114 (winter 1987) 1-28.

Ruland, Vernon. Eight sacred horizons; the religious imagination east & west. NY & london (1985) See 2, Chinese-japanese tao, 25-50.

Rule, Paul. T'ien-hsia: all under (the chinese) heaven. RTrad 1.1 (apr 1978) 19-32.

Santangelo, Paolo. The concept of good and evil, positive and negative forces in late imperial china: a preliminary appraisal. E&W n.s. 37 (dec 1987) 373-398.

Santangelo, Paolo. The origin of good and evil in human nature according to neo-confucianism. Some aspects of the question. E&W 40.1-4 (dec 1990) 231-259.

Schwartz, Benjamin I. The world of thought in ancient china. Harvard univ (1985) 490 p, notes, sel bibliog, gloss, index. See passim.

Seidel, Anna. Afterlife: chinese concepts. EncyRel 1 (1987) 124b-127b. Deals only with pre-buddhist notions.

Seiwert, Hubert. Ausgrenzung der dämonen, am beispiel der chinesischen religions geschichte. Saeculum 34.3/4 (1983) 316-333.

Seiwert, Hubert. Orakelwesen und zukunfs deutung im chinesischen altertum. Eine religionsgeschichtliche untersuchung zur entwicklung der

38

welt- und menschenbildes während der zhou-dynastie. Bonn (1979) 352 s, tabellen, anmerkungen, literaturverzeichnis.

Sitompul, A. A. Nature and the natural in asian thinking—asian animism and primal religion. EAJT 1.1 (1983) 15-27.

Stein, Rolf A. Le monde en petit. Paris (1987) 345 p, char list, notes, illus, char list. 3 up-dated art: Jardins en miniature d'extrême-orient; l'Habitation, aspects réels; Le monde et l'architecture dans la pensée religieuse. See engl tsl sep listed by Phyllis Brooks.

Stein, Rolf A. Tsl by Phyllis Brooks. Intro by Edward H. Schafer. The world in miniature. Container gardens and dwellings in far eastern religious thought. Stanford univ (1990) 396 p, illus 104 halftones, 36 line drawings, notes, bibliog, secondary sources, char list, index. Tsl of foregoing item.

Swan-Liat, K. Dualism and wholeness in a chinese perspective. ZMR 66.2 (1982) 118-134. Chin concern with man contrasted with western concern with truth.

Teng Ssu-yü. Orthodoxy and heterodoxy in ancient chinese patterns of thought. ASBIHP 55.3 (sept 1984) 339-414. From oracle bones to tung chung-shu.

Thomas, Léon. Les états de conscience inhabituels dans le zhuangzi. RHR 204 (may 1987) 25-38.

Thompson, Laurence G. On the prehistory of hell in china. JCR 17 (1989) 27-41.

Thompson, Laurence G. T'ien. EncyRel 14 (1987) 508a-510a.

Tilak, S. John. Nature and the natural in asian thinking . . . the response and the reaction to the paper read by dr. a. a. sitompul. EAJT 1.1 (1983) 28-30.

Tober, Linda M. & F. Stanley Lusby. Heaven and hell. EncyRel 6 (1987) See sec, Chinese traditions, 242a-242b.

Tran, Van Doan. Comments by Vincent Shih. Is chinese humanism atheistic? In ISCI (1983) 746-776. Same title in Eunts docete; commentaria urbaniana 37.2 (1984) 257-271.

Ts'ai, Yüan-p'ei. Tsl by Douglas Lancashire. Aesthetics as a substitute for religion. In CERF (1981) 240-251.

Tu, Wei-ming. The continuity of being: chinese visions of nature. In Leroy S. Rouner (ed) On nature, univ notre dame (1984) Repr in author's CT (1985) 35-50.

Tu, Wei-ming. Soul: chinese concepts. EncyRel 13 (1987) 447a-450a.

Waddell, N. A. (tsl) A selection from the ts'ai ken t'an ('vegetable-root discourses') EB 2.2 (nov 1919) 88-98.

Wilson, William Scott (tsl) The roots of wisdom: saikontan by hung ying ming. Tokyo etc (1985) 160 p, notes, bibliog. Ming text: ts'ai ken-t'an. A sort of three traditions eclecticism.

Yearley, Lee H. A comparison between classical chinese thought and thomistic christian thought. JAAR 51.3 (sept 1983) 427-458.

Yearley, Lee H. Mencius and aquinas; theories of virtue and conceptions of courage. SUNY (1990) 280 p, notes, chin terms, sel bibliog, indexes. Comparative study of relig ethics.

Yeung, Arnold Mik. Nature and the natural in asian thinking: classical asian religions. EAJT 1.1 (1983) 45-59.

Yü, Pin. Tsl by Douglas Lancashire. The meaning of religion. In CERF (1981) 155-159.

Yü, Ying-shih. New evidence on the early chinese conception of afterlife. JAS 16.1 (nov 1981) 81-85 Rev art on Michael Loewe, Ways to paradise q.v.

Yü, Ying-shih. Tung Chung-shu. EncyRel 15 (1987) 81b-83a.

Yü, Ying-shih. Wang Ch'ung. EncyRel 15 (1987) 332a-333a.

Zito, Angela Rose. Re-presenting sacrifice: cosmology and the editing of texts. CSWT 5.2 (dec 1984) 47-78. Re imperial sacrifice, li, and ritual text editing.

II.7 "Confucius" and "Confucianism"

Adler, Joseph. Descriptive and normative principle (li) in confucian moral metaphysics: is/ought from the chinese perspective. Zygon 16.3 (sept 1981) 285-293.

Alexander, George Gardiner. Confucius the great teacher. London (1890) xx + 314 p.

Algoud, Philippe. Le monde spirituel de l'asie orientale. Paris (1978) See 4, Le confucianisme, 83-89.

Allinson, Robert E. The ethics of confucianism and christianity: the delicate balance. CF 33.3 (sept 1990) 158-175.

Allinson, Robert E. The golden rule in confucianism and christianity. ACQ 16.4 (winter 1988) 1-15.

Ames, Roger T. The common ground of self-cultivation in classical taoism and confucianism. TJ 17.1-2 (dec 1985) 65-97. Repr in TaoRes 1.1 (autumn 1988) 23-54.

Ames, Roger T. Religiousness in classical confucianism: a comparative analysis. ACQ 12.2 (summer 1984) 7-24.

Ames, Roger T. Rites as rights: the confucian alternative. In HR&WR (1988) 199-216.

Beattie, Paul H. The religion of confucius: the first humanist. RH 22.1 (winter 1988) 11-17.

Becker, Gerhold K. The quest for the ultimate in confucianism and christianity. CF 32.4 (1989) 202-217.

Berling, Judith A. Ku Yen-wu. EncyRel 8 (1987) 408b-409b.

Berling, Judith A. Tai chen. EncyRel 14 (1987) 246a-247b.

Berthrong, John H. The problem of mind: mou tsung-san's critique of chu hsi. JCR 10 (1982) 39-52.

Berthrong, John. Trends in the interpretation of confucian religiosity. CF 32.4 (dec 1989) 224-244. Incl lengthy bibliog.

Bishop, Donald H. Confucianism and its contemporary relevance. CC 26.4 (dec 1985) 41-45.

Bishop, Donald H. Confucianism in contemporary taiwan. CC 24 (1983) 69-83.

Bloom, Alfred. Confucian and buddhist values in modern context. PW n.s.4 (fall 1988) 60-68.

Bloom, Irene. Wang yang-ming, lo chin-shun, and concepts of personal identity in ming neo-confucianism. ProcICS (1981) Thought & philos vol 1, 263-276.

Bosell, Eric. The confucian revival. Areopagus (trinity 1990, 3.4) 47-49.

Bresciani, Umberto. The religious thought of confucius. CF 29.2/3 (sept 1986) 129-144.

Buri, Fritz. Die gespräche des konfuzius und gotthelfs bernerkalendar. ZRGG 37.3 (1985) 216-252.

Cai, Xiqin (Ts'ai Hsi-ch'in) Tsl by Rosemary A. Roberts. A visit to confucius' hometown. Beijing (1986) 106 p, illus col photos, 2 maps, 2 app.

Carmody, Denise Lardner & John Tully Carmody. Peace & justice in the scriptures of the world religions: reflections on non-christian scriptures. NY & mahwan nj (1988) See chap 4, Confucianism and the analects, 70-95.

Chan, Wing-tsit. Confucian thought: foundations of the tradition. EncyRel 4 (1987) 15a-24a.

40

Chan, Wing-tsit. Exploring the confucian tradition. PEW 38.3 (july 1988) 234-250.

Chang, Aloysius. The confucian jen: a christian interpretation. CC 27.3 (sept 1986) 29-39.

Chang, Aloysius B. Liberative elements in the confucian tradition. JJRS 16.2 (july 1990) 24-42.

Chang, Chi-yun. Confucianism and western culture. SAR 10.4 (winter 1984) 19-43.

Chang, Chi-yun. Tsl by Orient Lee. Confucius' religious philosophy. CC 23.4 (dec 1982) 39-63.

Chang, Chi-yun. The great confucius. CC 21.2 (june 1980) 1-55.

Chang, Chi-yun. A system of cardinal values for ideal personality and ideal society: confucianism as a world religion. CC 21.3 (sept 1980) 39-70. Similar title in APQCSA 14.1 (spring 1982) 1-23.

Chang, Chi-yun. A system of cardinal values for the ideal society: confucianism as a world religion. APQCSA 14.1 (spr 1982) 1-23 Similar title in CC 21,3 (Sept 1980) 39-70.

Chang, Hao. K'ang Yu-wei. EncyRel 8 (1987) 246a-247b.

Chang, Kathy. Confucius' 2533rd birthday celebration. FCR 33.11 (nov 1983) 64-70, illus col photos incl covers.

Chao, Denise. Confucianism on happiness. CC 25.4 (1984) 9-18.

Chao, Samuel H. Confucian chinese and the gospel: methodological considerations. AJT 1.1 (apr 1987) 17-40.

Chen, Jingpan. Confucius as a teacher. Beijing (1990) 518 p, notes, bibliog. Originally ph.d. dissertation, univ of toronto (1940—sic)

Chen, Junmin. Clarifications on confucius' confucianism: concerning the rise of confucianists and the confucian school founded by confucius and its historical position. JCP 14.1 (1987) 91-95.

Cheng, Anne. Die bedeutung des konfuzianismus in frankreich: gestern, heute, morgen. In S. Krieger & R. Trauzettel (ed) Konfuzianismus und die modernisierung chinas, mainz (1990) 535-542.

Cheng, Anne. Etude sur le confucianisme des han: l'élaboration d'une tradition exégétique sur les classiques. Paris (1985) 322 p.

Cheng, Anne. La trame et la chaîne: aux origines de la constitution d'un corpus canonique de la tradition confucéene. EOEO 5 (1984) 13-26.

Ching, Julia. Confucian spirituality. JD 10.1 (jan-mar 1985) 75-81. Same title in german: Konfuzianische spiritualität, in Hans Waldenfels & Thoman Immos (ed) Fernöstliche weisheit und christlicher glaube, mainz (1985) 161-176.

Ching, Julia. Confucius. EncyRel 4 (1987) 38b-42b.

Ching, Julia. The mirror symbol revisited: confucian and taoist mysticism. MRT (1983) 226-246.

Chou, Yün-jin. Matteo ricci and his accomodation with confucianism. NPMB 24.6 (jan-feb 1990) 1-14.

Cohen, Stanley G. The religiousness of k'ung-fu-tzu (confucius) ZRGG 35.1 (1983) 34-39.

Coppel, Charles A. Confucian religion in indonesia. Proc 31st ICHS, Tokyo, vol 1 (1984) 268-269. Abstr.

Coppel, Charles A. From christian mission to confucian religion: the nederlandische zendingsvereeniging and the chinese of west java. In David Chandler & M.C.Ricklefs (ed) Nineteenth and twentieth century indonesia, monash univ (1986) 15-40.

Coppel, Charles A. "Is confucianism a religion?": a 1923 debate in java. Archipel 38 (1989) 125-135. Debate within chin community.

Coppel, Charles A. The origins of confucianism as an organized religion in java, 1900-1923. JSEAS 12.1 (mar 1981) 179-196.

Covell, Ralph R. Confucius, the buddha, and christ. A history of the gospel in chinese. Maryknoll NY (1986) 304 p. See passim.

Cua, A. S. Ethical uses of the past in early confucianism: the case of hsün tzu. PEW 35.2 (apr 1985) 133-156.

Dawson, Raymond. Confucius. NY (1982) 91 p, further reading, index, ref to analects.

DeBary, Wm Theodore. Human rites—an essay on confucian and human rights. CN 22.4 (fall 1984) 307-313.

DeBary, Wm Theodore. The prophetic voice in the confucian nobleman. CF 33.1 (apr 1990) 3-19.

Deverge, M. Confucianisme et succès économique à taiwan. Etudes 367.1-2 (1987) 5-13.

Dubs, Homer H. The victory of han confucianism. JAOS 58 (1938) 435-449. Rev version of this art in HFHD 2 (1944) app 2, 435-449.

Düssel, Reinhard. Aspects of confucianism in elias canetti's notes and essays. TR 18.1-4 (aut 1987-sum 1988) 333-341.

Dy, Manuel B. Jen in confucian and neo-confucian thought and christian love. Philippine studies 31.4 (4th qtr 1983) 430-450.

Eber, Irene (ed) Confucianism. The dynamics of tradition. NY (1986) 224 p. Relevant art sep listed in this bibliog; abbrev CDT

Ebrey, Patricia. Education through ritual: efforts to formulate family rituals during the sung period. In NCEduc (1989) 277-306.

Elvin, Mark. The collapse of scriptural confucianism. PFEH 41 (mar 1990) 45-76.

Eno, Robert. The confucian creation of heaven; philosophy and the defense of ritual mastery. SUNY (1990) 352 p, 3 app, notes, gloss, abbrev, bibliog, index.

Etiemble. Confucius et confucianisme EncyUniv 6 (1990) 360a-369b.

Fellows, Ward J. Religions east and west. NY etc (1979) See 5, Confucianism, 199-241.

Feng, Youlan (Fung Yu-lan) The historical role of confucian thought in the formation of the chinese nation. CSP 12.4 (summer 1981) 48-62.

Franke, Wolfgang. Confucian and taoist traditions as evident in chinese epigraphy in southeast asia. Proc 31st ICHS, Tokyo, vol 1 (1984) 267-268. Abstr.

Fry, C. George. Confucianism. In C. George Fry et al (ed) Great asian religions, grand rapids (1984) 87-110.

Fu, Charles Wei-hsun. Philosophical reflections on the modernization of confucianism as traditional morality. In RIID (1989) 303-323.

Fu, Charles Wei-hsun. Postwar confucianism and western democracy: an ideological struggle. In MIWR (1987) chap 9, 177-196.

Fu, Pei-jung. The concept of t'ien in classical confucianism. Bulletin of the college of liberal arts, natl taiwan univ 33 (dec 1984) 327-402.

Fu, Pei-jung. Photos by Lin Bor-liang. Confucian ritual in modern form. FCR 38.1 (jan 1988) 46-49, col photos. Issue devoted mainly to relig.

Fu, Pei-jung. A philosophical reflection on the christian-confucian dialogue. In RIID (1989) 533-554.

Fu, Yunlung. Tsl by William A. Wycoff. Studies on confucius since construction. CSP 12.2 (winter 1980-81) 25-51.

Fung, Hu-hsiang. The concept of god in confucianism. Tunghai journal 24 (jun 1983) 15-21.

42

Gálik, Marián. Controversies about confucius and confucianism in china (1898-1978) Asian & african studies 18, institute of literary sciences, dept of oriental studies, bratislavia (1982) 171-186. Rev art on various writings.

Garrett, William R. The confucian conundrum in "the religions of china" D&A 4.2 (summer 1990) 90-107. Re max weber's work.

Geden, Alfred S. Studies in the religions of the east. London (1913) repr delhi (1983). See Confucianism, 618-660.

Greenlees, Duncan. The gospel of china. Adyar, madras (1949—sic) lxxi + 177 p. Re the four books.

Gurdak, Thaddeus J. Benevolence: confucian ethics and ecstasy. In James Gaffney (ed) Essays in morality and ethics, ?place of publ (1980) 76-84.

Hall, David L. & Roger T. Ames. Getting it right: on saving confucius from the confucians. PEW 34.1 (jan 1984) 3-23. Why everybody else misunderstands yi ("righteousness") and what it really means.

Hwang, Philip Ho. Confucianism and theism. In Henry O. Thompson (ed) The wisdom of faith: essays in honor of sebastian alexander matezak, lanham md (1989) 51-62.

Hwang, Philip Ho. Fingarette's interpretation of confucius' view of ritual. D&A 4.1 (spring 1990) 96-104.

International confucian-christian conference, june 1988, hong kong. CF 31.2/3 (aug 1988) Entire issue devoted to papers; see passim.

Jin, Chunfeng. The confucian philosophy of man in the han period. CSH 23.3 (spring 1990) 22-31.

Jullien, Francois (tsl) Annexe: en prenant les textes canonique comme source (liu xie, wenxin diaolong, chap III, zong jing) EOEO 5 (1984) 129-134.

Jullien, Francois. Ni écriture sainte ni oeuvre classique: du statut du texte confucéene comme texte fondateur vis-à-vis de la civilisation chinoise. EOEO 5 (1984) 75-127.

Kamenarovic, Ivan P. Lumière et joie dans le confucianisme de l'antiquité CEC 8 (1989) 141-149.

Kelen, Betty. Confucius in life and legend. NY (1971) 160 p, bibliog. Repr singapore (1976)

Kelleher, Theresa. Confucianism. In WWR (1987) 135-159.

Kim, Sung-hae. Confucian understanding of woman: cultivation of self through learning. Pastoral theology (july 1986) 61-73.

Kong Demao & Ke Lan. In the mansion of confucius' descendants. An oral history . . . Beijing (1984) 292 p, sec of photos, map of kong mansion.

Kramers, R. P. Confucian apologetics in modern times. In LSS (1981) 177-190. "modern times" means pre-1949.

Kramers, R. P. The development of the confucian schools. In CHC vol l: The ch'in and han empires, 221 b.c.-a.d.220. (1986) Sec 14: 747-765.

Kramers, R. P. Konfuzius, china's entthronter heiliger? Bern (1979) 136 p, anmerkungen, anhang, quellen angaben, bibliog. Re the life and teachings.

Kramers, R. P. Der volkommene mensch in konfuzianischer und in christlicher sicht. In T. Müller-Krüger (heraus) Confrontations, stuttgart (l966)

Kupperman, Joel. Confucian ethics and weakness of will. JCP 8.1 (mar 1981) 1-8.

Lai, Whalen. Growing up rational, puritanical and weaned of gods: confucian education of the son after age six. CF 4 (dec 1990) 232-247.

Lai, Whalen. Of one mind or two? Query on the innate good in mencius. RS 26.2 (june (1990) 247-255.

Lai, Whalen. Yung and the tradition of the shih: the confucian restructuring of heroic courage. RS 21.2 (june 1985) 181-203.

Lauridsen, Kristen Ronbol. Long live confucius: some remarks on creel, confucius, and humanistic values. In AnHaf (1988) 78-81.

Lee, Shui Chuen. The confucian conception of reason and faith. D&A 1.1 (spring 1987) 58-65.

Legge, James. The religions of china. Confucianism and taoism described and compared with christianity. London (1880) 310 p. Repr folcroft, penn (1976) norwood, penn (1977) philadelphia (1978)

Leo, Juat Beh & John Clammer. Confucianism as folk religion in singapore: a note. In CFRSM (1983) 175-178.

Li, Tung-fang. Confucius: a short biographical sketch. Taipei (1983) 200 p.

Li, Zehou. A re-evaluation of confucius. Social sciences in china [beijing] 1.2 (june 1980) 99-127. Same title in Anna-Teresa Tymieiecka (ed) Phenomenology of life in a dialogue between chinese and occidental philosophy, dordrecht (1984) 153-178.

Lin, Shuen-fu. Confucius in the "inner chapters" of the chuang tzu. TR 18.1-4 (aut 1987-sum 1988) 379-401.

Lin, Tian-min. Thought and action in confucius. RH 22.1 (winter 1988) 7-10, 17.

Lin, Yü-sheng. The unity of heaven and man in classical confucianism and taoism and its philosophical and social implications. Proc 31st ICHS, Tokyo, vol 1 (1984) 258-259. Abstr.

Liu, Weihua. The methodological question in the study of confucius. CSP 17.3 (spring 1986) 78-101.

Luo, Chenglie & "Zhou Yi" (pseud) Feudal confucianism. Areopagus (trinity 1990, 3.4) 50-51.

Mak, M. H. June. Moral education. ACQ 18.3 (autumn 1990) 62-71.

Martinson, Paul V. Confucius lives: a theological critique of current chinese marxist reappraisal of the confucian tradition. CF 24.4 (dec 1981) 215-240. Similar title in Theology & life 4 (1982) 60-74.

Meng, Te-sheng & Paul K. T. Sih. God in confucian thought. In GCR (1977) 97-111.

Metzger, Thomas. Max weber's analysis of the confucian tradition: a critique. Bulletin of historical research; li-hsüeh hsüeh-pao, natl taiwan normal univ 11 (june 1983) 1-38. German version in MWSt (1983) 229-270.

Mindich, Jeffrey H. Painting eyes on the dragon. FCR 40.11 (nov 1990) 30-33, col photos. Re carvings in tainan confucian temple.

Mindich, Jeffrey H. A paragon for all generations. FCR 40.11 (nov 1990) 22-29, col photos. Re history and present aspect of tainan's confucian temple.

Mindich, Jeffrey H. Restored grandeur. FCR 40.11 (nov 1990) 4-21. Re restoration of tainan confucian temple.

Mo, Yi-moh. La personne dans l'éthique du confucianisme ancien. Taipei (1985) 278 p, notes, bibliog, index de traduction.

Mou Tsung-san. Tsl by Douglas Lancashire. Confucianism as religion. In CERF (1981) 21-43.

Na, Chae-Woon. Filial piety in confucian thought. NEAJT 28/29 (mar-sept 1982) 13-48.

Neville Robert C. Individuation in christianity and confucianism. CF 32.1 (mar 1989) 3-23.

Nikkilä, Pertti. Early confucianism and inherited thought in the light of some key terms of the confucian analects. I. The terms in shuching and shihching. Helsinki, studia orientalia vol 53 (1982) 275 p, primary sources, literature, abbrev, index.

Ogden, Graham S. Biblical and confucian thought:

a consideration of some common teachings. TJT 4 (mar 1982) 215-227.

Ogden, Graham S. Numerical sayings in israelite wisdom and in confucius. TJT 3 (mar 1981) 145-176.

Okada, Takehiko. Tsl by Rodney L. Taylor. Zazen to seiza: a prefatory discussion. Translation and discussion. JCR 10 (1982) 19-38.

Palmer, Spencer J. Confucian rituals in korea. Berkeley & seoul (n.d.=1985) 270 p, app, notes, gloss, geogr names, dynasties and kingdoms (china and korea) bibliog , index, illus with 111 pl (many in col) chin char in apparatus.

Parkin, Harry. Confucian thoughts on women. CN 22.2/3 (spring-summer 1984) 294-298. "Confucian underpinnings" of traditional society.

Paul, Diana. Portraits of the feminine: buddhist and confucian historical perspectives. In SHB (1980) 209-221.

Ren, Jiyu. How confucianism evolved into a religion. Social sciences in china [beijing] 1.2 (june 1980) 128-152.

Riley, Woodbridge. Men and morals; the story of ethics. NY (1929; repr 1960) See part 3, chap 2, Confucianism, 116-125.

Ro, Young-chan. The place of ethics in the christian tradition and the confucian tradition: a methodological prolegomenon. RS 22.1 (1986) 51-62.

Ro, Young-chan. The significance of the confucian texts as 'scripture' in the confucian tradition. JCP 15.3 (1988) 269-287.

Robinet, Isabelle. La notion de hsing dans le taoïsme et son rapport avec celle du confucianisme. JAOS 106.1 (jan-mar 1986) 183-196.

Rosemont, Henry jr. Kierkegaard and confucius: on finding the way. PEW 36.3 (july 1986) 201-212. Same title in CN 25.1 (winter 1986-87) 429-433.

Rosemont, Henry jr. Why take rights seriously? A confucian critique. In HR&WR (1988) 167-182.

Rosso, A. S. Confucius and confucianism. NCE 4 (1967) 156a-165a.

Rothfork, John. Confucianism in timothy mo's the monkey king. TR 18.1-4 (aut 1987-sum 1988) 403-442. Re novel publ 1978.

Rubin, Vitaly A. Values of confucianism. Numen 28.1 (1981) 72-79. Rev art on Tu Wei-ming's Humanity & self cultivation (1979) q.v.

Rule, Paul A. K'ung-tzu or confucius. The jesuit interpretation of confucianism. Sidney etc (1986) xiii + 303 p, bibliog, char index, notes, index.

Schluchter, Wolfgang. Einleitung. Max webers konfuzianismusstudie—versuch einer einordnung. In MWSt (1983) 11-54.

Schluchter, Wolfgang. Tsl by Neil Solomon. Rationalism, religion, and domination; a weberian perspective. Univ calif (1989) See chap 3, Confucianism and taoism: world adjustment, 85-116.

Schmidt-Glintzer, Helwig. Viele pfade oder ein weg? Betrachtungen zur durchsetzung der konfuzianischen orthopraxie. In MWSt (1983) 298-341.

Senger, Harro von. Rückbesinnung auf konfuzius in der volksrepublic china? ZDMG 133.2 (1983) 377-392.

Shen, Yifan. Confucian thought and theological reflection in china today. CF 31 (aug 1988) 166-176.

Sheng, C. L. Confucian moral philosophy and utilitarian theory. CC 23.1 (mar 1982) 33-46.

Sih, Paul K. T. Will confucianism thought (sic) survive in the modern age? CC 17.2 (june 1976) 27-30.

Skaja, Henry G. Li (ceremonial) as a primal concept in confucian spiritual humanism. CC 25 (mar 1984) 1-26.

Smith, D. Howard. Confucianism. EncyWF (1987) 273-278.

Sontag, Frederick. The analects of confucius: the universal man. JCP 17.4 (dec 1990) 427-438.

Standaert, N. Yang tingyun [1562-1627] confucian and christian in late ming china. Leiden (1988) 263 p, notes, bibliog, index index.

Steinhardt, Nancy Shatzman. Kong family mansion. In CTA (1984) 151-157, arch fig.

Steinhardt, Nancy Shatzman. Temple: Confucian temple compounds. EncyRel 14 (1987) 381b-383a.

Stevenson, Frank. Dwelling at ease and awaiting destiny: "taoism" in the "confucian" chung yung. TR 20.3 (spring 1990) 265-316.

Streng, Frederick J. Three approaches to authentic existence: christian, confucian and buddhist. PEW 32.4 (oct 1982) 371-392. Comparison of Paul Tillich, Chün-i T'ang, Keiji Nishitani.

Sunoo, Harold Hakwon. China of confucius: a critical interpretation. Virginia beach va (1985) 201 p, notes, bibliog, index. See passim.

Swart. Paula & Barry Till. A revival of confucian ceremonies in china. In TT:RCT (1989) 210-221.

Tan, Chung. Trial and triumph of confucian harmony ethics in modern china. Proc31stICHS, Tokyo, vol 1 (1984) 255-256. Abstr.

T'ang Chün-i. Tsl by Douglas Lancashire. The spirit of religion and modern man. In CERF (1981) 44-52.

Tang, Yijieh. An inquiry into the possibility of a third-phase development of confucianism. CSP 15.2 (winter 1983-84) 3-8. Confucianism lives?

Taylor, Rodney L. Compassion, caring, and the religious response to suffering. In Rodney L. Taylor & Jean Watson (ed) They shall not hurt; human suffering and human caring, colorado assoc univ press. boulder (1989) 11-32. See sec, Suffering in the confucian model, 23-31.

Taylor, Rodney L. Confucianism and the political order: religion poised in risk. In author's RDC (1990) 7-22.

Taylor, Rodney L. Confucianism: scripture and the sage. In Frederick M. Denny & Rodney L. Taylor (ed) The holy book in comparative perspective, univ south carolina (1985) 181-203. Republ as Scripture and the sage: on the question of a confucian scripture, in RDC (1990) 23-37.

Taylor, Rodney L. Modernity and religion: a contemporary confucian response. In author's RDC (1990) 135-147. "Response by Okada Takehiko"

Taylor, Rodney L. Of animals and men: the confucian perspective. In Tom Regan (ed) Animal sacrifices: religious perspectives on the use of animals in science, temple univ (1986) 239-263.

Taylor, Rodney L. The problem of suffering: christian and confucian dimensions. In author's RDC (1990) 115-134.

Taylor, Rodney L. The religious dimensions of confucianism. SUNY (1990) xiii + 198 p, notes, gloss, bibliog, index. Collection of essays, 6 republ and 3 previously unpubl, sep listed in this bibliog; abbrev RDC.

Taylor, Rodney L. The sage as saint: the confucian tradition. In Richard Kieckhefer & George D. Bond (ed) Sainthood: its manifestations in world religions (1988) 218-242. Republ as The saint as sage: a study in religious categories, in author's RDC (1990) 39-52.

Taylor, Rodney L. The way of heaven. An introduction to the confucian religious life. Leiden (1986) xi + 37 p, 48 pl. Iconography of relig series.

Tchang, F.-j. Religions de la chine. AnnEPHE 90 (1981-82) 121-126. Re confucianism.

Tchang, F.-j. Religions de la chine. AnnEPHE 91 (1982-83) 139-145. Re certain confucian classics.

Tchang, F.-j. Religions de la chine. AnnEPHE 92 (1983-84) 145-150. Re confucian classics.

Teng, Yung S. A study of the confucian thought in tu mu's literary works. TJ n.s.13.1/2 (dec 1981) 133-159.

The hero pattern and the life of confucius. JCStudies 1.3 (oct 1984) 241-260.

Thompson, Laurence G. Confucian thought: the state cult. EncyRel 4 (1987) 36a-38b.

Thompson, Laurence G. Confucianism and state orthodoxy. ProcC&S (1987) 5-12.

Tse, Chung M. Confucianism and contemporary ethical issues. In S. Cromwell Crawford (ed) World religions and global ethics, NY (1989) 91-125.

Tu, Wei-ming. Confucian ethics today; the singapore challenge. Singapore (1984) 247 p, gloss, sel bibliog, index. Intended as background and proposal for primary school ethics course.

Tu, Wei-ming. A confucian perspective on learning to be human. In Frank Whaling (ed) The world's religious traditions, edinburgh (1984) Repr in author's CT (1985) 51-65.

Tu, Wei-ming. The confucian sage: exemplar of personal knowledge. In John S. Hawley (ed) Saints and virtues, univ calif (1987) 73-86.

Tu, Wei-ming. Confucian studies in the people's republic. Humanities 8 (sept-oct 1987) 14-16, 34-35.

Tu, Wei-ming. Confucian thought. Selfhood as creative transformation. SUNY (1985) 203 p, gloss, bibliog of author. Collection of author's essays, sep listed in this bibliog; abbrev CT.

Tu, Wei-ming. The confucian tradition: a confucian perspective in learning to be human. In Frank Whaling (ed) The world's religions...NY (1986) 55-71.

Tu, Wei-ming. The confucian tradition in chinese history. Chap 5 in Paul S. Ropp (ed) Heritage of china, univ calif (1990) 112-137.

Tu, Wei-ming. Jen as a living metaphor in the confucian analects. PEW 31.1 (jan 1981) 45-54.

Repr in author's CT (1985) 81-92.

Tu, Wei-ming. Pain and suffering in confucian self-cultivation. PEW 34.4 (oct 1984) 379-388.

Tu, Wei-ming. Selfhood and otherness: father-son relationship in confucian thought. In Anthony Marsella et al (ed) Culture and self, london (1985) Repr in author's CT (1985) 113-130.

Tu, Wei-ming. The value of the human in classical confucian thought. Humanities 15.2 (may 1979) Repr in author's CT (1985) 67-80.

Vandermeersch, Léon. Aspects rituels de la popularization du confucianisme sous les han. In T&L (1990) 89-107.

Vandermeersch, Léon. Le confucianisme à l'époque des han postérieurs. AnnEPHE 94 (1985-86) 161-171.

Vandermeersch, Léon. Le confucianisme des "trois-royaumes" aux "jin occidentaux" Pénétration de l'influence taoïste. AnnEPHE 95 (1986-87) 121-126.

Vandermeersch, Léon. l'Eclipse du confucianisme sous les dynasties du nord et du sud de la chine désunifiée. AnnEPHE 96 (1987-88) 93-99.

Vandermeersch, Léon. Religions de la chine. AnnEPHE 89 (1980-81) 175-183. Re confucianism.

Vandermeersch, Léon. Ritualisme et juridisme. In EsurR (1990) 45-56.

Vandermeersch, Léon. I. La scolastique confucianiste sous les han: néo-canonique et archéo-canonique. II. De la reprise de vitalité du confucianisme à jia yi. III. Dong zhong-shu. AnnEPHE 93 (1984-85) 121-128.

Vandermeersch, Léon. Une tradition réfractaire à la théologie: la tradition confucianiste. EOEO 6 (1985) 9-21. Theme of this issue: "Une civilisation sans théologie?"

Wang, Chia-yu. Le confucianisme. In Livre des religions, paris (1989) 230-233.

Wang, Gung-wu. Lu xun, lim boon keng and confucianism. PFEH 39 (mar 1989) 75-91.

Wawrytko, Sandra A. Confucius and kant: the ethics of respect. PEW 32.3 (july 1982) 237-257.

Wu, John C. H. The real confucius. THM 1.1 (aug 1935) 11-20. Repr China academy, Bulletin of the institute of pacific research 1 (mar 1967) 77-89.

Wu, Lei-ch'uan. Tsl by Douglas Lancashire. Christianity and confucianism. In CERF (1981) 197-207.

Yearley, Lee H. Classical confucians and thomistic christians: contrasts that arise from the presence and absence of deity. D&A 1.3 (fall 1987) 23-36. A "somewhat different version" of author's art: A comparison between classical chinese thought and thomistic christian thought, JAAR 51.3 q.v.

Yearley, Lee H. A confucian crisis: mencius' two cosmogonies and their ethics. In C&EO (1985) 310-327.

Yearley, Lee H. Mencius and aquinas; theories of virtue and conceptions of courage. SUNY (1990) 280 p, notes, chin terms, sel bibliog, indexes. Comparative study of relig ethics.

Yeo, Khiok-Khng. Amos (4:4-5) and confucius: the will (ming) of god (thien) AJT 4.2 (oct 1990) 472-488.

Yokomatsu, Takashi. The fundamental characteristics of ancient confucianism. MexICHS 2: China (1976) 165-168.

Young, John D. Confucianism and christianity, the first encounter. Univ HK (1983) 182 p, gloss, notes, bibliog, index.

Yu, David C. Confucianism, maoism, and max weber. In TLLP (1985) 141-167.

Yu, Paul. Confucian ethics and western ethics: a comparative study. Commentary [singapore] 6.1 (sept 1983) 10-18.

Yü, Pin. Tsl by Douglas Lancashire. Roman catholicism and confucianism. In CERF (1981) 160-166.

Yu, Thomas Chi-ping. Filial piety: some observations on its ritual and meaning in confucian understanding. Theology & life 8 (dec 1985) 15-32.

Zhang, Hengshou. Theories of "humaneness" in the spring and autumn era and confucius' concept of humaneness. CSP 12.4 (summer 1981) 3-36. "Humaneness" is tsl of jen.

Zürcher, Erik. Chinese ch'an and confucianism. In ZCJEAA (1985) 29-46.

II.8 Religious Elements in "Neo-Confucianism"

Allinson, Robert E. The ethics of confucianism and christianity: the delicate balance. CF 33.3 (sep 1990) 158-175.

Berthrong, John. Chu hsi's ethics: jen and ch'eng. JCP 14.2 (june 1987) 161-178.

Ch'ien, Edward T. The neo-confucian confrontation with buddhism: a structural and historical analysis. JCP 9 (1982) 307-328.

Chafee, John & Wm Theodore DeBary (ed) Neo-confucian education: the formative stage. Univ calif (1989) Relevant art sep listed in this bibliog; abbbrev NCEduc.

Chan, Wing-tsit. Chu hsi and buddhism. In author's CH:NS (1989) Chap 29, 509-536.

Chan, Wing-tsit (ed). Chu hsi and neo-confucianism. Univ hawaii (1986) Papers fr intl conference at Honolulu, july 1982; relevant papers sep listed in this bibliog; abbrev CH&NC.

Chan, Wing-tsit. Chu hsi and quiet-sitting. In author's CH:NS (1989) Chap 17, 255-270.

48

Chan, Wing-tsit. Chu hsi and taoism. In author's CH:NS (1989) Chap 28, 486-508.

Chan, Wing-tsit. Chu hsi on t'ien. In author's CH:NS (1989) Chap 12, 184-196.

Chan, Wing-tsit. Chu hsi's religious life. In ISCI (1983) 52-74.

Chan, Wing-tsit. Confucian thought: neo-confucianism. EncyRel 4 (1987) 24a-36a.

Chan, Wing-tsit. Neo-confucian philosophical poems. Renditions 4 (spring 1975) 5-21. As much relig as philos.

Chang, Hao. Neo-confucian moral thought and its modern legacy. JAS 39.2 (feb 1980) 259-272. Rev symposium.

Ching, Julia. Chu hsi and ritual. In EsurR (1990) 57-76.

DeBary, Wm Theodore. Chen te-hsiu and the "learning of the heart and mind" ProcICS, Thought and philos vol 1 (1981) 393-394.

DeBary, Wm Theodore. Human rites—an essay on confucian and human rights. CN 22.4 (fall 1984) 307-313.

DeBary, Wm Theodore. Neo-confucianism and human rights. In HR&WR (1988) 183-198.

Fu, Charles Wei-hsun. Chu hsi on buddhism. In CH&NC (1986) 377-407.

Gernet, Jacques. Techniques de recueillement, religion et philosophie: à propos du jingzuo néo-confucéen. ProcICS, History and archeology vol 1 (1981) 475-493. Same title in BEFEO 69 (1981) 289-305.

Jan, Yün-hua. Li p'ing-shan and his refutation of neo-confucian criticism of buddhism. In DBT (1979) 162-193. Li's dates are 1185-1231.

Jiang, Paul Yun-ming. The concept of mind in chu hsi's ethics. Philosophical review [taipei] 7 (jan 1984) 27-53.

Kim, Yung Sik. Kuei-shen in terms of chi: chu hsi's discussion of kuei-shen. TJ 17.1-2 (dec 1985) 149-163.

Liu, Shu-hsien. Postwar neo-confucian philosophy: its development and issues. In RIID (1989) 277-302.

Masson, Michel E. Neo-confucianism: ethics of fung yu-lan. In GCR (1977) 113-154.

Ren, Jiyu. Chu hsi and religion. In CH&NC (1986) 355-376.

Rule, Paul. Neo-confucianism: theism, atheism or neither? In Victor C. Hayes (ed) Identity issues and world religions, South australian college of advanced education (1986) 135-144. This vol is Sel ProcIAHR.

Santangelo, Paolo. The origin of good and evil in human nature according to neo-confucianism. Some aspects of the question. E&W 40.1-4 (dec 1990) 231-259.

Shirokauer, Conrad. Ch'eng hao. EncyRel 3 (1987) 228a-229b.

Shirokauer, Conrad. Ch'eng i. EncyRel 3 (1987) 229b-231a.

Shirokauer, Conrad. Chu hsi. EncyRel 3 (1987) 469b-472a.

Taylor, Rodney L. The centered self: religious autobiography in the neo-confucian tradition. HR 17.3/4 (feb-may 1978) 266-283. Republ as The centered self: confucian religious autobiography, in author's RDC (1990) 53-64.

Taylor, Rodney L. Chang tsai. EncyRel 3 (1987) 200a-201a.

Taylor, Rodney L. Chou tun-i. EncyRel 3 (1987) 337b-339b.

Taylor, Rodney L. The confucian way of contemplation. Okada Takehiko and the tradition of quiet-sitting. Univ south carolina (1988) 230 p, 4 pl, notes, index, sel bibliog of Okada's works.

Taylor, Rodney L. Journey into self: the autobiographical reflections of hu chih. HR 21.4 (may 1982) 321-328.

Taylor, Rodney L. Meditation in ming neo-orthodoxy. JCP 6.2 (june 1979) 149-182. Republ as Meditation and ming neo-orthodoxy in author's RDC (1990) 93-114.

Taylor, Rodney L. Proposition and praxis: the dilemma of neo-confucian syncretism. PEW 32.2 (apr 1982) 187-199. Republ as Proposition and praxis in neo-confucian syncretism, in author's RDC (1990) 65-75.

Taylor, Rodney L. The study of confucianism as a religious tradition: notes on some recent publications. JCR 18 (fall 1990) 143-159. Rev art on a no of works.

Taylor, Rodney L. Subitist and gradualist: a simile for neo-confucian learning. MS 36 (1984-85) 1-32.

Taylor, Rodney L. The sudden/gradual paradigm and neo-confucian mind cultivation. PEW 33.1 (1983) 77-91. Republ in author's RDC (1990) 77-91.

Tillman, Hoyt Cleveland. Consciousness of t'ien in chu hsi's thought. HJAS 47.1 (1987) 31-50.

Tu, Wei-ming. Lu hsiang-shan. EncyRel 9 (1987) 48a-50a.

Tu, Wei-ming. Neo-confucian ontology: a preliminary questioning. JCP (1980) Repr in author's CT (1985) 149-170; german tsl in MWSt (1983) 271-297.

Tu, Wei-ming. On neo-confucianism and human relatedness. In author's CT (1985) 131-148. Orig publ in RFEA (1986—copyright 1984) 111-125, as Neo-confucian religiosity and human relatedness.

Tu, Wei-ming. Wang yang-ming. EncyRel 15 (1987) 335a-337b.

Yü, Chün-fang. Some ming buddhists' responses to neo-confucianism. JCP 15.4 (1988) 371-413.

II.9 Ethics - Morals

Adler, Joseph. Descriptive and normative principle (li) in confucian moral metaphysics: is/ought from the chinese perspective. Zygon 16.3 (sept 1981) 285-293.

Allinson, Robert E. The golden rule in confucianism and christianity. ACQ 16.4 (winter 1988) 1-15.

Berthrong, John. Chu hsi's ethics: jen and ch'eng. JCP 14.2 (june 1987) 161-178.

Bishop, Donald H. Themes in taoist ethics. CC 29.2 (june 1988) 67-74.

Carmody, Denise Lardner & John Tully Carmody. How to live well: ethics in the world religions. Belmont, calif (1988) See chap 6, Chinese ethics, 137-159.

Cartier, Michel. Dette et propriété en chine. In Dette (1988) 17-30.

Chang, Hao. Neo-confucian moral thought and its modern legacy. JAS 39.2 (feb 1980) 259-272. Rev symposium.

Ch'en, Li-fu. Tsl by Andrew Morton. The way of heaven, the way of man, and the chinese moral ethics. ACQ 17.1 (spring 1989) 1-14.

Cheng, Chung-ying. Totality and mutuality: confucian ethics and economic development. In Conference on confucianism and economic development in east asia: proceedings, taipei (1989) 15-56.

Ch'ien, Edward T. The transformation of neo-confucianism as transformative leverage. JAS 39.2 (feb 1980) 255-258. Rev symposium.

Ching, Julia. Ethical encounter: chinese and christian. In Jacques Pohier & Dietmar Mieth (ed) Christian ethics (1981) 30-35.

Cua, Antonio S. The concept of li in confucian moral theory. In Robert E. Allinson (ed) Understanding the chinese mind, chin univ of HK (1989) 209-235.

Cua, A. S. Ethical uses of the past in early confucianism: the case of hsün tzu. PEW 35.2 (apr 1985) 133ff.

Cua, A. S. Li and moral justification: a study in the li chi. PEW 33.1 (jan 1983) 1-16.

Fu, Charles Wei-hsun. Philosophical reflections on the modernization of confucianism as traditional morality. In RIID (1989) 303-323.

Girardot, Norman J. Behaving cosmogonically in early taoism. In C&EO (1985) 67-97.

Gurdak, Thaddeus J. Benevolence: confucian ethics and ecstasy. In James Gaffney (ed) Essays in morality and ethics, ?place of publ (1980) 76-84.

Huang, Chun-chieh. Three interpretations of mencian morality in t'ang times. ACQ part I, 10.1; part II, 10.2 (spring-summer 1982) 68-81; 38-50.

Ihara, Craig K. Guiltless morality. In Benjamin J. Hubbard & Bradley E. Starr (ed) Anxiety, guilt and freedom: religious perspectives (1990) 5-22. "Confucian" morality.

Ivanhoe, Philip J. Ethics in the confucian tradition: the thought of mencius and wang yang-ming. Atlanta (1990) 186 p, 3 app, notes, works cited, index.

Jiang, Paul Yun-ming. The concept of mind in chu hsi's ethics. Philosophical review [taipei] 7 (jan 1984) 27-53.

Jullien, Francois. Essai: "fonder" la morale, ou comment légitimer la transcendance de la moralité sans le support du dogme ou de la foi (au travers du mencius) EOEO 6 (1985) 23-81. Theme of this issue: "Une civilisation sans théologie?"

Kupperman, Joel. Confucian ethics and weakness of will. JCP 8.1 (mar 1981) 1-8.

Lai, Whalen. The chinese universe of moral

discourse—a postmodern appreciation. CF 32.2 (june 1989) 85-100.

Mak, M. H. June. Moral education. ACQ 18.3 (autumn 1990) 62-71.

Makeham, John. Ming-chiao in the eastern han: filial piety, reputation, and office. HHYC:CS 8.2 (dec 1990) 79-107.

Masson, Michel E. Neo-confucianism: ethics of fung yu-lan. In GCR (1977) 113-154.

Meyer, Jeffrey F. Moral education in taiwan. Comparative education review 32.1 (1988) 20-38.

Meyer, Jeffrey F. Teaching morality in taiwan schools: the message of the textbooks. CQ 114 (june 1988) 267-284.

Mo, Yi-moh. La personne dans l'éthique du confucianisme ancien. Taipei (1985 278 p, notes, bibliog, index du traduction.

Myers, Philip Van Ness. History as past ethics; an introduction to the history of morals. Boston etc (1913) See chap 5, Chinese morals: an ideal of filial piety, 53-76.

Ng, Margaret N. Internal shame as a moral sanction. JCP 8.1 (mar 1981) 75-86.

Qiu, R-z. Medicine, the art of humaneness: on the ethics of traditional chinese medicine. JMP 13.3 (1988) 277-300.

Riley, Woodbridge. Men and morals; the story of ethics. NY (1929; repr 1960) See part 3, chap 2, Confucianism, 116-125.

Ro, Young-chan. The place of ethics in the christian tradition and the confucian tradition: a methodological prolegomenon. RS 22.1 (1986) 51-62.

Robertson, J. M. A short history of morals. NY (1920; repr 1971) See part 3, chap 3, Chinese ethical doctrines, 151-163.

Rudd, H. F. Chinese moral sentiments before

confucius: a study in the origin of ethical valuations. Shanghai (1914) 220 p.

Saunders, Kenneth. The ideals of east and west. NY & cambridge univ (1934) See chap 2, The ethics of the chinese, 42-81.

Seiwert, Hubert. Ethik in der chinesischen kulturtradition. In R. Mokrosch, S. H. Pfürtner, H. Schmidt (heraus) Ethik in nichtchristlichen kulturen, stuttgart etc (1984) 136-167.

Sheng, C. L. Confucian moral philosophy and utilitarian theory. CC 23.1 (mar 1982) 33-46.

Tan, Che-Bin. Ethical particularism as a chinese contextual issue. In Dean S. Gilliland (ed) The word among us: contextualizing theology for mission today, dallas (1989) 262-281.

Tan, Chung. Trial and triumph of confucian harmony ethics in modern china. Proc31stICHS, tokyo, vol 1 (1984) 255-256. Abstr.

Thompson, Kirill Ole. Ethics and morality according to chinese philosophy. ACQ 9.2 (summer 1981) 1-20.

Tse, Chung M. Confucianism and contemporary ethical issues. In S. Cromwell Crawford (ed) World religions and global ethics, NY (1989) 91-125.

Tu, Wei-ming. Confucian ethics today; the singapore challenge. Singapore (1984) 247 p, gloss, sel bibliog, index. Background and proposal for primary school ethics course.

Tu, Wei-ming. The "moral universe" from the perspectives of east asian thought. In Gunther S. Stent (ed) Morality as a biological phenomenon, berlin (1978) Repr with comm by Clifford Geertz in PEW 31.3 (july 1981) also repr in author's CT (1985) 19-33.

Übelhör, Monika. The community compact (hsiang-yüeh) of the sung and its educational significance. In NCEduc (1989) 371-388.

Wawrytko, Sandra A. Confucius and kant: the ethics of respect. PEW 32.3 (july 1982) 237-257.

Whitehead, Raymond L. K. Ethics in post-mao china. In L. Rasmussen (ed) Annual of the society of christian ethics (1983) 161-184.

Wilson, Richard W., Sidney L. Greenblatt, & Amy Auerbach Wilson (ed) Moral behavior in chinese society. NY (1981) 199 p. See passim.

Wu, Kuang-ming. Deconcentration of morality: taoist ethics of person-making. HHYC:CS 1.2 (dec 1983) 625-654. Re chuang tzu and morality.

Yearley, Lee H. A confucian crisis: mencius' two cosmogonies and their ethics. In C&EO (1985) 310-327.

Yearley, Lee H. Mencius and aquinas: theories of virtue and conceptions of courage. SUNY (1990) 280 p, notes, chin terms, sel bibliog, indexes. Comparative study of relig ethics.

Yu, Paul. Confucian ethics and western ethics: a comparative study. Commentary [singaporc] 6.1 sept 1983) 10-18.

II.10 Filiality

Cheng, Zhong-ying. On confucian filial piety and its modernization: duties, rights, and moral conduct. CSP 20.2 (winter 1988-89) 48-88.

Chow, Lien-hwa. Christian responses to filial piety in chinese classical literature. In CAAP (1983) 135-146.

Davis-Friedman, Deborah. Long lives: chinese elderly and the communist revolution. Stanford univ (1983; rev ed 1991) See 5, Funerals and filial piety, 60-70.

Ho, Y. F. & L. Y. Lee. Authoritarianism and attitude toward filial piety in chinese teachers. Journal of social psychology 92 (1974) 305-306. Significant correlation was found.

Hsiao, Harry Hsin-o. Concepts of hsiao (filial piety) in the classic of poetry and the classic of documents. JICS:CUHK 10.2 (1979) 425-443.

Hsu, Francis L. K. Filial piety in japan and china: borrowing, variation and significance. Journal of

52

comparative family studies 2 (1971) 67-74.

Jordan, David K. Folk filial piety in taiwan: the twenty-four filial examplars. In Walter H. Slote (ed) The psycho-cultural dynamics of the confucian family: past and present, seoul (1986) 47-106.

Leu, Chien-ai. Filial piety modernized. FCR 39.3 (mar 1989) 18-21, illus.

Levi, Jean. Dong yong le fils pieux et le mythe formosan de l'origine des singes. JA 272.1-2 (1984) 83-132.

Major, John S. Hsiao. EncyRel 6 (1987) 474a-475a.

Makeham, John. Ming-chiao in the eastern han: filial piety, reputation, and office. HHYC:CS 8.2 (dec 1990) 79-107.

Myers, Philip Van Ness. History as past ethics: an introduction to the history of morals. Boston etc (1913) See chap 5, Chinese morals: an ideal of filial piety, 53-76.

Na, Chae Woon. Filial piety in confucian thought. NEAJT 28/29 (mar/sept 1982) 13-48.

Raddock, D. M. Growing up in new china: a twist in the circle of filial piety. History of childhood quarterly: the journal of psychohistory 2 (1974) 201-220.

Schopen, Gregory. Filial piety and the monk in the practice of indian buddhism: a question of 'sinicization' viewed from the other side. TP 70.1-3 (1984) 110-126.

Strong, John S. Filial piety and buddhism: the indian antecedents to a "chinese problem" In Peter Slater & Donald Wiebe (ed) Traditions in contact and change, wilfrid laurier univ (1983) 171-186.

Yu, Chi-ping. Filial piety and chinese pastoral care. AJT 4.1 (apr 1990) 316-328.

Yu, Thomas Chi ping. Filial piety: some observations on its ritual and meaning in confucian understanding. Theology & life [HK] 8 (dec 1985) 15-32.

Yu, Chi-ping. Theology of filial piety: an initial formulation. AJT 3.2 (oct 1989) 496-508.

Zito, Angela R. City gods, filiality, and hegemony in late imperial china. ModCh 13.3 (july 1987) 333-371.

II.11 Death - Afterlife - Ancestral Cult

N.B. Relevant items classified in other categories in 1985 bibliography have been brought together with new items here.

A. L. Chinese notions as to the moment of death. ChRev 10 (1881-82) 431.

Aijmer, Göran. Birth and death in china: musings on a taiwan corpus. Ethnos (1984) 5-41.

Antoni, Klaus. Death and transformations: the presentation of death in east and southeast asia. AsFS 41.2 (1982) 147-162.

Baker, Hugh D. R. Ancestral images: a bibliographical note. JHKBRAS 23 (1983) 221-232.

Baker, Hugh D. Burial, geomancy and ancestor worship. In ASONT (1965) 36-39.

Berger, Patricia. An ideology of one: the offering shrine of wu liang. EC 15 (1990) 223-235. Rev art on Wu Hung, The wu liang shrines . . .q.v.

Berliner, Nancy. Depictions of hell in chinese painting and shadow puppets. Orientations 17.4 (apr 1986) 42-49.

Bodde, Derk. The chinese view of immortality: its expression by chu hsi and its relationship to buddhist thought. RofR 6 (1942) 369-383. Repr ECC (1981) 316-330.

Bokenkamp, Stephen. Death and ascent in ling-pao taoism. TaoRes 1.2 (winter 1989) 1-20.

Brandon, S. G. F. The judgment of the dead. The idea of life after death in the major religions. NY (1967) See chap 9, The judgment of the dead bureaucratically organized, 178-188.

Bredon, Juliet. Hell 'à la chinoise.' The several wards of the taoist inferno. Asia 25 (1925) 138-141.

Brook, Timothy. Funerary ritual and the building of lineages in late imperial china. HJAS 49.2 (1989) 465-499.

Buckens, F. Les antiquités funéraires du honan central et la conception de l'âme dans la chinese primitive. MCB 8 (1946-47) 1-101.

Bulling, Anneliese Guttkind. Rites mentioned in han tomb inscriptions and the funerary art of han and pre-han periods. Proc31stICHS, Tokyo, vol 2 (1984) 929. Abstr.

Ch'iu, K'un-liang. Mu-lien "operas" in taiwanese funeral rituals. In RO/OR (1989) 105-125.

Chen, Chung-min. Ancestor worship and clan organization in a rural village of taiwan. ASBIE 23 (1967) engl summ 192-193.

Cheng, Te-k'un. Ch'in-han mortuary architecture. JICS:CUHK (1980) 193-269, illus.

Childs-Johnson, Elizabeth. The jue and its ceremonial use in the ancestor cult of china. AA 48.3/4 (1987) 171-196. Re a bronze vessel.

Chou, Chao-ming. Death, funerals and sacrifices in wang ch'ung's philosophy. TR 17.2 (winter 1986) 175-195.

Chow, Lien-hwa. Christian response to filial piety in chinese classical literature. In CAAP (1985) 135-146.

Christy, Anita. Articles of the spirit—the schloss collection of chinese tomb sculpture. Orientations 19.8 (aug 1988) 44-49.

Chuang, Ying-chang. A comparison of hokkien and hakka ancestor worship. ASBIE 69 (1990) 133-159.

Clarke, G. W. (tsl) The yü-li or precious records. JNCBRAS 28.2 (1918) 233-400. Deals with hells and punishments.

Croissant, Doris. Grabkult und jenseitsvorstellung in der han-zeit. In WGM (1989) 115-121.

Croissant, Doris. Der unsterbliche leib. Ahneneffigies und reliquienporträt in der porträtplastik chinas und japans. In M. Kratz (ed) Das bildnis in der kunst des Orients. Abhandlungen für die kunde des morgenlandes 50.1 (1990) 235-268, illus.

Davis-Friedman, Deborah. Long lives: chinese elderly and the communist revolution. Stanford univ (1983; rev ed 1991) See 5, Funerals and filial piety, 60-70.

Dean, Kenneth. Funerals in fujian. CEA 4 (1988) 19-78.

Dean, Kenneth. Lei yu-sheng ("thunder is noisy") and mu-lien in the theatrical and funerary traditions of fukien. In RO/OR (1989) 46-104.

Dehergne, Joseph. l'Exposé der jesuites de pékin sur le culte des ancêtres présenté à l'empereur k'anghi en novembre 1700. In RECEL (1980) 185-229.

Delahaye, H. Recherches récentes sur le thème de l'ascension céleste. BEFEO 72 (1983) 299-307. Summ of recent archeological finds.

Demiéville, Paul. Une descente aux enfers sous les t'ang: la biographie de houang che-k'iang. In Etudes d'histoire et de littérature chinoises offerts au professeur jaroslav prusek. (1976) 71-84.

DeWoskin, Kenneth J. Music and entertainment themes in the han funerary sculptures. Orientations 18.4 (apr 1987) 34-40.

Eberhard, Wolfram. Guilt and sin in traditional china. Univ calif (1967) 141 p, gloss, bibliog, illus, index.

Ebrey, Patricia. Cremation in sung china. American historical review 95 (apr 1990) 406-428. Broader historical survey than title indicates.

Elder, Gove. Responses of thai-chinese churches to the ancestor problem. In CAAP (1983) 225-233.

Erkes, Eduard. Ssu er pu wang [death without annihilation] AM 3.2 (1953) 156-161.

Erkes, Eduard. Die totenbeigaben im alten china. AA 6 (1936-37) 17-36.

Evans, John Karl. The cult of the dead in ancient rome and modern china: a comparative analysis. JHKBRAS 25 (1985) 119-151.

Falkenhausen, Lothar von. Ahnenkult und grabkult im vordynastischen qin: der religiöse hintergrund der terracotta armee. In Lothar Ledderose & Adele Schlombs (ed) Jenseits der grossen mauer: der erste gottkaiser von qin und seine terracotta armee, munich (1990) 35-48. Exhibition catalog art.

Fitch, R. F. A study of a taoist hell. ChRec 45.10 (oct 1914) 603-606, photos.

Fong, Mary H. T'ang line-engraved stone reliefs from shensi. ArsO 17 (1987) 43-71, 27 fig. T'ang tomb art.

Fong, Peng-Khuan. Khoo clan temple of penang. AofA 11.1 (jan-feb 1981) 104-111.

Girard-Geslan, Maud. La tombe à linceul de jade du roi de nanyue à canton. ArtsAs 41 (1986) Chin ruler of independent kingdom during 2nd century b.c.e.

Groot, J. J. M. de. The religious system of china. Leiden (1892-1910) Six vol: 1-3, Disposal of the dead; 4-6, The soul and ancestral worship. Repr taipei (1964) Compte rendu par E. Chavannes in RHR 37 (1898) 81-89.

Habenstein, Robert W. & William M. Lamers (ed) Funeral customs the world over. Milwaukee (1963) See chap 1, China, 1-40. Publ by the national funeral directors assoc of the united states, inc.

Hardacre, Helen. Ancestors: ancestor worship. EncyRel 1 (1987) 263a-268a.

Harrell, C. Stevan. When a ghost becomes a god. In RRCS (1974) 193-206.

Hase, Patrick. Observations at a village funeral. In David Faure, James Hayes, & Alan Birch (ed) From village to city: studies in the traditional roots of hong kong society, univ HK (1984) 129-163; 254-260.

Hase, Patrick H. Traditional funerals. JHKBRAS 21 (1981) 192-196, 10 photos. Re punti villages in new territories.

Hayes, James W. Graves. In RC/HK (1983) 209-212.

Hayes, James W. Graves in a chinese landscape. In RC/HK (1983) 137-145.

Hayes, James W. Moving ancestors. In RC/HK (1983) 199-201.

Hegel, Robert E. Heavens and hells in chinese fictional dreams. In P-S (1988) 1-10.

Ho Hao-tien (preface) Wei Po-ju (Paul Vidor) intro. Ten kings of hades. The vidor collection. Taipei (1984) 80 p, 66 b-&-w and col pl; bilingual. The evolution of traditional chin views about the nether world; app in chin only.

Hodous, Lewis. Chinese conceptions of paradise. ChRec 45.6 (june 1914) 358-371.

Hooyman & Vogelaar. Relation abrégée du tien-bing, vulgairement appelé la fête de morts, chez les chinois do batavia. JA 2 (1923) 236-243. Tirée des Mémoires de la société de batavia 6 (1792) et trad du hollandais.

Hu, Shih. The concept of immortality in chinese thought. Harvard divinity school bulletin (1946) 23-43.

Huang, WeiWei C. Chinese perspectives on death and dying. In Arthur Berger et al (ed) Perspectives on death and dying, philadelphia (1989) Chap 11, 126-130.

Hung, Daniel M. Mission blockade: ancestor worship. Evangelical missions quarterly (jan 1983) Repr in CAAP (1985) 199-208; repr in Chinese around the world (apr 1983) 3-6.

James, Jean M. The dating of the left wu family offering shrine. OA n.s.31.1 (spring 1985) 34-41. Re Wu liang tz'u.

James, Jean M. The iconographic program of the wu family offering shrines (a.d.151-ca.170) AA 39-72

James, Jean M. Interpreting han funerary art: the importance of context. OA n.s.31.3 (autumn 1985) 283-292.

James, Jean M. The role of nanyang in han funerary iconography. OA n.s.36.4 (winter 1990/91) 222-232.

Janelli, Roger L. & Dawnhee Yim Janelli. Ancestor worship and korean society. Stanford univ (1982) See chap 7, Ancestor cults in east asia compared, 177-195.

Jernigan, Homer L. Some reflections on chinese patterns of grief and mourning. SEAJT 15.1 (1973) 21-47. Re singapore chin.

Johnson, David. Actions speak louder than words: the cultural significance of chinese ritual opera. In RO/OR (1989) 1-45.

Johnson, David (ed) Ritual opera, operatic ritual. "Mu-lien rescues his mother" in chinese popular culture. Univ calif (1989) 324 p. 8 art sep listed in this bibliog; abbrev RO/OR.

Johnson, Elizabeth L. Grieving for the dead, grieving for the living: funeral laments of hakka women. In DeathRit (1988) 135-163.

Johnson, W. S. A chinese view of immortality. HJ 36 (1937-38) 287-292. Re hu shih and his "social immortality"

Jordan, David K. Two forms of spirit marriage in rural taiwan. BTLVK 127.1 (1971) 181-189.

Juliano, Annette L. Teng-hsien: an important six dynasties tomb. AA suppl (1980) 84 p, gloss, bibliog, 149 pl.

Karetzky, Patricia Eichenbaum. A scene of the taoist afterlife on a sixth century sarcophagus discovered in loyang. AA 44.1 (1983) 5-20, 9 fig.

Knapp, Ronald G. The changing landscape of the chinese cemetery. The china geographer 8 (1977) 1-13.

Knapp, Ronald G. Chinese vernacular burial. Orientations 13.7 (july 1982) 28-33.

Kramer, Kenneth. The sacred art of dying; how world religions understand death. Mahwah n.j. (1988) See chap 6, Chinese attitudes toward death, 81-93.

Kuwayama, George. The sculptural development of ceramic funerary figures in china. In QE (1987) 63-93, illus, notes.

Lai, David Chuen-yan. A feng-shui model as a location index. AAAG 64.4 (dec 1974) 506-513.

Lai, T. C. To the yellow springs; the chinese view of death. HK (1983) 133 p, illus. Anthol of sel fr traditional lit.

Langlois, Jack. Festival of the lonely ghosts. Echo 3.7 (july-aug 1973) 16-21, illus.

Ledderose, Lothar. A king of hell. In Suzuki kei sensei kanreki kinen: chugoku kaiga shi ronshu, tokyo (1981) 33-42.

Lei, Congyun. Catalogue of the exhibition, by lei conyun ... In QE (1987) 95-154.

Lemaître, Solange. Le mystère de la mort dans les religions d'asie. Paris (1943) xi + 151 p.

Li, O. Religions de la chine. ACF 92 (1983-84) 153-154. Re tomb goods, esp fr korea.

Li, Rui. Marriage of the dead. CL (autumn 1989) 30-37. Fictional descr of "marriage by burial" of deceased couple, set in lüliang mt rural area.

Li, Yih-yuan. On conflicting interpretations of chinese family rituals. In CFRB (1985) 263-281.

Liao, David. Christian alternatives to ancestor worship in taiwan. In CAAP (1985) 209-218.

Liaw, Stephen. Ancestor worship in contemporary taiwanese society and evangelism of the chinese. In CAAP (1985) 181-197.

Liebenthal, Walter. The immortality of the soul in chinese thought. MN 8 (1952) 327-397.

Lim, Guek Eng. Christianity encounters ancestor worship in taiwan. ERTh 8.2 (1984) 225-235.

Lim, Guek Eng. Christianity versus ancestor worship in taiwan. TCGB 11.2 (oct 1983) 4-10.

Lin, Chi-ping. Ancestor worship: the reactions of chinese churches. In CAAP (1985) 147-161.

Lin, Yueh-hwa. The golden wing. A sociological study of chinese families. London (1948) Repr westport, conn (1974) On death and its rituals see chap 10, 103-112.

Lisowski, F. P. The practice of cremation in china. EH 19.6 (june 1980) 6-10.

Lu, Shaochen. Catalogue of the exhibition, by...lu shaochen. In QE (1987) 95-154.

Luo, Feng. Lacquer painting on a northern wei coffin. Orientations 21.7 (july 1990) 18-29.

Mahdihassan, S. T'ao-t'ieh, a motif of chinese funerary art as the iconographic counterpart of cinnamon, an alchemical drug. AJCM 10.1-4 (1982) 5-13.

Martin, Emily. Gender and ideological differences in representations of life and death. In DeathRit (1988) 164-179.

Maspero, Henri. Sur quelques objets de l'époque des han. In EORL (1932) 403-418. Tomb furnishings.

Mew, James. Traditional aspects of hell (ancient and modern) london (1903) Repr ann arbor, mich (1971) See Buddhist hell, esp 43-102; incl H. A. Giles tsl of yü li ch'ao chuan, with illus.

Mozer, M. J. Death in china: a two-dimensional analysis. Journal of thanatology 3 (1975) 169-185.

Munford, T. F. 'Till death do us unite': xunzang and joint burial in ancient china. PFEH 27 (mar 1983) 1-19.

Naquin, Susan. Funerals in north china: uniformity and variations. In DeathRit (1988) 37-70.

Overmyer, Daniel L. China. Chap 6 in Frederick H. Holck (ed) Death and eastern thought, nashville & NY (1974) 198-225.

Paludan, Ann. The chinese spirit road, part I: The period of formation; part II: Imperial display. Orientations 19.9 (sept 1988; apr 1989) 56-65; 64-73.

Paludan, Ann. Huangling and zuling, two early ming mausolea. Orientations 19.1 (jan 1988) 28-37.

Paludan, Ann. The imperial ming tombs. Yale univ (1981) xviii + 251 p, illus b-&-w and col and col photos, tables, charts, notes, gloss, bibliog, app, index. Foreword by L. Carrington Goodrich.

Paludan, Ann. Some foreigners in the spirit roads of the northern sung imperial tombs. OA 29.4 (winter 1983-84) 377-388.

Parker, Jeannie. Chinese stone tomb sculpture in the royal ontario museum. Orientations 19.8 (aug 1988) 50-53.

Poo, Mu-chou. Ideas concerning death and burial in pre-han and han china. AM 3rd ser 2 (1990) 25-62.

Powers, Martin J. Hybrid omens and public issues in early imperial china. BMFEA 55 (1983) 1-56. Re offering shrines of wu clan, d 147-167. "Hybrid" ref to "confucian" and taoist inspirations.

Powers, Martin J. A late western han tomb near yangzhou and related problems. OA n.s.29.3 (autumn 1983) 275-290.

The quest for eternity. Chinese ceramic sculptures from the people's republic of china. Los angeles county museum of art, & san francisco chronicle books (1987) xiv + 161 p. Catalogue of exhibition; 5 essays sep listed in this bibliog; abbrev QE.

Rawski, Evelyn S. A historian's approach to chinese death ritual. In DeathRit (1988) 20-34.

Rawski, Evelyn S. The imperial way of death: ming and ch'ing emperors and death ritual. In DeathRit (1988) 228-253.

Ro, Bong Rin (ed) Christian alternatives to ancestor practices. Taichung (1985) Indiv art sep listed in this bibliog; abbrev CAAP.

Robinson, Natalie V. Chinese funerals in singapore. Sawaddi (july-aug 1981) 31-34.

Russell, T. C. Coffin pullers' songs: the macabre in medieval china. PFEH (mar 1983) 99-130.

Sanford, J. H. The nine faces of death: su tung-po's kuzo-shih. EB n.s.21.2 (1988) 54-77. Budd ideas in lit, text attributed to chin poet.

Schwab, Philip. Biblical understanding of ancestor practices. In CAAP (1983) 93-116.

Seaman, Gary. Mu-lien dramas in puli, taiwan. In RO/OR (1989) 155-190.

Seidel, Anna. Afterlife: chinese concepts. EncyRel 1 (1987) 124b-127b. Deals only with pre-budd notions.

Seidel, Anna. Geleitbrief an die unterwelt: jenseitsvorstellungen in den graburkunden der späteren han zeit. In RPO-A (1985) 161-183.

Seidel, Anna. Post-mortem immortality—or: the taoist resurrection of the body. In Saul Shaked et al (ed) Gilgul: essays on transformation, revolution & permanence in the history of religions, leiden (1987) 223-237.

Seidel, Anna. App by Marc Kalinowski. Tokens of immortality in han graves. Numen 29.1 (1982) 79-122. Rev art on Michael Loewe, Ways to paradise ... q.v.

Seidel, Anna. Traces of han religion in funeral texts found in tombs. In TGRC (1987) Engl text 23-57.

Shi, Yazhu. Catalogue of the exhibition, by ... shi yazhu ... In QE (1987) 95-154.

Shih, Joseph. l'Eschatologie dans le monde chinois. SM 32 (1983) 181-194.

Smith, Henry N. Ancestor practices in contemporary hong kong: religious ritual or social custom? AJT 3 (apr 1988) 31-45.

Smith, Henry N. Christianity and ancestor practices in hong kong: toward a contextual strategy. Missiology 17.1 (jan 1989) 27-38.

Smith, Henry. A typology of christian responses to chinese ancestor worship. Journal of ecumenical studies 26 (fall 1989) 628-647.

Steinhardt, Nancy Shatzman. Yuan period tombs and their decoration: cases at chifeng. OA n.s.36.4 (winter 1990/91) 198-221. Chifeng county is in present inner mongolian "autonomous region"

Stevens, Keith G. Portrait and ancestral images on chinese altars. AofA 19.1 (jan-feb 1989) 135-145.

Swart, Paula. The tomb of the king of nan yue. Orientations 21.6 (june 1990) 56, 66, illus.

Tan, Kim-sai. Christian alternatives to ancestor worship in malaysia. In CAAP (1985) 219-224.

Teiser, Stephen F. The ghost festival in medieval china. Princeton univ (1988) xvii + 275 p, char gloss, bibliog, index.

Teiser, Stephen F. Ghosts and ancestors in medieval chinese religion: the yü-lan-p'en festival as mortuary ritual. HR 26.1 (aug 1986) 47-67.

Teiser, Stephen F. "Having once died and returned to life": representations of hell in medieval china. HJAS 48.2 (dec 1988) 433-464.

Teiser, Stephen F. The ritual behind the opera: a fragmentary ethnography of the ghost festival, a.d.400-1900. In RO/OR (1989) 191-223.

The ten courts of hades. Echo 4.7 (july-aug 1974) 37-51, 60, illus.

58

Thompson, Laurence G. On the prehistory of hell in china. JCR 17 (1989) 27-41.

Thompson, Laurence G. Yu ying kung: the cult of bereaved spirits in taiwan. In author edited StAs (1975) 267-277.

Thompson, Stuart E. Death, food, and fertility. In DeathRit (1988) 71-108.

Thorp, Robert L. The qin and han imperial tombs and the development of mortuary architecture. In QE (1987) 17-37, illus, notes.

Thorp, Robert. The sui xian tomb: re-thinking the fifth century. AA 43.1/2 (1981-82) 67-92, 31 fig. Tomb in northern hupei.

Thote, Alain. Une tombe princière chinoise du Ve siècle avant notre ère. CRAIBL (avr-juin 1986) 393-413. Tomb no 1 at leigudun, that of marquis yi of tseng.

Till, Barry. The eastern mausoléums of the qing dynasty. Orientations 13.2 (feb 1982) 26-31.

Till, Barry. Ming tombs at guilin. Orientations 15.11 (nov 1984) 37-41.

Till, Barry. Qian ling. A tang dynasty imperial mausoleum. Orientations 13.7 (july 1982) 22-27.

Till, Barry. The tomb of a ming emperor's younger brother. AofA 19.3 (may-june 1989) 91-96. Tomb of chu i-liu (1568-1614) in hsin-hsiang, honan.

Till, Barry & Paula Swart. Funerary sculptures of the northern sung dynasty. In RDChArch (1984) 81-89.

Tober, Linda M. & F. Stanley Lusby. Heaven and hell. EncyRel 6 (1987) See sec: Chinese traditions, 242a-242b.

Vandier-Nicolas, Nicole. Le jugement des morts en chine. In Le jugement des morts, paris (1961) 231-254.

Voss, Gustav. Missionary accomodation to an-

cestral rites in the far east. Theological studies 43 (1943) 525-560. See passim.

Wakeman, Frederic jr. Mao's remains. In DeathRit (1988) 254-288.

Wang, Chongren. Stone sculpture of the han and tang tombs. In RDChArch (1984) 27-30.

Wang, Renbo (tsl by Julia F. Andrews) General comments on chinese funerary sculpture. In QE (1987) 39-61, illus, notes.

Watson, James L. Funeral specialists in cantonese society: pollution, performance, and social hierarchy. In DeathRit (1988) 109-134.

Watson, James L. Of flesh and bones: the management of death pollution in cantonese society. In Maurice Bloch & Jonathan Parry (ed) Death and the regeneration of life, london (1982) 155-186.

Watson, James. The structure of chinese funerary rites: elementary forms, ritual sequence, and the primacy of performance. In DeathRit (1988) 3-19.

Watson, James L. & Evelyn S. Rawski (ed) Death ritual in late imperial and modern china. Univ calif (1988) xv + 334 p, gloss-index. 12 essays sep listed in this bibliog; abbrev DeathRit.

Watson, Rubie S. Remembering the dead: graves and politics in southeastern china. In DeathRit (1988) 203-227.

Wei, Yongye. Catalogue of the exhibition by . . . wei yongye . . . In QE (1987) 95-154.

Wei, Yuan-kwei. Historical analysis of ancestor worship in ancient china. In CAAP (1983) 119-133.

Werblowsky, R. J. Zwi. On mortuary symbolism and a chinese hell-picture. In J. H. Kamstra et al (ed) Funerary symbols and religion, kampen, netherlands (1988) 154-164.

Whyte, Martin K. Death in the people's republic of china. In DeathRit (1988) 289-316.

Wilhelm, Richard. Tod und erneuerung nach der ostasiatischen welt-auffassung. CDA (1929-30) 49-69. Engl tsl by Jane A. Pratt, Death and renewal, in Spring (1962) 20-44; also tsl by Irene Eber, same title, in tsl's Lectures on the i ching. Constancy and change, princeton univ (1979) 135-165.

Wu, Hung. From temple to tomb: ancient chinese art and religion in transition. EC 13 (1988) 78-115. The "revolution" within ancestral cult.

Wu, Hung. Myths and legends in han funerary art: their pictorial structure and symbolic meanings as reflected in carvings on sichuan sarcophagi. In SCP (1987) 72-81.

Yang, Hsi-chang. The shang dynasty cemetery system. In K. C. Chang (ed) Studies of shang archaeology, yale univ (1986) 49-63.

Yu, Anthony C. 'Rest, rest, perturbed spirit!' Ghosts in traditional chinese prose fiction. HJAS 47.2 (1987) 397-434.

Yü, Ying-shih. Life and immortality in the mind of han china. HJAS 25 (1964-65) 80-122.

Yü, Ying-shih. New evidence on the early chinese conception of afterlife—a review article. JAS 16.1 (nov 1981) 81-85. Rev art on Michael Loewe, Ways to paradise q.v.

Yü Ying-shih. 'O soul, come back!' A study in the changing conceptions of the soul and afterlife in pre-buddhist china. HJAS 47.2 (1987) 363-395.

II.12 Feng-shui

Bennett, Steven J. Patterns of sky and earth: a chinese system of applied cosmology. Chinese science 3 (1978) 1-26.

Bonhoure, Frédérique, Mile Sun, & Oscar Lax. La maison de la réussite: astrologie et géomancie chinoise. Paris (1983) 215 p.

Bräutigam, Herbert. Der Drachenpalast: Sagen aus China über der Handwerkmeister Lu Ban. Berlin (1987)

Edde, Gérard. Feng shui: santé et habitat selon les traditions chinoises. Paris (1988) 192 p.

Eitel, Ernest J. Feng-shui: or, the rudiments of natural science in china. London (1873) 84 p. Repr cokaygne (1973) bristol, engl (1979) singapore (1986) french tsl by L. de Milloué, AMG 1 (1880) german tsl (1983).

Fong, Lo Yik. Geomancy (feng-shui) in relation to mankind. SarGaz 111, no 1494 (dec 1985) 34-38.

Hayes, James W. The disturbance of feng-shui. In RC/HK (1983) 206-208.

Ho, Mun-Gang. Géomancie ou "système de vent et de l'eau" en corée. Revue de corée [seoul] 12.3 (1980) 28-51.

Knapp, Ronald G. China's traditional rural architecture. Univ hawaii (1986) See chap 5, 108-121.

Lai, David Chuen-yan. A feng-shui model as a location index. AAAG 64.4 (dec 1974) 506-513.

Lip, Evelyn. Chinese geomancy. Singapore (1953 and 1979) x + 126 p, bibliog, gloss, profusely illus col photos and paintings by author. Repr with subtitle, A layman's guide to chinese geomancy, union city, calif (1987)

Lip, Evelyn Mong Har. Feng shui; chinese colours and symbolism. Journal of the singapore institute of architects (1978) 79-87.

Lip, Evelyn Mong Har. Geomancy and building, development and construction. Singapore (1977)

Lip, Evelyn Mong Har. Symbols, colours and decoration of chinese temples in malaysia and singapore. Journal of the malaysian institute of architects (1978)

Ma, J. Lawrence. Peking as a cosmic city. MexICHS, 2: china (1976) 141-164.

60

March, Andrew L. The winds, the waters and the living qi. Parabola 3.1 (1978) 28-34.

Morgan, Carole. l'Ecole des cinq noms dans les manuscrits de touen-houang. CETH 3 (1984) 255-261, 1 pl. Re a "forgotten school of geomancy"

Nemeth, David. Graven images and cosmic landscapes on cheju island. Korean culture 4.1 (mar 1983) 5-19, illus photos, fig.

Rossbach, Sarah. Feng shui; the chinese art of placement. NY (1983) 169 p, chronol, gloss, engl bibliog.

Seaman, Gary. Only half-way to godhead: the chinese geomancer as alchemist and cosmic pivot. AsFS 45 (1986) 1-18.

Skinner, Stephen. The living earth manual of feng-shui. London etc (1982) 129 p, sel bibliog, vocab, index.

Spiegel, H. Die architektur der graeber. Wiener beitraege zur kunst- und kulturgeschichte asiens 7: 66-87. (1932-33)

Walters, Derek. Feng shui. The chinese art of designing a harmonious environment. NY etc (1988) 112 p, illus.

Yoon, Hong-key The image of nature in geomancy. Geographical journal 4.4 (1980) 341-348.

II.13 Religion and State

Dubs, Homer H. The sacred field. Chap 4, app 2 in HFHD 1 (1938) 281-283. Re field personally ploughed by emperor to open planting season.

Eichhorn, W. The ministry of ceremony (li pu) EtSong sér 1 no 3 (1976) 237-258. Tsl fr sung-shih, chap 163.

Eide, Elling O. Li po's naming cloud-ritual hsü in relation to the feng sacrifice of 742 and the great heavenly treasure scandal . . . TS 1 (1983) 8-20.

Falkenhausen, Lothar von. Ahnenkult und grabkult im vordynastischen qin: der reliöse hintergrund der terracotta-armee. In Lothar Ledderose &

Adele Schlombz (ed) Jenseits der grossen mauer: der erste gottkaiser von qin und seine terracotta-armee, munich (1990) 35-48. Exhibition catalogue art.

Herbert, Penelope. Taoism and the t'ang state. ProcC&S (1987) 59-68.

Ho, Yun-i. Ideological implications of major sacrifices in early ming. MingSt 6 (spring 1978) 55-73. Re imperial sacrifices.

Ho, Yün-yi. The ministry of rites and suburban sacrifices in early ming. Taipei (preface 1980) 327 p, 9 app, illus, notes, bibliog.

Ho, Yün-yi. Revitalization of the cult of heaven: ceremonial politics in the early ming. National chengchi univ journal 42 (dec 1980) 17-30.

Hucker, Charles O. A dictionary of official titles in imperial china. Stanford univ (1985) Engl and chin indexes, chin char throughout. See relevant entries for official titles related to relig.

Kohl, Louis von. Die grundlagen des altchinesischen staates und die bedeutung der riten und der musik. Baessler-archiv 17.2 (1934) 55-98.

Levi. Jean. Bureaucratie et sacerdoce dans l'empire céleste. RHR 207.3 (juil-sept 1990) 227-260. Re "the close-knit and ambiguous relations between mandarins and their gods," esp as reflected in a 16th c story.

Levi, Jean. Les fonctions religieuses de la bureaucratie céleste. l'Homme 27.1 (1987) 35-57.

Li, Thomas Shiyu & Susan Naquin. The baoming temple: religion and the throne in ming and ching china. HJAS 48.1 (june 1988) 131-188. Re temple near peking, a "small buddhist nunnery"

Liu, Kwang-ching (ed) Orthodoxy in late imperial china. Univ calif (1990) Relevant art sep listed in this bibliog; abbrev OLIC.

Liu, James T. C. The sung emperors and the ming-t'ang or hall of enlightenment. In EtSong 2 (1973) 45-58.

Ma, J. Lawrence. Peking as a cosmic city. MexICHS 2: China (1976) 141-146.

McMullen, D. L. A note on the feng ritual of 742—in response to professor elling eide. TS 2 (winter 1984) 37-40.

Meyer, Jeffrey F. Peking as a sacred city. Taipei (1976) 225 p, map, illus, bibliog. Rev ed titled The dragons of tiananmen: beijing as a sacred city, univ south carolina (1991) xii + 208 p, illus, bibliog, index.

Meyer, Jeffrey F. Traditional peking: the architecture of conditional power. In Bardwell Smith & Holly Bauer Reynolds (ed) The city as a sacred centre, leiden etc (1987) 113-133.

Overmyer, Daniel L. Attitudes toward popular religion in ritual texts of the chinese state: the collected statutes of the great ming. CEA 5 (1989-1990) 191-221.

Paludan, Ann. The chinese spirit road, part I: The period of formation; part II: Imperial display. Orientations 19.9 and 20.4 (sept 1988 & apr 1989) 56-65; 64-73, illus.

Paludan, Ann. The imperial ming tombs. Yale univ (1981) xviii + 251 p, illus b-&-w and col photos, tables, charts, notes, gloss, bibliog, app, index. Forward by L. Carrington Goodrich.

Paludan, Ann. Some foreigners in the spirit roads of the northern sung imperial tombs. OA n.s.29.4 (winter 1983-84) 377-388.

Rawski, Evelyn S. The imperial way of death: ming and ch'ing emperors and death ritual. In DeathRit (1988) 228-253.

Reiter, Florian C. Fan tsu-yü's (1041-1098) lectures on t'ang emperors and their taoist inclinations. Oriens 31 (1986) 290-313.

Reiter, Florian C. Vision, traum und wirklichkeit, aspekte religöser propaganda im chinesischen kaiserreich. ZRGG 42.2 (1990) 122-135.

Rule, Paul. Traditional kingship in china. In I. W. Mabbett (ed) Patterns of kingship and authority in traditional asia, london etc (1985) 44-57.

Schmidt-Glintzer, Helwig. Die manipulation von omina und ihre beurteilung bei hofe. Die beispiel der himmelsbriefe wang ch'in-jo (962-1025) unter chen-tsung tregierte 998-1023. AS 35.1 (1981) 1-14.

Seaman, Gary. The emperor of the dark heavens and the han river gateway into china. In Ec&Emp (1989) 165-177.

Segalen, Victor. Notes pour le culte du ciel (inédit) Commentaries de Annie Joly-Segalen. La revue francaise de pékin [paris & beijing] 1 (1982) 13-27.

Shek, Richard. Religion in chinese society: orthodoxy versus heterodoxy. In ProcC&S (1986) 35-42.

Steinhardt, Nancy Shatzman. Altar to heaven complex. In CTA (1984) 139-149, photo, arch fig.

Steinhardt, Nancy Shatzman. Chinese imperial city planning. Univ hawaii. (1990) See passim for relevant material.

Taylor, Romeyn. An imperial endorsement of syncretism: ming t'ai-tsu's essay on the three teachings. Translation and commentary. MingSt 16 (spring 1983) 31-38.

Taylor, Romeyn. Ming t'ai-tsu and the gods of the walls and moats. MingSt 4 (spring 1977) 31-49.

Taylor, Romeyn. Official and popular religion and the political organization of chinese society in the ming. In OLIC (1990) 126-157.

Teng, Shu-p'ing. Tsl and and adapted by Susan Naquin & Curtis H. Brizendine. Two sets of jade tablets in the national palace museum collection. NPMB 11.6 (jan-feb 1977) 1-17. Tablets used in feng and shan sacrifices during t'ang and sung.

Teng, Ssu-yü. Orthodoxy and heterodoxy in ancient chinese patterns of thought. ASBHIP 55.3 (sept 1984) 339-414.

Thompson, Laurence G. Confucian thought: the state cult. EncyRel 4 (1987) 36a-38b.

Thompson, Laurence G. Confucianism and state orthodoxy. In ProcC&S (1987) 5-12.

Thorp, Robert L. The qin and han imperial tombs and the development of mortuary architecture. In QE (1987) 17-37, illus, notes.

Thorp, Robert (ed) Son of heaven: imperial arts of china. Seattle (1988)_ Exhibition catalog. See esp 1, The altar; 3, The temple; 5, The tomb. Profusely illus col photos, maps, suggested readings.

Till, Barry. The eastern mausoleums of the qing dynasty. Orientations 13.2 (feb 1982) 26-31.

Till, Barry. Qian ling. A tang dynasty imperial mausoleum. Orientations 13.7 (july 1982) 22-27.

Verellen, Franciscus. Liturgy and sovereignty: the role of taoist ritual in the foundation of the shu kingdom (907-925) AM 3rd ser 2.1 (1989) 59-78.

Wagner, Rudolf G. Imperial dreams. In P-S (1988) 11-24. Re dreams of emperors.

Waida, Manabu. Kingship in east asia. EncyRel 8 (1987) 330a-333b.

Wechsler, Howard J. Offerings of jade and silk. Ritual and symbol in the legitimation of the t'ang dynasty. Yale univ (1985) xi + 313, notes, sel bibliog, gloss-index.

Weller, Robert. Bandits, beggars, and ghosts: the failure of state control over religious interpretation in taiwan. AmEtht 12 (1985) 46-61.

Yu, Zhuoyun (chief comp) et al. Palaces of the forbidden city. Copyright HK (1984) orig chin publ (1982).

Zito, Angela R. City gods, filiality, and hegemony in late imperial china. ModCh 13.3 (july 1987) 333-371.

Zito, Angela Rose. Re-presenting sacrifice: cosmology and the editing of texts. CSWT 5.2 (dec 1984) 47-78. Re imperial sacrifice, li, and ritual text editing.

II.14 Taoism: General Treatments

Algond, Philippe. Le monde spirituelle de l'asie orientale. Paris (1978) See 5, Le taoïsme, 91-97.

Baldrian, Farzeen. Tsl fr french by Charles LeBlanc. Taoism: an overview. EncyRel 14 (1987)

Barrett, T. H. Religious traditions in chinese civilization: buddhism and taoism. Chap 6 in Paul S. Ropp (ed) Heritage of china, univ calif (1990) 138-163.

Chamberlayne, John H. Taoism. In EncyWF (1987) 279-287.

Chang, Stephen T. The great tao. San francisco (1985) 464 p, illus, index. A miscellany of topics, only marginally related to relig.

Cooper, J. C. Taoism. The way of the mystic. NY (1972) 128 p, index. Rev ed (1990) 142 p, index.

Creel, Herrlee G. The changing shapes of taoism. ProcICS, taipei, Thought & philosophy vol 1 (1981) 1-35.

DeMarco, Michael A. Taoism in new china-hands. CC 30.3 (sept 1989) 41-49. Re expansion of taoist studies in the west.

Fellows, Ward J. Religions east and west. NY etc (1979) See 5, Taoism, 243-269.

Fischer-Schreiber, Ingrid. The encyclopedia of eastern philosophy and religion. Boston (1988) See for budd and taoism, passim, art by Ingrid Fischer-Schreiber. Tsl of Lexicon der östlichen weisheitslehren, bern & munich (1986)

Franke, Wolfgang. Confucian and taoist traditions as evident in chinese epigraphy in southeast asia. Proc31stICHS, Tokyo, vol 1 (1984) 267-268. Abstr.

Geden, Alfred S. Studies in the religions of the east. London (1913) repr delhi (1983). See Taoism, 661-674.

Hou, Cai. The contents of the daoist religion and its cultural function. CSP 22.2 (winter 1990-91) 24-42.

Kao Chung-hsin. Tsl by T. C. Chang. The taoist way to truth. FCR 38.1 (jan 1983) 22-27, col photos.

King, James R. The taoist tradition. In Great asian religions, ed by C. George Fry et al, grand rapids (1984) 111-138.

Lagerwey, John. Worship and cultic life: taoist cultic life. EncyRel 15 (1987) 482b-486b.

Legge, James. The religions of china. Confucianism and taoism described and compared with christianity. London (1880) 310 p. Repr folcroft, penn (1976) norwood penn (1977) philadelphia (1978)

Maspero, Henri. Tsl by Frank A. Kierman. Taoism and chinese religion. Univ massachusetts (1981) 656 p. Tsl of Le taoïsme et les religions chinoises (1971)

Noss, John B. Man's religions. NY (1949). See pt 3, chap 9, Chinese religion and the taoists, 327-368. This textbook issued in new ed (1956, 1963, 1969 . . .) Retitled A history of the world's religions (1990)

Raguin, Yves. Lecons sur le taoïsme. Taipei (1981) vi + 175 p.

Rosso, A. S. Taoism. NCE 13 (1967) 935b-936b.

Schipper, K. M. Le corps taoïste. ZDMG Suppl 4 (1980) 431-433.

Schipper, Kristofer. Le corps taoïste; corps physique—corps social. Paris (1982) 334 p, illus, notes, chart of dyn, bibliog, index. See rev by Livia Knaul, AsFS 42.1 (1983) 147-149; N. J. Girardot, HR 23.2 (nov 1983) 169-180; I. Robinet, TP 72 (1986) 165-174.

Schipper, Kristofer. Taoïsme. In EncyUniv 22 (1990) 51b-57b

Schluchter, Wolfgang. Tsl by Neil Solomon. Rationalism, religion, and domination: a weberian perspective. Univ calif (1989) See chap 3, Confucianism and taoism: world adjustment, 85-116.

Seidel, Anna. Chronicle of taoist studies in the west 1950-1990. CEA 5 (1989-1990) 223-347. With extensive analysis and bibliographical references.

Siklós, Bulcsu. Philosophical and religious taoism. In S. Sutherland et al (ed) The world's religions, boston (1988) 542-551.

Special issue on taoist studies I; "en honneur de Maxime Kaltenmark" CEA 4 (1988) Indiv essays sep listed in this bibliog.

Wang, Chia-yu. Le taoïsme religieux. In Le livre des religions, paris (1989) 234-237.

Zhong, Weimin. Taoist priests keep alive the ancient beliefs. The east [tokyo] 20.5 (oct 1984) 9-11.

II.15 Lao Tzû and Tao Tê Ching

N.B. This category does not include new translations of the tao tê ching.

Barrett, T. H. Taoist and buddhist mysteries in the interpretation of the tao-te ching. JRAS 1 (1982) 35-43. Reflections on reading I. Robinet's Les commentaires du tao tö king jusqu'au VIIe siècle q.v.

Boltz, Judith Magee. Lao-tzu. EncyRel 8 (1987) 454a-459b.

Boltz, William G. The lao tzu text that wang pi and ho-shang kung never saw. BSOAS 48.3 (1985) 493-501.

Boltz, William G. The religious and philosophical significance of the 'hsiang erh' lao tzu in the light of the ma-wang-tui silk manuscripts. BSOAS 45.1 (1982) 95-117.

Boltz, William G. Textual criticism and the ma wang tui lao tzu. HJAS 44.1 (jan 1984) 185-224.

Carmody, Denise Lardner & John Tully Carmody. Peace and justice in the scriptures of the world religions: reflections on non-christian scriptures. NY & mahwah n.j. (1988) See chap 5, Taoism and the tao te ching, 96-121.

Chan, Wing-tsit. Influences of taoist classics on chinese philosophy. In LB (1981) 139-153.

Graham, A. C. The origins of the legend of lao tzu. ProcICS, Thought & philosophy vol 1 (1981) 59-71.

Grison, P. Les "dits" de lao-tseu. EtTrad 84 no 482 (1983) 166-172.

Haas, Hans. Lao tsze und konfuzius. Einleitung in ihr spruchgut. Leipzig (1920) 60 s.

Hsiao, Paul Shih-yi. Heidegger and our translation of the tao te ching. In HET (1987) 93-103.

Izutsu, Toshihiko. Sufism and taoism; a comparative study of key philosophical concepts. Tokyo (1983) 493 p. Rev 1-vol version of 2-vol publ of (1967) q.v.

Kohn, Livia. Die emigration des laozi. Mythologische entwicklungen vom bis 2. bis 6 jahrhundert. MS 38 (1988-89) 49-68.

LaFargue, Michael. Interpreting the aphorisms in the tao te ching. JCR 18 (1990) 25-43.

Lee, Agnes C. J. Echoes of karma liberation in the tao te ching. CF 29.4 (dec 1986) 180-198.

Lee, Agnes C. J. Francis of assisi and chuang tzu: a comparative study in religious consciousness. CF 27.2-3 (july 1984) 94-114.

Loy, David. Chapter one of the tao te ching: a new interpretation. RS 21 (sept 1985) 369-379.

May, Robert M. Physicians of the soul; the psychologies of the world's great spiritual teachers. NY (1982) See chap 1, Lao tzu, the old sage, 9-43.

Pas, Julian F. Recent translations of the tao te ching. JCR 18 (1990) 127-141. Rev art on works by Robert Henricks, Ellen M. Chen, Victor Mair.

Pelphrey, Brant. Meditation on a bowl: the daode jing and kenotic christology. Areopagus (christmas 1990, 4.1) 21-27.

Pöggeler, Otto. West-east dialogue: heidegger and lao-tzu. In HET (1987) 47-78.

Raguin, Yves E. Lao-tzu et son importance pour le taoïsme. SM 23 (1984) 165-179.

Reiter, Florian C. Die einundachtzig bildtexte zu den inkarnationen und wirkungen lao-chün's. Dokumente einer tausendjährigen polemik in china. ZDMG 136 (1984) 450-491.

Robinet, Isabelle. Polyséisme du text canonique et syncrétisme des interpretations: étude taxonomique des commentaires du daodejing au sein de la tradition chinoise. EOEO 5 (1984) 27-47.

Schmidt, Hans-Hermann. Die hundertachtzig vorschriften von lao-chün. In RPO-A (1985) 149-159.

Wang, Hsien-chih. Concept of nature of tao-te-ching and its theological meaning: a search of a methodology of chinese contextual theology. SEAJT 19.1 (1978) 118-131.

Wu, Kathleen Johnson. On lao tzu's idea of the self. Zygon 16 (june 1981) 165-180.

II.16 Taoist Texts-The Canon

Andersen, Poul. The study of the daozang. SCEAR 3 (1990) 81-94.

Baldrian-Hussein, Farzeen. Procédés secrets du joyau magique—traité d'alchimie taoïste du XIe siècle. Présentation et traduction du chinois par... Paris (1984) 322p. See rev by Isabelle Robinet, CEA 2 (1986) 241-252, sep listed in this bibliog.

Bokenkamp, Stephen R. Sources of the ling-pao scriptures. In T&TStudies 2 (MCB 21) (1983) 434-486.

Bokenkamp, Stephen. Taoist literature, part I: Through the t'ang dynasty. In ICTCL (1986) 138-152. Incl canonical texts and other materials.

Boltz, Judith M. A survey of taoist literature, tenth to seventeenth centuries. Univ calif, berkeley, center for chinese studies (1987) xiv + 417 p, intro, 2 app, notes, bibliog, list of names, index.

Boltz, Judith Magee. Taoist literature. EncyRel 14 (1987) 317a-329b.

Boltz, Judith Magee. Taoist literature, part II: Five dynasties to the ming. In ICTCL (1986) 152-174. Incl canonical and other materials.

Boltz, Judith M. Tao-tsang. In ICTCL (1986) 763-766.

Ch'en, Shou-yi. A brief note on the tao tsang. Blaisdell institute journal, claremont, calif, 1.2 (june 1966) 11-13.

Chavannes, Edouard. Rev of L. Wieger, Taoïsme, vol 1. TP 12 (1911) 749-753. See further, author's Melanges, Ibid. 13 (1912) 126-127.

Chen, Z. Un recueil d'épigraphie taoïste: le daojia jinshi zhilüe. AnnEPHE 96 (1987-88) 88-89.

Cleary, Thomas (tsl) The book of balance and harmony. San francisco (1989) xxxii + 153 p. Tsl of li tao-ch'un, chung-ho chi (?13th c)—ch'üan chen school.

Cleary, Thomas (tsl) Fifteen statements on the establishment of a teaching, by wang zhe (12th century) TaoRes 1.1 (autumn 1988) 13-17.

Cleary, Thomas (tsl) The inner teachings of taoism by chang po-tuan, commentary by liu i-ming. Boston & london (1986) xix + 118 p, intro, related texts. Tsl of chin tan ssu pai tzu chieh. German tsl münchen (1990).

Cleary, Thomas (tsl) The taoist i ching. Boston & london (1986) 333 p, gloss. Tsl of version by liu i-ming (1796) of ch'üan chen school.

Cleary, Thomas (tsl) Understanding reality: a taoist alchemical classic by chang po-tuan, with a concise commentary by liu i-ming. Univ of hawaii (1987) Tsl of wu chen p'ien.

Decaux, Jacques. The huangdijing [the canon of the yellow emperor] CC 26.4 (dec 1985) 47-58.

Decaux, Jacques. Les quatre livres de l'empereur jaune: le canon taoïque retrouvé. Taipei (1989)

Decaux, Jacques (tsl and comm) The true classic of the original word of laozi by master guanyin. CC 31.1; 31.2 (mar & june 1990) 1-43; 1-46.

Demiéville, Paul. Zhuangzi. In EncyUniv 23 (1990) 994a-995c.

Huang, Jane (tsl) in colaboration with Michael Wurmbrand. The primordial breath. An ancient chinese way of prolonging life through breath control. Torrance, calif, vol 1 (1987) 169 p, gloss, bibliog. 7 treatises of the taoist canon, tao-tsang.

Jan, Yün-hua. The bridge between man and cosmos: the philosophical foundation of music in the t'ai p'ing ching. STR&MT (1989) 15-27.

Kaltenmark, Max. Quelques remarques sur le t'ai-shang ling-pao wu-fu siu. Zinbun 18 (1982) 1-10.

Knaul, Livia. Lost chuang tzu passages. JCR 10 (1982) 53-79.

Kohn, Livia. The teaching of t'ien-yin-tzu. JCR 15 (1987) 1-28. Re tao-tsang s. 1026.

Kroll, Paul W. Spreading open the barrier of heaven. AS 40.1 (1986) 22-39. Tsl of shang ch'ing taoist text (HY no 1304)

Lagerwey, John. Wu-shang pi-yao; somme taoïste du VIe siècle. Paris (1981) 290 p, chin char used

66

throughout, listes des ouvrages cités, notes bibliog, bibliog, index. Intro and "traduction de la table des matières complète retrouvée à tun-huang; résumé du texte . . ."

Larre, Claude. La symphonie de l'empereur jaune (un extrait du zhuangzi, ch. 14) Paris (1985).

Larre, Claude. Le traité VII du houai nan tseu. Les esprits légers et subtils animateurs de l'essence. Paris (1982) viii + 300 p.

Lin, Shuen-fu. Confucius in the "inner chapters" of the chuang tzu. TR 18.1-4 (aut 1987-sum 1988) 379-401.

Loon, Piet van der. Taoist books in the libraries of the sung period: a critical study and index (sung tai shou ts'ang tao shu k'ao) London (1984) 189p.

Mansvelt-Beck, B. J. The date of the taiping jing. TP 66.4-5 (1980) 149-182.

Maspero, Henri. Tsl by Frank A. Kierman. Taoism and chinese religion. Amherst, mass (1981) 656 p. Tsl of Le taoïsme et les religions chinoises (1971) q.v.

Mei, Y. P. Lieh-tzu. EncyRel 8 (1987) 540b-541b.

Mollier, Christine. Une apocalypse taoïste du Ve siècle: les incantations divines des grottes abyssales. Paris (1990) 239 p.

Pelliot, Paul. Rev of L. Wieger, Taoïsme, vol 1. JA ser 10, 20 (1912) 141-156.

Penny, Benjamin. A system of fate calculation in taiping jing. PFEH 41 (1990) 1-8.

Petersen, Jens Ostergard. The anti-messianism of the taiping jing. SCEAR 3 (1990) 1-41.

Petersen, Jens Ostergard. The early traditions relating to the han dynasty transmission of the taiping ching, Part 1. AO 50 (1989) 133-171.

Reiter, Florian C. Der perlenbeutel aus den drei höhlen (san-tung chu-nang). Arbeitsmaterialen zum taoismus der frühen t'ang zeit. Wiesbaden (1990) x + 200 p, indexes. Re a taoist encyclopedia.

Reiter, Florian C. The scripture of the hidden contracts (yin-fu ching), a short survey on facts and findings. NachrDGNVO 136 (1984) 75-83.

Reiter, Florian C. Studie zu den übertieferungen von mutmasslich unsterblichen (i-hsien chuan) aus dem taoistischen kanon. Oriens 29/30 (1983) 351-396.

Robinet, Isabelle. Chuang-tzu et le taoïsme "religieux" JCR 11 (1983) 59-105.

Robinet, Isabelle. Polyséisme du text canonique et syncrétisme des interpretations: étude taxonomique des commentaires du daode jing au sein de la tradition chinoise. EOEO 5 (1984) 27-47.

Robinet, Isabelle. Le révélation du shangqing dans l'histoire du taoïsme. Paris, 2 vols (1984) vol 1: 262 p, tables, charts indices; vol 2: 464 p, bibliog, indices.

Robinet, Isabelle. Le ta-tung chen-ching; son authenticité et sa place dans les textes du shang-ch'ing ching. In T&TStudies (MCB 21, 1983) 394-433.

Russell, Terry Secret anatomic terminology in the mao shan scriptures BCAR 1 (1987) 83-89.

Saso, Michael. The chuang-tzu nei-p'ien: a taoist meditation. In Victor H. Mair (ed) Experimental essays on chuang-tzu, univ of hawaii (1983) 140-157.

Schafer, Edward H. Table of contents to wang hsüan-ho, san tung chu nan (tao tsang 780-82, HY no 1131)—a t'ang taoist anthology. SSP no 12 (1984) 3 p.

Schipper, K. M. Les canons taoïstes des song. AnnEPHE 90 (1981-82) 115-119.

Schipper, Kristofer M. La compilation du canon taoïste des ming. Proc31st ICHS, Tokyo, vol 1 (1984) 256-257. Abstr.

Schipper, Kristofer. Religions de la chine. AnnEPHE 89 (1980-81) 171-173. Re taoist canon.

Schipper, Kristofer M. Yün-chi ch'i-ch'ien. In ICTCL (1986) 966-968.

Seidel, Anna. Le sutra merveilleux du ling-pao suprême, traitant de lao tseu qui convertit les barbares (le manuscrit s.2081) Contribution à l'étude du bouddho-taoïsme des six dynasties. CETH 3 (1984) 305-352, 8 pl.

Sellman, James D. The 'cosmic talisman' of liturgical taoism: an analysis of the structure and content of the ling pao chen wen. CC 24.3 (sept 1983) 57-69.

Switkin, Walter. Immortality; a taoist text of microbiotics. San francisco (1975) 66 p, notes, bibliog, chin char used throughout. Intro and annot tsl of yang-hsing yen ming lu, chap 2 and 3.

Thompson, Laurence G. Taoism: classic and canon. In Frederick M. Denny & Rodney L Taylor (ed) The holy book in comparative perspective, univ south carolina (1985) 204-223.

Walters, Derek. The t'ai hsüan ching: the hidden classic. Wellingsborough, Northamptonshire, engl (1983) 224 p.

Watson, Burton. Chuang-tzu. EncyRel 3 (1987) 467a-469b.

Wieger, Léon. Taoïsme. T. 1: Bibliographie générale. I. Le canon (patrologie) II. Les index officiels et privés. Ho-kien-fou (1911) 336 p. See rev listed under Chavannes in TP and Pelliot in JA.

Yao, Tao-chung. The historical value of the ch'üan-chen sources in the tao-tsang. Sung studies newsletter (later titled BSYS) 13 (1977) 67-76.

II.17 Taoist Arts and Iconography

Hall, Dickson. Sculpture at kongwangshan. Orientations 13.3 (mar 1982) 50-55. North chiangsu.

Shows both budd and taoist influence. Dated 160-180 c.e.

Cahill, Suzanne. The word made bronze: inscriptions on medieval chinese bronze mirrors. AAA 39 (1986) 62-70. Mirrors as numinous objects to taoists.

Ebert, Jorinde. Ein daoistisches priestergewand vom anfang des 19. jahrhunderts. In WQGM (1989) 105-110.

Gyss-Vermande, Caroline. Démons et merveilles: vision de la nature dans une peinture liturgique due XVe siècle. ArtsAS 43 (1988) 106-122. Study of one of a large no of taoist liturgical paintings relating to shui-lu chai.

Hoffman-Ogier, Wayne H. Dragonflight: chinese calligraphy and the mystical spirit of taoism. Studia mystica 6.4 (winter 1983) 3-43.

James, Jean M. Some idiosyncratic problems in early daoist-buddhist sculptures in china. AAA 42 (1989) 71-76. Re some votive sculptures fr shanhsi in chicago's field museum.

Ledderose, Lothar. Some taoist elements in the calligraphy of the six dynasties. TP 70.4-5 (1984) 246-278.

Lee, Wayne. The painter immortal: wu tao-tzu. ACQ 11.2 (summer 1983) 27-40.

Liao, Ping (ed) Hou Bo & Gao Mingyi (photos) The yongle palace murals. Peking (1985) 109 p, col pl. Taoist paintings of 13th-14th c in shanhsi.

Nelson, Susan E. Intimations of immortality in chinese landscape painting of the fourteenth century. OA n.s.33.3 (autumn 1987) 275-292.

Pontynen, Arthur. Philosophia perennis ars orientalis. A buddhist-taoist icon in the freer gallery of art. OA n.s.28.4 & 29.2 (winter & summer 1982/83) 359-367; 143-158. Re a gilt-bronze sculpture.

Reiter, Florian C. The visible divinity. The sacred icon in religious taoism. NachrDGNVO 144 (1988) 51-70.

68

Schafer, Edward H. The dance of the purple culmen. TS 5 (1987) 45-68. Re taoist temples, music and dances of 8th c in ch'angan.

Sorensen, Henrik H. A survey of the religious sculptures of anyue. Univ copenhagen (1989) Anyue county is in sichuan province. Re budd and taoist sculptures.

Steinhardt, Nancy Shatzman. Temple: taoist temple compounds. EncyRel 14 (1987) 380a-381b.

Thompson, Laurence G. Taoist iconography. EncyRel 7 (1987) 50b-54a.

II.18 Taoist Thought

Barnett, Raymond J. Taoism and biological science. Zygon 21.3 (sept 1986) 297-317.

Bokenkamp, Stephen. Death and ascent in ling-pao taoism. TaoRes 1.2 (winter 1989) 1-20.

Bokenkamp, Stephen R. The peach flower font and the grotto passage. JAOS 106.1 (jan-mar 1986) 65-77.

Bokenkamp, Stephen R. Stages of transcendence: the bhumi concept in taoist scripture. In CBA (1990) 119-147.

Chang, Aloysius. Concept of the tao. In Sebastian A. Matczak (ed) God in contemporary thought, NY etc (1977) 79-95.

Chang, Aloysius. Destiny in the taoist tradition: lieh tzu's yang chu and li ming chapters reexamined. CC 28.1 (mar 1987 41-48.

Chang, Yao Shiu-yen. The non-perfection and natural value concepts in taoism. Proc31stICHS, Tokyo, vol 1 (1984) 250-251. Abstr.

Cho, Kat Kyung. Das absolute in der taoistischen philosophie. In Dietrich Papenfuss & Jürgen Söring (ed) Tranzendenz und immanenz; philosophie und theologie in der veränderten welt, stuttgart etc (1977) 239-255.

Cooper, J. C. Yin and yang; the taoist harmony of opposites. Wellingborough, northamptonshire, engl (1981) 128 p, illus.

Copleston, Frederick. Religion and the one; philosophers east and west. NY (1982) See chap 3, The one in taoism and buddhism, 40-67.

Decaux, Jacques. Taoist philosophy and jungian psychology. CC 22.4 (dec 1981) 95-110.

Decaux, Jacques. Life and existence. CC 23.1 (mar 1982) 61-77.

Demariaux, J.C. Du tao aux dix mille êtres. EtTrad 87 no 491 (1986) 10-16. Cosmology and numerology fr passages in tao te ching, chuang tzu, lieh tzu.

Demiéville, Paul. Zhuangzi. In EncyUniv 23 (1990) 994a-995c.

Garner, Richard T. The deconstruction of the mirror and other heresies: ch'an and taoism as abnormal discourse. JCP 12.2 (1985) 155-168.

Girardot, Norman J. Behaving cosmogonically in early taoism. In C&EO (1985) 67-97.

Girardot, Norman J. Myth and meaning in early taoism. The theme of chaos (hun-tun) Univ calif (1983) 422 p, app, notes, gloss chin char, sel bibliog, index.

Grison, Pierre. A propos de la triade. EtTrad 82 no 473 (1981) 131-139. From the one, two; from the two, three . . .

Hendrischke, Barbara. How the celestial master proves heaven reliable. In RPO-A (1985) 77-86. Re thought system of t'ai-p'ing ching.

Inada, Kenneth. Zen and taoism: common and uncommon grounds of discourse. JCP 15.1 (1988) 51-65.

Ishida, Hidemi. Body and mind: the chinese perspective. In TMLT (1989) 41-71.

Izutsu, Toshihiko. Sufism and taoism. A comparative study of key philosophical concepts.

Tokyo (1983) 493 p. Rev version of author's 2 vol wk, A comparative study of key philosophical concepts in sufism and taoism, keio univ (1966-67), q.v.

Jan, Yün-hua. Tao, principle, and law: the three key concepts in the yellow emperor taoism. JCP 7.3 (sept 1980) 205-228.

Jan, Yün-hua. Tao yüan or tao: the origin. JCP 7.3 (sept 1980) 195-204.

Kalinowski, Marc. La transmission du dispositif de neuf palais sous le six-dynasties. In T&TStudies 3 (MCB 22, 1985) 773-811.

Kaltenmark, Max. King yu pa-king [ching yü pa-ching] In Fukui Kojun festschrift, Toya bunka ronshu, tokyo (1969) 1147-1154. Re important term in mao shan texts.

Kao, Hsin-sheng C. Taoist mirror: ching-hua yuan and lao-chuang thought. JCP 15.2 (1988) 151-172.

Karetzky, Patricia Eichenbaum. The engraved designs on the late sixth century sarcophagus of li ho. AA 47.2 (1986) 81-106, 14 fig. Taoist cosmological themes.

Karetzky, Patricia Eichenbaum. A scene of the taoist afterlife in a sixth century sarcophagus discovered in loyang. AA 41.1 (1983) 5-20.

Kirkland, J. Russell. The roots of altruism in the taoist tradition. JAAR 54.1 (spring 1986) 59-77.

Knaul, Livia. Kuo hsiang and the chuang tzu. JCP 12 (1985) 429-447.

Knaul, Livia. The winged life; kuo hsiang's mystical philosophy. JCStudies 2 (april 1985)

Koch, Philip J. Solitude in ancient taoism. Diogenes 148 (winter 1989) 78-91.

Kojima, Hajime. Die jodo-lehre shinrans und der taoismus in china. In RPO-A (1985) 233-238.

Lagerwey, John. Chen-jen. EncyRel 3 (1987) 231a-233a.

Lagerwey, John. Ecriture et corps divin en chine. TdelaR 7 (1986) 275-285. Writing in taoism, and vital breath (ch'i)

Levi, Jean. The body: the taoist's coat of arms. Zone 3 (1989) 105-126.

Levi, Jean. Connais le masculin, garde le féminin. Stratégies du yin et du yang. Le sexe des nombres. Genre humain 10 (1984) Le masculin, 75-89.

Levi, Jean. Vers des céréales et dieux du corps dans le taoïsme. TdelaR 7 (1986) 99-119.

Lin, Yü-sheng. The unity of heaven and man in classical confucianism and taoism and its philosophical and social implications. Proc31stICHS, tokyo, vol 1 (1984) 258-259. Abstr.

Lin, Shuen-fu. Confucius in the "inner chapters" of the chuang tzu. TR 18.1-4 (aut 1987-sum 1988) 379-401.

Lindseth, Thomas. Preventative medicine according to taoist principles. International journal of holistic health and medicine 1.2 (nov 1982-mar 1983) 6-7.

Ma, Hing Keung. The chinese taoistic perspective on human development. International journal of intercultural relations 14.2 (1990) 235-249.

Mitsuda, Masato. Taoist philosophy and its influence on t'ang naturalist poetry. JCP 15.2 (june 1988) 199-216.

Mollier, Christine. Eschatology and demonology in early taoism. Proc31stICHS, tokyo, vol 2 (1984) 882-884. Abstr.

Murakami, Yoshimi. Conceptions of equality and human nature in taoism. In R. Siriwardena (ed) Equality and the religious traditions of asia, london (1987) 114-134. Based on lao tzu and chuang tzu.

Paper, Jordan. From shamanism to mysticism in the chuang-tzu. Scottish journal of religious studies 3 (1982) 27-45.

70

Parkes, Graham. Thoughts on the way: being and time via lao-chuang. In HET (1987) 105-144. Re heidegger's thought.

Raguin, Yves. Themes of classical taoism. Areopagus (trinity 1990, 3.4) 32-36.

Reiter, Florian C. Ch'ung-yang sets forth his teachings in fifteen discourses; a concise introduction to the taoist way of life of wang che. MS 36 (1984/85) 33-54.

Robinet, Isabelle. Chuang-tzu et le taoïsme "religieux" JCR 11 (1983) 59-105.

Robinet, Isabelle. Kuo hsiang. EncyRel 8 (1987) 404a-405a.

Robinet, Isabelle. Kuou siang ou le monde comme absolu. TP 69 (1983) 87-112.

Robinet, Isabelle. La notion de hsing dans le taoïsme et son rapport avec celle de confucianisme. JAOS 106.1 (jan-mar 1986) 183-196.

Robinet, Isabelle. The place and meaning of the notion of taiji in taoist sources prior to the ming dynasty. HR 29 (may 1990) 373-411, illus.

Robinet, Isabelle. Le révélation du shangqing dans l'histoire du taoïsme. Paris (1984) vol 1: 262 p, tables, charts, indx; vol 2: 464 p, bib, indices.

Robinet, Isabelle. Sexualité et taoïsme. In M. Bernos (ed) Sexualité et religions, paris (1988) 50-71.

Robinet, Isabelle. (1) La transmission des textes sacrés (2) Les paradis terrestres et cosmiques (3) La marche sur les étoiles (4) La pratique du tao. In Mythes et croyances du monde entier, t 6, la chine, paris (1989) 369-398.

Robinet, Isabelle. l'Unité transcendante des trois enseignements selon les taoïstes des song et des yuan. In RPO-A (1985) 103-125.

Robinet, Isabelle. Visualization and ecstatic flight in shangqing taoism. In TMLT (1988) 159-191.

Ross, R. R. N. Non-being and being in taoist and western traditions. RTrad 2.2 (oct 1979) 24-38.

Roth, Harold D. The early taoist concept of shen: a ghost in the machine? In Kidder Smith jr (ed) Sagehood and systematizing thought in warring states and han china, bowdoin college (1990) 11-32.

Schafer, Edward H. The grand aurora. Chinese science 6 (1983) 21-32. Term used in taoist cosmological speculation.

Schipper, Kristofer. Tchouang-tseu et les rites. In André Caquot & Pierre Caniver (ed) Ritualisme et vie intérieur . . . paris (1989) 105-115.

Seidel, Anna. Post-mortem immortality—or, the taoist resurrection of the body. In Saul Shaked et al (ed) Gilgul: essays on transformation, revolution and permanence in the history of religions, leiden (1987) 223-237.

Shih, Joseph. l'Eschatologie dans le monde chinois. SM 32 (1983) 181-194.

Stambaugh, Joan. Heidegger, taoism, and the question of metaphysics. In HET (1987) 79-91.

Stevenson, Frank. Dwelling at ease and awaiting destiny: "taoism" in the "confucian" chung yung. TR 20.3 (spring 1990) 265-316.

Stines, James W. I am the way: michael polanyi's taoism. Zygon 20.1 (mar 1985) 59-77.

Strickmann, Michel. Therapeutische rituale und das problem des bösen im frühen taoismus. In RPO-A (1985) 185-200.

Thomas, Léon. l'Absolu dans deux pensées apophatiques: basilide et le taoïsme. Revue d'histoire et de philosophie religieuses 67.2 (1987) 181-191.

Thomas, Léon. Cosmogonie et cosmologie du taoïsme philosophique. Connaissance des religions 4.1-2 (1988) 59-68.

Thomas, Léon. Les états de conscience inhabituels dans le "zhuangzi" RHR 204.2 (1987) 129-149. On the mystical experiencing of the tao.

Tominaga, Thomas T. Taoist and wittgensteinian mysticism. JCP 9.3 (sept 1982) 269-289.

Vervoorn, A. Zhuang zun: a daoist philosopher of the late first century b.c. MS 38 (1988-89) 69-94.

Visvader, John & William C. Doub. The problem of desire and emotions in taoism and ch'an. In ECCT (1983) 281-297.

Wayman, Alex. Male, female, and androgyne. Per buddhist tantra, jacob boehme, and the greek and taoist mysteries. In T&TStudies 2 (MCB 21, 1983) 592-631.

Wong, Yuk. The concepts of language and immortality in early medieval china. CC 28.3 (sept 1987) 29-36.

Wu, Kuang-ming. Deconstructing morality: taoist ethics of person-making. HHYC:CS 1.2 (dec 1983) 625-654. Chuang tzu and morality.

Wu, Yi. On chinese ch'an in relation to taoism. JCP 12 (1985) 131-154.

Yu, David C. The creation myth and its symbolism in classical taoism. PEW 31.4 (oct 1981) 479-500.

Yu, David C. The creation myth of chaos in the daoist canon. JOS 24.1 (1986) 1-20.

Yu, David C. The mythos of chaos in ancient taoism and contemporary chinese thought. JCP 8.3 (sept 1981) 325-348.

Zimmerman, Georg. Die bedeutung des herzens in taoistischen texten. AS 39.1-2 (1985) 45-53.

II.19 Taoism and History

Barrett, T. H. Ko hung. EncyRel 8 (1987) 359b-360b.

Barrett, T. H. Li shao-chün. EncyRel 8 (1987) 558a-558b.

Bell, Catherine M. Lu hsiu-ching. EncyRel 9 (1987) 50a-51a.

Bell, Catherine M. T'ao hung-ching. EncyRel 14 (1987) 287a-288b.

Benn, Charles. Religious aspects of emperor hsüan-tsung's taoist ideology. In BTS-II (1987) 127-145.

Cahill, Suzanne E. Taoism at the sung court: the heavenly text affair of l008. BSYS 16 (1981) 23-44.

Cheung, Frederick Hok-ming. Religion and politics in early t'ang china: taoism and buddhism in the reigns of kao-tsu and t'ai-tsung. JICS/CUHK 18 (1987) 265-275.

Decaux, Jacques. Dao jia: an attempt at evaluating its position at the time of the warring kingdoms. CC 28.4 (dec 1987) 85-93.

Dehergne, Joseph. Les historiens jésuites du taoïsme. In Jacques Gernet et al, La mission francaise de pékin aux XVIIe et XVIIIe siècles, paris (1976) 59-67.

Herbert, Penelope. Taoism and the t'ang state. ProcC&S (1987) 59-68.

Jagchid, Sechin. Chinese buddhism and taoism during the mongolian rule of china. Mongolian studies 6 (1980) 61-98.

Jagchid, Sechin. The mongol khans and chinese buddhism and taoism. JIABS 2.1 (1979) 7-28.

Jan, Yün-hua. Tao, principle, and law: the three key concepts in the yellow emperor taoism. JCP 7.3 (sept 1980) 205-228.

Kaltenmark, Max. Les communautés taoïstes. In L. Lanciotti (ed) Sviluppi scientifici prospettive (1975) 89-102. Re late han—three kingdoms.

Kirkland, J. Russell. Chang kao—noteworthy tang taoist? TS 2 (1984) 31-35.

Kirkland, Russell. From imperial tutor to taoist priest: ho chih-chang at the t'ang court. JAH 23 (1989) 101-133.

Kirkland, J. Russell. The last taoist grand master

72

at the t'ang imperial court: li han-kuang and t'ang hsüan-tsung. TS 4 (1986) 43-67.

Kobayashi, Masayoshi. Engl tsl of summ by Author & Florian Deleanu. A study on the history of the taoist religion during the six dynasties. Tokyo (1990) In jap, with engl summ 1-36.

Lagerwey, John. Les lignes taoïstes du nord de taiwan. CEA 4 (1988) 127-143.

Lagerwey, John. The taoist religious community. EncyRel 14 (1987) 306a-317a.

Leung, Man Kam & Julian F. Pas (tsl) A survey of the history of taoism. A review article. JCR 15 (1987) 61-80. Tsl of art fr Research in the history of chinese philosophy (Zhongguo jexue shi yanjiu) 1 (1983) 41-50.

Miyakawa, Hisayuki. Taoism under the confucian order in sung and ming times. MexICHS 2: china (1976) 169-175.

Raguin, Yves. Emergence of the daoist community. Areopagus (christmas 1990, 4.1 35-39.

Reed, Barbara. [Women in] Taoism. In WWR (1987) 161-181.

Reiter, Florian C. A chinese patriot's concern with taoism: the case of wang o (1190-1273) OE 33.2 (1990) 95-131. Inscriptions of wang o indicating his opposition to mongol rule of force.

Reiter, Florian C. Ch'iu ch'u-chi, ein alchemist im china des 13. jahrhundert. Neue gesichtspunkte für ein historische bewertung. ZDMG 139 (1987) 184-207.

Reiter, Florian C. Fan Tsu-yü's (1041-1098) lecture on t'ang emperors and their taoist inclinations. Oriens 31 (1988) 290-313.

Reiter, Florian C. Grundelemente und tendenzen des religiösen taoismus. Das spannungsverhältnis von integration in seiner geschte zur chin-, yüan- und frühen ming-zeit. Wiesbaden 1988 vii + 174 p, literatur-verzeichnis, zeichenliste, register zu names und begriffen.

Reiter, Florian C. Das selbstverständnis des taoismus zur frühen t'ang-zeit in der darstellung wang hsüan-ho's. Saeculum 33.3/4 (1982) 240-257.

Reiter, Florian C. Some observations concerning taoist foundations in traditional china. ZDMG 133.2 (1983) 363-376. Re taoist monasteries and monachism.

Reiter, Florian C. The soothsayer hao ta-t'ung (1140-1212) and his encounter with ch'üan-chen taoism. OE 28.2 (1981) 198-205.

Robinet, Isabelle. Chang chüeh. EncyRel 3 (1987) 197a-197b.

Robinet, Isabelle. Chang lu. EncyRel 3 (1987) 198b-199b.

Robinet, Isabelle. Chang tao-ling. EncyRel 3 (1987) 199b-200a.

Robinet, Isabelle. Nature et rôle du maître spirituel dans le taoîsme non liturgique. In M. Meslin (dir) Maître et disciples dan les traditions religieuses. Colloque (1988). Paris (1990) 37-50.

Robinet, Isabelle. Le révélation du shangqing dans l'histoire du taoïsme. Paris (1984) vol 1: 262 p, tables, charts, indices; vol 2: 464 p, bibliog, indices.

Robinet, Isabelle. Ssu-ma ch'eng-chen. EncyRel 14 (1987) 40b-41a.

Sakai, Tadao. Dissemination of taoistic religion over the regions surrounding china. Proc 31st ICHS, tokyo, vol 1 (1984) 247-248. Abstr.

Schafer, Edward H. Aspects of mao-shan taoism in t'ang. MexICHS 2: china (1976) 239-244.

Schafer, Edward H. The dance of the purple culmen. TS 5 (1987) 45-68. Re taoist temples, music and dances of 8th c in ch'angan.

Schafer, Edward H. Mao shan in t'ang times. Boulder, colo (1980) 72 p, notes, diagram. SSCR monograph no 1; 2nd rev ed (1989) 97 p.

Schafer, Edward H. The princess realized in jade. TS 3 (1985) 1-25. Re 8th c princesses who became taoist priestesses.

Schipper, Kristofer M. Une banque de données informatisée sur l'histoire du taoïsme. EtCh 1 (1983) 48-54.

Schipper, Kristofer M. Master chao i-chen (? — 1382) and the ch'ing-wei school of taoism. In TRC (1987) Engl text 4-20.

Schipper, Kristofer M. Recherches sur le taoïsme ancien. AnnEPHE 96 (1987-88) 82-87.

Schipper, Kristofer M. Religions de la chine. ACF 89 (1980-81) 171-173. Re taoism.

Schipper, Kristofer M. Religions de la chine: les maîtres célestes à l'époque song. AnnEPHE 91 (1982-83) 133-137. Re history of so-called "taoist papacy"

Schipper, Kristofer M. Taoist ritual and local cults of the t'ang dynasty. ProcICS, Folk custom & culture vol (1981) 101-115. Same title in T&TStudies 3 (MCB 22, 1985) 812-834.

Schlegel, Gustave A. Problèmes géographiques. 18: san sien chan, les trois îles enchantées. TP 6 (1895) 1-64.

Seidel, Anna. Imperial treasures and taoist sacraments; taoist roots in the apocrypha. In T&TStudies 2 (MCB 21, 1983) 291-371. Rise of taoism in han.

Seidel, Anna. Le sutra merveilleux du ling-pao suprême, traitant de lao tseu qui convertit les barbares (le manuscrit s.2081) Contribution à l'étude du bouddho-taoïsme des six dynasties. CETH (1984) 305-352, sec of pl.

Seidel, Anna. Taoist messianism. Numen 31.2 (1984) 161-174.

Seidel, Anna. Traces of han religion in funeral texts found in tombs. In TRC (1987) Engl text 23-57.

Strickmann, Michel. The tao amongst the yao: taoism and the sinification of south china. Rekishi ni okeru minshu to bunka (Sakai Tadao festschrift) tokyo (1982) 22-30.

Strickmann, Michel. Le taoïsme du mao chan. Chronique d'une révélation. Paris (1981) 278 p, bibliog, notes.

Sun, K'o-k'uan. Yü chi and southern taoism during the yüan period. In John D. Langlois jr (ed) China under mongol rule, princeton univ (1981) 212-253.

Tang, Yijie. On the emergence of the daoist religion and its characteristics. CSP 20.1 (spring 1989) 33-54.

Tsui, Bartholomew P. M. The transmission of the taoist complete perfection sect in south china. CF 33.4 (dec 1990) 248-257.

Verellen, C. Franciscus. Liturgy and sovereignty: the role of taoist ritual in the foundation of the shu kingdom (907-925) AM 3rd ser 2 (1989) 59-78).

Yao, Tao-chung. Ch'iu ch'u-chi and chinggis khan. HJAS 46.1 (june 1986) 201-219.

Yao, Tao-chung. The historical value of the ch'üan-chen sources in the tao-tsang. Sung studies newsletter (later titled BSYS) 13 (1977) 67-76.

II.20 Taoism and Literature

Addiss, Stephen. Blake, taoism and zen. In SpF (1982) 281-287. "Parallel passages" showing "similar visions"

Bokenkamp, Stephen. Taoist literature, part I: through the t'ang dynasty. In ICTCL (1986) 138-152. Both canonical and other material.

Boltz, Judith M. Taoist literature, part II: Five dynasties to the ming. In ICTCL (1988) 152-174.

Endres, Günther (tsl) Die sieben meister der volkommenen verwirklichung: der taoistische lehrroman ch'i-chen chuan in übersetsung und im spiegel seiner quellen. Frankfurt am main (1985)

Güntsch, Gertrud. Das shen-hsien chuan und das erscheinungsbild eines hsien. Frankfurt/M etc. (1988)

Hawkes, David. Quanzhen plays and quanzhen masters. BEFEO 69 (1981) 153-170.

Holzman, Donald. Ts'ao chih and the immortals. AM 3rd ser 1.1 (1988) 15-57. Reviews all of ts'ao chih's prose and poetry on the subject.

Idema, Wilt & Stephen H. West. Chinese theater 1100-1450; a source book. Wiesbaden (1982) See chap 7, Chung-li of the han leads lan ts'ai-ho to enlightenment. Tsl of "anonymous comedy" with intro.

Kao, Hsin-sheng C. Taoist mirror: ching-hua yuan and lao-chuang thought. JCP 15.2 (june 1988) 151-172.

Kroll, Paul W. In the halls of the azure lad. JAOS 105.1 (jan-mar 1985) 75-94.

Kroll, Paul W. Li po's rhapsody on the great p'eng-bird. JCR 12 (1984) 1-17.

Kroll, Paul W. Li po's transcendent diction. JAOS 106.1 (jan-mar 1986) 99-117.

Kroll, Paul W. Notes on three taoist figures of the t'ang dynasty. SSCRB 9 (1981) 19-41. Re Szu-ma ch'eng-chen, refined mistress chia, and the lady of the highest prime.

Kroll, Paul W. Verses from on high: the ascent of t'ai shan. TP 69.4/5 (1983) 223-260.

Li, Wai-yee. Dream visions of transcendence in chinese literature and painting. AsArt 3.4 (fall 1990) 53-78. Taoism and immortality.

Mitsuda, Masato. Taoist philosophy and its influence on t'ang naturalist poetry. JCP 15.2 (june 1988) 199-216.

Palandri, Angela Jung. The taoist vision: a study of t'ao yuanming's nature poetry. JCP 15.2 (june 1988) 97-121.

Schafer, Edward H. Aspects of mao-shan taoism in t'ang. MexICHS 2: china (1976) 239-244.

Schafer, Edward H. Cantos on "one bit of cloud at shamanka mountain" AS 36.2 (1982) 102-124.

Schafer, Edward H. Cosmic metaphors: the poetry of space. SSP 5 (1984) 18 p.

Schafer, Edward H. The cranes of mao shan. In T&TStudies 2 (MCB 21, 1983) 372-393. Mostly on cranes in t'ang lit.

Schafer, Edward H. Empyreal powers and chtonian edens: two notes on t'ang taoist literature. JAOS 106.4 (oct-dec 1986) 667-677.

Schafer, Edward H. Mirages on the sea of time. The taoist poetry of ts'ao t'ang. Univ calif (1985) 153 p, notes, bibliog, gloss, index.

Schafer, Edward H. The snow of mao shan: a cluster of taoist images. JCR 13/14 (1985/86) 107-126.

Schafer, Edward H. Transcendent elder mao. CEA 2 (1986) 111-122.

Schafer, Edward H. Two taoist bagatelles. SSCRB 9 (1981) 1-18. Re the yin-transmitting lithophones; the mutations of mercurial maid.

Schafer, Edward H. Ways of looking at the moon palace. AM 3rd ser 1.1 (1988) 1-14.

Schafer, Edward H. The world between: ts'ao t'ang's grotto poems. SSP 32 (1988) 12 p.

Schafer, Edward H. Wu yün's 'cantos on pacing the void' HJAS 41.2 (1981) 77-115.

Schafer, Edward H. Wu yün's stanzas on "saunters in sylphdom" (yu hsien shih) MS 35 (1981-83) 309-345.

Yeh, Michelle. Taoism and modern chinese poetry. JCP 15.2 (1988) 173-197.

Yu, Shiao-ling. Taoist themes in yuan drama (with emphasis on the plays of ma chih yuan) JCP 15.2 (1988) 123-149.

II.21 Taoist Biography

Arbuckle, Gary. When did ge hong die? BCAR 2 (1988) 1-7.

Bell, Catherine. Tu kuang-t'ing. EncyRel 15 (1987) 80a-81a.

Cleary, Thomas (tsl) Transformations of the tao. TaoRes 1.1 (autumn 1988) 11-12. Re Tan jingshan, 10th c.

Corless, Roger J. T'an-luan: taoist sage and buddhist bodhisattva. In BTS-II (1987) 36-45.

Kirkland, J. Russell. Chang kao—noteworthy tang taoist. TS 2 (1984) 31-35.

Kirkland, J. Russell. From imperial tutor to taoist priest: ho chih-chang at the t'ang court. JAH 23 (1989) 101-133

Kirkland, J. Russell. The last taoist grand master at the t'ang imperial court: li han-kuang and t'ang hsüan-tsung. TS 4 (1986) 43-67.

Knaul, Livia. Leben und legende des ch'en t'uan [ca 906-989] Frankfurt am main (1981) 242 p.

Kohn, Livia. The mother of the tao. TaoRes 1.2 (winter 1989) 37-113. Study and tsl of tu kuang-t'ing's yung-ch'eng chi hsien lu.

Kroll, Paul W. Notes on three taoist figures of the t'ang dynasty. SSCRB 9 (1981) 19-41. Re Szu-ma ch'eng-chen, refined mistress chia, and the lady of the highest prime.

Kubo, Noritada. Tsl by James C. Dobbins. Hsiao pao-chen. EncyRel 6 (1987) 475a-475b. Re founder of the t'ai-i sect of taoism.

Kubo, Noritada. Tsl by James C. Dobbins. Liu hai-ch'an. EncyRel 9 (1987) 3a.

Kubo, Noritada. Tsl by James C. Dobbins. Liu te-jen. EncyRel 9 (1987) 3a-3b. Re founder of chen-ta sect of taoism.

Kubo, Noritada. Tsl by James C. Dobbins. Wang Che. EncyRel 15 (1987) 331a-331b.

Mather, Richard B. K'ou ch'ien-chih. EncyRel 8 (1987) 377b-379a.

Reiter, Florian C. Ch'iu ch'u-chi, ein alchemist im china des 13. jahrhunderts. Neue gesichspunkte für ein historische bewertung. ZDMG 139 (1984) 184-207.

Reiter, Florian C. Ch'ung-yang sets forth his teachings in fifteen discourses: a concise introduction to the taoist way of life of wang che. 36 (1984/85) 33-54.

Robinet, Isabelle. Chang tao-ling. EncyRel 3 (1987) 199b-200a.

Robinet, Isabelle. Ssu-ma ch'eng-chen. EncyRel 14 (1987) 40b-41a.

Russell, T. C. Chen tuan at mount huangbo: a spirit-writing cult in late ming china. AS 44.1 (1990) 107-140.

Schipper, Kristofer M. Master chao i-chen (?—1382) and the ch'ing-wei school of taoism. In TRC (1987) Engl text 4-20.

Verellen, Franciscus. Du guangting (850-933) taoïste de cour à la fin de la chine médiévale. Paris (1989) 263 p, chronol, bibliog of tu's works.

Wong, Shiu Hou. Investigations into the authenticity of the chang san-feng ch'uan-chi, the complete works of chang san-feng. Australian natl univ (1982) 205 p, bibliog, index. Author concludes text is "spurious"

II.22 Taoist Immortals - Hagiography

Baldrian-Hussein, Farzeen. Lü tung-pin in northern sung literature. CEA 2 (1986) 133-169, 2 maps, illus fr blockprints.

Cahill, Suzanne. Reflections of a metal mother: tu kuang-t'ing's biography of hsi wang mu. JCR 13/14 (1985/86) 127-142.

76

Cleary, Thomas (ed & tsl) Immortal sisters. Secrets of taoist women. Boston & london (1989) 96 p. Re six chin women, 4th-12th c.

Despeux, Catherine. Immortelles de la chine ancienne: taoïsme et alchimie féminine. Paris (1990) 371 p.

Girardot, N. J. Hsien. EncyRel 6 (1987) 475b-477a

Güntsch, Gertrud. Das shen-hsien chuan und das erscheinungsbild eines hsien. Frankfurt/M etc. (1988)

Jan Yün-hua. The change of images: the yellow emperor in ancient chinese literature. JOS 19 (1981) 117-137.

Kagan, Alan L. Eight immortals longevity blesssings: symbolic and ritual perspectives of the music. In STR&MT (1989) 121-135.

Kohn, Livia. Transcending personality: from ordinary to immortal life. TaoRes 2.2 (1990) 1-22.

Kroll, Paul W. In the halls of the azure lad. JAOS 105.1 (jan-mar 1985) 75-94.

Kwok, Man Ho & Joanne O'Brien (tsl & ed) The eight immortals of taoism; legends and fables of popular taoism. London, NY etc (1990) 156 p, 3 app. Intro by Martin Palmer.

Lagerwey, John. Chen-jen. EncyRel 3 (1987) 231a-233a.

Laufer, Berthold. The prehistory of aviation. Chicago (1928) See 1, The romance of flying in ancient china. Some stories connected with fang-shih.

Little, Stephen. Realm of the immortals. Daoism in the arts of china. Cleveland museum of art in conjunction with indiana univ (1988) 67 p, intro, col pl, catalog, chronol, gloss, bibliog, index.

Porkert, Manfred. Biographie d'un taoïste légendaire: tcheou tseu-yang. Paris (1979) 169 p.

See rev art with corrections and additions by Isabelle Robinet in TP 67 (1981) 123-136.

Raguin, Yves Emile. Le patriarche lü, le grand immortel (lü tung-pin) SM 35 (1986) 369-394.

Reiter, Florian C. Die einundachtzig bildtexte zu den inkarnationen und wirkungen lao-chün's. Dokumente einer tausend jährigen polemik in china. ZDMG 136 (1984) 450-491.

Reiter, Florian C. Leben und wirken lao-tzu's in schrift und bild. Lao-chün pa-shih-i-hua t'u-shuo. Würzburg (1990) 240 s, übersetzung, literaturveraeichnis, register. Good repro of wood-cuts and texts.

Reiter, Florian C. Der nahme tung-hua ti-chün und sein umfeld in der taoistischen tradition. In RPO-A (1985) 87-101.

Reiter, Florian C. Studie zu den übertieferungen von mutmasslich insterblichen (i-hsien chuan) aus dem taoistischen kanon. Oriens 29/30 (1983) 351-396.

Robinet, Isabelle. The taoist immortal: jesters of light and shadow, heaven and earth. JCR 13/14 (1985/86) 87-106.

Schafer, Edward H. Transcendent elder mao. CEA 2 (1986) 111-122.

Schipper, K. Religions de la chine. ACF 88 (1979-80) 129-136. Etude de genre hagiographique taoïste.

Schlegel, Gustave A. Problèmes géographiques. 18: San sien chan, les trois îles enchantées. TP 6 (1895) 1-64.

Tsui, Bartholomew P. M. Descriptions of the immortals and the taoist identity. In Victor C. Hayes (ed) Identity issues and world religions . . . south australian college of advanced education (1986) 125-134.

Verellen, Franciscus. Luo gongyuan. Légende et culte d'un saint taoïste. JA 275.3/4 (1987) 283-332.

Wong, Shiu Hou. Investigations into the authenticity of the chang san-feng ch'uan-chi, the complete works of chang san-feng. Australian natl univ (1982) 205 p, bibliog, index. Author concludes text is "spurious".

II.23 Taoist Pantheon - Cults

Cahill, Suzanne. Performers and female taoist adepts: hsi wang mu as the patron deity of women in medieval china. JAOS 106.1 (jan-mar 1986) 155-168.

Lagerwey, John. Envoyés et démons dans le taoïsme. In Julien Ries et Henri Limet (ed) Anges et démons, louvain-la-neuve, belge (1989) 71-83.

Levi, Jean. Le panthéon taoïste: la légende dorée. In MetC (1985) 354-367.

Reiter, Florian C. "The investigation commissioner of the nine heavens" and the beginning of his cult in northern chiang-hsi in 731 a.d. Oriens 31 (1988) 266-289.

Reiter, Florian C. Der nahme tung-hua ti-chün und sein umfeld in der taoistischen tradition. In RPO-A (1985) 87-101.

Roth, Harold D. Huang-lao chün. EncyRel 6 (1987) 483b-484b.

Seidel, Anna. Huang-ti. EncyRel 6 (1987) 484b-485b.

Steinhardt, Nancy Shatzman. Zhu haogu reconsidered: a new date for the rom [royal ontario museum] painting and the southern shanxi buddhist-daoist style. AA 48.1/2 (1987) 5-20, 33 fig. Cp W. C. White's Chinese temple frescoes (1940).

II.24 Professional Taoism - Monachism

Bertuccioli, Giuliano. Mao-shan revisited. E&W 35 (1985) 277-279 "Continuation and conclusion" of author's art of 1974 in E&W 24, 403-415, q.v.

Despeux, Catherine. l'Ordination des femmes taoïstes sous le t'ang. EtCh 5.1-2 (prin-aut 1986) 53-100.

Ebert, Jorinde. Ein daoistisches priestergewand vom anfang des 19. jahrhunderts. In WGM (1989) 105-110.

Eskildsen, Steve. Asceticism in ch'üan-chen taoism. BCAR 3/4 (1990) 153-191.

Hahn, Thomas H. New developments concerning buddhist and taoist monasteries. In TT:RCT (1989) 79-101.

Hawkes, David. Quanzhen plays and quanzhen masters. BEFEO 69 (1981) 153-170.

Jan, Yün-hua. Cultural borrowings and religious identity: a case study of the taoist religious codes. HHYC:CS 4.1 (june 1986) 281-294. Taoist borrowing fr budd.

Kate, Sister. Some descriptive notes on an american taoist cloister. TaoRes 1.1 (autumn 1988) 18-21.

Lagerwey, John. Taoist priesthood. EncyRel 11 (1987) 547b-550b.

Lagerwey, John. The taoist religious community. EncyRel 14 (1987) 306a-317a.

Luo, Zhufeng. Tsl by Donald MacInnis. The current situation of daoism in qingchengshan, sichuan province. Tripod 47 (1988) 57-59.

Ozaki, Masaharu. The taoist priesthood: from tsai-chia to ch'u-chiao. SES 11 (1984) 97-110. Repr RFEA (1986) 97-109.

Picture album of mt wudang taoist shrine. n.p. (Hua yi publ house) (1990) 64 p, col photos with chin and engl captions.

Reiter, Florian C. Some observations concerning taoist foundations in traditional china. ZDMG 133.2 (1983) 363-376. Re taoist monasteries and monachism.

Reiter, Florian C. The soothsayer hao ta-t'ung

78

(1140-1212) and his encounter with ch'üan-chen taoism. OE 28.2 (1981) 198-205.

Robinet, Isabelle. Chang tao-ling. EncyRel 3 (1987) 199b-200a.

Robinet, Isabelle. Nature et rôle du maître spirituel dans le taoïsme non liturgique. In M. Meslin (ed) Maîtres et disciples dans les traditons religieuses, paris (1990) 37-50.

Robinet, Isabelle. Le révélation du shangqing dans l'histoire du taoïsme. Paris (1984) vol 1: 262p, tables, charts, indices; vol 2: 464 p, bibliog, indices.

Schafer, Edward H. Mao shan in t'ang times. Boulder, colo (1980) 72 p, notes, diagram. SSCR monograph no 1; 2nd rev ed (1989) 97 p.

Schipper, Kristofer M. Les maîtres célestes à l'époque song. ACF 91 (1982-83) 133-137.

Schipper, Kristofer M. Master chao i-cheng (?—1382) and the ch'ing-wei school of taoism. In TRC (1987) Engl text 4-20.

Schipper, Kristofer. Le monachisme taoïste. In Incontro (1984) 199-216.

Schipper, Kristofer M. Taoist ordination ranks in the tunhuang manuscripts. In RPO-A (1985) 127-148.

Strickmann, Michel. Le taoïsme du mao chan. Chronique d'une révélation. Paris (1981) 278 p, bibliog, notes.

Tsui, Bartholomew P. M. The transmission of the taoist complete perfection sect in south china. CF 33 (dec 1990) 248-257.

II.25 Taoist Self-Cultivation: Yoga, Alchemy, etc.

Akahori, Akira. Drug taking and immortality. In TMLT (1989) 73-98.

Ames. Roger T. The common ground of self-cultivation in classical taoism and confucianism. TJ 17.1-2 (dec 1985) 65-97. Repr in TaoRes 1.1 (autumn 1988) 23-54.

Baldrian-Hussein, Farzeen. Inner alchemy: notes on the origin and use of the term neidan. CEA 5 (1989-90) 163-190.

Baldrian-Hussein, Farzeen. Procédés secrets du joyau magique—traité d'alchimie taoïste du XIe siècle. Présentation et traduction du chinois par... Paris (1984) 322 p. See rev by Isabelle Robinet, CEA 2 (1986) 241-252, sep listed in this bibliog.

Baldrian-Hussein, Farzeen. Yüeh-yang and lü tung-pin's ch'in-yüan ch'un: a sung alchemical poem. In RPO-A (1985) 19-31.

Bokenkamp, Stephen R. Death and ascent in ling-pao taoism. TaoRes 1.2 (1989) 1-20.

Bokenkamp, Stephen R. The entheogenic herb calamus in taoist literature. PTP 15 (1983) 6-22.

Boltz, Judith M. Opening the gates of purgatory; a twelfth-century taoist meditation technique for the salvation of lost souls. In T&TStudies 2 (MCB 21, 1983) 487-511. Re manual of instruction for internal meditation and external rite of salvation.

Cleary, Thomas (tsl) Awakening to the tao, by liu i-ming. Boston & shaftesbury (1990) 105 p. No chin title given; liu was born in 1737.

Cooper, Jean C. Chinese alchemy: the taoist quest for immortality. Wellingsborough, northamptonshire, engl (1984) 160 p.

Despeux, Catherine. Le chemin de l'éveil. Illustré par le dressage du buffle dans le bouddhisme chan, le dressage du cheval dans le taoïsme, le dressage de l'éléphant dans le bouddhisme tibétaine. Paris (1981) 139 p.

Despeux, Catherine. Gymnastics: the ancient tradition. In TMLT (1989) 225-261.

Despeux, Catherine. Les lectures alchimiques du hsi-yu chi. In RPO-A (1985) 61-75.

Despeux, Catherine. La moelle du phénix rouge.

Santé et longue vie dans la chine du XVIe siècle. Paris (1988)

Despeux, Catherine. Taiji quan: art martial, technique de longue vie. Paris (1981)

Despeux, Catherine (tsl) Zhao pichen, traité d'alchimie et de physiologie taoïste. Paris (1979) Chao was born 1860.

Engelhardt, Ute. Qi for life: longevity in the tang. IN TMLT (1989) 263-296.

Engelhardt, Ute. Theorie und technik des taijiquan. Schorndorf (1981)

Eskildsen, Steve. Asceticism in ch'üan-chen taoism. BCAR 3/4 (1990) 153-191.

Fukui, Fumimasa. On perennial youth and longevity: a taoist view on health of the elderly. Journal of religion and aging 4.3-4 (1988) 119-126.

Harper, Donald. The sexual arts of ancient china as described in a manuscript of the second century b.c. HJAS 47.2 (1987) 539-593. From tomb 3, ma-wang-tui.

Ho, Peng Yoke (Ho Ping-yü). Li, qi and shu: an introduction to science and civilization in china. Univ HK (1985) See part 4: Chinese alchemy, 171-217, chin char, illus, bibliog.

Huang, Jane (tsl) in collaboration with Michael Wurmbrand. The primordial breath. An ancient chinese way of prolonging life through breath control. Torrance, calif (1987) 169 p, gloss, bibliog. Seven treatises fr the taoist canon (tao tsang)

Kaltenmark, Max. King yu pa-king [ching yü pa-ching] In Fukui Kojun festschrift, Toya bunka ronshu, tokyo (1969) 1147-1154. Re important term in mao shan taoist texts.

Knaul, Livia. That sleep of death—a note on the structure of taoist mysticism. Proc31st ICHS, tokyo, vol 1 (1984) 248-250. Abstr.

Kohn, Livia. Eternal life in taoist mysticism. JAOS 110.4 (oct-dec 1990) 622-640.

Kohn, Livia. Guarding the one: concentrative meditation in taoism. In TMLT (1989) 125-158.

Kohn, Livia. Medicine and immortality in t'ang china. JAOS 108.3 (july-sept 1988) 465-469. Rev art on Ute Engelhardt, Die klassische tradition der qi-übungen, q.v.

Kohn, Livia. Seven steps to the tao: sima chengzhen's zuowanglun. St augustin, germany (1987) 205 p, app, chin texts, bibliog, index, chin char used throughout. Discussion and tsl.

Kohn, Livia. Taoist insight meditation: the tang practice of neiguan. In TMLT (1989) 193-224.

Kohn, Livia. The teaching of t'ien-yin-tzu. JCR 15 (1987) 1-28. Re tao-tsang s. 1026.

Kohn, Livia, in cooperation with Sakade Yoshinobu. Taoist meditation and longevity techniques. Univ michigan (1989) xii 384 p. Essays sep listed in this bibliog; abbrev TMLT.

Lagerwey, John. Worship and cultic life. EncyRel 15 (1987) 482b-486b.

Lai, Whalen. The interiorization of the gods. TaoRes 1.1 (autumn 1988) 1-10.

Lee, Agnes C. J. Movement within stillness and stillness within movement: the contemplative character of t'ai chi chuan. CF 30 (may1987) 25-38.

Levi, Jean. l'Abstinence des céréales chez les taoïstes. EtCh 1 (1983) 3-47.

Levi, Jean. Vers des céréales et dieux du corps dans le taoïsme. TdelaR 7 (1986) 99-119.

Lu, K'uan-yü (Charles Luk) The secrets of chinese meditation. Self-cultivation by mind control as taught in the ch'an, mahayana and taoist schools in china. London (1964) 240 p, gloss, illus, index. Repr london (1984) German tsl by H.-U. Rieker, Geheimnisse der chinesischen meditation, zürich & stuttgart (1967)

Mahdihassan, S. Cinnabar-gold as the best alchemical drug of longevity, called makaradhwaja in india. AJCM 13.1-4 (1985) 93-108.

Mahdihassan, S. Outline of the beginnings of alchemy and its antecedents. AJCM 12.1-4 (1984) 32-42.

Mahdihassan, S. Tan, cinnabar, as drug of longevity prior to alchemy. AJCM 12.1-4 (1984) 50-54.

Mahdihassan, S. T'ao-t'ieh, a motif of chinese funerary art as the iconographic counterpart of cinnabar, an alchemical drug. AJCM 10.1-4 (1982) 5-13.

Maliszewski, Michael. Martial arts: an overview. EncyRel 9 (1987) See sec: China, 225b-226a.

Maspero, Henri. Engl tsl by Frank A. Kierman. Taoism and chinese religion. Amherst, mass (1981) 656 p. Tsl of author's Le taoïsme et les religions chinoises (1971) q.v.

Miura, Kunio. The revival of qi: qigong in contemporary china. In TMLT (1989) 331-362.

Miyuki, Mokusen (übers & kommentiert) Die erfahrung der goldenen blüte... Meditation aus d. china d. 12.jahrh. Bern, etc (1984) 254 s.

Needham, Joseph et al. Science and civilization in china. Vol 5, Chemistry and chemical technology; part 4, Spagyrical discovery and invention: apparatus, theories and gifts. Cambridge univ (1980) See esp (h) with Nathan Sivin; Comparative macrobiotics, 210-323; extensive bibliog 323-509.

Odier, Daniel. Nirvana tao; techniques de méditation. Paris (1974) See for ch'an, 149-169; for taoism, 173-203.

Odier, Daniel & Marc de Smedt. Les mystiques orientales. Paris (1972) See Le taoïsme, 56-74. Rev ed (1984)

Pregadio, Fabrizio. Two recent books on the taoist 'cultivation of life' CEA 5 (1989-90) 387-404. Rev art on Kohn, TMLT q.v. and a jap work.

Prensky, William L. Tai chi: a spiritual martial art. Parabola 4.2 (1979) 68-73.

Robinet, Isabelle. l'Alchimie interne dans le taoïsme. CEA 2 (1986) 241-252. Rev art on Farzeen Baldrian-Hussein, Procédés secrets du joyau magique . . . q.v.

Robinet, Isabelle. Chuang-tzu et le taoïsme "religieux" JCR 11 (1983) 59-105.

Robinet, Isabelle. Original contributions of neidan to taoism and chinese thought. In TMLT (1989) 297-330.

Robinet, Isabelle. Recherche sur l'alchimie intérieure (neidan): l'école zhenyuan. CEA 5 (1989-90) 141-162.

Robinet, Isabelle. Taoïsme et mystique. CEC 8 (1989) 65-103.

Robinet, Isabelle. Visualization and ecstatic flight in shangqing taoism. In TMLT (1989) 159-191.

Sakade, Yoshinobu. Longevity techniques in japan: ancient sources and contemporary studies. In TMLT (1989) 1-40. The "ancient sources" incl chin texts.

Sakade, Yoshinobu. The p'eng-tsu legend and the p'eng-tsu-ching—ideas for keeping in good health in ancient china. Proc31stICHS, tokyo, vol 1 (1984) 259-260. Abstr.

Sakade, Yoshinobu. The taoist character of the 'chapter on nourishing life' of the ishinpo. KDBR (1986) 775-798.

Schafer, Edward H. Two taoist bagatelles. SSCRB 9 (1981) 1-18. Re the yin-transmitting lithophones and the mutations of mercurial maid.

Sivin, Nathan. Chinese alchemy. EncyRel 1 (1987) 186a-190b.

Soo, Chee. Taoist yoga; the chinese art of k'ai men. Northamptonshire, engl (1984) 160 p.

Switkin, Walter. Immortality; a taoist text of macrobiotics. San francisco (1975) 66 p, notes, bibliog. Intro and annot tsl of yang-hsing yen-min lu, chap 2 & 3; chin char used throughout.

Tu, Wei-ming. T'ai-chi. EncyRel 14 (1987) 247b-249a.

Whiting, Joshua C. Tai chi chuan, the water-course way: its spiritual and mystical features. Journal of religious and psychical research 4 (july 1988) 141-145.

Yamada, Toshiaki. Longevity techniques and the compilation of the lingbao wufuxu. In TMLT (1989) 99-124.

II.26 Taoist Liturgy and Ritual

Andersen, Poul. The practice of bugang. CEA 5 (1989-90) 15-53. Re taoist ritual dance.

Bell, Catherine. Ritualization of texts and textualization of ritual in the codification of taoist liturgy. HR 27.4 (may 1988) 366-392.

Boltz, Judith M. Opening the gate of purgatory: a taoist meditation technique for the salvation of lost souls. In T&TStudies 2 (MCB 21, 1983) 487-511. Re manual of instruction for internal meditation and external rite of salvation.

Cedzich, Ursula-Angelika. Das ritual der himmelsmeister im spiegel früher quellen—übersetzung und untersuchung des liturgischen materials im dritten chüan der teng-chen yin-chüeh. Würzburg (1987) 174 p + chin text, bibliog. See rev art by Anna Seidel in CEA 4 (1988) 199-204.

Chan, Wing-hoi. The dangs of kam tin and their jiu [chiao] festival. JHKBRAS 29 (1989) 302-375.

Chan, Wing-hoi. Observations at the jiu [chiao] festival of shek o and tai long wan, 1986. JHKBRAS 26 (1986) 78-101.

Dean, Kenneth. Field notes on two taoist jiao observed in zhangzhou in december 1985. CEA 2 (1986) 191-209.

Girardot, Norman J. "Let's get physical": the way of liturgical taoism. HR 23.2 (nov 1983) 169-180. Rev art on K. Schipper, Le corps taoïste, q.v.

Kagan, Alan L. Eight immortals longevity blessings: symbolic and ritual perspectives of the music. In STR&MT (1989) 121-135.

Lagerwey, John. Taoist ritual in chinese society and history. NY & london (1987) 364 p, bibliog, index, 4 app, 27 b-&-w pl. See rev by J. Pas in JCR 16 (1988) 99-106; David Yu in CC 29.3 (sept 1988) 89-94.

Lagerwey, John. Rapport sur une conférence taoïste, tenue à hongkong en décembre 1985. CEA 2 (1986) 185-190. Conference on taoist ritual and music. See papers sep listed in this bibliog in vol abbrev STR&MT.

Lagerwey, John. "Les têtes des démons tombent par milliers": le fachang, rituel exorciste du nord de taiwan. l'Homme 27.1 (1987) 101-116.

Lagerwey, John. Worship and cultic life: taoist cultic life. EncyRel 15 (1987) 482b-486b.

Lü, Ch'ui-k'uan. Enquête préliminaire sur la musique taoïste de taiwan. Sommaire en francais par j. l. [john lagerwey] CEA 4 (1988) 112-126.

Lu, Ping-chuan & Tsao Pen-yeh. The ritual music of taoist "chiao"—studies made in lin-chueng and p'eng-hu. Proc31stICHS, tokyo, vol 2 (1984) 656-658. Abstr.

Malek, Roman. Das chai-chieh lu: materialien zur liturgie im taoismus. Frankfurt am main etc (1985) 374 s, schlussbemerkungen, anhang, index, bibliog.

Pas, Julian. Rituals of cancellation of evil (hsiao-chai) In STR&MT (1989) 28-35.

Saso, Michael. The liturgical heritage of the hsinchu taoists. CEA 4 (1988) 175-180.

82

Saso, Michael. The structure of taoist liturgy. Trans of the intl conference of orientalists in japan 32, tokyo (1987) 43-51.

Saso, Michael. Taoism and the rite of cosmic renewal. Washington state univ (1972) 120 p, notes, bibliog, illus. 2nd ed (1990) 152 p.

Schafer, Edward H. Two taoist bagatelles. SSCRB 9 (1981) 1-18. Re The yin-transmitting lithophones & the mutations of mercurial maid.

Schipper, Kristofer. Mu-lien plays in taoist liturgical context. In RO/OR (1989) 126-154.

Schipper, K. Recherche sur le rituel taoïste: la structure. AnnEPHE 95 (1986-87) 108-114.

Schipper, K. Recherches sur le rituel taoïste. AnnEPHE 92 (1983-84) 139-144.

Schipper, K. Recherches sur le rituel taoïste. AnnEPHE 93 (1984-85) 115-120.

Schipper, K. Recherches sur le rituel taoïste. AnnEPHE 94 (1985-86) 155-158.

Schipper, Kristofer. A study of buxu: taoist liturgical hymn and dance. In STR&MT (1989) 110-120.

Schipper, K. M. Taoist ritual and local cults of the t'ang dynasty. ProcICS, taipei, Folk customs and culture vol (1981) 101-115. Same title in T&TStudies 3 (MCB 23, 1985) 812-834.

Schipper, Kristofer. Vernacular and classical ritual in taoism. JAS 45.1 (nov 1985) 21-57.

Schipper, Kristofer & Wang Hsiu-huei. Progressive and regressive time cycles in taoist rituals. In Lawrence Fraser & ??? Haber (ed) Time, science, and society in china and the west, univ mass (1986) 185-205.

Seidel, Anna. Early taoist ritual. CEA 4 (1988) 199-204. Rev art on Ursula-Angelika Cedzich, Das ritual der himmelsmeister im spiegel früher quellen . . . q.v.

Shen, Yi and Hilary Fraser. The twelve-year cycle of festivals at shuili. FCR 34.2 (sept 1984) 45-52. Re chiao.

Soymié, Michel. Les dix jours de jeûne de taoïsme. In Yoshioka hakase kanreki kinen: dokyo kenkyu ronshu, tokyo (1977) 1-27.

Tanaka, Issei. The jiao festival in hong kong and the new territories. In TT:RCT (1989) 271-198.

Thompson, Laurence G. Chiao. EncyRel 3 (1987) 239a-240b.

Thompson, Laurence G. Taoist iconography. EncyRel 7 (1987) 50b-54a.

Tsao, Pen-yeh. Variation technique in the formal structure of music of taoist jiao-shih in hongkong. JHKBRAS 23 (1983) 172-181.

Tsao, Pen-yeh and Daniel P. L. Law (ed) Studies of taoist rituals and music of today. HK: chinese univ of HK (1989) 1985 conference; engl language papers sep listed in this bibliog; abbrev STR&MT.

Tsui, Bartholomew P. M. Taoist ritual books of the new territories. In STR&MT (1989) 136-143.

Verellen, Franciscus. Liturgy and sovereignty: the role of taoist ritual in the foundation of the shu kingdom (907-925) AM 3rd ser 2.1 (1989) 59-78.

II.27 Meditation - Mysticism - Personal Religious Experience

Blanchon, Flora. Mystique et politique en chine: histoire d'un itinéraire et éléments d'une interaction. CEC 8 (1989) 17-44.

Campany, Robert. Return-from-death narratives in early medieval china. JCR 18 (1990) 91-125.

Chan, Wing-tsit. Chu hsi and quiet-sitting. Chap 17 in author's CH:NS (1989) 255-270.

Chan, Wing-tsit. Memories, dreams, divination, and popular beliefs. Chap 7 in author's CH:NS (1989) 106-125.

Chao, Tze-chiang (tsl) A chinese garden of serenity. Epigrams from the ming dynasty 'discourse on vegetable roots' Mount vernon, NY (1959) 60 p. Eclectic views by hung tzu-ch'eng.

Ching, Julia. The mirror symbol revisited: confucian and taoist mysticism. In MRT (1983) 226-246.

Emmons, Charles F. Chinese ghosts and ESP. A study of paranormal beliefs and experiences. Metuchen, n.j. & london (1982) 297 p, bibliog, index. ". . . based on a total of over 3,600 interviews, questionnaires, and observations made in hong kong from june 1980 through january 1981"

Hegel, Robert E. Heavens and hells in chinese fictional dreams. In P-S (1988) 1-10.

Jou, Tsung-hwa. The tao of meditation; way to enlightenment. Piscataway, n.j. (1983) 176 p, illus col and b-&-w.

Kaltenmark, Maxime. La mystique taoïste. In A. Ravier (ed) La mystique et les mystiques, paris (1965) 649-669.

Katz, Steven T. (ed) Mysticism and religious traditions. Oxford univ (1983) Abbrev MRT

Knaul, Livia. That sleep of death—a note on the structure of taoist mysticism. Proc31stICHS, tokyo, vol 1 (1984) 248-250. Abstr.

Li, Wai-yee. Dream visions of transcendence in chinese literature and painting. AsArt 3.4 (fall 1990) 53-78. The "dream of daoist reconciliation" and "the dream of the divine woman"

Lu, K'uan-yü (Charles Luk) The secrets of chinese meditation. Self-cultivation by mind control as taught in the ch'an, mahayana and taoist schools in china. London (1964) 240 p, gloss, illus, index. Repr london (1984) German tsl by H. U. Rieker, Geheimnisse der chinesischen meditation, zürich & stuttgart (1967)

Mathieu, Rémi. Le songe de chao jianzi. Etude sur les rêves d'ascension céleste et les rêves d'esprits dans la chine ancienne. AS 37 (1983) 120-138.

McClenon, James. Chinese and american anomalous experiences: the role of religiosity. Sociological analysis: a journal in the sociology of religion 51 (spring 1990) 53-67.

McClenon, James. A survey of chinese anomalous experiences and comparison with western representative national examples. JSSR 27 (spring 1988) 421-426.

McFarlane, S. Bodily awareness in the wing chun system. Religion 19 (1989) 241-253.

Odier, Daniel. Nirvana tao; techniques de méditation. Paris (1974) See for ch'an, 149-169; for taoism, 173-203.

Okada, Takehiko. Tsl by Rodney L. Taylor. Zazen to seiza: a prefatory discussion. JCR 10 (1982) 19-38. Tsl and discussion.

Pas, Julian F. Journey to hell: a new report of shamanistic travel to the courts of hell. JCR 17 (1989) 43-60.

Robinet, Isabelle. Taoïsme et mystique. CEC 8 (1989) 65-103.

Robinet, Isabelle. La transmission des textes sacrés, paradis terrestres et cosmiques, la marche sur l'étoiles, la pratique du tao. In MetC (1985) 369-398.

Strickmann, Michel. Dreamwork of psycho-sinologists: doctors, taoists, monks. In P-S (1988) 25-46.

Thomas, Léon. Les états de conscience inhabituels dans le "zhuangzi" RHR 204.2 (1987) 129-149. On the mystical experiencing of the tao.

Thompson, Laurence G. Dream divination and chinese popular religion. JCR 16 (1988) 73-82.

Underwood, Frederic B. Meditation: an overview. EncyRel 9 (1987) 327b-331a.

Vervoorn, Aat. Men of the cliffs and caves; the development of the chinese eremitic tradition to the end of the han dynasty. HK (1990) 368 p.

Vervoorn, Aat. The origins of chinese eremitism. JICS:CUHK 15 (1984) 249-295.

Waddell, N. A. (tsl) A selection from the ts'ai ken t'an ('vegetable-root discourses') EB 2.2 (nov 1919) 88-98.

Wagner, Rudolf G. Imperial dreams. In P-S (1988) 11-24. Re dreams of emperors.

Wilson, William Scott (ts) The roots of wisdom: saikontan by hung ying ming. Tokyo etc (1985) 160 p, notes, bibliog. Ming text: ts'ai ken-t'an. A sort of 3 traditions eclecticism.

II.28 Popular Religion and "Superstitions": General

Bell, Catherine. Religion and chinese culture: toward an assessment of 'popular religion' HR 29 (aug 1989) 35-57. Rev art on several recent books.

Chan, Wing-tsit. Memories, dreams, divination, and popular beliefs. Chap 7 in author's CH:NS (1989) 106-125.

Clammer, John R. (ed) Studies in chinese folk religion in singapore and malaysia. Singapore (1983) 178 p. Essays sep listed in this bibliog; vol abbrev CFRSM.

Cohen, Alvin P. Chinese religion: popular religion. EncyRel 3 (1987) 289a-296b.

Cohen, Alvin P. Completing the business of life: the vengeful dead in chinese folk religion. In Folk culture, vol 2: Folkways in religion, gods, spirits, and men, cuttack, india (1983) 59-66.

Cohen, Myron L. Souls and salvation: conflicting themes in chinese popular religon. In DeathRit (1988) 180-202.

Eastman, Lloyd E. Family, field, and ancestors. Constancy and change in china's social and economic history, 1550-1949. Oxford univ (1988).

See chap 3, Gods, ghosts, and ancestors: the popular religion, 41-61.

Feuchtwang, Stephen. The study of chinese popular religion. Revue européene des sciences sociales 27 (1989) 84ff.

Harper, Donald. A chinese demonography of the third century b.c. HJAS 45 (1985) 459-498.

Harrell, Stevan. The concept of fate in chinese folk ideology. ModCh 13.1 (jan 1987) 90-109.

Harrell, C. Stevan. Domestic observances: chinese practices. EncyRel 4 (1987) 410b-413b.

Hayes, James W. Village beliefs and practices. In RC/HK (1983) 197-198.

Hou, Ching-lang. Les monnaies de la trésorerie et la notion de destin fondamental. In Dette (1988) 81-93.

Johnson, David, Andrew J. Nathan & Evelyn S. Rawski (ed) Popular culture in late imperial china. Univ calif (1985) See pertinent art sep listed in this bibliog; abbrev PopCult.

Kaltenmark, Maxime & Michel Soymié. Symbolisme traditionel et religions populaire. EncyUniv 5 (1990) 621b-625b.

Li, Rui. Marriage of the dead. CL (autumn 1989) 30-37. Fictional descr of "marriage by burial" of deceased couple, set in lüliang mt rural area.

Lip, Evelyn. Chinese beliefs and superstitions. Singapore (1985) 80 p, illus by author.

Liu, Joyce C. H. The protest from the invisible world; the revenge ghost in yuan drama and the elizabethan drama. TR 19.1-4 (aut 1988-sum 1989) 755-776.

M. K. [Max Kaltenmark] & M. S. [Michel Soymié] Symbolisme traditionelle et religions populaires. EUF 4 (1968) Chine, sec 5, 362a-365c. Same title in EncyUniv 5 (1990) 621b-625b.

Moes, Robert. (comp) Auspicious spirits: korean folk paintings and related subjects. Washington, d.c. (1983) 200 p, sel bibliog, topical index, profusely illus. Exhibition catalog; altho korean in subj matter, much material relates to china.

Stockard, Janice E. Daughters of the canton delta; marriage patterns and economic strategies in south china, 1860-1930. Stanford univ (1989) See chap 5, Arranging a spirit marriage, 90-101.

Tseng, Li-ling. Photos by Joseph Chen & Lin Borliang. Temple figures, toys and tradition in dough. FCR 39.5 (may 1989) 60-75, illus col photos.

Weller, Robert P. & Hill Gates. Hegemony and chinese folk ideologies: an introduction. ModCh 13 (1987) 3-16.

Yazawa, Toshihiko. Christianisme et religions populaires en chine. In BetSA (1990) 189-203.

II.29 Local Studies: Mainland China

Dean, Kenneth. Funerals in fujian. CEA 4 (1988) 19-78.

Dean, Kenneth. Lei yu-sheng ("thunder is noisy") and mu-lien in the theatrical and funerary traditions of fukien. In RO/OR (1989) 46-104.

Dean, Kenneth. Revival of religious practices in fujian: a case study. In TT:RCT (1989) 51-78.

Dean, Kenneth. Taoism in southern fujian: field notes, fall, 1985. In STR&MT (1989) 74-87.

Doolittle, Justus. Social life of the chinese . . . with special but not exclusive reference to fuhchau. NY (1865) repr singapore (1986) vol 1, xvi + 459 p; vol 2, 490 p; illus, index for both vol at end of vol 2. Well over half of this work deals with relig. Sep entries for various subj listed in this bibliog; abbrev SLC

Dudbridge, Glen. Yü-ch'ih chiang at an-yang: an eighth century cult and its myths. AM 3rd ser 1 (1990) 27-49. Local popular cult.

Groot, J. J. M. de. Les fêtes annuellement célébrées à emoui (amoy) Etude concernant la religion populaire chinois. Being AMG 11 and 12 (1886) Repr in 2 vol, taipei (1977) NY (1981)

Haar, Barend J. Ter. The genesis and spread of temple cults in fukien. In FukienD&D (1990) 349-396.

Hsu, Francis L. K. Exorcising the trouble makers. Magic, science, and culture. Westport, conn (1983) xvi + 164 p, 2 app, bibliog, index. Incorporates author's 1942 study, Religion, science, and human crisis q.v.

Liu, Chiang. Religion in foochow. ChRec 66.2 (feb 1935) 89-94)

Luo, Zhufeng. Tsl by Donald MacInnis. The current situation of daoism in qingchengshan, sichuan province. Tripod 47 (1988) 57-59.

Schafer, Edward H. The empire of min. Rutland, vt and tokyo (1954) See chap 6, Religion, 90-109.

Schafer, Edward H. Mao shan in t'ang times. Boulder, colo (1980) 72 p, notes, diagram. SSCR monograph no 1; 2nd rev ed (1989) 97 p.

II.30 Deities and Images: General

Carlyon, Richard. A guide to the gods. NY (1981) See Chinese, 78-96.

Chamberlain, Jonathan. Chinese gods. HK & taipei (1983) 162 p, 16 col illus, tables, charts.

Delahaye, Hubert. Les antécédents magiques des statues chinoises. Revue d'esthétique 5 (1983) 45-53.

Goidsenhoven, Jacques van. Héros et divinités de la chine. Bruxelles (1971) 194 p of text + album of artworks. Informative handbook.

Levi, Jean. Les fonctions religieuses de la bureaucratie céleste. l'Homme 27 no 101 (jan-mars 1987) 35-57.

Lip, Evelyn. Chinese temples and deities. Singapore (1981) 107 p, gloss, bibliog, profusely

86

illus. Same title, also publ singapore (1986) 112 p.
Author states, "Some of the material for this book
has been extracted from Chinese temples and
deities published in 1981 . . ."

Pederson, Bent Lerbaek. A painted qing pantheon. AO 49 (1988) 49-104. Re popular prints.

Pederson, Bent L. Popular pantheons in old china.
JOS 26.1 (1988) 28-59. Re popular prints.

Stein, Rolf A. Grottes-matrices et lieux saints de
la déesse en asie-orientale. Paris (1988) 83 p, 21
pl, liste des ouvrages cités. See passim.

Tong, Fung-wan (i.e. Tung Fang-yüan) Vibrant,
popular pantheon. FCR 38.1 (jan 1988) 9-15, illus
col photos.

II.31 Specific Deities and Cults

Berthier, Brigitte. La dame-du-bord-de-l'eau: la
fémininité à travers un culte de la religion populaire
chinoise. Nanterre (1988) 300 p, illus, photos,
notes, bibliog.

Boltz, Judith Magee. In homage to t'ien-fei.
JAOS 106.1 (jan-mar 1986) 211-232.

Cahill, Suzanne. Performers and female taoist
adepts: hsi wang mu as the patron deity of women
in medieval china. JAOS 106.1 (jan-mar 1986)
155-168.

Chan, Wing-hoi. The dangs of kam tin and their
jiu [chiao] festival. JHKBRAS 29 (1989) 302-
375.

Chard, Robert L. Folktales on the god of the stove.
HHTC:CS 8.1, vol 1 (june 1990) 149-182.

Diesinger, Gunter. Kuan-yü-darstellung in china
und japan: vom idealporträt zum klischeebild. In
ZDMG Supplementa 7 (1989) 681-691.

Diesinger, Gunter. Vom general zum gott: kuan
yü (gest.220 n.chr.) und seine "poshume karriere"
Heidelberg univ (1984) 314 s, engl summ, bibliog,
abbildungsverz, register, bildanhang (44 abb)

Duara, Prasenjit. Superscribing symbols: the
myth of guandi, chinese god of war. JAS 47.4
(nov 1988) 778-795.

Dudbridge, Glen. The goddess hua-yüeh san-
niang and the cantonese ballad ch'en-hsiang t'ai-
tzu. HHYC:CS 8.1, vol 2 (june 1990) 627-646. Fr
medieval cult to contemporary ballad text.

Dudbridge, Glen. Miao-shan on stone. HJAS 42.2
(dec 1982) 589-614. Re early 12th c inscriptions.

Dudbridge, Glen. Yü-chih chiang at an-yang: an
eighth century cult and its myths. AM 3rd ser 1
(1990) 27-49.

Eno, Robert. Was there a high god ti in shang
religion? EC 15 (1990) 1-26.

Fong, Mary H. The iconography of the popular
gods of happiness, emolument, and longevity (fu
lu shou) AA 44.2/3 (1983) 159-199, 21 fig.

Fong, Mary H. Wu daozi's legacy in the popular
door gods (menshen) qin shubao and yuchi gong.
AAA 42 (1989) 6-24.

Irwin, Lee. Divinity and salvation: the great
goddesses of china. AsFS 49.1 (1990) 53-68.

Johnson, David The wu tzu-hsü pien-wen and its
sources. HJAS 40.1; 40.2 (june & dec 1980) 93-
156; 465-505. Re legend of yangtzu river god.

Katz, Paul. Demons or deities?—The wangye of
taiwan. AsFS 46.2 (1987) 197-215.

Katz, Paul. Wen ch'iung—the god of many faces.
HHYC:CS 8.1, vol 1 (june 1990) 183-219. One
of the best-known faces is as a "plague god" in
taiwan.

Kinsley, David R. The goddesses' mirror; visions
of the divine from east and west. SUNY (1989)
See chap 2, Kuan-yin, the chinese goddess of
mercy, 25-51.

Lai, Whalen. The crossing of paths in the cult of
kuan-kung. CF 32 (dec 1989) 218-223.

Lai, Whalen. Looking for mr ho po: unmasking the river god of ancient china. HR 29 (may 1990) 335-350, illus.

Lang, Graeme & Lars Ragvald. Official and oral traditions about hong kong's newest god [i.e. wong tai sin] JHKBRAS 27 (1987) 93-97.

Lang, Graeme & Lars Ragvald. Upward mobility of a refugee god: hong kong's huang daxian. Univ stockholm (1986) 32 p, ref.

Levi, Jean. Identité et bureaucratie divines en chine ancienne. RHR 225.4 (1988) 447-465.

Lin, Kai-shyh. The eternal mother and the heavenly father: two deities of rebellion in late imperial china. ASBIE 69 (1990) 161-180. White lotus and taiping myths.

Little, Stephen. The demon queller and the art of qiu ying [ch'iu ying] AA 46.1/2 (1985) 8-80, 62 fig.

Loewe, Michael. The cult of the dragon and the invocation for rain. In CINS (1987) 195-213.

Major, John S. New light on the dark warrior. JCR 13/14 (1985/86) 65-86.

Major, John S. Shang-ti. EncyRel 13 (1987) 223a-224a.

Meyer, Roger D. Shou lao sells. FCR 37.5 (may 1987) 2-10, col illus.

Paper, Jordan. The persistence of female dieties in patriarchal china. Journal of feminist studies in religion 6 (spring 1990) 25-40.

Ragvald, Lars & Graeme Lang. Confused gods: huang daxian and huang yeren at mt. luofu. JHKBRAS 27 (1987) 74-92.

Riegel, Jeffrey. Kou-mang and ju-shou. CEA 5 (1989-90) 55-83. Re a pair of warring states deities of life and death.

Sangren, P. Steven. Female gender in chinese religious symbols: kuan yin, matsu, and the "eternal mother" Signs 9 (1983) 4-25.

Sangren, P. Steven. History and the rhetoric of legitimacy: the matsu cult of taiwan. CSSH 30 (oct 1988) 674-697.

Schipper, Kristofer. The cult of pao-sheng ta-ti and its spread to taiwan—a case study of fen-hsiang. In FukienD&D (1990) 397-416.

Schipper, Kristofer. Seigneurs royaux, dieux des épidémies. ASSR 59.1 (1985) 31-40.

Seaman, Gary. The emperor of the dark heavens and the han river gateway into china. In Ec&Emp (1989) 165-177.

Seidel, Anna. Yü-huang. EncyRel 15 (1987) 541a-541b.

Silk, Michael A. The apotheosis of kuan-yü. ACQ 11.2 (summer 1983) 41-47.

Siu, Anthony K. K. Tam kung: his legend and worship. JHKBRAS 27 (1987) 278-279.

Stevens, Keith. Fukienese wang yeh (ong ya) JHKBRAS 29 (1989) 34-60.

Stevens, Keith. The jade emperor and his family, yu huang ta ti. JHKBRAS 29 (1989) 18-33.

Tay, C. N. Kuan-yin: the cult of half asia. Taipei (1984) 179 p.

Thompson, Laurence G. Popular and classical modes of ritual in a taiwanese temple. SSCRB 9 (1981) 106-122. Matsu is the deity of this temple.

Thompson, Laurence G. T'ien. EncyRel 14 (1987) 508a-510a.

Tirone, Gail (text) & Lin Bor-liang (photos) A gathering of deities occasions folk celebrations. FCR 36.7 (july 1986) 36-41. Re Peikang matsu festival 27 apr 86.

Wang, H.-h. Le culte de guan-di. AnnEPHE 92 (1983-84) 151-152.

Watson, James L. Standardizing the gods: the promotion of t'ien hou ("empress of heaven") along the south china coast, 960-1960. In PopCult (1985) 292-324.

Yang, Winston L. Y. From history to fiction: the popular image of kuan yu. Renditions 15 (1981) 67-79.

Zito, Angela R. City gods, filiality, and hegemony in late imperial china. ModCh 13.3 (july 1987) 333-371.

II.32 Religious Calendar - Festivals - Popular Customs

Ancient chinese woodblock new year prints. Peking (1985) 184 p.

Bredon, Juliet. Chinese new year festivals: a picturesque monograph of the rites, ceremonies and observances in relation thereto. Shanghai (1930) 29 p. Repr singapore (1989) 29 p, illus b-&-w and col.

Burkhardt, Valentine R. Chinese creeds and customs. HK vol 1 (1953) vol 2 (1955) vol 3 (1958) 181, 201, 164 p, each vol profusely illus, indexes. Repr HK (1983)

Chan, Wing-hoi. Observations at the jiu [chiao] festival of shek o and tai long wan, 1986. JHKBRAS 26 (1986) 78-101, photos, gloss.

Chang, Toy Len. Chinese festivals the hawaiian way. Honolulu, privately publ (1983) 74 p, drawings, index, brief bibliog.

Chen, C. P. Chinese culture and chinese new year. Asian outlook 17.2 (feb 1982) 17-19.

Chiang, Kuei. Tsl by Timothy A. Ross. Whirlwind. San francisco (1977) See chap 13 of this novel for descr of new year observances in wealthy shantung gentry family in 1920s, 150-166.

Choi, Chi-cheung. The chinese "yue lan" ghost festival in japan: a kobe case study. JHKBRAS 24 (1984) 230-263, illus photos, tables, app, documents.

Festivals and fine arts, taiwan, republic of china. Taipei (n.d. 1985?) 80 p, illus col photos.

Foh, Chang Pat. Ching ming festival. SarGaz 111, no 1493 (oct 1985) 22-29.

Garrett, Valery M. A hoklo wedding. JHKBRAS 27 (1987) 112-116.

Groot, J. J. M. de (tsl fr dutch by C. G. Chavannes) Les fêtes annuellement célébrées à émoui (amoy) Etude concernant la religion populaire des chinois. Being AMG 1 and 2 (1886) Repr taipei (1977) repr NY (1981)

Hayes, James. Lantern festival, cheung chau, 10th february 1971. JHKBRAS 26 (1986) 267-270.

Holzman, Donald. The cold food festival in early medieval china. HJAS 46.1 (june 1986) 51-80.

Huang, Yu-mei. Braving the 'bees' FCR 34 (sic) (apr 1983) 60-61, illus col photos. Re release of "bee" firecrackers during lantern festival at yenshui, tainan county.

Huang, Yu-mei. China's first festival. FCR 32.11 (nov 1982) 68-72, illus col photos.

Huang, Yu-mei. The light arts. FCR 34.4 (apr 1983) 56-59, illus col photos. Re lantern festival and its lanterns.

Huang, Yu-mei. The making of a dragon boat. FCR 34 (sic) (july 1983) 49-53, illus col photos.

Johnson, David. The city-god cults of t'ang and sung china. HJAS 45.2 (dec 1985) 363-457.

Jones, Douglas. Chinese festivals. In Alan Brown (ed) Festivals in world religions, NY (1986) 60-73.

Lai, Kuan Fook. The hennessy book of chinese festivals. Kuala lumpur (1984) 93 p.

Latsch, Marie-Luise. Chinese traditional festivals. Beijing (1984) 107 p.

Law, Joan (photos) & Barbara E. Ward (text)

Chinese festivals in hong kong. HK (1982) 95 p, 85 col pl, index, gloss, festival calendar.

Lee, Peter K. H. A chinese new year interreligious celebration (hong kong) CF 25.1 (mar 1982) 32-36.

Mindich, Jeffrey. Chu yuan—a man mourned 2,200 years. He died for truth and justice. FCR 35.6 (june 1985) 2-9, many illus. Re traditon behind tuan wu festival.

Modder, Ralph P. Chinese temple festivals. HK (1983) 69 p.

Ng, Greer Anne. The dragon and the lamb: chinese festivals in the life of chinese canadian/american christians. RelEd 84 (summer 1989) 368-383.

Sellman, James D. From myth to festival: a structural analysis of the chinese new year celebration. CC 23.2 (june 1982) 41-58.

Shiratori, Yoshiro (ed) The dragon boat festival in hong kong. Tokyo, sophia univ (1985)

Siu, Helen F. Recycling tradition: culture, history, and political economy in the chrysanthemum festivals of south china. CSSH 32.4 (oct 1990) 765-794.

Teiser, Stephen F. The ghost festival in medieval china. Princeton univ (1988) xvii + 275 p, char gloss, bibliog, index.

Teiser, Stephen F. Ghosts and ancestors in medieval chinese religion: the yü-lan-p'en festival as mortuary ritual. HR 26.1 (aug 1986) 47-67.

Teiser, Stephen F. The ritual behind the opera: a fragmentary ethnography of the ghost festival, a.d.400-1900. In RO/OR (1989) 191-223.

Thompson, Laurence G. Dancing lions. JCR 15 (1987) 29-43. Lions in various festival contexts.

Thompson, Laurence G. Chinese religious year. EncyRel 3 (1987) 323a-328a.

Tirone, Gail (text) & Lin Bor-liang (photos) A gathering of deities occasions folk celebrations.

FCR 36.7 (july 1986) 36-41. Re peikang matsu festival, 27 apr 86.

Wang, Emily. New year prints. FCR 35.3 (mar 1985) 42-53, many col illus.

Yang, Chongguang. Fêtes traditionelles de chine. Revue francaise de pékin 2 (1983) 82-101.

II.33 Temples and Mountains - Pilgrimage

Andersen, Poul. A visit to hua-shan. CEA 5 (1989-90) 349-364.

Bertuccioli, Giuliano. Mao-shan revisited. E&W 35 (1985) 277-279. "Continuation and conclusion" of author's art of 1974 in E&W 24, 403-415, q.v.

Chen, Dacan. Tsl fr unpubl ms by J. L. (John Lagerwey?) Notes sur un voyage à gezaoshan. CEA 4 (1988) 167-173. Re a taoist mt in chianghsi.

Dove, Victor. Temples, tombs and gardens in szechwan. AA 15 (1985) 72-79.

Faure, David & Lee Lai-mui. The po tak temple in sheung shui market. JHKBRAS 22 (1982) 271-279.

Fong, Peng-Khuan. Khoo clan temple of penang. AofA 11.1 (jan-feb 1981) 104-111.

Goodrich, Anne Swann. Chinese hells. The peking temple of eighteen hells and chinese conceptions of hell. St augustin, germany (1981) 167 p, app, bibliog, index, 32 pl.

Hahn, Thomas. The standard taoist mountain and related features of religious geography. CEA 4 (1988) 145-156, photos.

Hase, Patrick H. Old han wong temple, tai wai, sha tin. JHKBRAS 23 (1983) 233-240.

Hayes, James W. The kwun yam-tung-shan temple of east kowloon 1840-1940. JHKBRAS 23 (1983) 212-218.

90

Hayes, James. Notes on temples and shrines, hong kong island. JHKBRAS 27 (1987) 285-291.

Hayes, James W. Secular non-gentry leadership of temple and shrine organizations in urban british hong kong. JHKBRAS 23 (1983) 113-136.

Hayes, James. The tai sheung lo kwan temple, chaiwan. JHKBRAS 28 (1988) 217-218.

Hua, Cecilia Ng Siew. The sam poh neo neo keramat: a study of a baba chinese temple. In CFRSM (1983) 98-131.

Humphrey, Peter. Temples in the city of xian: a reflection of the religious situation in china. RCL 8 (winter 1980) 274-278.

Jong, Kiam Chun. Tua pek kong temple of kuching. SarGaz 1478 (dec 1981) 39-45.

Kroll, Paul W. Verses from on high: the ascent of t'ai shan. TP 69.4/5 (1983) 223-260.

Lagerwey, John. Le pèlinerage taoïque en chine. In Jean Chelini & Henry Branthomme (ed) Histoire des pèlinerages non chrétien ... paris (1987) 311-327.

Leu, Chien-ai. Photos by Chung Yung-ho. Temple roof art. FCR 40.11 (nov 1990) 34-45, col photos. Re ornamentation of temple roofs in chien nien technique.

Li, Shiyu. Investigation and research of the temple of shun-tian bao-ming. Proc31stICHS, tokyo, vol 2 (1984) 876. Abstr.

Lip, Evelyn. Chinese temple architecture. Architect 94 (mar 1987) 17-19. Re temples in china mainland, singapore, malaysia.

Lip, Evelyn. Chinese temple architecture in singapore. Singapore univ (1983) 114 p, col photos, drawings, fig, app, bibliog, chin char used throughout.

Lip, Evelyn. Chinese temples and deities. Singapore (1981) 107 p, gloss, bibliog, profusely illus. Same title, also publ in singapore (1986) 112 p. Author states, "Some of the material for this book has been extracted from Chinese temples & deities published in 1981 ..."

Mount taishan. n.p. (Hua yi publ house) (1988) 78 p, illus.

Ng, Teng Seng. Siang on kong temple. Jernal persatuan sej mal sar 5 (june 1980) 24-34.

Picture album of mt wudang taoist shrine. n.p. (Hua yi publ house) (1990) 64 p, col pix with chin and engl captions.

Reiter, Florian C. Die ausführungen li tao-yüans zur geschichte und geographie des berges lu (chiang-hsi) in kommentar zum wasserklassiker, und ihre bedeutung für die regionale geschichtsschreibung. OE 28 (1981) 15-29.

Reiter, Florian C. Bergmonographien als geographische und historische quellen, dargestellt an ch'en shun-yüs bericht über den berg lu (lushan chi) aus dem 11. jahrhundert. ZDMG 130 (1978) 397-407.

Reiter, Florian C. Der bericht über den berg lu (lushan chi) von ch'en shun-yü, ein historiographischer beitrag aus der sung zeit zum kulturraum des lu shan. SYSN 15 (1979) 132-133. Abstr.

Schmidt-Glintzer, Helwig. Bergesteigungen in china—zu wandlungen und dauerhaftigkeit einer daseinmetapher. ZDMG Supplementa 7 (1989) 469-481. Re mainly to lit.

Tirone, Gail (text) Shen Yi (photos) A very brief visit to the halls of hell. FCR 35.7 (july 1985) 62-65. Re tung-yüeh miao in tainan.

Tseng, Yung-li (text) Joseph Chen (photos) Chinese temple rococo. FCR 38.1 (jan 1988) 50-56.

Tseng, Yung-li (text) Shen Yi (photos) Spirit of a temple. FCR 36.2 (feb 1986) 50-57. Re taipei's lung-shan ssu.

Wells, Mariann Kaye. Chinese temples in california. Univ calif (1962) 108 p, app, photos, fig. Repr of univ of calif thesis.

II.34 Ritual

Ahern, Emily Martin. Chinese ritual and politics. Cambridge univ (1981) 144 p, notes, bibliog, char list, index.

Ames, Roger T. Rites as rights: the confucian alternative. In HR&WR (1988) 199-216.

Blacking, John. Problems in the documentation and analysis of ritual. In STR&MT (1989) 10-14.

Bulling, Anneliese Guttkind. Rites mentioned in han tomb inscriptions and the funerary art of han and pre-han periods. Proc31stICHS, tokyo, vol 2 (1984) 929. Abstr.

Chiao, Chien. Cognitive play: some minor rituals among hong king chinese. EAC-2 (1983) 138-144.

Ching, Julia. Chu hsi and ritual. In EsurR (1990) 57-76.

Cua, A. S. Li and moral justification: a study in the li chi. PEW 33.1 (jan 1983) 1-16.

DeBary, Wm Theodore. Human rites—an essay on confucian and human rights. CN 22.4 (fall 1984) 307-313.

Ebrey, Patricia. Education through ritual: efforts to formulate family rituals during the sung period. In NCEduc (1989) 277-306.

Gates, Hill. Money for the gods. ModCh 13.1 (jan 1987) 259-277.

Hayes, James. Occasional protective rites. In RC/HK (1983) 165-178.

Hayes, James. Periodic protective rites. In RC/HK (1983) 156-164.

Hayes, James W. Supplication and thanksgiving ceremonies. In RC/HK (1983) 204-205.

Ho, Yun-i. Chinese ritual and sacrifice. In Ainslee T. Embree (ed in chief) Encyclopedia of asian history, NY & london, vol 1 (1988) 296a-299a.

Ho, Yun-i. Ideological implications of major sacrifices in early ming. MingSt 6 (spring 1978) 55-73. Re imperial sacrifices.

Ho, Yün-yi. The ministry of rites and suburban sacrifices in early ming. Taipei (preface 1980) 327 p, 9 app, illus, notes, bibliog.

Ho, Yün-yi. Revitalization of the cult of heaven: ceremonial politics in the early ming. National chengchi univ journal 42 (dec 1980) 17-30.

Hwang, Philip H. Fingarette's interpretation of confucius' view of ritual. D&A 4.1 (spring 1990) 96-104.

Jao, Tsung-i. Le canon des rites et quelques théories majeures du ritualisme suivant le commentaire de zuo des annales des printemps et automnes. In EsurR (1990) 27-44.

Kurihara, Keisuke. On the yin-ssu in ancient china. MexICHS, China, vol 2 (1976) 3-7. Re ancient sacrifice.

Levi, Jean. Le silence du rite. TdelaR 6 (1985) 75-80. Education, incl relig aspects, in ancient china.

Liu, Chiang. Religion, funeral rites, sacrifices and festivals in kirin. ChRec 65 (1934) 227-238. Same title in ACCS (1958-59) 8-20.

McCreery, John. Why don't we see some real money here? Offerings in chinese religion. JCR 18 (fall 1990) 1-24.

McMullen, David. Bureaucrats and cosmology: the ritual code of t'ang china. In D. Cannadine & S. Price (ed) Rituals of royalty, cambridge univ (1987) 181-236.

McMullen, D. L. A note on the feng ritual of 742 in response to professor elling eide. TS 2 (winter 1984) 37-40.

Naundorf, Gert. Raumvorstellung in den chiao-opfern bis zur han-zeit. In RPA-O (1985) 323-330.

92

Paper, Jordan. The ritual core of chinese religion. Religious studies and theology 7 (may-sept 1987) 19-35.

Ruitenbeck, Klaas. Craft and ritual in traditional chinese carpentry. ChSci 7 (dec 1986) 1-23. Ritual and magic; lu pan ching; special footrules.

Sangren, P. Steven. Orthodoxy, heterodoxy, and the structure of value in chinese rituals. ModCh 13.1 (jan 1987) 63-89.

Sato, Koji. "Chao-sheng"—the religious ritual to save departed souls in taiwan. TJR 22 (dec 1988) 91-104.

Schipper, Kristofer. Chiens de paille et tigres en papier: une pratique rituelle et ses gloses au cours de la traditon chinois. EOEO 6 (1985) 83-94. Theme of this issue: "Une civilisation sans théologie?"

Schipper, K. M. Le rituel du corps de remplacement en chine. Quatrième colloque pluridisciplinaire franco-japonaise, paris (1985)

Schipper, Kristofer. Tchouang-tseu et les rites. In André Caquot & Pierre Caniver (ed) Ritualisme et vie intérieure: religion et culture . . . paris (1989) 105-115.

Seaman, Gary. Spirit money: an interpretation. JCR 10 (1982) 80-91.

Skaja, Henry G. Li (ceremonial) as a primal concept in confucian spiritual humanism. CC 25 (mar 1984) 1-26.

Smith, Richard J. Ritual in ch'ing culture. In OLIC (1990) 281-310.

Steinhardt, Nancy Shatzman. The han ritual hall. In CTA (1984) 69-77.

Steinhardt, Nancy Shatzman. The mingtang of wang mang. Orientations 15.11 (1984) 42-48.

Strickmann, Michel. Therapeutische rituale und das problem des bösen im frühen taoismus. In RPO-A (1985) 185-200.

Sutton, Donald S. Ritual drama and moral order: interpreting the gods' festival troupes of southern taiwan. JAS 49.3 (aug 1990) 535-554.

Sutton, Donald S. Rituals of self-mortification: taiwanese spirit-mediums in comparative perspective. JRS 4.1 (1990) 99-125.

Swart, Paula & Barry Till. A revival of confucian ceremonies in china. In TT:RCT (1989) 210-221, illus.

Teng, Shu-p'ing. Tsl and adapted by Susan Naquin & Curtis H. Brizendine. Two sets of jade tablets in the national palace museum collection. NPMB 11.6 (jan-feb 1977) 1-17. Tablets used in feng and shan sacrifices during t'ang and sung.

Tham, Seong Chee. Religion and modernization: a study of changing rituals among singapore's chinese, malays, and indians. East asian cultural studies 23.1-4 (mar 1984) entire issue, 186 p, illus b-&-w photos.

Thompson, Laurence G. Confucian thought: the state cult. EncyRel 4 (1987) 36a-38b.

Thompson, Laurence G. Popular and classical modes of ritual in a taiwanese temple. SSCRB 9 (1981) 106-122.

Tsien, Tsuen-hsuin. Paper and printing. Being vol 5 pt 1 of Joseph Needham, Science & civilisation in china. (1985) See 32(d) (3) Ceremonial uses of paper, 102-109.

Vandermeersch, Léon. Aspects rituels de la popularization du confucianisme sous les han. In T&L (1990) 89-107.

Vandermeersch, Léon. Ritualisme et juridisme. In EsurR (1990) 45-56.

Verellen, Franciscus. Liturgy and sovereignty: the role of taoist ritual in the foundation of the shu kingdom (907-925) AM 3rd ser 2.1 (1989) 59-78.

Vidal, Jacques. [Material on china] In J. Ries & H. Limet (ed) Les rîtes d'initiation, louvain-la-neuve (1986) 41-48.

Wechsler, Howard J. Offerings of jade and silk. Ritual and symbol in the legitimation of the t'ang dynasty. Yale univ (1985) xi + 313 p, notes, sel bibliog, gloss-index.

Zito, Angela Rose. Re-presenting sacrifice: cosmology and the editing of texts. CSWT 5.2 (dec 1984) 47-78. Re imperial sacrifice, li, and ritual text editing.

II.35 Divination

Aune, David E. Oracles. EncyRel 11 (1987) 81-87.

Banck, Werner. Der Chinese tempelorakel; teil II: übersetzung und analysen. Wiesbaden (1985) xxx + 393 s.

Berthier, Brigitte. Enfant de divination, voyageur du destin. l'Homme 101 (jan-mar 1987) 86-100. Re chi-t'ung medium; "destin" is space-time.

Bielenstein, Hans. Han portents and prognostications. BMFEA 56 (1984) 97-112.

Bonhoure, Frédérique, Mile Sun & Oscar Lax. La maison de la réussite: astrologie et géomancie chinoise. Paris (1989) 215 p.

Brown, Chappel. Inner truth and the origin of the yarrow stalk oracle. JCP 9 (1982) 190-211.

Chan, Wing-tsit. Memories, dreams, divination, and popular beliefs. Chap 7 in author's CH:NS (1989) 106-125.

Chang, Cheng-lang. Tsl by H. Huber, R. Yates, et al. An interpretation of the divinatory inscriptions on early chou bronzes. EC 6 (1980-81) 80-96.

Choong, Ket Che. Chinese divination—an ethnographic case study. In CFRSM (1983) 49-97.

Despeux, Catherine. La divination en chine. In MetC (1985) 318-326.

Drège, Jean-Pierre. Notes d'onirologie chinoise. BEFEO 70 (1981) 271-289.

Fracasso, Riccardo. Teratoscopy or divination by monsters: being a study of the wu-tsang shan-ching. HHYC:CS 1.2 (dec 1983) 657-700. Text is first 5 books of shan hai ching.

Gernet, Jacques. Petits écarts et grands écarts. In J. P. Vernant et al, Divination et rationalité, ?paris (1974) 52-69.

Harlez, C. de. Miscellanées chinois. 1—Le rêve dans les croyances chinoises. Bruxelles (date ?) 22 p.

Hegel, Robert E. Heavens and hells in chinese fictional dreams. In P-S (1988) 1-10

Heinze, Ruth-Inge. Social implications of the relationships between mediums, entourages and clients in singapore today. SEAJSocSci 7 (1979) 60-80.

Ho, Kwok Man, Martin Palmer & Joanne O'Brien. Lines of destiny. How to read faces and hands the chinese way. Boston (1986) 190 p.

Hou, Ching-lang. Physiognomie d'après le teint sous la dynastie des t'ang. CETH vol 1 (1979) 55-66, 2 fig, 6 pl.

Jordan, David. Eufunctions, dysfunctions, and oracles: literary miracle making in taiwan. In PCCS (1990) 98-115.

Jordan, David K. Taiwanese poe divination: statistical awareness and religious belief. JSSR 21 (1982) 114-118.

Kalinowski, Marc. La littérature divinatoire dans le daozang. CEA 5 (1989-90) 85-114. Re some 40 texts on divination.

Kalinowski, Marc. Les traités de shuihudi et l'hémérologie chinois à la fin des royaumes-combattants. TP 72.4-5 (1986) 175-228. Fr tomb excavation at shuihudi in hupei.

Keightley, David N. Late shang divination: the magico-religious legacy. In Henry Rosemont (ed) Explorations in early chinese cosmology, chico, calif (1984) 11-34.

Keightley, David N. Shang divination and meta-physics. PEW 38.4 (1988) 367-397.

Kermadec, Jean-Michel Huon de. Tsl by N. Derek Poulsen. The way of chinese astrology. The four pillars of destiny. London (1983) Orig french ed titled Les huit signes de votre destin, publ in paris (date?)

Kohn, Livia. A mirror of auras: chen tuan on physiognomy. AsFS 47 (1988) 215-256.

Kohn, Livia. A textbook of physiognomy: the tradition of the shenxiang quanbian. AsFS 45.2 (1986) 227-258. Re standard work by yuan chung-ch'e, ming dyn.

Kudo, Motoo. Tsl by P. A. Herbert. The ch'in bamboo strip book of divination (jih-shu) and ch'in legalism. ActaA 58 (mar 1990) 24-37.

Lackner, Michael. Der chinesische traumwald: traditionelle theorien des traumes und seiner deutung im spiegel der ming-zeitlichen anthologie meng-lin hsuan-chieh. Frankfurt etc (1985)

Lau, Theodora. The handbook of chinese horoscopes. London (1981)

Lessa, William A. The chinese trigrams in micronesia. JAFL 82, no 326 (oct-dec 1969) 353-362.

Loewe, Michael. The almanacs (jih-shu) from shui-hu-ti: a preliminary survey. AM 3rd ser 1.2 (1988) 1-27. Texts fr recent excavations in hupei.

Loewe, Michael. China. In M. Loewe & Carmen Blacker (ed) Oracles and divination, london & boulder, colo (1981) 38-62.

Loewe, Michael. Divination by shells, bones and stalks during the han period. TP 74.1-3 (1988) 81-118.

Loewe, Michael. The oracles of the clouds and the winds. BSOAS 51.3 (1988) 500-520.

Martel, Francois. Les boussoles divinatoires chinoises. Communications 19 (1972) 115-137.

Morgan, Carole. A propos des fiches oraculaires de huang daxian. JA 275 (1987) 163-191. Re oracle slips in huang daxian temple, HK.

Morgan, Carole. La divination d'après les cris de corbeaux. CEC 8 (1989) 57-76.

Morgan, Carole. La divination d'après les croassements des corbeaux dans les manuscrits de dunhuang. CEA 3 (1987) 55-76.

Morgan, Carole. Dog divination from a dunhuang manuscript. JHKBRAS 23 (1983) 184-193.

Morgan, Carole. Les "neuf palais" dans les manuscrits de touen-houang. In NCET (1981) 251-260.

Palmer, Martin (ed & tsl) with Mak Hin Chung, Kwok Man Ho & Angela Smith. T'ung shu. The ancient chinese almanac. Boston (1986) 240 p, chin text and illus, app incl notes, gloss, bibliog.

Pas, Julian. Temple oracles in a chinese city. A study of the use of temple oracles in taichung, central taiwan. JHKBRAS 24 (1984) 1-15.

Penny, Benjamin. A system of fate calculation in taiping jing. PFEH 41 (mar 1990) 1-8.

Russell, T. C. Chen tuan at mount huangbo: a spirit-writing cult in late ming china. AS 44.1 (1990) 107-140.

Schmidt-Glintzer, Helwig. Die manipulation von omina und ihre beurteilung bei hofe. Das beispiel der himmelsbriefe wang ch'in-jo (962-1025) unter chen-tsung treierte 998-1023. AS 35.1 (1981) 1-14.

Seiwert, Hubert Michael. Orakelwesen und zukunfsdeutung im chinesischen altertum. Eine religionsgeschichtliche untersuchung zur entwicklung der welt- und menschenbildes während der zhou-dynastie. Bonn (1979) 352 s, tabellen, anmerkungen, literaturverzeichnis.

Smith, Richard J. Knowing fate: divination in late imperial china. JCStudies 3.2 (oct 1986) 153-190.

Thompson, Laurence G. Dream divination and chinese popular religion. JCR 16 (1988) 73-82.

Thompson, Laurence G. The moving finger writes: a note on revelation and renewal in chinese religion. JCR 10 (1982) 92-147.

Tsui, Bartholomew P. M. The place of fu-chi (spirit-writing) in modern taoist sects in hong kong. CF 33 (sept 1990) 176-189.

Vandermeersch, Léon. Origine et évolution de l'achilléomancie chinoise. CRAIBL (nov-dec 1990, fasc 4) 949-961. With a few comments by Jacques Gernet, 962-963.

Vandermeersch, Léon. Les origines divinatoires de la tradition chinoise du parallélisme littéraire. EOEO 11 (1989) 11-33.

Vandermeersch, Léon. De la tortue à l'achillée. In J. P. Vernant et al, Divination et rationalité ? paris (d ?) 29-51.

Wagner, Rudolf G. Imperial dreams. In P-S (1988) 11-24. Re dreams of emperors.

Zhang, Yachu & Liu Yu. Tsl by . Some observations about milfoil divination based on shang and zhou bagua numerical symbols. EC 7 (1981-82) 46-55.

II.36 Shamanism - Spirit Mediums

Berthier, Brigitte. Enfant de divination, voyageur du destin. l'Homme 27 no 101 (jan-mars 1987) 86-100. Re chi-t'ung medium; "destin" is space-time.

Chang, Kwang-chih. Art, myth, and ritual. The path to political authority in ancient china. Harvard univ (1983) 160 p, 38 photos, 24 line drawings. See chap 3, Shamanism and politics, 44-55; chap 4, Art as the path to authority, 56-80. Chap 4 "published in slightly different form" as The animal in shang and chou bronze art, HJAS 41 (dec 1981) 527-554.

Chow, Tse-tsung. Ancient chinese wu shamanism and its relationship to sacrifices, history, dance-music, and poetry. TJ n.s. 13.1/2 (dec 1981) Engl summ 23-25.

Ecsedy, I. The new year's tree and other traces of ancient shamanistic cult in china. In Mihály Hoppál (ed) Shamanism in eurasia, part 1 [of 2] göttingen (1984) 107-121.

Harvey, E. D. Shamanism in china. In Studies in the science of society presented to a. g. keller, yale univ (1937) 247-266.

Heinze, Ruth-Inge. Automatic writing in singapore. In CFRSM (1983) 146-160.

Huey, Ju Shi. Chinese spirit mediums in singapore: an ethnographic study. In CFRSM (1983) 3-48.

Izutsu, Toshihiko. Celestial journey: mythopoesis and metaphysics. EJ 51 (1982) 449-477. As exemplified by ch'ü yüan, "shaman-poet"

Jordan, David K. & Daniel L. Overmyer. The flying phoenix. Aspects of chinese sectarianism in taiwan. Princeton univ (1986) xiv + 329 p, 8 photo-illus, app, works cited, index. See rev by H. Seiwert in MS 37 (1986-87) 380-383.

Kagan, Richard C. & Anna Wasescha. The taiwanese tang-ki: the shaman as community healer and protector. In SICS (1982) 112-141.

Kendall, Laurel. Korean shamanism: women's rites and a chinese comparison. In RFEA (1986) 57-73.

Kendall, Laurel. Supernatural traffic—east asian shamanism. CM&P 5.2 (1981) 171-191. Rev art on studies of shamanism in korea, japan and taiwan.

Lee, Raymond L. M. Continuity and change in chinese spirit mediumship in urban malaysia. BTLVK 142.2-3 (1986) 198-214.

Lee, Raymond L. M. Dancing with the gods: a spirit medium festival in urban malaysia. Anthropos 78 (1983) 355-368.

Mathieu, Rémi. Chamanes et chamanisme en chine ancienne. l'Homme 27 no 101 (1987) 10-34.

Pas, Julian F. Journey to hell: a new report of shamanistic travel to the courts of hell. JCR 17 (1989) 43-60.

Sawatsky, Sheldon. Chinese shamanism. TJT 12 (mar 1990) 121-143.

Seaman, Gary. The divine authorship of pei-yu chi [journey to the north] JAS 45.3 (may 1986) 483-497.

Sutton, Donald. Pilot survey of chinese shamans, 1875-1945; a spatial approach to social history. Journal of social history 15.2 (fall 1981) 39-50.

Sutton, Donald S. Rituals of self-mortification: taiwanese spirit-mediums in comparative perspective. JRS 4.1 (1990) 99-125.

Wolf, Margery. The woman who didn't become a shaman. AmEth 17.2 (aug 1990) 419-430. Taiwan case.

Yen, Alsace. Shamanism as reflected in the folktale. AsFS 39.2 (1980) 105-121.

II.37 Magic - Witchcraft - Sorcery

Cahill, Suzanne. The word made bronze: inscriptions on medieval chinese bronze mirrors. AAA 39 (1986) 62-70. Mirrors as numinous objects to taoists.

Cavendish, Richard (ed in chief) Man, myth and magic. NY etc (1983) An 11-vol encyclopedia, profusely illus; see Index vol, under china.

Chard, Robert. Magicians as artisans: a han usage of the word kung. PTP 16 (1984) 61-81.

Cochod, Louis. Occultisme et magie en extrême-orient: inde, indochine, chine. Paris (1949). See chap 3, La magie primitive de la chine, 229-316.

Delahaye, Hubert. Les antécédents magiques des statues chinoises. Revue d'esthétique n.s. 2 (1983) 45-53.

Dubs, Homer H. The kang-mao amulets. Chap 99, app 3 in HFHD 3 (1955) 537-543.

Glum, Peter. Rain magic at anyang? Speculations about two ritual bronze vessels of the shang dynasty filled with revolving dragons. BMFEA 54 (1982) 241-272.

Harper, Donald. Magic: magic in east asia. EncyRel 9 (1987) 112b-115a.

Harper, Donald. A note on nightmare magic in ancient and medieval china. TS 6 (1988) 69-76.

Hsu, Francis L. K. Exorcising the trouble makers. Magic, science, and culture. Westport, conn (1983) xvi + 164 p, 2 app, bibliog, index. Incorporates author's 1942 study, Religion science, and human crisis, q.v.

Hsu, Francis L. K. Religion, science and human crisis. London (1952) 142 p. Incorporated in author's Exorcising the troublemakers, westport, conn & london (1983)

Kuhn, Philip A. Soulstealers. The chinese sorcery scare of 1768. Harvard univ (1990) 299 p, notes, bibliog, maps, illus, index.

Lackner, Michael. Der chinesische traumwald: traditionelle theorien d. traumes u. seiner deutung im spiegel d. ming-zeitl. Anthologie meng-lin-hsüan-chieh. Frankfurt am main, bern, NY (1985)

Murray, Julia K. & Suzanne E. Cahill. Recent advances in understanding the mystery of ancient chinese "magic mirrors"; a brief summary of chinese analytical and experimental studies. ChSci 8 (jan 1987) 1-8.

Parrinder, Geoffrey. Exorcism. EncyRel 5 (1987) See sec, China and north asia, 227a-228b.

Qui, Xigui. Tsl by Vernon K. Fowler. On the burning of human victims and the fashioning of clay dragons in order to seek rain as seen in the shang dynasty oracle-bone inscriptions. EC 9-10 (1983-85) 290-306.

Riegel, Jeffrey K. Early chinese target magic. JCR 10 (1982) 1-18.

Roth, Harold D. Fang-shih. EncyRel 5 (1987) 282b-284a.

Ruitenbeck, Klaas. Craft and ritual in traditional chinese carpentry. ChSci 7 (dec 1986) 1-23. Ritual and magic; lu pan ching; special footrules...

Topley, Marjorie. China. In Man, myth and magic (see under Cavendish, Richard, ed) (1985) 456-464.

II.38 Religion and Medicine

Akahori, Akira. Drug taking and immortality. In TMLT (1989) 73-98.

Anderson, E. N. & Marja L. Folk medicine in rural hong kong. In CE (1973) 121-126.

Belgum, David. Medicine and morals and mao. Journal of religion and health 17 (oct 1978) 261-273.

Birnbaum, Raoul. Chinese buddhist traditions of healing and the life cycle. In Lawrence E. Sullivan (ed) Healing and restoring: health and medicine in the world's religious traditions, ?place of publ (1989) 33-57.

Browning, Don S. Medicine, modernization and religion in the people's republic of china. Second opinion: health, faith and ethics 4 (1987) 10-29.

Cass, Victoria B. Female healers in the ming and the lodge of ritual and ceremony. JAOS 106.1 (jan-mar 1986) 233-240.

Chen, Lucy H. (Chen Hsiu-mei) Spirit calling. In author's collection, Spirit calling: tales about taiwan, taipei (1962) 73-87. Fictional account of calling sick person's spirit by taoist priest.

Despeux, Catherine (tsl). Préscriptions d'acuponcture valant mille onces d'or. Paris (1987) Text is last 2 chap of ch'ien-chin fan by sun ssu-mo (t'ang dyn)

Despeux, Catherine. Taiki k'iuan: technique de combat, technique de longue vie. Paris (1976)

Engelhardt, Ute. Die klassische tradition der qi-übungen (qigong). Eine darstellung anhand des tang zeitlichen textes fuqi jinyi lun von sima chengzhen. Wiesbaden (1987) 328 p + engl summ.

Hillier, S. M. & J. A. Jewell. Health care and traditional medicine in china, 1800-1982. London etc (1983) See chap 7, Theoretical basis of chinese traditional medicine, 221-241, passim.

Hsu, Francis L. K. Exorcising the trouble makers. Magic, science, and culture. Westport, conn (1983) xvi + 164 p, 2 app, bibliog, index. Incorporates author's 1942 work, Religion, science, and human crisis, q.v.

Huang, William & Mary Stark. Chinese medical tradition: the way of tai ji. Interculture (engl ed) 21 (oct-dec 1988) 19-40.

Klein, H. Die esoterik in der medizinphilosophie chinas. Untersuchen zu leben und werk der arztphilosophen der ming-zeit chang chieh-pin. ?place of publ (1986) 275 s.

Kleinman, Arthur & James L. Gale. Patients treated by physicians and folk healers: a comparative outcome study in taiwan. CM&P 6.4 (dec 1982) 405-423.

Kleinman, Arthur et al (ed) Medicine in chinese cultures: comparative studies of health care in chinese and other societies. Washington d.c. (1975) Art sep listed in this bibliog; abbrev MCC.

Kohn, Livia. Medicine and immortality in t'ang china. JAOS 108.3 (july-sept 1988) 465-469. Rev art on Ute Engelhardt, Die klassische tradition der qi-übungen... q.v.

Lindseth, John. Preventative medicine according to taoist principles. International journal of holistic health and medicine 1.2 (nov 1982-mar 1983) 6-7.

Miura, Kunio. The revival of qi: qigong in contemporary china. In TMLT (1989) 331-362.

Morris, Brian. Thoughts on chinese medicine. The eastern anthropologist [lucknow, india] 42.1 (jan-mar 1989) 1-33.

Porkert, Manfred. Greifbarkeit und ergriffensein: das körperverständnis in der chinesischen medizin. EJ 52 (1983) 389-429.

Qiu, R.-z. Medicine, the art of humaneness: on the ethics of traditional chinese medicine. JMP 13.3 (1988) 277-300.

Sakade, Yoshinobu. Longevity techniques in japan: ancient sources and contemporary studies. In TMLT (1989) 1-40. The "ancient sources" incl chin texts.

Sakade, Yoshinobu. The p'eng-tsu legend and the p'eng-tsu-ching—ideas for keeping in good health in ancient china. Proc31stICHS, tokyo, vol 1 (1984) 259-260. Abstr.

Sakade, Yoshinobu. The taoist character of the 'chapter on nourishing life' of the ishinpo. KDBR (1986) 775-798.

Schiffeler, John William. Chinese folk medicine. A study of the shan-hai ching. AsFS 39.2 (1980) 41-83. Same title in AJCM 12.1-4 (1984) 2-31.

Straten, N. H. van. Concepts of health, disease and vitality in traditional china. A psychological interpretation. Based on the research materials of George Koeppen. Wiesbaden (1983) 193 p, bibliog, index.

Strickmann, Michel. Dreamwork of psychosinologists: doctors, taoists, monks. In P-S (1988) 25-46.

Strickmann, Michel. Therapeutische rituale und das problem des bösen frühen taoismus. In RPO-A (1985) 185-200.

Thompson, Laurence G. Medicine and religion in late ming china. JCR 18 (1990) 45-59.

Trying to tempt back the soul of an unconscious

invalid. Annual report of the church missionary society, london (1906) 319.

Unschuld, Paul U. The chinese reception of indian medicine in the first millenium a.d. BHM 53.3 (fall 1979) 329-345.

Unschuld, Paul U. Medicine in china. A history of ideas. Univ calif (1985) See first 6 chap, passim.

Veith, Ilza. Medicine and religion in eastern traditions. EncyRel 9 (1987) 312b-319a.

II.39 Religion in Folklore, Tract, Literature and Drama

Ang, A. C. Taoist-buddhist elements in wang wei's poetry. CC 30.1 (mar 1989) 79-89.

Baldrian-Hussein, Farzeen. Yüeh yang and lü tung-pin's ch'in yüan ch'un: a sung alchemical poem. RPO-A (1985) 19-31.

Berling, Judith A. Religion and popular culture: the management of moral capital in the romance of the three teachings [san-chiao k'ai-rui kuei- cheng yen-i] In PopCult (1985) 188-218.

Bonnet, J. Un roman initiatique chinois. EtTrad 88 no 495 (1987) 27-37. Re shui hu chuan.

Brokaw, Cynthia. Guidebooks to social and moral success: the morality books in 16th and 17th century china. ICfO 27 (1982) 137-141. Re pao-chuan.

Brokaw, Cynthia. Yüan huang (1533-1606) and the ledgers of merit and demerit. HJAS 47.1 (june 1987) 137-195.

Cahill, Suzanne. Beside the turquoise pond: the shrine of the queen mother of the west in medieval chinese poetry and religious practice. JCR 12 (1984) 19-32.

Cahill, Suzanne. Sex and the supernatural in medieval china: cantos on the transcendent who presides over the river. JAOS 105.2 (1985) 197-220.

Cahill, Suzanne. A white clouds appointment with the queen mother of the west. JCR 16 (1988) 43-53.

Campany, Robert. Cosmogony and self-cultivation: demonic and the ethical in two chinese novels. JRE 14.1 (spring 1986) 81-112. Re hsi yu chi and feng shen yen-i.

Campany, Robert F. Demons, gods and pilgrims: the demonology of the hsi-yu chi. ChLit 7.1-2 (1985) 95-115.

Campany, Robert. Return-from-death narratives in early medieval china. JCR 18 (1990) 91-125.

Carlitz, Katherine. The conclusion of the jin ping mei. MingSt 10 (spring 1980) 23-29.

Carlitz, Katherine. The rhetoric of the chin p'ing mei. Indiana univ (1986) See chap 3, Religion in chin p'ing mei, 53-69.

Ch'iu, K'un-liang. Mu-lien "operas" in taiwanese funeral rituals. In RO/OR (1989) 105-125.

Chan, Alan K. L. Goddesses in chinese religions. In Goddesses (1990) 9-81. Focuses particularly on taoist female deities.

Chan, Stephen Chingku. The return of the ghost woman: a critical reading of three sung hua-pen stories. ACQ 15.3 (autumn 1987) 47-72.

Chan, Wing-tsit. Neo-confucian philosophical poems. Renditions 4 (spring 1975) 5-21. As much relig as philos.

Chang, H. C. Chinese literature 3: Tales of the supernatural. Columbia univ (1984) 169 p, genl intro.

Chard, Robert L. Folktales on the god of the stove. HHYC:CS 8.1, vol 1 (june 1990) 149-182.

Chiang, Kuei. Tsl by Timothy A. Ross. Whirlwind. San francisco (1977) See chap 13 of this novel for descr of new year's observances in wealthy shantung gentry family in 1920s, p 150-166.

Cohen, Alvin P. A taiwanese puppeteer and his theatre. AsFS 40 (1981) 33-49.

Cohen, Alvin. Tales of vengeful souls. A sixth century collection of chinese avenging ghost stories. Taipei, paris, HK (1982) xxiv + 166 p. Re yüan hun chih.

Dean, Kenneth. Lei yu-sheng ("thunder is noisy") and mu-lien in the theatrical and funerary traditions of fukien. In RO/OR (1989) 46-104.

Delahaye, Hubert. Les antécédents magiques des statues chinoises. Revue d'esthétique 5 (1983) 45-53.

Demiéville, Paul. l'Oeuvre de wang le zélateur (wang fan-tche) suivi des "instructions domestiques de l'aïeul" (t'ai-kong kia-kiao). Poèmes populaires des t'ang (viiie-xe siècles), édités, traduits et commentés d'après de manuscrits de touen-houang. Paris (1983) 890 p.

Despeux, Catherine. Les lectures alchimiques du hsi-yu chi. In RPO-A (1985) 61-75.

Diény, J.-P. Pour une lexique de l'imagination littéraire en chine. Le symbolisme du soleil. BEFEO 69 (1981) 119-152.

Dragon tales. A collection of chinese stories. Beijing (1988) 232 p, illus sketches. Various comp and tsl into engl.

Dudbridge, Glen. The goddess hua-yüeh san niang and the cantonese ballad ch'ien-hsiang t'ai-tzu. HHYC:CS 8.1, vol 2 (june 1990) 627-646. From medieval cult to contemporary ballad text.

Endres, Günther (tsl) Die sieben meister der volkommenen verwirklichung: der taoistische lehrroman ch'i-chen chuan in übersetzung und im spiegel seiner quellen. Frankfurt am main (1985)

Frodsham, J. D. (ts) Goddesses, ghosts and demons: the collected poems of li he (790-816) San francisco (1983) lx + 290 p, bibliog, index. Rev ed of The poems of li ho, oxford univ (1970)

100

Fu, James S. Mythic and comic aspects of the quest: hsi yu chi as seen through don quixote and huckleberry finn. Singapore univ (1977) 125 p, bibliog, index.

Gjertson, Donald E. The early chinese buddhist miracle tale, a preliminary survey. JAOS 101.3 (july-sept 1981) 287-301.

Gjertson, Donald E. Miraculous retribution: a study and translation of t'ang ling's ming-pao chi. Univ calif center for south & southeast asia studies (1989) 312 p, bibliog, index.

Grant, Beata. The spiritual saga of woman huang: from pollution to purification. In RO/OR (1989) 224-311. Re "one of the many story cycles that... make up the rich complexity of the chinese popular narrative tradition"

Hargett, James M. Playing second fiddle: the luan-bird in early and medieval chinese literature. TP 75.4-5 (1989) 235-262.

Hawkes, David. Quanzhen plays and quanzhen masters. BEFEO 69 (1981) 153-170.

Hegel, Robert E. Heavens and hells in chinese fictional dreams. In P-S (1988) 1-10.

Holzman, Donald. Songs for the gods: the poetry of popular religion in fifth-century china. AM 3rd ser 3.1 (1990) 1-19.

Holzman, Donald. Ts'ao chih and the immortals. AM 3rd ser 1.1 (1988) 15-57. Reviews all of ts'ao chih's prose and poetry on the subj.

Idema, Wilt & Stephen H. West. Chinese theater 1100-1450; a source book. Wiesbaden (1982) See chap 7, Chung-li of the han leads lan ts'ai-ho to enlightenment. Tsl of "anonymous comedy" with intro.

Izutsu, Toshihiko. Celestial journey: mythopoesis and metaphysics. EJ 51 (1982) 449-477. As exemplified by ch'ü yüan, "shaman-poet"

Johnson, David. Actions speak louder than words: the cultural significance of chinese ritual opera. In RO/OR (1989) 1-45.

Johnson, David (ed). Ritual opera, operatic ritual. "Mu-lien rescues his mother" in chinese popular culture. Univ calif (1989) Essays sep listed in this bibliog; abbrev RO/OR.

Johnson, David. The wu tzu-hsü pien-wen and its sources. HJAS 40.1; 40.2 (june & dec 1980) 93-156; 465-505. Re legend of yangtzu river god.

Kao, Hsin-sheng C. Taoist mirror: ching-hua yuan and lao-chuang thought. JCP 15.2 (1988) 151-172.

Kao, Karl S. Y. (ed) Classical chinese tales of the supernatural and the fantastic: selections from the third to the tenth century. Indiana univ (1985) 406 p, bio-bibliog, notes, 2 app, bibliog.

Kroll, Paul. Meng Hao-jan. Boston (1981)

Lackner, Michael. Der chinesische traumwald: traditionelle theorien des traumes und seiner deutung im spiegel der ming-zeitlichen anthologie meng-lin hsuan-chieh. Frankfurt etc (1985)

Lai, Whalen. Popular moral tracts and the chinese personality. CF 25.1 (mar 1982) 22-31. "su-xun" or "popular instructions"

Larsen, Jeanne. Women of religion in t'ang poetry: toward a new pedagogy of reading traditional genres. JCLTA 22.3 (oct 1987) 1-25.

Lauwaert, Francoise. Comtes des dieux, calculs des hommes: essai sur la notion de rétribution dans les contes en langue vulgaire du 17e siècle. TP 76.1-3 (1990) 62-94.

Lee, Peter K. H. Two stories of loyalty. CF 32.1 (mar 1989) 25-40. Ruth in old testament and kuan han-ch'ing's injustice to tou-o.

Levi, Jean. Les fonctionnaires et le divin: luttes de pouvoirs entre divinités et administrateurs dans les contes des six dynasties et des tang. CEA 2 (1986) 81-110. Engl summ 107-110.

Liu, James J. Y. Poetry: chinese religious poetry. EncyRel 11 (1987) 378a-380a.

Liu, Joyce C. H. The protest from the invisible world: the revenge ghost in yuan drama and the elizabethan drama. TR 19.1-4 (aut 1988-sum 1989) 755-776.

Liu, Ts'un-yan. Buddhist sources of the novel feng-shen yen-i. JHKBRAS 1 (1960-61) 68-97.

Loon, Piet van der. Les origines rituelles du théâtre chinois. JA 265.1/2 (1977) 141-168.

Lynn, Richard John. The sudden and gradual in chinese poetry criticism: an examination of the ch'an poetry analogy. In S&G (1987) 381-427.

Ma, Y. M. & Joseph S. M. Lau. Metamorphoses of monkey. JR 58 (july 1978) 309-313.

Mair, Victor H. The contribution of t'ang and five dynasties transformation texts (pien-wen) to later chinese popular literature. Sino-platonic papers no 12, dept of oriental studies, univ penn (1989) 71 p.

Mair, Victor H. Language and ideology in the written popularizations of the sacred edict. In PopCult (1985) 325-359.

Mair, Victor H. & Maxine Belmont Weinstein. Popular literature. In ICTCL (1986) Part 1: Essays: 75-82. Much of this popular literature is relevant to relig.

Martinson, Paul V. The chin p'ing mei as wisdom literature: a methodological essay. MingSt 5 (fall 1977) 44-56. On utilizing novels as source for relig studies.

Mathieu, Rémi. Etude sur la mythologie et l'ethnologie de la chine ancienne. paris, t 1. Traduction annotée du shanhai jing; t 2. Index du shanhai jing. (1983) cxvi + 1223 p.

Overmyer, Daniel L. Attitudes toward the ruler and state in chinese popular religious literature: sixteenth and seventeenth century pao-chüan. HJAS 44 (1984) 347-379.

Overmyer, Daniel L. Values in chinese sectarian literature: ming and ch'ing pao-chüan. In PopCult (1985) 219-254.

Paper, Jordan. Riding on a white cloud: aesthetics as religion in china. Religion 15 (1985) 3-27. Humanities in traditional china and their relig aspects.

Ptak, Roderich. Cheng hos abenteuer im drama und roman der ming-zeit. Stuttgart (1986) See 4, Das konfuzianische weltbild in hsia hsi-yang ... 101-103; 5, Cheng ho und die göttin der seefahrer, 104-111; 19.6, Chang t'ien-shih, 252-254; 19.7, Chin pi feng, 254-257; 20, Die drei lehren, 258-268.

Ptak, Roderich. Hsi-yang chi—an interpretation and some comparisons with hsi-yu chi. ChLit 7.1-2 (july 1985) 117-141.

Ropp, Paul S. Dissent in early modern china. Ju-lin wai-shih and ch'ing social criticism. Univ michigan (1981) See chap 5, The use and abuse of the supernatural: ju-lin wai-shih, literati skepticism, and popular religion, 152-191.

Roth, Robert Paul. Chinese stories and religion. Areopagus (christmas 1990, 4.1) 14-20. Both budd and others.

Rothfork, John. Confucianism in timothy mo's the monkey king. TR 18.1-4 (aut 1987-sum 1988) 403-442. Re novel publ 1978.

Rousselle, Erwin (tsl) Ch'ung-p'ien chu-t'ien-chuan, the revised edition of the record of the gods. Peking (1928)

Rust, Ambros (tsl) Meng hao-jan (691-740): sein leben und religiöses denken nach sein gedichten. Ingenbohl, switzerland (1960)

Sanford, J. H. The nine faces of death: su tung-po's kuzo-shih. EB n.s.21.1 (1988) 54-77. Budd ideas in lit, text attributed to the chin poet.

Schafer, Edward H. Ways of looking at the moon palace. AM 3rd ser 1.1 (1988) 1-14.

Schipper, Kristofer. Mu-lien plays in taoist liturgical context. In RO/OR (1989) 126-154.

Schmidt-Glintzer, Helwig. Bergbesteigungen in china—zu wandlungen und dauerhaftigkeit einer daseinmetapher. ZDMG Supplementa 7 (1989) 469-481. Refers mainly to lit.

Seaman, Gary. The divine authorship of pei-yu chi [journey to the north] JAS 45.3 (may 1986) 483-497.

Seaman, Gary. Journey to the north. An ethnohistorical analysis and annotated translation of the chinese folk novel pei-yu chi. Univ calif (1987) 236 p, intro, map, gloss to intro, bibliog, char index.

Seaman, Gary. Mu-lien dramas in puli, taiwan. In RO/OR (1989) 155-190.

Tan, Sooi Beng. An introduction to the chinese glove puppet theatre in malysia. JMBRAS 57.1 (1984) 40-55, photos, fig. "The po te hi is performed only during religious occasions" in lieu of much more expensive live opera.

Teiser, Stephen F. The ghost festival in medieval china. Princeton univ (1988) xvii + 275 p, char gloss, bibliog, index.

Teiser, Stephen F. The ritual behind the opera: a fragmentary ethnography of the ghost festival, a.d.400-1900. In RO/OR (1989) 191-223.

Thomas, Léon. La source aux fleurs de pêches de tao yuan-ming. RHR 202.1 (1985) 57-70. Source is seen to be shamanist and taoist thought.

Ting, Nai-t'ung. The holy man and the snake-woman. Fabula 8.3 (1966) 145-191. The "king and the lamia" tale in comparative study (in china it is the story of white snake)

Vandermeersch, Léon. Les origines divinatoires de la tradition chinoise du parallélisme littéraire. EOEO 11 (1989) 11-33.

Wang, Betty. Flower deities mark the lunar months with stories of love and tragedy. FCR 34.10 (oct 1984) 18-32, illus paintings.

Wang, Betty. The traditional world of string puppets. FCR 32.10 (oct 1982) 31-36, illus col photos.

Wang, Hsiu-huei. Vingt-sept récits retrouvés du jijian zhi. TP 75.4-5 (1989) 191-208. Yi-chien chih by hung mai (1123-1202)

Wang, Wen-hsing. Tsl by Chen Chu-yun. The day of the sea-goddess. ChPen (spring 1986) 70-90. Fictional re-creation of matsu festival in taiwanese fishing harbor.

Wilson, Graeme. Tao-buddha-zen: Appearance and reality in the poetry of the far east. ACQ 11.2 (summer 1983) 14-26.

Wong, Eva (tsl) Seven taoist masters. A folk novel of china. Boston (1989) 208 p, line drawings. Novel about wang ch'ung-yang and seven disciples set in sung dyn.

Xu, Zhonglin. The tale of nezha—three chapters from the canonization of the gods. CL (july 1983) 71-113.

Yang, Winston L. Y. From history to fiction: the popular image of kuan yu. Renditions 15 (1981) 67-79.

Yao, Dajuin. The mu-lien operas: a selective bibliography. In RO/OR (1989) 312-324.

Yen, Alsace. Shamanism as reflected in the folktale. AsFS 39.2 (1980) 105-121.

Yu, Anthony C. 'Rest, rest, perturbed spirit!' Chosts in traditonal chinese prose fiction. HJAS 47.2 (1987) 397-434.

Yu, Shiao-ling. Taoist themes in yuan drama (with emphasis on the plays of ma chih-yuan) JCP 15.2 (june 1988) 123-149.

II.40 Sects - Secret Societies - New Religions

An, Ming. Resolutely hit the sabotage activities of reactionary taoist sects in rural districts. SCMP 1092 (20 july 1955) 17-20.

Asai, Motoi. On the teachings of long-hua-jing and other bao-chuan in the ming-qing period. Proc31stICHS, tokyo, vol 2 (1984) 879-880.

Barrett, T. H. Chinese sectarian religion. Modern asian studies 12 (1978) 333-352. Rev art on Overmyer, Folk buddhist religion & Naquin, Millenarian rebellion, q. q.v.

Bays, Daniel H. Christianity and the chinese sectarian tradition. CF 32.4 (dec 1989) 202-217.

Evils of forming illegal associations; prohibition of magicians, leaders of sects, and teachers of false doctrines; renunciation of allegiance; the tea sect &c. ChRep 14.2 (feb 1845) 69-77.

Faure, David. Secret societies, heretic sects, and peasant rebellions in nineteenth century china. JCUHK 5.1 (1979) 187-206.

Favre, Benoit. Les révolutions chinoises et les sociétés secrèts. Revue de paris ann 38, t5 (1931) 679-697.

Fong, Mak Lau. The sociology of secret societies. A study of chinese secret societies in singapore and peninsular malaysia. Oxford univ (1981) 178 p, tables, maps, diagr, 7 app, bibliog, index.

Harrell, Stevan & Elizabeth J. Perry. Syncretic sects in chinese society: an introduction. ModCh 8.3 (july 1982) 283-303.

Jin, Chongji. The relationship between the boxers and the white lotus sect. CSH 20.3-4 (spr-sum 1987) 87-97.

Jochim, Christian. Flowers, fruit, and incense only: elite versus popular in taiwan's religion of the yellow emperor. ModCh 16.1 (jan 1990) 3-38.

Jordan, David K. "Causes and effects" tales in sectarian revelation. ProcICS, Folk customs and culture vol (1981) 73-99.

Jordan, David K. Eufunctions, dysfunctions, and oracles: literary miracle making in taiwan. In PCCS (1990) 98-115.

Jordan, David K. The recent history of the celestial way: a chinese pietistic association. ModCh 8.4 (oct 1982) 435-462.

Jordan, David K. & Daniel L. Overmyer. The flying phoenix. Aspects of chinese sectarianism in taiwan. Princeton univ (1986) xiv + 329 p, 8 photo-illus, app, works cited, index. See rev by H. Seiwert in MS 37 (1986-87) 380-383.

Kelley, David E. Temples and tribute fleets: the luo sect and boatmen's association in the eighteenth century. ModCh 8.3 (july 1982) 361-391.

Lee, Raymond L. M. & Susan E. Ackerman. Ideology, authority and conflict in a chinese religious movement in west malaysia. In CFRSM (1983) 132-145.

Li, Jikui. How to view the boxers' religious superstitions. CSH 20.3-4 (spr-sum 1987) 98-112.

Li, Thomas Shiyu & Susan Naquin. The baoming temple: religion and the throne in ming and qing china. HJAS 48.1 (june 1988) 131-188. Re a "small buddhist nunnery" near peking, and white lotus sectarianism.

Meyer, Jeffrey F. The sacred truth society. Studies in religion 11 (1982) 285-298.

Moran, Craig. Rev art on Susan Naquin's Millenarian rebellion in china (1976) q.v. CF 29.4 (dec 1986) 221-229.

Munro, Robin (ed & tsl). Synthetic sects and secret societies: revival in the 1980s. CSA 21.4 (summer 1989) 3-101. Topic title for entire issue.

Naquin, Susan. Connections between rebellions: sect family networks in qing china. ModCh 8.3 (july 1982) 337-360.

Naquin, Susan. Millenarian rebellion in china. The eight trigrams uprising of 1813. Yale univ (1976) 384 p, maps, 3 app, notes, sel bibliog, gloss-index. See rev by Timothy Jensen in HR 18.1 (aug 1978) by Craig Moran in CF 29.4 (dec 1986) 221-229.

Naquin, Susan. Shantung rebellion. The wang lun uprising of 1774. Yale univ (1981) 228 p, app, notes, gloss, bibliog, index. Re white lotus sects in ch'ing society.

104

Naquin, Susan. The transmission of white lotus sectarianism in late imperial china. In PopCult (1985) 255-291.

Noguchi, Tetsuro. Revolts and religious sects in chiang-hsi in the end of the 19th century. Proc31stICHS, tokyo, vol 2 (1984) 878-879. Abstr.

Overmyer, Daniel L. Alternatives: popular religious sects in chinese society. ModCh 7.2 (apr 1981) 153-190.

Overmyer, Daniel L. Attitudes toward the ruler and state in chinese popular religious literature: sixteenth and seventeenth century pao-chüan. HJAS 44 (1984) 347-379.

Overmyer, Daniel L. Preface. In RRR (1984) 338-341. Preface to sec titled Modern china.

Overmyer, Daniel L. Values in chinese sectarian literature: ming and ch'ing pao-chüan. In PopCult (1985) 219-254.

Overmyer, Daniel L. The white cloud sect in sung and yüan china. HJAS 42 (1982) 615-642.

Perry, Elizabeth J. Taipings and triads: the role of religion in inter-rebel relations. In RRR (1984) 342-353.

Perry, Elizabeth J. Worshipers and warriors: white lotus influence on the nien rebellion. ModCh 2.1 (jan 1976) 4-22.

Pettus, William B. Chinese secret societies and their similarity to freemasonry. New age magazine 34 (1926) 540-547, 601-603.

Reid, Gilbert. New religious movements in china. Church missionary review 76 no 849 (mar 1925) 15-26.

Rosner, Erhard. Frauen als anführerinnen chinesischer sekten. In RPO-A (1985) 239-246. Re women in ch'ing sectarianism.

Shek, Richard. Chinese millenarian movements. EncyRel 9 (1987) 532b-536b.

Shek, Richard. Millenarianism without rebellion: the huangtian dao in north china. ModCh 8.3 (july 1982) 305-335. Re a late 19th-early 20th c sect.

Shek, Richard. The practices and aspirations of ming-qing sectarians. Proc31stICHS, tokyo, vol 2 (1984) 877-878. Abstr.

Shek, Richard. The revolt of the zaili, jindan sects in rehe (jehol) ModCh 6.2 (apr 1980) 161-196. Re white lotus sects in north china.

Shek, Richard. Sectarian eschatology and violence. In VC (1990) 87-114.

Siaw, Laurence K. L. Chinese society in rural malaysia. Oxford univ (1983) See 7, The role of the secret societies, 1948-1955, p 108-131.

Smolin, Georij Jakovlevic. La révolte de la société secrète du mi-le-chiao conduite par wang tsê (1047-1048) EtSong sér 1 no 2 (1971) 143-170.

T'ao Ch'eng-chang. Tsl by Teng Ssu-yü. The evolution of china's secret sects and societies. Renditions 15 (spring 1981) 81-102. Same title in George Kao (ed) The translation of things past: chinese history and historiography, univ HK (1982) 81-102.

Tai, Hsüan-chih. Tsl by Ronald Suleski. The red spears, 1916-1949. Univ michigan (1985) See 3, Organization and beliefs, 31-40; 4, Ceremonies and ritual practices, 41-58.

Tan, Chee-Beng. The development and distribution of dejiao associations in malaysia and singapore: a study on a chinese religious organization. Singapore (1985) 87 p, maps, illus, 2 app.

Teng, Ssu-yü. An introductory study of chinese secret societies. ProcICS, History & archeology vol 3 (1981) 1147-1181.

Thaxton, Ralph. The fate of the heavenly gates: rebellion, religion and repression in republican china. In RRR (1984) 373-389. Heavenly gates was a millenial movement in honan, 1925-32.

Tristan, F. La société du ciel et de la terre. EtTrad 86 no 487, no 488; no 489-90; no 493 (1985 & 1986) 12-18; 51-58; 155-162; 129-140.

Tsui, Bartholomew. Tan tse tao: a contemporary chinese faith-healing sect in hong kong. JHKBRAS 25 (1985) 1-16.

Waltner, Ann. T'ang-yang-tzu and wang shih-chen: visionary and bureaucrat in the late ming. LIC 8.1 (june 1987) 105-133. T'ang is female visionary worshiped in cult; wang is prominent literatus.

Ward, John S. M. & W. G. Stirling. The hung society, or, the society of heaven and earth. London (1925-26) 3 vol, diagrams, illus. Repr NY (1973) repr taipei (1983)

Weller, Robert. Ideology, organisation and rebellion in chinese sectarian religion. In RRR (1984) 390-406. Re "heterodox" sects in taiwan.

Weller, Robert P. Sectarian religion and political action in china. ModCh 8.4 (oct 1982) 463-483.

Weng, T'ung-wen. Identity of wan yun lung, founder of t'ien-ti hui. Proc31stICHS, tokyo, vol 2 (1984) 880-881. Abstr.

Yoshihara, Kazuo. Dejiao: a chinese religion in southeast asia. JJRS 15 (1988) 199-221.

Yoshihara, Kazuo. "Dejiao": a study of an urban chinese religion in thailand. In John R. Clammer (ed) Studies in urban anthropology, singapore (1987) 61-79.

Young, Richard Fox. Sanctuary of the tao. The place of christianity in a sino-japanese unity sect (tao yüan) JCR 17 (1989) 1-26.

II.41 Modern (Pre-1949) Religion

Drake, F. S. Religion in a manchurian city. ChRec 66.2 & 66.3 (feb & mar 1935) 104-111; 161-170.

Overmyer, Daniel L. Preface In RRR (1984) 338-341. Preface to sec entitled Modern china.

Reid, Gilbert. New religious movements in china. Church missionary review 76 no 849 (mar 1925) 15-26.

Thaxton, Ralph. The fate of the heavenly gates: rebellion, religion and repression in republican china. In RRR (1984) 373-389. Heavenly gates was a millenial movement in honan, 1925-32.

Wang, Gungwu. Lu xun, lim boon keng and confucianism. PFEH 39 (mar 1989) 75-91.

II.42 Religion under Communism

An, Ming. Resolutely hit the sabotage activities of reactionary taoist sects in rural districts. SCMP 1092 (20 july 1955) 17-20.

Anagnost, Ann S. Politics and magic in contemporary china. ModCh 13.1 (jan 1987) 40-62.

Belgum, David. Medicine and morals and mao. Journal of religion and health 17 (oct 1978) 261-273.

Bishop, Donald H. Maoism as a religion. RH 10.1 (winter 1976) 26-30.

Bonavia, David. Self-confidence paves the way for a revival [of religion in china] FEER 109.34 (aug 15, 1980) 24-25.

Bosell, Eric. The confucian revival. Areopagus (trinity 1990, 3.4) 47-49.

Browning, Don S. Medicine, modernization and religion in the people's republic of china. Second opinion: health, faith and ethics 4 (1987) 10-29.

Bush, Richard C. Religion in china and japan. In Robert F. Weir (genl ed) The religious world: communities of faith, NY & london (1982) 171-196.

Bush, Richard C. et al (ed) The religious world. NY & london (1988) 171-196, notes, gloss, suggested readings, 209-212.

Chang, Chi-p'eng. The ccp's policy toward religion. I&S 19.9 (sept 1983) 55-70.

Chao, Jonathan T. China's religious policy: what does it mean? In James A. Scherer (ed) Western christianity and the people's republic of china (1979) 31-37.

Chao, Jonathan. Church and state in socialist china, 1949-1987. Crux [Regent coll, vancouver b.c.] 25 (july 1989) 8-20.

Chao, Jonathan. Function and role of the state: the place of religion and education (a case study: china) In John C. VanderStelt (ed) The challenge of marxist and neo-marxist ideologies for christian scholarship (1982) 187-209.

Chen, Fu Tien. The current religion policy of people's republic of china (january 1, 1976-march 15, 1979) Norwalk, calif (1983).

Chen, Kenneth K. S. Religious changes in communist china. CC 11.4 (1970) 56-62. Same title in Sah Mong-wu et al (ed) Chinese political science, taipei (1980) 347-353.

Chih, Hung. Chinese daily life as a locus for ethics. Concilium 126 (1979) 33-41.

Ching, Julia. Religion, politics, and protest in the people's republic. San francisco etc (1990) See 6, Is there religious freedom in china? 125-144.

Davis-Friedman, Deborah. Long lives: chinese elderly and the communist revolution. Stanford univ (1983; rev ed 1991) See 5, "Funerals and filial piety" 60-70.

Dean, Kenneth. Field notes on two taoist jiao observed in zhangzhou in december, 1985. CEA 2 (1986) 191-209.

Dean, Kenneth. Funerals in fujian. CEA 4 (1988) 19-78.

Dean, Kenneth. Revival of religious practices in fujian: a case study. In TT:RCT (1989) 51-78.

Dean, Kenneth. Taoism in southern fujian: field notes, fall, 1985. In STR&MT (1989) 74-87.

Deng, Zhaoming. Some prejudiced understandings of religion in the press of china. CF 26.4 (1983) 208-211.

Douglas Lancashire (tsl) A communist newspaper report and editorial. In CERF (1981) 268-275. Re the regime and religion.

Edsman, Carl-Martin. Die hauptreligionen des heutigen asiens. Tübingen (1971) See Chinas religionene, 28-38; 116-136.

Ewing, W. Carroll jr. & Teresa Chu. Religion in china today. EH 19.6 (june 1980) 6-10.

Feibleman, James K. Understanding oriental philosophy. A popular account for the western world. NY (1976) See Pt 2, chap 28, Chinese communism; chap 29, Mao tse-tung, 155-171.

Feuchtwang, Stephen. The problem of "superstition" in the people's republic of china. In Gustavo Benavides & M. W. Daly (ed) Religion and political power, SUNY (1989) 43-68.

Freedom of (from?) religion. CNA 1222 (18 dec 1981) 1-8.

Fu, Charles Wei-hsun & Gerhard E. Spiegler (ed) Movements and issues in world religions. A sourcebook and analysis of developments since 1945. Religion, ideology, and politics. NY etc (1987) Pertinent art sep list ed in this bibliog; abbrev MIWR.

Fu, Charles Wei-hsun & Gerhard E. Spiegler (ed) Religious issues and interreligious dialogues. An analysis and sourcebook of developments since 1945. NY etc (1989) Pertinent art sep listed in this bibliog; abbrev RIID.

Goldman, Merle. Religion in post-mao china. In Robert J. Myers (ed) Religion and the state [i.e. Annals of the amer acad of pol sci 483] (1986) 146-156.

Gong, Jianlong. Why are superstitious activities on the rise again? An investigation of rural superstitious activities in chuansha county, shanghai municipality. CSA 16.1-2 (fall-winter 1983-84) 204-211.

Gordon, Arvan. A change in the chinese understanding of "religion" RCL 14.2 (summer 1986) 210-212.

Gordon, Arvan. Religion and the new chinese constitution. RCL 11 (summer 1983) 130-134.

Government functionary discusses religion. RCDA 28.3 (summer 1989) 84-86.

Haglund, Ake. Maoism: a new religious formation in the people's republic of china. In Haralds Biezais (ed) New religions, stockholm (1975) 43-54,

Hahn, Thomas H. New developments concerning buddhist and taoist monasteries. In TT:RCT (1989) 79-101.

Hahn, Thomas H. On doing fieldwork in daoist studies in the people's republic—conditions and results. CEA 2 (1986) 211-217.

Hendrischke, Barbara. Chinese research into daoism after the cultural revolution. AS 34 (1984) 25-42.

Heuser, R. (tsl) Satzung der chinesischen taoistischen gesellschaft (zhongguo dao jiao xiehui zhangcheng) China heute 8 (1989) 37-39.

Hsieh, Jiann & Chou Ying-hsing. Public aspirations in the new year couplets: a comparative study between the people's republic and taiwan. AsFS 40.2 (1981) 125-149.

Hsing, Kuo-ch'iang. The ccp's united front with religious groups. I&S 16.2 (feb 1980) 45-56.

Humphrey, Peter. Temples in the city of xian: a reflection of the religious situation in china. RCL 8 (winter 1980) 274-278.

Hunter, Neale. Religion and the chinese revolution. In R. Wylie (ed) China. The peasant revolution, NY (1972) 81-97.

Jan, Yün-hua. Recent chinese research publications on religious studies. In TT:RCT (1989) 25-42.

Jan, Yün-hua. The religious situation and the studies of buddhism and taoism in china: an incomplete and imbalanced picture. JCR 12 (fall 1984) 37-64.

Kramers, R. P. On religion and religious values in china today. CF 27.4 (dec 1984) 196-203. From mainland booklet publ jan 1983, "talks on religion"

Kuo, Z. Y. & Y. H. Lam. Chinese religious behavior and the deification of mao tse-tung. Psychological record 18 (1968) 455-468.

Lazzarotto, Angelo S. The chinese communist party and religion. Missiology 11.3 (july 1983) 267-290.

Liang, Heng & Judith Shapiro. Intellectual freedom in china after mao, with a focus on 1983. NY (1984) See Religious freedom, 46-54; mimeo.

Lin, Ying. A study on the history of chinese religions during the past thirty years. In McGill univ publ Re-examination of china's religious legacy: a chinese perspective (1982) 1-12. Mimeo fr 1980 conference paper.

Luo Zhufeng. Tsl by Donald MacInnis. The current situation of religion in qinchengshan, sichuan province. Tripod 47 (1988) 57-59.

MacInnis, Donald E. Maoism: the religious analogy. ChrCent 85 (10 jan 1968) 39-42.

MacInnis, Donald. Religion: china. IDOC; international documentation no 67 (nov 1974) 16-20.

MacInnis, Donald E. Religion in china today; policy and practice. Maryknoll NY (1989) 458 p, gloss, sel list of sources, index. See passim.

MacInnis, Donald E. Secularism and religion in china: the problem of transcendence. In F. J. Adelmann (ed) Contemporary chinese philosophy, the hague (1982) 117-133.

Mackerras, Colin. Chinese society since mao: religion and family. Brisbane (1984) 27 p. Aquinas memorial lecture sep publ as booklet.

Martin, Helmut. Cult and canon. The origins and development of state maoism. Armonk NY (1982)

Martinson, Paul V. Confucius lives: a theological critique of the current chinese marxist reappraisal of the confucian tradition. CF 24.4 (dec 1981) 215-240.

Martinson, Paul V. Some theological reflections on current marxist studies of the confucian tradition. Theology and life 4 (1982) 60-74.

Meienberger, Norbert. Religionskritik unter mao. AS 39.1-2 (1985) 127-146.

Morris, Christopher (tsl) Religion and feudal superstitions. In CERF (1981) app 1, 277-280. Editorial in People's daily 15 mar 79.

Morrison, Peter. Religious policy in china and its implementation in the light of document no 19. RCL 12 (winter 1984) 244-255.

Munro, Robin (ed & tsl) Syncretic sects and secret societies: revival in the 1980s. CSA 21.4 (summer 1989) 3-101. Topic title for entire issue.

Murphy, Laurence T. Religion and politics in china. JD 7.1 (jan-mar 1982) 46-55.

Newell, William H. Limitations on the right to believe on the chinese mainland. RCL 16 (summer 1988) 135-145.

Niu, Yu-hsien. Criticize thoroughly the "theory of genius" of confucius and mencius. CEd 7.1-2 (1974) 162-165. In SCMP 5529 (8 jan 1974) 34-36.

Paper, Jordan. Religion and art in contemporary china. JCR 15 (1987) 51-60.

Pas, Julian. Religion in china today. Canada-china journal 5.1-2 (1985) 18, 21.

Pas, Julian F. Revival of temple worship and popular religious traditons. In TT:RCT (1989) 158-209.

Pas, Julian F. (ed) The turning of the tide; religion in china today. Oxford univ for HKBRAS (1989) 15 art sep listed in this bibliog; abbrev TT:RCT

Pas, Julian F. Introduction: chinese religion in transition. In TT:RCT (1989) 1-24.

Piediscalzi, Nicholas. China's new policy on religion. ChrCent 102 (19-26 june, 1985, 611-614. Per 1982 constitution and ccp document 19.

Pong, Raymond & Carlo Caldarola. China: religion in a revolutionary society. In Carlo Caldarola (ed) Religion and societies: asia and the middle east, berlin etc (1982) 551-577, bibliog.

Raddock, D. M. Growing up in new china: a twist in the circle of filial piety. History of childhood quarterly: the journal of psychohistory 2 (1974) 201-220.

Red china's non-existent religious "freedom" Asian outlook [taipei] 15.2 (feb 1980) 42-45.

Religion in the people's republic of china. Tunbridge wells, kent, engl (1982) 44 p. China study project booklet.

Religions in china. CNA 1186 (aug 1980) 1-7.

Seiwert, Hubert et al. The institutional context of the history of religions in china. In Michael Pye (ed) Marburg revisited; institutions and strategies in the study of religion, marburg (1989) 127-141. Report of IAHR working group, june 1988.

Seiwert, Hubert. Loyalitäts- und orientierungskonflikte in der religions forschung: religionstheorie in china 1979-1988. In FestColpe (1990) 162-175.

Senger, Harro von. Rückbesinnung auf konfuzius in der volksrepublic china? ZDMG 133.2 (1983) 377-392.

Shen, Yifan. Confucian thought and theological reflection in china today. CF 31 (aug 1988) 166-176.

Siu, Helen F. Recycling rituals: politics and popular culture in contemporary rural china. In Perry Link et al (ed) Unofficial china: popular culture and thought in the people's republic, boulder, colo etc (1989) 121-137.

Smart, Ninian. Discontinuities and continuities between mao zedong thought and the traditional religions of china. D&A 4.2 (sum 1990) 42-50.

Swart, Paula & Barry Till. A revival of confucian ceremonies in china. In TT:RCT (1989) 210-221, illus 7 b & w photos.

Tan, Chung. Trial and triumph of confucian harmony ethics in modern china. Proc31stICHS, tokyo, vol 1 (1984) 255-256. Abstr.

Tang, Runhua. Religion in china. New china quarterly 17 (aug 1990) 119-124. General survey.

The religious policy of the people's republic of china: our party's basic policy on religious questions during the period of socialism. Missiology 11.3 (july 1983) 291-307. Editorial fr Red flag 12, 16 june 82, 2-8.

Thompson, Laurence G. Observations on religion in communist china: introductory comments. JCR 12 (1984) 33-36.

Tu, Wei-ming. Confucian studies in the people's republic. Humanities 8 (sept-oct 1987) 14-16, 34-35.

Tu, Wei-ming. The religious situation in the people's republic of china. In Frank Whaling (ed) Religion in today's world, edinburgh (1987) 279-291.

Wakeman, Frederic jr. Mao's remains. In DeathRit (1988) 254-288.

Wang, Jack. Chinese communists' religious policy. Asian outlook [taipei] 18.6 (june 1983) 40-45.

Whitehead, Raymond L. Ethics in post-mao china. In L. Rasmussen (ed) Annual of the society of christian ethics (1983) 161-184.

Whitehead, Raymond L. Love and struggle in the ethic of mao. ChrCent 91.2-3 (23 jan 1974) 75-77.

Whyte, Martin K. Death in the people's republic of china. In DeathRit (1988) 289-316.

Whyte, Martin King & William L. Parish. Urban life in contemporary china. Univ chicago (1984) See Religion and social values, 302-331.

Wickeri, Philip L. Seeking the common ground: protestant christianity, the three-self movement, and china's united front. Maryknoll, NY (1988) 356 p, notes bibliog, index. See passim.

Winters, Clyde-Ahmad. China's new religious freedom. Contemporary review 247 no 1439 (dec 1985) 319-323.

Woo, Franklin J. The political challenge of china to western christianity and chinese religion. CN 24.1 (winter 1984-85) 326-328.

Wood, James E. Religion and the state in china: winter is past. Journal of church and state 28 (autumn 1986) 393-407.

Wood, James E. jr. La religion et l'état en chine: l'hiver est passé. Conscience and liberty 35 (1988) 38-53. Apparently french version of author's art publ in Journal of church and state (1986) q.v.

Xiao, Zhitian. Tsl by J. Wickeri. Some opinions on present religious phenomena: thoughts on "eight problems in social investigation" CF 26.4 (1983) 212-221.

Yu, David C. Confucianism, maoism, and max weber. In TLLP (1985) 141-167.

Yu, David. The meaning of religion in contemporary china. CN 21.2 (spring 1983) 249-250.

Yü, David. Religion and politics in the asian communist nations. In MIWR (1987) Chap 17, 371-392.

Yu, David C. Religious studies in china at crossroads. JCR 18 (1990) 167-172.

Zhao, Fusan. Religion, spiritual culture and national unity. Chinese theological review [HK] 1 (1985) 101-107.

110

Zhuo, Xin-ping. Theorien über religion und christentum im chinesischen raum. China heute 7.5 (1988) 72-81.

II.43 Taiwan

Ahern, Emily Martin. The thai ti kong festival. In AnthroTS (1981) 397-425.

Aijmer, Göran. Birth and death in china: musings on a taiwan corpus. Ethnos 49.1-2 (1984) 5-42.

Berthier, Brigitte. Enfant de divination, voyageur du destin. l'Homme 27 no 101 (jan-mars 1987) 86-100. Re chi-t'ung medium; "destin" is space-time.

Bishop, Donald H. Confucianism in contemporary taiwan. CC 24 (1983) 69-83.

Ch'iu, K'un-liang. Mu-lien "operas" in taiwanese funeral rituals. In RO/OR (1989) 105-125.

Chang, Chiao-hao. Religious strength in diversity. FCR 38.1 (jan 1988) 40-45, col photos. Issue mainly devoted to religion.

Chang, I-chu. Woodcarvers, gods, and profits. FCR 38.11 (nov 1988) 54-63, illus col photos. Carving of relig and secular themes by chiu hua-hai et al in sanyi, miaoli, taiwan.

Chiu, Hei-yuan. Faiths in transition. FCR 38.1 (jan 1988) 4-8 illus col photos. Issue mainly devoted to relig.

Chiu, Milton M. Taiwanese religions. EncyRel 14 (1987) 252a-255a.

Chu, Hai-yuan. The impact of different religions on the chinese family in taiwan. In CFRB (1985) 221-231.

Chuang, Ying-chang. A comparison of hokkien and hakka ancestor worship. ASBIE 69 (1990) 133-159.

Cohen, Alvin P. A taiwanese puppeteer and his theatre. AsFS 40 (1981) 33-49.

DeMarco, Michael A. Taiwan temples: where heaven and earth mingle. Rosicrucian digest 67.3 (may-june 1989) 30-35.

Deverge, M. Confucianisme et succès économique à taiwan. Etudes 367.1-2 (1987) 5-13.

Ebert, Jorinde, Barbara M. Kaulbach & Martin Kraatz. Religiöse malerei aus taiwan. Köln (1981) Catalog of exhibit oct-nov 1980 at marburg univ.

Festivals and fine arts, taiwan, republic of china. Taipei (n.d. 1985?) 80 p, illus col photos.

Folk arts. FCR 40.4 (apr 1990) Almost entire issue devoted to folk arts and their "shaky state"in taiwan. All this intimately connected with relig.

Fu, Pei-jung (text) Lin Bor-liang (photos). Confucian ritual in modern form. FCR 38.1 (jan 1988) 46-49. Issue devoted mainly to relig.

Gates, Hill. Money for the gods. ModCh 13.1 (jan 1987) 259-277.

Gates, Hill. Chinese working-class lives: getting by in taiwan. Cornell univ (1987) See chap 8, Folk religions, old and new, 175-204.

Gods, ghosts, and ancestors. FCR 38.1 (jan 1988) Issue devoted mainly to relig; this is editorial.

Gutheinz, Luis & Edmond Tang. Economic development and quality of life: a socio-religious survy of taiwan. Pro-mundi vita asia-australia, dossier no 33 (1985) 1-29.

Harrell, Stevan. The concept of fate in chinese folk ideology. ModCh 13.1 (jan 1987) 90-109.

Harrell, Stevan. Men, women, and ghosts in taiwanese folk religion. In G&R (1986) Chap 4, 97-116.

Harrell, C. Stevan. Ploughshare village. Culture and context in taiwan. Univ washington (1982) See chap 6, The organization of religion, 182-206.

Ho, Chuan-Kun. Burial patterns of prehistoric taiwan (part I) JICS 19 (1988) 433-468.

Hsi, Ju-chi. Religious practices in hsinchuang. In TTV (1976) Chap 7, 140-150.

Hsieh, Jiann & Chou Ying-hsiung. Public aspirations in the new year couplets; a comparative study between the people's republic and taiwan. AsFS 40.2 (1981) 125-149.

Hu, Tai-li. My mother-in-law's village. Rural industrialization and change in taiwan. Taipei (1984) See sec, The myth of the liu lineage temple, 37-40; chap 7, Religious activities and the surname opera, 161-180.

Huang, Yu-mei. Braving the "bees" FCR 34 (sic) 4 (apr 1983) 60-61 illus col photos. Re release of "bee" firecrackers during lantern festival at yenshui, tainan county.

Huang, Yu-mei. China's ghost festival. FCR 32.11 (nov 1982) 68-72 illus col photos.

Huang, Yu-mei. The light arts. FCR 34.4 (apr 1983) 56-59 illus col photos. Re lantern festival and its lanterns.

Huang, Yu-mei. The making of a dragon boat. FCR 34 (sic) 7 (july 1983) 49-53 illus col photos.

Huang, Yu-mei. Presto! A 'new' ancient landmark. FCR 34 (sic) 8 (aug 1983) 56-63 illus col photos. Re restoration of old bldgs, incl several confucian temples.

Hung, Daniel M. Mission blockade: ancestor worship. Chinese around the world (apr 1983) 3-6. Repr fr Evangelical missions quarterly (jan 1983) Repr in CAAP (1985) 199-208.

Jacobs, J. Bruce, Jean Hagger & Anne Sedgeley (comp) Taiwan: a comprehensive bibliography of english-language publications. La trobe univ & columbia univ (1984) For relig see esp sec 7, Society, and 8, Culture.

Jochim, Christian. Flowers, fruit, and incense only: elite versus popular in taiwan's religion of the yellow emperor. ModCh 16.1 (jan 1990) 3-38.

Jordan, David K. "Causes and effects" tales in sectarian revelation. ProcICS, taipei, Folk customs & culture vol (1981) 73-99.

Jordan, David K. Chinese pietism: syncretic movements in modern taiwan. In C. R. Das (ed) Folk culture, new delhi (1983)

Jordan, David K. Eufunctions, dysfunctions, and oracles: literary miracle making in taiwan. In PCCS (1990) 98-115.

Jordan, David K. Folk filial piety in taiwan: the twenty-four filial exemplars. In Walter H. Slote (ed) The psycho-cultural dynamics of the confucian family: past and present, seoul (1986) 47-106.

Jordan, David K. The recent history of the celestial way: a chinese pietistic association. ModCh 8.4 (oct 1982) 435-462.

Jordan, David K. The repression of hostility and the representation of hell in south taiwan religious processions. In Ruth-Inge Heinze (ed) Asian concepts of hell, berkeley, calif (1983) 17-31, 82-83.

Jordan, David K. Taiwanese poe divination: statistical awareness and religious belief. JSSR 21 (1982) 114-118.

Jordan, David K. & Daniel L. Overmyer. The flying phoenix. Aspects of chinese sectarianism in taiwan. Princeton univ (1986) xix + 329 p, 8 photo-illus, app, works cited, index.

Kagan, Richard C. & Anna Wasescha. The taiwanese tang-ki: the shaman as community healer and protector. In SICS (1982) 112-141.

Kao, Chung-hsin. Tsl by T. C. Chang. The taoist way to truth. FCR 38.1 (jan 1988) 22-27, illus col photos.

Katz, Paul. Demons or deities?—The wangye of taiwan. AsFS 46.2 (1987) 197-215.

Katz, Paul. Wen ch'iung—the god of many faces. HHYC:CS 8.1, vol 1 (june 1990) 183-219. One of the best-known faces is as a "plague god" in taiwan.

112

Kaulbach, B. & B. Proksch. Photos by Kuo Tung-tai. Arts and culture in taiwan. Taipei (1984) 125 p, illus col photos. See relevant sec.

Kendall, Laurel. Supernatural traffic—east asian shamanism. CM&P 5.2 (1981) 171-191. Rev art on studies of shamanism in korea, japan and taiwan.

Kleinman, Arthur & James L. Gale. Patients treated by physicians and folk healers: a comparative outcome study in taiwan. CM&P 6.4 (dec 1982) 405-423.

Lagerwey, John. The fachang ritual in northern taiwan. In STR&MT (1989) 66-73.

Lagerwey, John. Taoist ritual in chinese society and history. NY & london (1987) 364 p, bibliogs, 4 app incl tables, 27 b-&-w photos, index.

Lagerwey, John. Les têtes des démons tombent par milliers. Le "fachang" rituel du nord de taiwan. l'Homme 27 no 101 (1987) 101-116.

Leu, Chien-ai. Filial piety modernized. FCR 39.3 (mar 1989) 18-21, illus.

Leu, Chien-ai (text) Chung Yung-ho (photos) Temple roof art. FCR 40.11 (nov 1990) 34-45. Re ornamentation of temple roofs in chien nien technique.

Li, Wen-lang. Hsinchuang: a participant observation study of a cane-growing village. Chap 9 in TTV (n.d.1976) See relevant sec.

Li, Wen-lang. Shuichuet'ou: a participant observation study of a rice-growing village. Chap 10 in TTV (n.d.1976) See relevant sec.

Li, Yih-yuan. On conflicting interpretations of chinese family rituals. In CFRB (1985) 263-281.

Li, Yih-yuan. Social change, religious movements, and personality adjustments: an anthropological view. In Tseng Wen-shing & David Y. H. Yu (ed) Chinese culture and mental health, orlando, florida (1985) 57-66.

Liao, David. Christian alternatives to ancestor worship in taiwan. In CAAP (1985) 209-218.

Liaw, Stephen. Ancestor worship in contemporary taiwanese society and evangelism of the chinese. In CAAP (1985) 181-197.

Lim, Guek Eng. Christianity encounters ancestor worship in taiwan. ERTh 8.2 (1984) 225-235.

Lim, Guek Eng. Christianity versus ancestor worship in taiwan. TCGB 11.2 (oct 1983) 4-10.

Lin, Chi-ping. Ancestor worship: the reactions of chinese churches. In CAAP (1985) 147-161.

Lü, Ch'ui-k'uan. Enquête préliminaire sur la musique taoïste de taiwan. Sommaire en francais par J. L. (John Lagerwey?) CEA 4 (1988) 112-126.

Lu, Ping-chuan & Tsao Pen-yeh. The ritual music of taoist "chiao"—studies made in lin-chuang and p'eng-hu. Proc31stICHS, tokyo, vol 2 (1984) 656-658. Abstr.

Markbreiter, Stephen. Fukienese wood carvings; a survival in taiwan. AofA 19.3 (may-june 1989) 97-104. Mostly relig carvings.

Marlière, M. Les cultes traditionnels à taiwan: un syncretism en évolution. Ethnographie 77 no 85 (1981) 125-136.

McCreery, John. Why don't we see some real money here? Offerings in chinese religion. JCR 18 (1990) 1-24.

Meyer, Jeffrey. The image of religion in taiwan textbooks. JCR 15 (1987) 44-50.

Meyer, Jeffrey F. Moral education in taiwan. Comparative education review 32.1 (1988) 20-38.

Meyer, Jeffrey F. The sacred truth society. Studies in religion 11 (1982) 285-298.

Meyer, Jeffrey F. Teaching morality in taiwan schools: the message of the textbooks. CQ 114 (june 1988) 267-284.

Meyer, Roger D. Shou lao sells. FCR 37.5 (may 1987) 2-10, col illus.

Mindich, Jeffrey. Chu yuan—a man mourned for 2,200 years. He died for truth and justice. FCR 35.6 (june 1985) 2-9 many illus. Re tradition behind tuan wu festival.

Mindich, Jeffrey H. Painting eyes on the dragon. FCR 40.11 (nov 1990) 30-33 col photos. Re carvings in tainan confucian temple.

Mindich, Jeffrey H. A paragon for all generations. FCR 40.11 (nov 1990) 22-29 col photos. Re history and present aspects of tainan's confucian temple.

Mindich, Jeffrey H. Restored grandeur. FCR 40.11 (nov 1990) 4-21 col photos, plan. Re restoration of tainan confucian temple.

Nadeau, Randall. Manifestations of spiritual efficacy in taiwanese temples. BCAR 1 (1987) 57-68.

Nadeau, Randall. Religious studies in taiwan: a review article. BCAR 2 (1988) 57-68.

P'eng, Yung-hai. Customs and traditions in plains and highlands of taiwan. Yung-chen, taipei-hsien (1972) 185 p, illus, bibliog. See chap 1, 3, 5, 7, 9 for taiwanese chin beliefs and customs.

Pas, Julian F. Journey to hell: a new report of shamanistic travel to the courts of hell. JCR 17 (1989) 43-60.

Pas, Julian. Temple oracles in a chinese city. A study of the use of temple oracles in taichung, central taiwan. JHKBRAS 24 (1984) 1-45.

Ross, Daniel G. Chinese and western religious symbols as used in taiwan. Fu jen univ (1980) 226 p. Recognition and meaning of sel symbols by 414 taiwanese.

Sangren, P. Steven. Female gender in chinese religious symbols: kuan yin, matsu, and the "eternal mother" Signs 9 (1983) 4-25.

Sangren, P. Steven. History and magical power in a chinese community. Stanford univ (1987) 268 p, bibliog, char list, tables, maps, fig, index. Re Ta-ch'i and surrounding villages; "magical power" ref to ling, or spiritual efficacy; anthropological fieldwork done 1976-77.

Sangren, P. Steven. History and the rhetoric of legitimacy; the matsu cult of taiwan. CSSH 30 (oct 1988) 674-697.

Sangren, P. Steven. Orthodoxy, heterodoxy, and the structure of value in chinese rituals. ModCh 13.1 (jan 1987) 63-89.

Saso, Michael. The liturgical heritage of the hsinchu taoists. CEA 4 (1988) 175-180.

Saso, Michael. Taiwan: old gods and modern society. In Carlo Caldarola (ed) Religion and societies: asia and the middle east, berlin etc (1982) 579-605, bibliog.

Sato, Koji. "Chao-sheng"—the religious ritual to save departed souls in taiwan. TJR 22 (dec 1988) 91-104.

Sawatsky, Sheldon. Chinese shamanism. TJT 12 (mar 1990) 121-143.

Sawatzky, Sheldon. State-church conflict in taiwan: its historical roots and contemporary manifestations. Missiology 9 (1981) 449-463. Some historical ref to non-christian cases.

Schipper, Kristofer. The cult of pao-sheng ta-ti and its spread to taiwan—a case study of fen-hsiang. In FukienD&D (1990) 397-416.

Schipper, Kristofer. Seigneurs royaux, dieux des épidémies. ASSR 59.1 (1985) 31-40.

Seaman, Gary. Mu-lien dramas in puli, taiwan. In RO/OR (1989) 155-190.

Seaman, Gary. The sexual politics of karmic retribution. In AnthroTS (1981) 381-396.

Seiwert, Hubert. Religious response to modernization in taiwan: the case of i-kuan tao. JHKBRAS 21 (1981) 43-70.

114

Seiwert, Hubert. Volksreligion und nationale tradition in taiwan. Studien zur regionalen religionsgeschichte einer chinesischen provinz. Wiesbaden (1985) 284 s, gloss chines. zeichen, literatgurverzeichnis, 2 maps, index und glossar.

Shen Yi & Hilary Fraser. The twelve-year cycle of festivals at shuili. FCR 34.2 (feb 1984) 45-52. Re chiao.

Shepherd, John R. Sinicized siraya worship of a-li-tsu. BIEAS 58 (1984) 1-81, photo-illus. Many comparisons of aboriginal siraya relig with taiwanese chin relig.

Stevens, Keith G. Portrait and ancestral images on chinese altars. AofA 19.1 (jan-feb 1989) 135-145.

Stevens, Keith. Temples and deities: religion. In Insight guides: Republic of china: taiwan, singapore (1984) 75-90.

Suenari, Michio. The "religious family" among the chinese of central taiwan. SES 11 (1984) 169-184 Repr RFEA (1986) 169-184.

Sutton, Donald S. Ritual drama and moral order: interpreting the gods' festival troupes of southern taiwan. JAS 49.3 (aug 1990) 535-554.

Sutton, Donald S. Rituals of self-mortification: taiwanese spirit-mediums in comparative perspective. JRS 4.1 (1990) 99-125.

Temple carvings and sculptures in ancient style. FCR 22.11 (nov 1972) 33-44. Photo-story re carvings at a temple in sanhsia, outskirts of taipei.

Thompson, Laurence G. Dancing lions. JCR 15 (1987) 29-43.

Thompson, Laurence G. Chinese religious year. EncyRel 3 (1987) 323a-328a.

Thompson, Laurence G. Dream divination and chinese popular religion. JCR 16 (1988) 73-82.

Thompson, Laurence G. The moving finger writes: a note on revelation and renewal in chinese religion. JCR 10 (1982) 92-147.

Thompson, Laurence G. Obiter dicta on chinese religion as play. ProcICS, Folk customs and culture vol (1981) 59-72

Thompson, Laurence G. Popular and classical modes of ritual in a taiwanese temple. SSCRB 9 (1981) 106-122.

Tirone, Gail (text) Lin Bor-liang (photos). A gathering of deities occasions folk celebrations. FCR 36.7 (july 1986) 36-41. Re Peikang matsu festival 27 apr 86.

Tirone, Gail (text) Shen Yi (photos). A very brief visit to the halls of hell. FCR 35.7 (july 1985) 62-65. Re Tung-yüeh miao in tainan.

Tong, Fung-wan (Tung Fang-yüan) Tsl by Georgine G. Caldwell. Understanding of the social ethical dimensions of buddhism and christianity. TJT 7 (mar 1985).

Tong, Fung-wan (Tung Fang-yüan) Vibrant, popular pantheon. FCR 38.1 (Jan 1988) 9-15, col photos.

Tseng, Li-ling (text) Joseph Chen & Lin Bor-liang (photos). Temple figures, toys and tradition in dough. FCR 39.5 (may 1989) 60-75.

Tseng, Yung-li (text) Joseph Chen (photos). Chinese temple rococo. FCR 38.1 (jan 1988) 50-56.

Tseng, Yung-li (text) Shen Yi (photos). Spirit of a temple. FCR 36.2 (feb 1986) 50-57.

Wang, Betty. Buddhist images are shaped of emotion: the return of shao lai-cheng. FCR 34.8. (aug 1983) 66-71, illus col photos.

Wang, Betty. The traditional world of string puppets. FCR 32.10 (oct 1982) 31-36, illus col photos.

Wang, Emily. New year prints. FCR 35.3 (mar 1985) 42-53, many col illus.

Wang, Wen-hsing. Tsl by Chen Chu-yun. The day of the sea-goddess. ChPen (spring 1986) 70-90. Fictional recreation of matsu festival in taiwanese fishing harbor.

Weller, Robert P. Bandits, beggars, and ghosts: the failure of state control over religious interpretation in taiwan. AmEth 12 (1985) 46-61.

Weller, Robert P. & Hill Gates. Hegemony and chinese folk ideologies: an introduction. ModCh 13 (1987) 3-16.

Weller, Robert. Ideology, organization and rebellion in chinese sectarian religion. In RRR (1984) 390-406. Re "heterodox" sects in taiwan.

Weller, Robert P. The politics of ritual disguise: repression and response in taiwanese popular religion. ModCh 13.1 (1987) 17-39.

Weller, Robert P. Sectarian religion and political action in china. ModCh 8.4 (oct 1982) 463-484.

Weller, Robert P. Unities and diversities in chinese religion. Univ washington (1987) 215 p, app on geomancy, char list, notes, ref, index. "Chinese religion" as studied in taiwan by anthropologist.

Wolf, Margery. The woman who didn't become a shaman. AmEth 17.3 (aug 1990) 419-430.

II.44 Hong Kong and Overseas

Ackerman, Susan E. & Raymond L. M. Lee. Heaven in transition: non-muslim innovation and ethnic identity in malaysia. Univ hawaii (1988) See chap 8, The path of mystical dissent: the baitiangong alternative in chinese religion, 120-153.

Ackerman, Susan E. & Raymond L. M. Lee. Pray to the heavenly father: a chinese new religion in malaysia. Numen 29.1 (july 1982) 62-77.

Antoni, Klaus. Death and transformations: the presentation of death in east and southeast asia. AsFS 41.2 (1982) 147-162.

Beh, Leo Juat & John Clammer. Confucianism as folk religion in singapore: a note. In CFRSM (1983) 175-178.

Berndt, Manfred. Servanthood among para-

christian and non-christian religions in hong kong. CF 14.4 (1971) 157-182.

Blofeld, John. Chinese buddhist temples in singapore. Sawaddi 1 (jan-feb 1982) 24-28.

Bloomfield, Frena. The occult world of hong kong. HK (1980) 132 p.

Brown, Iem. Religions of the chinese in indonesia. In Leo Suryadinata (ed) The ethnic chinese in the ASEAN states: bibliographical essays, singapore (1989) 97-118.

Burkhardt, Valentine R. Chinese creeds and customs. HK vol 1 (1953) vol 2 (1955) vol 3 (1958) 181, 201, 164 p, each vol profusely illus, indexes. Repr HK (1983)

Chan, Ka Yan. Joss stick manufacturing: a study of a traditonal industry in hong kong. JHKBRAS 29 (1989) 94-120.

Chan, Wing-hoi. The dangs of kam tin and their jiu [chiao] festival. JHKBRAS 29 (1989) 302-375.

Chan, Wing-hoi. Observations at the jiu [chiao] festival of shek o and tai long wan, 1986. JHKBRAS 26 (1986) 78-101, photos, gloss.

Chang, Toy Len. Chinese festivals the hawaiian way. Honolulu, privately printed (1983) 74 p, illus drawings, brief bibliog, index.

Chiao, Chien. Cognitive play: some minor rituals among hong kong chinese. EAC-2 (1983) 138-144.

Choi, Chi-cheung. The chinese "yue lan" ghost festival in japan: a kobe case study, aug. 31-sept. 4, 1982. JHKBRAS 24 (1984) 230-263, illus photos, tables, app, documents.

Choong, Ket Che. Chinese divination—an ethnographic case study. In CFRSM (1983) 49-97.

Clammer, John R. Straits chinese society. Studies in the sociology of the baba communities of malaysia and singapore. Singapore univ (1980) See 4. Religion and assimilation, 45-60.

116

Clammer, John R. (ed) Studies in chinese folk religion in singapore and malaysia. Singapore (1983) 178 p. Essays sep listed in this bibliog; abbrev CFRSM.

Coppel, Charles A. Confucian religion in indonesia. Proc31stICHS, tokyo, vol 1 (1984) 268-269. Abstr.

Coppel, Charles. From christian mission to confucian religion: the nederlandische zendingsvereeniging and the chinese of west java. In David Chandler & M. C. Ricklefs (ed) Nineteenth and twentieth century indonesia, monash univ (1986) 15-40.

Coppel, Charles A. "Is confucianism a religion?": a 1923 debate in java. Archipel 38 (1989) 125-135. Debate within chin community.

Coppel, Charles A. The origins of confucianism as an organized religion in java, 1900-1923. JSEAS 12.1 (mar 1981) 178-196.

DeBernardi, Jean. The god of war and the vagabond buddha. ModCh 13.3 (1987) 310-332.

Elder, Gove. Responses of thai-chinese churches to the ancestor problem. In CAAP (1983) 225-233.

Elliott, Alan J. A. The significance of religion among the overseas chinese. ACSS (1951) 28-32

Faure, David. Folk religion in hong kong and the new territories today. In TT:RCT (1989) 259-270.

Faure, David. The structure of chinese rural society: lineage and village in the eastern new territories, hong kong. Oxford univ (1986) See chap 5, Religion and the representation of territory, 70-86.

Faure, David & Lee Lai-mui. The po tak temple in sheung shui market. JKHBRAS 22 (1982) 271-279.

Foh, Chang Pat. Ching ming festival. SarGaz 111 no 1493 (oct 1985) 22-29.

Fong, Lo Yik. Geomancy (feng-shui) in relation to mankind. SarGaz 111 no 1494 (dec 1985) 34-38.

Fong, Mak Lau. The sociology of secret societies. A study of chinese secret societies in singapore and peninsular malaysia. Oxford univ (1981) 178 p, tables, maps, diagr, 7 app, bibliog, index.

Fong, Pong-khuan. Khoo clan temple of penang. AofA 11.1 (jan-feb 1981) 104-111.

Franke, Wolfgang. Confucian and taoist traditions as evident in chinese epigraphy in southeast asia. Proc31stICHS, tokyo, vol 1 (1984) 267-268. Abstr.

Franke, Wolfgang. Notes on chinese temples and deities in northwestern borneo. In RPO-A (1985) 267-289. Notes fr field trips in 1974 and 1982.

Hase, Patrick. Observations at a village funeral. In David Faure, James Hayes & Alan Birch (ed) From village to city: studies in the traditional roots of hong kong society, univ HK (1984) 129-163, 254-260.

Hase, Patrick H. Old hau wong temple, tai wai, sha tin. JKHBRAS 23 (1983) 233-240.

Hase, Patrick H. Traditional funerals. JHKBRAS 21 (1981) 192-196, illus 10 photos. Re punti villages in new territories.

Hayes, James W. The disturbance of feng-shui. In RC/HK (1983) 206-208.

Hayes, James W. Graves. In RC/HK (1983) 209-212.

Hayes, James W. Graves in a chinese landscape. In RC/HK (1983) 137-145.

Hayes, James W. The kwun yam-tung shan temple of east kowloon, 1840-1940. JHKBRAS 23 (1983) 212-218.

Hayes, James W. Lantern festival, cheung chau, 10th february 1971. JHKBRAS 26 (1986) 267-270.

Hayes, James W. Moving ancestors. In RC/HK (1983) 199-201.

Hayes, James. New buildings. In RC/HK (1983) 202-203.

Hayes, James. Notes on temples and shrines, hong kong island. JHKBRAS 27 (1987) 285-291.

Hayes, James W. Occasional protective rites. In RC/HK (1983) 165-178.

Hayes, James W. Periodic protective rites. In RC/HK (1983) 156-164.

Hayes, James. The rural communities of hong kong; studies and themes. Oxford univ (1983) 308 p. Essays by author, sep listed in this bibliog; abbrev RC/HK

Hayes, James W. Secular non-gentry leadership of temple and shrine organizations in urban british hong kong. JHKBRAS 23 (1983) 113-136.

Hayes, James. Specialists and written materials in the village world. In PopCult (1985) 75-111. Incl much of relevance to relig.

Hayes, James W. Supplication and thanksgiving ceremonies. In RC/HK (1983) 204-205.

Hayes, James. The tai sheung lo kwan temple, chaiwan. JHKBRAS 28 (1988) 217-218.

Hayes, James W. Village beliefs and practices. In RC/HK (1983) 197-198.

Hayes, James W. Geomancy and the village. In TICHK (1967) 22-30. Repr in RCHK (1983) 146-152.

Hayes, James W. Removal of villages for fung shui reasons. Another example from lantau island, hong kong. JHKBRAS 9 (1969) 156-158. Repr in RCHK (1983) 153-155.

Heinze, Ruth-Inge. Automatic writing in singapore. In CFRSM (1983) 146-160.

Heinze, Ruth-Inge. The nine imperial gods of singapore. AsFS 40.2 (1981) 151-172. The star-gods of ursa major.

Heinze, Ruth-Inge. Social implications of the relationships between mediums, entourages and clients in singapore today. SEAJSocSci 7 (1979) 60-80.

Hooker, M. B. The "chinese confucian" and the "chinese buddhist" in british burma, 1881-1947. JSEAS 21.2 (1990) 384-401. With special ref to ambiguities in legal definitions.

Hua, Cecilia Ng Siew. The sam poh neo neo keramat: a study of a baba chinese temple. In CFRSM (1983) 98-131.

Huey, Ju Shi. Chinese spirit mediums in singapore: an ethnographic study. In CFRSM (1983) 3-48.

Jong, Kiam Chun. Tua pek kong temple of kuching. SarGaz no 1478 (dec 1981) 39-45.

Kate, Sister. Some descriptive notes on an american taoist cloister. TaoRes 1.1 (autumn 1988) 18-21.

Khoo, Betty L. True to temple tradition. Straits times A (1979) 112-116.

Lai, David Chuen-yan. A feng-shui model as a location index. AAAG 64.4 (dec 1974) 506-513.

Lai, Kuan Fook. The hennessy book of chinese festivals. Kuala lumpur (1984) 93 p.

Lang, Graeme & Lars Ragvald. Official and oral traditions about hong kong's newest god [i.e. wong tai sin] JHKBRAS 27 (1987) 93-97.

Lang, Graeme & Lars Ragvald. Upward mobility of a refugee god: hong kong's huang daxian. Univ stockholm (nov 1986) 32 p, ref.

Law, Jean (photos) & Barbara E. Ward (text). Chinese festivals in hong kong. HK (1982) 95 p, 85 col pl, gloss, festival calendar, index.

Lee, Peter K. H. A chinese new year interreligious celebration (hong kong) CF 25.1 (mar 1982) 32-36.

Lee, Raymond L. M. Continuity and change in chinese spirit mediumship in urban malaysia. BTLVK 142.2-3 (1986) 198-214.

Lee, Raymond L. M. Dancing with the gods: a spirit medium festival in urban malaysia. Anthropos 78 (1983) 355-368.

Lee, Raymond L. M. & Susan E. Ackerman. Ideology, authority and conflict in a chinese religious movement in west malaysia. In CFRSM (1983) 132-145.

Leo, Juat Beh & John Clammer. Confucianism as folk religion in singapore: a note. In CFRSM (1983) 175-178.

Lessa, William A. The chinese trigrams in micronesia. JAFL 82 no 326 (oct-dec 1969) 353-362.

Lin, Ting Kwong, Ho Kong Chong & Tong Chee Kiong. A multivariate approach to studying chinese customs and rites in singapore. SEAJSocSci 18.2 (1990) 70-84.

Lip, Evelyn. Chinese temple architecture. Architect 94 (mar 1987) 17-19. In china mainland, singapore and malaysia.

Lip, Evelyn. Chinese temple architecture in singapore. Singapore univ (1983) 114 p, col photos, drawings, fig, app, bibliog, index, chin char used throughout.

Lu, Ping-chuan & Tsao Pen-yeh. The ritual music of taoist "chiao"—studies made in lin-cheung and p'eng-hu. Proc31stICHS, tokyo, vol 2 (1984) 656-658. Abstr.

Morgan, Carole. A propos des fiches oraculaires de huang daxian. JA 275 (1987) 163-191. Re oracle-slips in huang daxian temple, HK.

Myers, John T. Traditional chinese religious practices in an urban-industrial setting: the example of kwun tong. In Ambrose Y. C. King & Rance P. L. Lee (ed) Social life and development in hong kong, HK (1981) 275-288.

Newell, William H. Treacherous river. A study of rural chinese in north malaya. Univ malaya (1962) See chap 5, Religion, 92-122.

Ng, Cecilia Siew Ha. The sam poh neo neo keramat: a study of a baba chinese temple. In CFRSM (1983) 98-131.

Ng, Greer Anne. The dragon and the lamb: chinese festivals in the life of chinese canadian/american christians. RelEd 84 (summer 1989) 368-383.

Ng, Teng Seng. Siang ong kong temple. Jernal persatuan sej mal sar 5 (june 1980) 24-34.

Parkin, Harry. Postscript: chinese religious studies today. In CFRSM (1983) 161-174.

Ragvald, Lars & Graeme Lang. Confused gods: huang daxian (wong tai sin) and huang yeren at mt. luofu. JHKBRAS 27 (1987) 74-92.

Robinson, Natalie V. Chinese funerals in singapore. Sawaddi (july-aug 1981) 31-34.

Sakai, Tadao. Some aspects of chinese religious practices and customs in singapore and malaya. JSEAS 12.1 (mar 1981) 133-141.

Salmon, Claudine & Denys Lombard. Les chinois de jakarta; temples et vie collective. Ann arbor, mich (1980) lxxviii (in engl) + 358 p (in french) 34 photo pl, notes, bibliog, tables, chin texts.

Scanlon, Phil jr. Southeast asia: a cultural study through celebration. Northern illinois univ (1985) See 1, Singapore and malaysia; 2, Malaysia; passim for chin relig.

Shen, Philip. Concerns with politics and culture in contextual theology: a hong kong chinese perspective. CF 25.3 (sept 1982) 129-137.

Shiratori, Yoshiro (ed) The dragon boat festival in hong kong. Tokyo, sophia univ (1985)

Siaw, Laurence K. L. Chinese society in rural malaysia. Oxford univ (1983) See 7, The role of the secret societies, 1948-1955, 108-131.

119

Siu, Anthony K. K. Tam kung: his legend and worship. JHKBRAS 27 (1987) 278-279.

Smith, Henry N. Ancestor practices in contemporary hong kong: religious ritual or social custom? AJT 3 (apr 1989) 31-45.

Smith, Henry N. Christianity and ancestor practices in hong kong: toward a contextual strategy. Missiology 17 (jan 1989) 27-38.

Song, Arthur. Chinese religion: the chinese community in southern africa. Religion in south africa 3.1 (1982) 19-30.

Sparks, Douglas W. Group dynamics of religious associations in hong kong. In Gerald H. Krausse (ed) Urban society in southeast asia, vol 2, HK (1988) 233-250. Focuses on teochiu relig associations.

Stevens, Keith G. Portrait and ancestral images on chinese altars. AofA 19.1 (jan-feb 1989) 135-145.

Suryadinata, Leo. Confucianism in indonesia: past and present. Southeast asia: an international quarterly 3.3 (spring 1974) 881-903. Same title in author's book, The chinese minority in indonesia; seven papers, singapore (1978) 33-62.

Tan, Chee-Beng. Chinese religion in malaysia: a general view. AsFS 42 (1983) 217-250.

Tan, Chee-Beng. The development and distribution of dejiao associations in malaysia and singapore: a study on a chinese religious organization. Singapore (1985) 87 p, illus, maps, 2 app.

Tan, Chee-Beng. Pernakan chinese in northeast kelantan with special reference to chinese religion. JMBRAS 55.1 (july 1982) 26-52. Illus in vol 55.2, p 135.

Tan, Kim-sai. Christian alternatives to ancestor worship in malaysia. In CAAP (1985) 219-224.

Tan, Sooi Beng. An introduction to the chinese glove puppet theatre in malaysia. JMBRAS 57.1 (1984) 40-55, photos, fig. "The po te hi is performed only during religious occasions" in lieu of much more expensive live opera.

Tanaka, Issei. The jiao festival in hong kong and the new territories. In TT:RCT (1989) 271-298.

Tham, Seong Chee. Religion and modernization: a study of changing rituals among singapore's chinese, malays, and indians. East asian cultural studies 23.1-4 (mar 1984) 186 p (entire issue) b-&-w photos.

Tom, K. S. Echoes from old china. Honolulu (1989) See 5, Celebrations and festivals, 19-43; 6, Popular gods and religious personages, 44-62; 10, Chinese hells, 94-97.

Tsao, Pen-yeh. Variation technique in the formal structure of the music of taoist jiao-shih in hong kong. JHKBRAS 23 (1983) 172-181.

Tsui, Bartholomew P. M. The place of fu-chi (spirit-writing) in modern taoist sects in hong kong. CF 33 (sept 1990) 176-189.

Tsui, Bartholomew P. M. Tan tse tao: a contemporary chinese faith-healing sect in hong kong. JHKBRAS 25 (1985) 1-16.

Tsui, Bartholomew P. M. Taoist ritual books of the new territories. In STR&MT (1989) 136-143.

Wells, Marian Kaye. Chinese temples in california. Univ calif (1962) 108 p, app, photos and fig. Repr of univ of calif thesis.

Willmott, Donald Earl. The chinese of semarang: a changing community in indonesia. Cornell univ (1960) See chap 9, Religion and magic, 182-259.

Wilson, B. D. Notes on some chinese customs in the new territories. JHKBRAS 23 (1983) 41-61.

Yoshihara, Kazuo. "De jiao": a study of an urban chinese religion in thailand. In John R. Clammer (ed) Studies in urban anthropology, singapore (1987) 61-79.

Yoshihara, Kazuo. Dejiao: a chinese religion in southeast asia. JJRS 15.2-3 (june-sept 1988) 199-221.

II.45 Comparisons - Interactions

Allinson, Robert E. The chinese case in a philosophy of world religions. In author (ed) Understanding the chinese mind, chin univ HK (1989) 48-74.

Allinson, Robert E. The ethics of confucianism and christianity: the delicate balance. CF 33.3 (sept 1990) 158-175.

Allinson, Robert E. The golden rule in confucianism and christianity. ACQ 16.4 (winter 1988) 1-15.

Ames, Roger T. The common ground of self-cultivation in classical taoism and confucianism. TJ 17.1-2 (dec 1985) 65-97. Repr in TaoRes 1.1 (autumn 1988) 23-54.

Ames, Roger T. Religiousness in classical confucianism: a comparative analysis. ACQ 12.2 (summer 1984) 7-23.

Antoni, Klaus. Death and transformations: the presentation of death in east and southeast asia. AsFS 41.2 (1982) 147-162.

Aubin, Francoise. La vision catholique de la religiosité chinoise et mongole. Mélanges de l'école francaise de rome, italie et méditerranée 101.2 (1989) 991-1035.

Barnett, Raymond J. Taoism and biological science. Zygon 21.3 (sept 1986) 297-317.

Bauer, Wolfgang. The hermit's temptation: aspects of eremitism in china and the west in the third and early fourth century a.d. ProcICS, taipei, Thought & philosophy vol 1 (1981) 73-115.

Bays, Daniel H. Christianity and chinese sects: religious tracts in the late nineteenth century. In Suzanne Wilson Barnett & John King Fairbank (ed) Christianity in china: early protestant missionary writings, harvard univ (1985) 121-134.

Bays, Daniel H. Christianity and the chinese sectarian tradition. CSWT 4.7 (june 1982) 33-55.

Bays, Daniel H. Popular religious movements in china and the united states in the nineteenth century. Fides et historia 15.1 (fall-winter 1982) 24-38.

Becker, Gerhold K. The quest for the ultimate in confucianism and christianity. CF 32.4 (dec 1989) 202-217.

Ben Yosef, I. J. Confucianism and taoism in the star of redemption. Journal for the study of religion [univ of durban, south africa] 1, (1988) 25-36. Franz Rosenszeig's Star of redemption is "probably the most significant contribution to a systematic jewish theology in the 20th century" acc to author of this art.

Berling, Judith A. Christianity and chinese religions: explorations of new possibilities. CN 27.3 (summer 1989) Rev art on book by Hans Küng & Julia Ching q.v.

Berndt, Manfred. Servanthood among para-christian and non-christian religions in hong kong. CF 14.4 (1971) 157-182.

Berthrong, John. Tao and logos: confucian - christian dialogue. CN 25.1 (winter 1986-87) 433-437.

Bertuccioli, Giuliano. Matteo ricci and taoism. In ISCI (1983) 41-49.

Blanchon, Flora. Mystique et esthétique en chine: histoire d'un itinéraire et éléments d'une interaction. CEC 8 (1989) 17-44.

Bock, Felicia G. (tsl) Classical learning and taoist practices in early japan, with a translation of books XVI and XX of the engi-shiki. Arizona state univ (1985) 100 p, notes, gloss, diagr, tables, bibliog.

Buri, Fritz. Die gespräche des konfuzius und gotthelfs bernerkalender. ZRGG 37.3 (1985) 216-252.

Campany, Robert F. "Survival" as an interpretive strategy: a sino-western comparative case study. Method & theory in the study of religion 2.1 (spring 1990) 2-26.

Ch'en, Tu-hsiu. Tsl by Douglas Lancashire. Christianity and the chinese people. In CERF (1981) 208-222.

Ch'ien, Edward T. The neo-confucian confrontation with buddhism: a structural and historical analysis. JCP 9 (1982) 307-328.

Chan, Wing-tsit. Chu hsi and taoism. Chap 28 in author's CH:NS (1989) 486-508.

Chan, Wing-tsit. Influence of taoist classics on chinese philosophy. In LB (1981) 139-153.

Chan, Wing-tsit. Perspectives on religion. SAR 14.4 (winter 1988) 50-64.

Chang, Aloysius. Chinese culture and christianity. CC 29.2 (june 1988) 51-66.

Chang, Aloysius. The confucian jen: a christian interpretation. CC 27.3 (sept 1986) 29-39.

Chang, Chi-yun. Confucianism and western culture. SAR 10.4 (winter 1984) 19-43.

Chao, Samuel H. Confucian chinese and the gospel: methodological considerations. AJT 1.1 (apr 1987) 17-40.

Chen, Chang-fang. Thoreau's orientalism: chinese thought in walden. TR 18.1-4 (aut 1987-sum 1988) 287-322. Confucianism and taoism.

Cheng, Anne. Die bedeutung des konfuzianismus in frankreich: gestern, heute, morgen. In S. Krieger & R. Trauzetiel (ed) Konfuzianismus und die modernisierung chinas, mainz (1990) 535-542.

Ching, Julia. Ethical encounter: chinese and christian. In Jacques Pohier & Dietmar Mieth (ed) Christian ethics, edinburgh (1981) 30-35.

Chou, Yun-jin. Matteo ricci and his accomodation with confucianism. NPMB 24.6 (jan-feb 1990) 1-14.

Chow, Lien-hwa. Christian response to filial piety in chinese classical literature. In CAAP (1983) 135-146.

Chow, Tse-tsung. Ancient chinese wu shamanism and its relationship to sacrifices, history, dance-music, and poetry. TJ n.s.13.1/2 (dec 1981) Engl summ 23-25.

Chryssides, George D. God and the tao. RS 19.1 (mar 1983) 1-11.

Chuang, Ying-chang. A comparison of hokkien and hakka ancestor worship. ASBIE 69 (1990) 133-159.

Clasper, Paul. Christian faith, asian wisdom traditions and the newly emerging paradigm shift. CF 26.4 (dec 1983) 195-207.

Clasper, Paul. Christian spirituality and the chinese context. CF 20.1 (1977) 2-17. Same title in SEAJT 18.2 (1977) 1-12.

Clavier, H. La foi, le mérite et la grâce dans les religions d'extrême-orient et dans le christianisme. Revue d'histoire et de philosophie religieuses 42.1 (1962) 1-16.

Cooper, Eugene. The potlatch in ancient china: parallels in the socio-political structure of the ancient chinese and the american indians of the northwest coast. HR 22.2 (1982) 103-128.

Copleston, Frederick. Religion and the one: philosophers east and west. NY (1982) See chap 3, The one in taoism and buddhism, 40-67.

Corless, Roger J. T'an-luan: taoist sage and buddhist bodhisattva. In BTS-II (1987) 36-45.

Corradini, Piero. Matteo ricci's approach to chinese civilization. D&A 4.2 (summer 1990) 51-59.

Covell, Ralph R. Confucius, the buddha, and christ. A history of the gospel in chinese. Maryknoll, NY (1986) 304 p.

Decaux, Jacques. Taoist philosophy and jungian psychology. CC 22.4 (dec 1981) 95-110.

Dehergne, Joseph. l'Exposé des jésuites de pékin sur le culte des ancêtres presenté à l'empereur k'anghi en novembre 1700. In RECEL (1980) 185-229.

122

Dehergne, Joseph. Les historiens jésuites du taoïsme. In Jacques Gernet et al, La mission francaise de pékin aux XVIIe et XVIIIe siècles, paris (1976) 59-67.

Despeux, Catherine. Le chemin de l'éveil. Illustré par le dressage du buffle dans le bouddhisme chan, le dressage du cheval dans le taoïsme, le dressage de l'éléphant dans le bouddhisme tibétaine. Paris (1981) 139 p.

Doolittle, Justus. Missionary topics. Chap 17 in author's SLC vol 2 (1895) 394-417. Re certain beliefs and practices esp relevant to christian missionary efforts.

Dorsey, John T. Confucianism, christianity, and social change in john hersey's The call. TR 18.1-4 (aut 1987-sum 1988) 323-331.

Düssel, Reinhard. Aspects of confucianism in elias canetti's notes and essays. TR 18.1-4 (aut 1987-sum 1988) 333-341.

Dy, Manuel B. Jen in confucian and neo-confucian thought and christian love. Philippine studies 31.4 (4th qtr 1983) 430-450.

Elder, Gove. Responses of thai-chinese churches to the ancestor problem. In CAAP (1985) 225-233.

Evans, John Karl. The cult of the dead in ancient rome and modern china: a comparative analysis. JHKBRAS 25 (1985) 119-151.

Eynon, Matthew. Form and function in the japanese mikoshi and the chinese chiaozu. TJR 21 (dec 1987) 69-94.

Franke, Herbert. The taoist elements in the buddhist great bear sutra (pei-tou ching) AM 3rd ser 1 (1990) 75-111. Compares non-canonical texts in mongolian, tibetan and uighur.

Freedman, Maurice & Marjorie Topley. Religion and social realignment among the chinese in singapore. JAS 21.1 (nov 1961) 3-23.

Fu, Charles Wei-hsun. Chu hsi on buddhism. In CH&NC (1986) 377-407.

Fu, Charles Wei-hsun. Postwar confucianism and western democracy: an ideological struggle. Chap 9 in MIWR (1987) 177-196.

Fu, James S. Mythic and comic aspects of the quest: hsi yu chi as seen through don quixote and huckleberry finn. Singapore univ (1977) 125 p, bibliog, index.

Fu, Pei-jung. A philosophical reflection on the christian-confucian dialogue. In RIID (1989) 533-554.

Fung, Hu-hsiang. Chinese philosophical foundations for interreligious dialogue. D&A 3.1 (spring 1989) 45-50.

Gelburd, Gail & Geri De Paoli. Asian philosophy in recent american art. Univ penn for hofstra museum (1990) 124 p, 11 col and b-&-w illus.

Gernet, Jacques. Chine et christianisme. Paris (1982) Engl tsl by Janet Lloyd, China and the christian impact, univ cambridge (1985) 310 p. German tsl, zürich & münchen (1984). See Index and passim.

Gernet, Jacques. Christian and chinese visions of the world in the seventeenth century. ChSci 4 (sept 1980) 1-17.

Hsiao, Paul Shih-yi. Heidegger and our translation of the tao te ching. In HET (1987) 93-103.

Hsieh, Jiann & Ying-hsiung Chou. Public aspirations in the new year couplets: a comparative study between the people's republic and taiwan. AsFS 40.2 (1981) 125-149.

Hsu, Francis L. K. Filial piety in japan and china: borrowing, variation and significance. Journal of comparative family studies 2 (1971) 67-74.

Hung, Daniel M. Mission blockade: ancestor worship. Chinese around the world (apr 1983) 3-6 Repr fr Evanglical missions quarterly (jan 1983) repr in CAAP (1985) 199-208.

Hwang, Philip Ho. Confucianism and theism. In Henry O. Thompson (ed) The wisdom of faith: essays in honor of sebastian alexander matczak, lanham, md (1989) 51-62.

Inada, Kenneth. Zen and taoism: common and uncommon grounds of discourse. JCP 15.1 (1988) 51-65.

International confucian-christian conference, june 1988, hongkong. CF 31.2/3 (aug 1988) Entire issue devoted to papers on this subj; see passim.

Izutsu, Toshihiko. Sufism and taoism. A comparative study of key philosophical concepts. Tokyo (1983) 493 p. Rev version of author's 2-vol wk, A comparative study of key philosophical concepts in sufism and taoism, keio univ (1966-67) q.v.

James, Jean M. Some iconographic problems in early daoist-buddhist sculptures in china. AAA 42 (1989) 71-76. Re some votive sculptures fr shanhsi in chicago's field museum.

Jan, Yün-hua. Cultural borrowing and religious identity: a case study of the taoist religious codes. HHYC:CS 4.1 (june 1986) 281-294. Re taoist borrowing fr buddhism.

Jan, Yün-hua. Li p'ing-shan and his refutation of neo-confucian criticism of buddhism. In DBT (1979) 162-193. Li's dates are 1185-1231.

Janelli, Roger L. & Dawnhee Yim Janelli. Ancestor worship and korean society. Stanford univ (1982) See chap 7, Ancestor cults in east asia compared, 177-195.

Jullien, Francois. La conception du monde naturel, en chine et en occident, selon tang junyi. EOEO 3 (1983) 117-125.

Kate, Sister. Some descriptive notes on an american taoist cloister. TaoRes 1.1 (autumn 1988) 18-21.

Kendall, Laurel. Korean shamanism: women's rites and a chinese comparison. In RFEA (1986) 57-73.

Kendall, Laurel. Supernatural traffic—east asian shamanism. CM&P 5.2 (1981) 171-191. Rev art on shamanism in korea, japan, and taiwan.

Kleinman, Arthur & James L. Gale. Patients treated by physicians and folk healers: a comparative outcome study in taiwan. CM&P 6.4 (dec 1982) 405-423.

Knaul, Livia. Chuang tzu and the chinese ancestry of ch'an. JCP 13 (1986) 411-428.

Kojima, Hajime. Die jodo-lehre shinrans und der taoismus in china. In RPO-A (1985) 233-238.

Kramers, R. P. Der volkommene mensch in konfuzianischer und in christlicher sicht. In T. Müller-Krüger (heraus) Confrontations, stuttgart (1966)

Küng, Hans & Julia Ching. Christianity and chinese religions. NY etc (1989) 309 p, basic lit, indexes. Engl tsl of Christentum und chinesische religion, münchen (1988) See passim for chin relig. Same title in SEDOS bulletin [rome] 22 (june 15 1990) 163-167.

Lagerwey, John. The oral and the written in chinese and western religion. In RPO-A (1985) 301-322.

Lai, Whalen. The crossing of paths in the cult of kuan-kung. CF 32.4 (dec 1989) 218-223. Title ref to mixing of relig "ways"

Lee, Agnes C. J. Francis of assisi and chuang tzu: a comparative study in religious consciousness. CF 27.2-3 (july 1984) 94-114.

Lee, Cyrus. Some reflections on chinese humanism and christian spirituality. CC 25.4 (dec 1984) 1-8.

Lee, Peter K. H. A chinese new year interreligious celebration (hong kong) CF 25.1 (mar 1982) 32-36.

Lee, Peter K. H. Christian spirituality in a chinese religious context. EAJT 3.1 (apr 1985) 16-30. Re motif of "hsin-hsing (heart-nature)"

Lee, Peter K. H. Christianized hsin-hsing spirituality. CF 27.2/3 (july 1984) 73-93.

Lee, Peter K. H. Two stories of loyalty. CF 32.1 (mar 1989) 25-40. Compares story about Ruth in old testament with kuan han-ch'ing's injustice to tou–o.

Lee, Peter K. H. & Yuk Wong. Ta-t'ung and the kingdom of god. CF 31.4 (dec 1988) 225-245. Li yün chap of li chi and certain biblical passages compared.

Legge, James. The religions of china. Confucianism and taoism described and compared with christianity. London (1880) 310 p. Repr folcroft, penn (1976) norwood, penn (1977) philadelphia (1978)

Lessa, William A. The chinese trigrams in micronesia. JAFL 82 no 326 (oct-dec 1969) 353-362.

Levi, Jean. Dong yong le fils pieux et le mythe formosan de l'origine des singes. JA 272.1-2 (1984) 83-132.

Liang, Shuming. A comparison of confucianism and buddhism. CSP 20.3 (spring 1989) 3-32.

Liao, David. Christian alternatives to ancestor worship in taiwan. In CAAP (1985) 209-218.

Liaw, Stephen. Ancestor worship in contemporary taiwanese society and evangelism of the chinese. In CAAP (1985) 181-197.

Lim, Guek Eng. Christianity encounters ancestor worship in taiwan. ERTh 8.2 (1984) 225-235.

Lim, Guek Eng. Christianity versus ancestor worship in taiwan. TCGB 11.2 (oct 1983) 4-10.

Lin, Chi-ping. Ancestor worship: the reactions of chinese churches. In CAAP (1985) 147-161.

Lin, Kai-shyh. The eternal mother and the heavenly father: two deities of rebellion in late imperial china. ASBIE 69 (1990) 161-180. Re white lotus and taiping myths.

Lin, S.-h. Le christianisme vu par la religion chinoise. Concilium 203 (1986) 101-110.

Lin, Xiaoping. Wu li's religious beliefs and A lake in spring. AAA 40 (1987) 24-35. Influence of catholicism on ch'ing painter's picture.

Liu, Joyce C. H. The protest from the invisible world: the revenge ghost in yuan drama and the elizabethan drama. TR 19.1-4 (aut 1988-sum 1989) 755-776.

Liu, Ming-wood. Fan chen's treatise on the destructibility of the spirit and its buddhist critics. PEW 35.4 (oct 1987) 402-428.

Liu, Chiang. Some challenges of china's religions to christianity. ChRec 65.4 (apr 1934) 217-221.

Loewe, Michael. Imperial china's reactions to the catholic missions. Numen 35.2 (dec 1988) 179-212.

Mahdihassan, S. Cinnabar-gold as the best alchemical drug of longevity, called makaradhasaja in india. AJCM 13.1-4 (1985) 93-108.

Mahdihassan, S. Indian and chinese cosmic elements. AJCM 7.4 (winter 1979) 316-323.

Mahdihassan, S. Indian and chinese cosmologies reconsidered. AJCM 13.1-4 (1985) 5-12.

Mahdihassan, S. Symbols designed by european alchemists incorporating elements of chinese origin. AJCM 15.1-2 (1987) 3-12.

Mahdihassan, S. Venus, the goddess of fertility, numerologically 15 in babylon and the origin of the chinese system of 8 designs, called pa-kua. AJCM 15.3-4 (1987) 81-97.

McClenon, James. Chinese and american anomalous experiences: the role of religiosity. Sociological analysis: a journal in the sociology of religion 51 (spring 1990) 53-67.

McClenon, James. A survey of chinese anomalous experiences and comparison with western representative national samples. JSSR 27 (spring 1988) 421-426.

Müller, Wilhelm. Matteo ricci's beitrag zur kenntnis der religionen chinas. In Johannes Triebel (ed) Der missionar als forscher, gütersloh (1988) 130-154.

Najarian, Nishan J. Religious conversion in nineteenth-century china: face-to-face interactions between western missionaries and the chinese. In SICS (1982) 67-111.

Neville, Robert C. A christian response to shu-hsien liu and pei-jung fu. In RIID (1989) 555-570.

Neville, Robert C. Individuation in christianity and confucianism. CF 32.1 (mar 1989) 3-23.

Ng, Greer Anne. The dragon and the lamb: chinese festivals in the life of chinese canadian/american christians. RelEd 84 (summer 1989) 368-383.

Ogden, Graham S. Biblical and confucian thought: a consideration of some common teachings. TJT 4 (mar 1982) 215-227.

Ogden, Graham S. Numerical sayings in israelite wisdom and in confucius. TJT 3 (mar 1981) 145-176.

Park, O'Hyun. Oriental ideas in recent religious thought. Lakemont, georgia (1974) See chap 5, Chinese religions and the religion of china, 155-185; same title as art in Perspectives in religious studies 2 (fall 1975) 160-190.

Parkes, Graham (ed) Heidegger and eastern thought. Univ hawaii (1987) Indiv art sep listed in this bibliog; abbrev HET.

Parkes, Graham. Thoughts on the way: being and time via lao-chuang. In HET (1987) 105-144. Re Heidegger's thought.

Paul, Diana. Portraits of the feminine: buddhist and confucian historical perspectives. In SHB (1980) 209-221.

Pelphrey, Brant. Meditation in a bowl: the dao-de-jing and kenotic christology. Areopagus (christmas 1990, 4.1) 21-27.

Perry, Elizabeth J. Taipings and triads: the role of religion in inter-rebel relations. In RRR (1984) 342-353.

Petzold, Bruno. Heraus von Horst Hammitzch. Die quintessenz der t'ien-t'ai-(tendai)lehre; eine komparative untersuchung. Wiesbaden (1982) xv + 619 s, bemerkungen zur herausgezogenen literatur, erganzende bibliographische angaben zu arbeiten von Bruno Petzold, zeichen glossar wesentlicher chinesischer und japanischer, termini und namen. Contains extensive discussion of relationships with taoism.

Pöggeler, Otto. West-east dialogue: heidegger and lao-tzu. In HET (1987) 47-78.

Provine, Robert C. The sacrifice to confucius in korea and its music. TKBRAS 50 (1975) 43-69, illus.

Ptak, Roderich. Hsi-yang chi—an interpretation and some comparisons with hsi-yu chi. ChLit 7.1-2 (july 1985) 117-141.

Ricci, Matteo. Tsl by Douglas Lancashire. The true meaning of the lord of heaven (t'ien-chu shih-i) Taipei (1985) xiv + 485 p, chin-engl text ed by Edward J. Malatesta.

Ro, Bong Rin (ed) Christian alternatives to ancestor practices. Taichung (1985) Indiv art sep listed in this bibliog; abbrev CAAP.

Ro, Young-chan. The place of ethics in the christian tradition and the confucian tradition: a methodological prolegomenon. RS 22.1 (1986) 51-62.

Robinet, Isabelle. Notes préliminaire sur quelques antinomies fondamentales entre le bouddhisme et le taoïsme. In Incontro (1984) 217-242.

Robinet, Isabelle. La notion de hsing dans le taoïsme et son rapport avec celle du confucianisme. JAOS 106.1 (jan-mar 1986) 183-196.

Rosemont, Henry jr. Kierkegaard and confucius: on finding the way. PEW 36.3 (july 1986) 201-212. Same title in CN 25.1 (winter 1986-87) 429-433.

Ross, Daniel G. Chinese and western religious

126

symbols as used in taiwan. Fu jen univ (1980) 226 p. Recognition and meaning of sel symbols acc to 414 taiwanese.

Ross, R. R. N. Non-being and being in taoist and western traditions. RTrad 2.2 (oct 1979) 24-38.

Sakade, Yoshinobu. Longevity techniques in japan: ancient sources and contemporary studies. In TMLT (1989) 1-40. The "ancient sources" ref to chin texts.

Sakade, Yoshinobu. The taoist character of the 'chapter on nourishing life' of the ishinpo. KDBR (1986) 775-798.

Sakai, Tadao. Dissemination of taoistic religion over the regions surrounding china. Proc31stICHS, tokyo, vol 1 (1984) 247-248. Abstr.

Saso, Michael. Taiwan: old gods and modern society. In Carlo Caldarola (ed) Religion and societies: asia and the middle east, berlin etc (1982) 579-605, bibliog.

Sawatsky, Sheldon. Chinese shamanism. TJT 12 (mar 1990) 121-143.

Schiltz, Véronique. Imagerie grecque et magie chinoise: spéculations sur le miroir de kelermès. In Lilly Kahil et al (ed) Iconographie classique et identités régionales, athens (1986) 273-283.

Schwab, Philip. Biblical understanding of ancestor practices. In CAAP (1983) 93-116.

Senda, Minoru. Taoist roots in japanese culture. JQ 35.2 (1988) 133-138.

Shaw, Yu-ming. Chinese culture in the mind of the west. Concilium 126 (1979) 1-18. Historical survey.

Shen, Yifan. Confucian thought and theological reflection in china today. CF 31 (aug 1988) 166-176.

Sheng, C. L. Confucian moral philosophy and utilitarian theory. CC 23.1 (mar 1982) 33-46.

Shepherd, John R. Sinicized siraya worship of a-

li-tsu. BIEAS 58 (1984) 1-81, illus photos. Many comparisons of aboriginal siraya relig with taiwanese chin relig.

Shih, J[oseph]. The chinese way and the christian way. SM 30 (1981) 191-205.

Shinohara, Koichi. Buddhism and confucianism in ch'i-sung's essay on teaching (yuan-tao) JCP 9.4 (dec 1982) 401-422. Ch'i-sung's dates are 1007-1072.

Smith, Huston. Chinese religion in world perspective. D&A 4.2 (summer 1990) 4-14.

Smith, Henry N. Christianity and ancestor practices in hong kong: toward a contextual strategy. Missiology 17.1 (jan 1989) 27-38.

Smith, Henry. A typology of christian responses to chinese ancestor worship. Journal of ecumenical studies 26 (fall 1989) 628-647.

Smith, D. Howard. Conflicting ideas of salvation in a.d. fifth century china. In M&HS (1973) 291-303.

Song, Shun-ching. Voltaire et la chine. Univ de provence (1989) See chap 4, Religion, 115-126.

Stambaugh, Joan. Heidegger, taoism, and the question of metaphysics. In HET (1987) 79-91.

Standaert, N. Yang tingyun [1562-1627] confucian and christian in late ming china. His life and thought. Leiden (1988) 263 p, notes, bibliog, index.

Stevenson, Frank. Dwelling at ease and awaiting destiny: "taoism" in the "confucian" chung yung. TR 20.3 (spring 1990) 265-316.

Stines, James W. I am the way: michael polanyi's taoism. Zygon 20.1 (mar 1985) 59-77.

Streng, Frederick J. Three approaches to authentic existence: christian, confucian and buddhist. PEW 32.4 (oct 1982) 371-392. Comparison of paul tillich, chün-i t'ang, and keiji nishitani.

Strolz, Walter. Heilswege der weltreligionen.

Band 2: Christliche begegnund mit hinduismus, buddhismus, und taoismus. ? place of publ (1986) 255 s.

Swan-Liat, K. Dualism and wholeness in a chinese perspective. ZMR 66.2 (1982) 118-134. Chin concern with man, contrasted with western concern with truth.

Tan, Kim-sai. Christian alternatives to ancestor worship in malaysia. In CAAP (1983) 219-224.

T'ang, Chün-i. Tsl by Douglas Lancashire. The spirit of religion and modern man. In CERF (1981) 44-52.

Taylor, Rodney L. Modernity and religion: a contemporary confucian response. In author's RDC (1990) 135-147. "Response" by Okada Takehiko.

Taylor, Rodney L. The problem of suffering: christian and confucian dimensions. In author's RDC (1990) 115-134.

Teng, Yung S. A study of the confucian thought in tu mu's literary works. TJ n.s.13.1/2 (dec 1981) 133-159.

Thomas, Léon. l'Absolu dans deux pensées apophatiques: basilide et le taoïsme. Revue d'histoire et de philosophie religieuses 67.2 (1987) 181-191.

Ting, Nai-t'ung. The holy man and the snake-woman. Fabula 8.3 (1966) 145-191. The "king and the lamia" tale in comparative study (in china it is the story of white snake)

Tominaga, Thomas T. Ch'an, taoism, and wittgenstein. JCP 10.2 (june 1983) 127-145.

Tominaga, Thomas T. Taoist and wittgensteinian mysticism. JCP 9.3 (sept 1982) 269-289.

Török, S. J. Multi-criteria decision making (MCDM) and the social psychology of religion in chinese, thai and japanese thought. JSiamSoc 78.2 (1990) 74-78.

Visvader, John & William C. Doub. The problem

of desires and emotions in taoism and ch'an. In ECCT (1983) 281-197.

Voss, Gustav. Missionary accomodation to ancestral rites in the far east. Theological studies 43 (1943) 525-560.

Wawrytko, Sandra A. Confucius and kant: the ethics of respect. PEW 32.3 (july 1982) 237-257.

Wayman, Alex. Male, female, and androgyne, per buddhist tantra, jacob boehme, and the greek and taoist mysteries. In T&TStudies 2 (MCB 21, 1983) 592-631.

Werblowsky, R. J. Z. l'Image occidentale de la religion chinois de leibnitz à de groot. Diogène 133 (1986) 113-121.

Werblowsky, R. J. Zwi. The western perception of china 1700-1900. D&A 4.2 (summer 1990) 60-70. Cp author's art in Diogène 133 (1986), l'Image occidental . . .

Wickeri, Philip L. Seeking the common ground: protestant christianity, the three-self movement, and china's united front. Maryville, NY (1988) 356 p, notes, bibliog, index. See passim.

Williams, Marjorie. Dragons, porcelains and demons: cultural exchange between china and persia. Orientations 17.8 (aug 1986) 22-32.

Wu, Lei-ch'uan. Tsl by Douglas Lancashire. Christianity and confucianism. In CERF (1981) 197-207.

Wu, Yi. On chinese ch'an in relation to taoism. JCP 12 (1985) 131-154.

Wyder, H. Chinesische religion und christliche botschaft. In Die religion in geschichte und gegenwart, bd 1, tübingen (1956) 1661a-1664b.

Yazawa, Toshihiko. Christianisme et religions populaires en chine. In BetSA (1990) 189-203.

Yearley, Lee H. Classical confucians and thomistic christians: contrasts that arise from the presence and absence of deity. D&A 1.3 (fall 1987) 23-36. A "somewhat different version" of author's art, A comparison between classical chinese thought and thomistic christian thought, JAAR 51.3, q.v.

Yearley, Lee H. A comparison between classical chinese thought and thomistic christian thought. JAAR 51.3 (sept 1983) 427-458.

Yearley, Lee H. Mencius and aquinas; theories of virtue and conceptions of courage. SUNY (1990) 280 p, notes, chin terms, sel bibliog, indexes. Comparative study of relig ethics.

Yeo, Khiok-Khng. Amos (4:4-5) and confucius: the will (ming) of god (thien) AJT 4.2 (oct 1990) 472-488.

Young, John D. Confucianism and christianity; the first encounter. Univ HK (1983) 182 p, gloss, notes, bibliog, index.

Young, Richard Fox. Sanctuary of the tao. The place of christianity in a sino-japanese unity sect (tao yüan) JCR 17 (1989) 1-26, illus.

Yu, Anthony C. Two literary examples of religious pilgrimage: the commedia and the journey to the west. HR 22 (1983) 202-230.

Yu, Chi-ping. Filial piety and chinese pastoral care. AJT 4.1 (apr 1990) 316-328.

Yu, Chi-ping. Theology of filial piety: an initial formulation. AJT 3.2 (oct 1989) 496-508.

Yü, Chün-fang. Some ming buddhists' responses to neo-confucianism. JCP 15.4 (1988) 371-413.

Yu, David C. Confucianism, maoism, and max weber. In TLLP (1985) 141-167.

Yu, Paul. Confucian ethics and western ethics: a comparative study. Commentary [singapore] 6.1 (sept 1983) 10-18.

Yü, Pin. Tsl by Douglas Lancashire. Roman catholicism and confucianism. In CERF (1981) 160-166.

Zhao, Dianpeng. Chinese culture and christian faith. Chinese theological review [holland, mich] (1988) 32-40.

Zürcher, Erik. The lord of heaven and the demons—strange stories from a late ming christian manuscript. In RPO-A (1985) 359-375. Re confrontation of christianity with chin popular relig.

II.46 Religion and Society

Ahern, Emily Martin. Chinese ritual and politics. Cambridge univ (1981) 144 p, notes, bibliog, char list, index.

Aijmer, Göran. Birth and death in china: musings on a taiwan corpus. Ethnos 49.1-2 (1984) 5-42.

Bak, Janos M. & Gerhard Benecke (ed) Religion and rural revolt. Manchester univ (1984) See sec Modern china, with preface by Daniel Overmyer, and art by Elizabeth Perry, Ralph Thaxton, and Robert Weller, sep listed in this bibliog; abbrev RRR.

Brook, Timothy. Funerary ritual and the building of lineages in late imperial china. HJAS 49.2 (1989) 465-499.

Chang, Kwang-chih. Art, myth and ritual: the path to political authority in ancient china. Harvard univ (1983) See chap 3, Shamanism and politics, 44-55; chap 4, Art as the path to authority, 56-80. Chap 4 publ "in slightly different form" in HJAS 41 (dec 1981) 527-554: The animal in shang and chou bronze art.

Cheng, Chung-ying. Totality and mutuality: confucian ethics and economic development. In Conference on confucianism & economic development in east asia: proceedings, taipei (1989) 15-56.

Chu, Hai-yuan. The impact of different religions on the chinese family in taiwan. In CFRB (1985) 221-231.

Cohen, Myron L. Lineage organization in north china. JAS 49.3 (aug 1990) 509-534.

Cooper, Eugene. The potlatch in ancient china: parallels in the socio-economic structure of the ancient chinese and the american indians of the northwest coast. HR 22.2 (1982) 103-128.

Deverge, M. Confucianisme et succès économique à taiwan. Etudes 367.1-2 (1987) 5-13.

DeVos, George. Religion and family: structural and motivational relationships. In RFEA (1986) 3-33.

DeVos, George A. & Takao Sofue (ed) Religion and the family in east asia. Univ calif (1986) SES 11 (1984); art sep listed in this bibliog; abbrev RFEA.

Eisenstadt, Shmuel N. Innerweltliche transzendenz und die strukturierung der welt; max webers studie über china und die gestalt der chinesischen zivilisation. In MWSt (1983) 363-411.

Eisenstadt, S. N. This worldly transcendentalism and the structuring of the world: weber's "religion of china" Journal of developing societies 1.2 (dec 1985) 168-186.

Freedman, Maurice. Religion and society in south eastern china. Man 57 no 62 (1957) 56-57.

Gates, Hill & Robert P. Weller. Hegemony and chinese folk ideologies: an introduction. ModCh 13.1 (1987) 3-16.

Gutheinz, Luis & Edmond Tang. Economic development and quality of life: a socio-economic survey of taiwan. Pro-mundi vita asia-australia dossier no 33 (1985) 1-29.

Hayes, James W. Secular non-gentry leadership of temple and shrine organizations in urban british hong kong. JHKBRAS 23 (1983) 113-136.

Ho, Y. F. & L. Y. Lee. Authoritarianism and attitude toward filial piety in chinese teachers. Journal of social psychology 92 (1974) 305-306. Significant correlation was found.

Hou, Ching-lang. Les monnaies de la trésorerie et la notion de destin fondamental. In Dette (1988) 81-93.

Houtart, Francois & Genevieve Lemercinier. The great asiatic religions and their social functions. Belgium & new delhi (1983 & 1984) See chap 2 sec 3, Confucianism, taoism and chinese buddhism, 51-62.

Hsu, Jing & Wen-shing Tseng. Family relations in classic chinese opera. IJSP 20 (1974) 159-172.

Jordan, David K. Sworn brothers: a study in chinese ritual kinship. In CFRB (1985) 232-262.

Kierman, V. C. The great asiatic religions and their social functions. Journal of contemporary asia [stockholm] 13.2 (1983) 229-235.

Kischkel, Heinz. Max weber und das tao. Zu einem neuen taoistischen paradigma der religionswissenschaft. ZRGG 40.4 (1988) 335-357.

Leutner, Mechthild. Geburt, heirat und tod in Peking: volkskultur und elitekultur vom 19. jahrhundert bis zur gegenwart. Berlin (1989)

Levi, Jean. Les fonctionnaires et le divin: luttes de pouvoirs entre divinités et administrateurs dans les contes des six dynasties et des tang. CEA 2 (1986) 81-110; engl summ 107-110.

Levy, Marion J. jr. The family revolution in modern china. Harvard univ (1949) See chap 7, The kinship structure of integration and expression: integration, 247-257.

Lin, Ting Kwong, Ho Kong Chong & Tong Chee Kiong. A multivariate approach to studying chinese customs and rites in singapore. SEAJSocSci 18.2 (1990) 70-84.

Linck, Gundula. Frau und familie in china. München (1988)

Liu, Kwang-ching (ed) Orthodoxy in late imperial china. Univ calif (1990) Relevant art sep listed in this bibliog; abbrev OLIC.

Liu, Kwang-chih. Socioethics as orthodoxy: a perspective. In OLIC (1990) 53-100.

Mackerras, Colin. Chinese society since mao: religion and the family. Brisbane (1984) 27 p.

Aquinas memorial lecture sep publ as booklet.

Metzger, Thomas. Mas weber's analysis of the confucian tradition: a critique. Bulletin of historical research: li-hsüeh hsüeh-pa, natl taiwan normal univ 11 (june 1983) 1-38. German version in MWSt (1983) 229-270.

Molloy, S. Max weber and the religions of china: any way out of the maze? BJS 31.3 (1980) 377-400.

Niida, Noboru. The industrial and commercial guilds of peking and religion and fellow-countrymanship as elements of their coherence. FS 9 (1950) 179-206.

Overmyer, Daniel L. Preface. In RRR (1984) 338-341.

Parkin, Harry. Confucian thoughts on women. CN 22.2/3 (spr-sum 1984) 294-298. "Confucian underpinnings" of traditional chin society.

Ross, Daniel G. Chinese and western religious symbols as used in taiwan: a sociological study. Fu jen univ (1980) 226p. Recognition and meaning of sel symbols acc to 414 taiwanese.

Schluchter, Wolfgang. Einleitung, max webers konfuzianismusstudie—versuch einer einordnung. In MWSt (1983) 11-54.

Schluchter, Wolfgang. Tsl by Neil Solomon. Rationism, religion, & domination: a weberian perspective. Univ calif (1989) See chap 3, Confucianism and taoism: world adjustments, 85-116; chap 10, Imperial china, 354-360. Orig german version of chap 3 is in Aspekte bürokratischer herrschaft, frankfurt am main (1985, 1988) chap 10 is in Religion und lebensführung, frankfurt am main (1988)

Seiwert, Hubert. The institutional context of the history of religions in china. In Michael Pye (ed) Marburg revisited; institutions and strategies in the study of religion, marburg (? d) 127-142.

Shih, Joseph. Religion against development: the case of china. In P. Land (ed) Theology meets progress, rome (1971) 207-248.

Shinohara, Koichi. 'Adjustment to the world' and 'rationalization' in max weber's study of chinese religious tradition. SR/SR 18.1 (1979) 27-34.

Siu, Helen F. Recycling rituals: politics and popular culture in contemporary rural china. In Perry Link et al (ed) Unofficial china; popular culture and thought in the people's republic, boulder, colo etc (1989) 121-137.

Siu, Helen F. Recycling tradition: culture, history, and political economy in the chrysamthemum festivals of south china. CSSG 32.4 (1990) 765-794.

Spiro, Melford E. Some reflections on family and religion in east asia. SES 11 (1984) 35-56. Repr in RFEA (1986) 35-54.

Twitchett, Denis. Law and religion: law and religion in east asia. EncyRel 8 (1987) 469a-472a.

Übelhör, Monika. The community compact (hsiang-yüeh) of the sung and its educational significance. In NCEduc (1989) 371-388.

Van der Sprenkel, O. B. Chinese religion. BJS 5 (1954) 272-275. Rev art on H. H. Gerth (tsl) Max weber's the religion of china, q.v.

Watson, James L. Funeral specialists in cantonese society: pollution, performance, and social hierarchy. In DeathRit (1988) 109-134.

Watson, James L. & Evelyn S. Rawski (ed) Death ritual in late imperial and modern china. Univ calif (1988) 334 p. 12 essays sep listed in this bibliog; abbrev DeathRit.

Watson, Rubie S. Remembering the dead: graves and politics in southeastern china. In DeathRit (1988) 203-227.

Wilson, Richard W., Sidney L. Greenblatt & Amy Auerbach Wilson (ed) Moral behavior in chinese society. NY (1981) 199 p. See passim.

Yang, C. K. The chinese family in the communist revolution. MIT (1959) Repr in author's Chinese communist society: the family and the village, MIT (1965) See chap 10, Secularization of the family institution, 183-190.

Yu, David C. Confucianism, maoism, and max weber. In TLLP (1985) 141-167.

II.47 Miscellaneous

Bauer, Wolfgang. The hermit's temptation: aspects of eremitism in china and the west in the third and early fourth century a.d. ProcICS, taipei, Thought & philosophy vol 1 (1981) 73-115.

Bauer, Wolfgang. The hidden hero: creation and disintegration of the ideal of eremitism. In Donald Munro (ed) Individualism and holism: studies in confucianism and taoism, univ mich (1985) 157-197.

Carroll, Owen. The religious implications of the choukoutien lower cave. Berkeley, calif (1981) 78 p.

Chan, Ka Yan. Joss stick manufacturing: a study of a traditional industry in hong kong. JHKBRAS 29 (1989) 94-120.

Despeux, Catherine. Le maître dans le taoïsme non liturgique. In M. Meslin (ed) Maître et disciples dans les traditions religieuses, paris (1990) 35-50.

Dingler, W. B. (ed) Youth and religion: a religious attitude study of hongkong secondary school students. HK (1969)

Eynon, Matthew. Form and function in the japanese mikoshi and the chinese chiaozu. TJR 21 (dec 1987) 69-94

Ferguson, John. War and peace in the world's religions. Oxford univ (1978) See 5, Religions of the far east, 62-77.

Hu, Shih. Tsl by Douglas Lancashire. Immortality—my religion. In CERF (1981) 252-267. "A radically altered English version of the article written by Hu Shih himself appeared in the January/February, 1931 issue of Forum under the title 'What I Believe'"

Hucker, Charles O. A dictionary of official titles in imperial china. Stanford univ (1985) Engl and chin indexes, chin char used throughout. See relevant entries for official titles relating to relig.

Jabouille, M. P. Le phénix fabuleux de la chine et le faisan ocellé. Bulletin des amis du vieux hué 16.4 (oct-déc 1929)

Kate, Sister. Some descriptive notes on an american taoist cloister. TaoRes 1.1 (autumn 1988) 18-21.

Lagerwey, John. The oral and written in chinese and western religion. In RPO-A (1985) 301-322.

Lewis, Mark Edward. Sanctioned violence in early china. SUNY (1990) 374 p, notes, works cited, index. See passim.

Mathieu, Rémi. Le songe de zhao jianzi. Etude sur les rêves d'ascension céleste et les rêves d'esprits dans la chine ancienne. AS 37 (1983) 120-138. Chao flourished ca 500 b.c.e. in state of chin, acc to shih chi.

McFarlane, S. Bodily awareness in the wing chun system. Religion 19 (1989) 241-253.

Russell, T. C. Coffin pullers' songs: the macabre in medieval china. PFEH 27 (mar 1983) 99-130.

Schipper, Kristofer M. Une banque de données informatisée sur l'histoire du taoïsme. EtCh 1 (1983) 48-54.

Seidel, Anna. Kokuho. Note à propos du terme "trésor national" en chine et au japon. BEFEO 69 (1981) 229-261. Chin "treasures" incl prophetic texts, ho-t'u, apocrypha, taoist registers, budd patriarchal transmission symbols, etc.

Selover, Thomas. San-chiao: religious dimensions of pacific culture. In Frank K. Flinn & Tyler Hendricks (ed) Religion in the pacific era, NY (1985) 95-110.

Shih, Joseph. Mediators in chinese religion. In M. Dhavamony (ed) Mediation in christianity and other religions - SM 21 (1972) 113-126.

132

Southland, Samuel & Donna. Demonizing and mental illness: the problem of identification. Pastoral psychology 33 (spring 1985) 173-188. Mostly on case studies of possible "demonizing" from HK.

Strickmann, Michel. Dreamwork of psychosinologists: doctors, taoists, monks. In P-S (1988) 25-46.

Thompson, Laurence G. Obiter dicta on chinese religion as play. ProcICS, taipei, Folk customs and cultures vol (1981) 59-72.

Toma, Seita. What could the overcoming of eschatalogical thought of ancient china bring to the east asian world? In Toru Yuse & Masaoki Doi (ed) Forms of control and subordination in antiquity, leiden (1988) 68-75.

Török, S. J. Multi-criteria decision making (MCDM) and the social psychology of religion in chinese, thai and japanese thought. JSiamSoc 78.2 (1990) 74-78.

Tsien, Tsuen-hsuin. Paper and printing. Cambridge univ (1985) Being vol 5, pt 1 of Joseph Needham, Science and civilisation in china; see 32 (d) (3) Ceremonial uses of paper, 102-109.

Wang, Zongyu. Confucianist or buddhist? An interview with liang shuming. CSP 20.2 (winter 1988-89) 39-47.

Part Three

Chinese Buddhism

134

III.1 Reference Materials

Catalogue des manuscrits chinois de touen-houan. Fonds pelliot chinois de la bibliothèque nationale, vol III, no 3001-3500. Paris (1983) xx + 482 p. Sec 1, Bouddhisme; sec 2, Taoïsme; sec 3, Textes divers; sec 4, Particularités diverses.

Conze, Edward. Ed and rev by Lewis Lancaster. Buddhist scriptures: a bibliography. NY & london (1982) xiv + 161 p comparative cat, indices.

Demiéville, Paul, Hubert Durt & Anna Seidel. Repertoire du canon bouddhique sino-japonais. Edition de taicho (taisho shinshu daizokyo) Paris & tokyo (1978) 372 p. Fasc annexe du hobogirin.

Durt, Hubert & Anna Seidel (ed). Hobogirin. Fasc V: Chootsusho - chuu; fasc VI: da - daiji zaiten. Paris & tokyo (1979; 1983)

Eitel, E. J. Handbook for the student of chinese buddhism. HK (1870) viii + 224 p. Repr of 3rd ed (1888) amsterdam (1970)

Eitel, E. J. Hand-book of chinese buddhism, being a sanskrit chinese dictionary with vocabularies of buddhist terms in pali, singhalese, siamese, burmese, tibetan, mongolian and japanese. HK 2nd ed (1888) 231 p in 2 col. Repr san francisco (1976) new delhi (1981)

Grönbold, Günter. Der buddhistische kanon; eine bibliographie. Wiesbaden (1984) 70 p, index. See 23-26; 30-31; sekundär literatur, 45-62 passim.

Howard, Diane. A survey of some western works on chinese buddhism from the han to the sui dynasty written since 1960. Newsletter for research in chinese studies (Han-hsüeh yen-chiu t'ung-hsün) 6.1, no 21 (mar 1987) 8-14.

Gardner, James L. Zen buddhism: a classified bibliography of western-language publications through 1990. Salt lake city (1991) 412p, author and subj indexes.

Kudara Kogi. Chinese buddhist manuscripts from central asia in the mannerheim collection [helsinki] Proc31stICHS, tokyo, vol 2 (1984) 995-997.

Lancaster, Lewis R. In collaboration with Sung-bae Park. The korean buddhist canon: a descriptive catalogue. Univ calif (1979) xxiii + 724 p, indexes of titles, authors/tsl, place names, case char; comparative catalogue index, bibliog.

Malalasekera, G. P. & Jotiya Dhirasekera (ed) Encyclopaedia of buddhism. Ceylon, 4 vol issued (1961, 1966, 1971-77, 1984) Vol 1-3 ed by Malalasekera; vol 4 ed by Dhirasekera. The 4 vol cover from A to Democracy. For chin budd see relevant entries.

Mayeda, Egaku. Japanese studies on the schools of the chinese agamas. In Heinz Bechert (heraus) Zur schulzugehövigkeit von werken der hinayana-literatur, göttingen (1985) 94-103.

Nanjio, Bunyiu (Nanjo, Bunyu) A catalogue of the chinese translation of the buddhist tripitaka, the sacred canon of the buddhists in china and japan. Oxford (1883) [ix] + xxxvi + 480 col. Repr tokyo (1929) san francisco (1975) india (1989)

Pfandt, Peter. Mahayana texts translated into western languages; a bibliographical guide. Köln (1983) 167 p; rev ed with supplement (1986) 208 p.

Reynolds, Frank E, John Holt & John Strong (ed) Guide to Buddhist religion. Boston (1981) See Contents passim for relevant topics.

Schmitt (sic), Gerhard, Thomas Thilo & Taijun Inokuchi. Katalog chinesischer buddhistischer textfragmente. Berlin (1975-85) Schriften zur geschichte und kultur des alten orients, berliner turfan texte 6.14.

Teiser, Stephen F. T'ang buddhist encyclopedias: a bibliographical introduction to fa-yüan chu-lin and chu-ching yao-chi. TS 3 (winter 1985) 109-128.

Thilo, Thomas. Katalog chinesischer buddhistischer textfragmente. Band 2: schriften zur geschichte und kultur des alten orients. Berlin (1985) 1-94, 52 pl.

Wurm, Paul. Religiöser eifer bei chines. buddhisten. AMZ 10 (1883) 501-503.

Yampolsky, Philip. New japanese studies in early ch'an history. In ECCT (1983) 1-11.

III.2 General Treatments

Barrett, T. H. Religious traditions in chinese civilization: buddhism and taoism. In Paul S. Ropp (ed) Heritage of china, univ calif (1990) Chap 6, 138-163.

Beal, Samuel. Buddhist literature in china. London (1882) xvi + 185 p, 5 pl. Repr delhi (1988)

Bush, Richard C. et al (ed) The religious world: communities of faith. NY & london (1982) See Buddhism in china, 141-152.

Cousins, L. S. Buddhism. In John R. Hinnells (ed) A handbook of living religions, NY etc (1984) See relevant material in this art.

Fang, Litian. A tentative discussion of the characteristics of chinese buddhism. CSP 20.4 (summer 1989) 3-71.

Gernet, Jacques & Catherine Meuwese. Bouddhisme chinois. In EncyUniv 4 (1990) 399b-404a.

Jan, Yün-hua. Buddhist literature. In ICTCL (1986) Part 1: Essays: 1-12. Incl texts and pop lit.

Kitagawa, Joseph M. & Mark D. Cummings (ed) Buddhism and asian history. NY etc (1989) This is collection of art extracted fr EncyRel (1987) See relevant art.

Kiyota, Minoru (ed) assisted by Elvin W. Jones. Mahayana buddhist meditation: theory and practice. Univ hawaii (1978) Art sep listed in this bibliog; abbrev MBM.

Ku, Cheng-mei. Chinese buddhism—past and present. D&A 4.2 (summer 1990) 31-41.

Lahiri, Miss Latika. China. Chap 9 in Sukumar Dutt (ed) Buddhism in east asia, bombay (1966) 127-158.

Lahiri, Latika. Variety and unity of buddhist thought and practice in china. BuddSt 8 (mar 1984) 77-87.

McFarlane, S[ewell S.]. Items on "chinese religion" and "chinese buddhism" In John R. Hinnells (ed) Facts on file dictionary of religions, penguin ed (1984) See passim.

Park, Sung Bae. Buddhist faith and sudden enlightenment. SUNY (1983) 211 p, notes, gloss of chin char, bibliog, index.

Raguin, Yves. Lecons sur le bouddhisme. Taipei (1982) iv + 142 p.

Robinson, Richard H. The buddhist religion; a historical introduction. Belmont, calif (1970) See chap 4, Developments outside of india, 77-99. 2nd ed, co-authored by Willard L. Johnson (1977) See chap 9, The buddhism of east asia, 145-183. 3rd ed by co-authors (1982) See chap 10, East asian buddhism, 155-213.

Siklós, Bulcsu. Buddhism in china. In S. Sutherland et al (ed) The world's religions, boston (1988) 756-767.

The encyclopedia of eastern philosophy and religion. Boston (1988) See for budd and taoism, art by Ingrid Fischer-Schreiber; for zen (ch'an) see art by Michael S. Diener. This is engl tsl of Lexicon der östlichen weisheitslehren, bern & munich (1986)

Wieger, Léon. Bouddhisme chinois. Siensien, 2 vol (1910-1913) Repr peking (1940) See entry under Texts in Translation, iii.3.

Zürcher, Erik. Buddhism in china. In Raymond Dawson (ed) The legacy of china, oxford (1964) 56-79. Repr boston (1990)

Zürcher, Eric (sic) Buddhismus und fremde religionen in china. In China: colloquium-verlag otto h. hess, berlin (1980) 98-108.

Zürcher, Erik. Perspectives in the study of chinese buddhism. JRAS 2 (1982) 161-176.

III.3 Texts in Translation

Beal, Samuel (comp and tsl) A catena of buddhist scriptures from the chinese. London (1871) 436 p. Repr taipei (1970) india (1988)

Beal, Samuel (tsl). The romantic legend of sakya buddha: from the chinese-sanskrit . . . London (1875) xii + 395 p. Repr delhi (1985)

Bechert, Heinz (ed). Valentina Stache-Rosen (tsl) Upalipariprccha sutra: ein text zur buddhistischen ordensdisziplin. Göttingen (1984) 120 s.

Bischoff, F. A. (ed, tsl, comm). Arya mahabalanama-mahayanasutra. Tibétain (mss de touen-houang) et chinois. Contribution à l'étude des divinités mineures du bouddhisme tantrique. Paris (1956) 138 p, 4 facsimiles.

BTTSoc (tsl) The song of enlightenment, with commentary. San francisco (1983) bi-lingual ed 85 p. Tsl of cheng-tao ko by t'ang dyn master yung-chia.

Buswell, Robert E. jr. The formation of ch'an ideology in china and korea: the vajrasamadhi-sutra, a buddhist apocryphon. Princeton univ (1989) 315 p, illus, gloss, works cited, index. Study and tsl.

Chang, Garma C. C. (genl ed). A treasury of mahayana sutras. Selections from the maharatnakuta sutra. Penn state univ in cooperation with institute for advanced study of world religions (1983) xv + 496 p. 22 sutras on 8 major topics in mahayana budd. Tsl fr chin by the budd assoc of the united states.

Cheng, Hsueh-li (tsl & comm). Nagarjuna's twelve gate treatise. Dordrecht etc (1982) xv + 151 p, bibliog, notes, index. Text exists only in chin as shih-er men lun.

Chou, Hsiang-kuang (tsl), The vigrahavyavartani sastra (gatha part) Calcutta etc (1962) Tsl fr chin ed of prajnaruchi and vimoksasena, with chin texts.

Cleary, Thomas (tsl). The buddhist i ching [by] chih-hsu ou-i [1599-1655] Boston & london (1987) xxi + 237 p.

Cleary, Thomas (tsl). Entry into the inconceivable. An introduction to hua-yen buddhism. Univ hawaii (1983) 230 p. With tsl of texts by tu shun, cheng-kuan, chih-yen, fa-tsang.

Cleary, Thomas (tsl). Entry into the realm of reality; the guide. A commentary on the gandavyuha, the final book of the avatamsaka sutra, [by li tongxuan] Boston & shaftesbury, dorset, engl (1989) 85 p.

Cleary, Thomas (tsl). The flower ornament scripture. A translation of the avatamsaka sutra. Boston & london (1984-87) 3 vol. The only apparatus is gloss with each vol.

Fabian, Ludwig & Peter Lengsfeld (heraus). Die torlose schranke—mumonkan—zen-meister mumons koan-sammlung. München (1989) Tsl of Yamada Koun's tsl of Gateless Gate.

Forte, Antonino. Political propaganda and ideology in china at the end of the seventh century; inquiry into the nature, authors and function of the tunhuang document s.6502 followed by an annotated translation. Napoli, instituto universitario oriental. (1976) 312 p. Text composed by a group of budd monks to legitimate ascension to throne of empress wu chao (r.683-707) See rev by M. Strickmann in EB n.s.10.1 (may 1977) 156-160.

Goddard, Dwight (comp). Self-realization of noble wisdom. The lankavatara sutra compiled by dwight goddard on the basis of d. t. suzuki's rendering from the sanskrit and chinese. Clearlake calif (1983) 166 p. Original version publ 1932.

Gokhale, Vasudev. Pratityasamutpadasastra des ullangha, kritisch behandeft und aus dem chinesischen ins deutsch übertragen. Bonn (1930)

Griffiths, Paul J., Noriaki Hakamaya, John P. Keenan & Paul L. Swanson (tsl and notes). The realm of awakening: a translation and study of the tenth chapter of asanga's mahayanasangraha.

Oxford univ (1989) xix + 399 p. Intro by Keenan. Incl tsl of chin comm.

Hanayama, Shoyu et al. A huge project to translate the chinese version of the buddhist tripitaka into english has started. YE n.s. 8.4 (autumn 1982) 3-5. In jap.

Hirakawa, Akira (tsl). Tripitaka, vinayapitaka, bhiksunivinaya. Monastic discipline for the buddhist nuns: an english translation of the chinese text of the mahasamghika-bhiksuni-vinaya. Patna (1982) xvi + 434 p, index.

Höke, Holger (übers). Das p'u-sa pen yüan ching (frühere leben des bodhisattva) Eine sammlung buddhistischer festschichten. Bochumer jahrbuch zur ostasienforschung 7 (1984) 113-214.

Hsüan-hua. A general explanation of the buddha speaks the sutra in forty-two section. BTTSoc (1979) 97 p.

Huyên-Vi, Thich (tsl). Ekottaragama (II) Traduit de la version chinoise par thich huyên-vi. BSR 2.1-2 (1985) 36-46. Same title format for Ekottaragama III (ibid 3.1, 1986) 31-38; IV (ibid 3.2, 1986) 132-142; V (ibid 4.1, 1987) 47-58; VI (ibid 4.2, 1987) 127-134; VII (ibid 5.1, 1988) 47-59.

Kim, Young-ho (tsl & annot). Tao-sheng's commentary on the lotus sutra. A study and translation. SUNY (1990) xix + 374 p, abbrev, gloss, bibliog, index.

La Vallée Poussin, Louis de. Tsl fr french by Leo M. Pruden. Abhidharmakosabhasyam. Berkeley calif, 3 vol: I and II (1988) III (1989) I, lxii + 363 p; II, xvi + p.365-765; III, xxii + p.767-1086.

Lai, Whalen W. The earliest folk buddhist religion in china: t'i-wei po-li ching and its historical significance. In BTS-II (1987) 11-35.

Lai, Whalen. Wonhyo (yüan hsiao) on the nirvana school: summation under the "one mind" doctrine. JIABS 8.2 (1985) 75-83. Tsl of nieh-p'an tsung-yao.

Lamotte, Etienne. Engl tsl by Leo M. Pruden.

Karmasiddhiprakarana. The treatise on action by vasubandhu. Berkeley calif (1988) 131 p, index. Has brief biog of lamotte.

Lu, K'uan Yü (Charles Luk) tsl. The surangama sutra (leng yen ching) Chinese rendering by master paramiti of central north india at chih chih monastery, canton, china, a.d.705, by ch'an master han shan (1546-1623) London (1966) 262 p. Repr new delhi (1978) london (1987)

Magnin, Paul. Un traité de bouddhisme chinois: sens des deux extrêmes de tous les dharma du grand véhicule (dacheng zhufa erbian yi) EOEO 6 (1985) 109-111. Présentation et trad.

Meisig, Konrad (heraus). Das sramanyaphala-sutra. Synoptische übersetzung und glossar der chinesischen fassungen verglichen mit dem sanskrit und pali. Wiesbaden (1987) 625 p, parallel chin and sanskrit and pali texts, gloss, engl summ.

Meisig, Konrad. Das sutra von der vier ständen. Das agganna-sutra im licht seiner chinesischen parallelen. Wiesbaden (1988) 249 p, parallel chin and sanskrit and pali texts, gloss.

Mukhopadhyaya, Sujitkumar. An outline of the principal methods of meditation. Santiniketan (1972) Tsl fr chin version of kumarajiva, Ssu wei yao lüeh fa, of ten kinds of meditation acc to sanskrit texts. Orig publ in VBQ 3 (1950)

Mus, Paul. Sadgatikarika de dharmika subhuti. Publiés, traduites et annotés à l'aide des versions en pali, chinois et tibétain. ?Paris (1939)

Nadeau, Randall (tsl & intro). "The decline of the dharma" in early chinese buddhism: a translation of the "scripture preached by the buddha on the total extinction of the dharma" BCAR 1 (1987) 133-140.

Nakamura, Hajime. The influence of confucian ethics on the chinese translations of buddhist sutras. SIS 5.3/4 (1957) 156-170.

Ogata, Shohaku (tsl) The transmission of the lamp: early masters, compiled by tao yuan, a ch'an monk of the sung dynasty. Wolfeboro, new hampshire (1990) 401 p, index.

138

Pajin, Dusan (tsl). On faith in mind—translation and analysis of the hsin-hsin ming. JOS 26.2 (1988) 270-288. Incl chin text, attrib to seng-ts'an.

Paul, Diana Y. (tsl & ed). Philosophy of mind in sixth-century china. Paramartha's "evolution of consciousness" Stanford univ (1984) 266 p, intro, tsl, app of ref materials.

Paul, Diana Y. With contributions by Frances Wilson. Women in buddhism. Images of the feminine in the mahayana tradition. Berkeley, calif (1979) 333 p, gloss, bibliog, index. Tsl mostly fr chin texts.

Powell, William F. (tsl). The record of tung-shan. Univ hawaii (1986) 99 p, notes, index of persons, bibliog. Tung-shan liang-chieh's dates are 807-869.

Red pine (tsl) The zen teaching of bodhidharma. San francisco (1989) 125 p, notes. Bi-lingual text.

Research soc of central asian culture (ed) Monumenta serindica: Vol I: Chinese buddhist texts from tunhuang. Kyoto (1958)

Robinson, Richard (tsl) Chinese buddhist verse. London (1954) 85 p, bibliog, notes, index of chin texts tsl. Repr westport, conn (1980)

Ryukoku university translation center (ed & annot) The sutra of contemplation on the buddha of immeasurable life as expounded by sakyamuni buddha. Kyoto (1984) xl + 169 p, facsimile, bibliog, indexes.

Soothill, W. E. (tsl). The lotus of the wonderful law or the lotus gospel: saddharma pundarika sutra, miao-fa lien hua ching. Oxford (1930) xii + 275 p. Repr san francisco (1977) london & new jersey (1987)

Tamura, Kwansei. A history of translation of buddhist canon. YE n.s. 9.1 (winter 1983) 3-8.

Tanaka, Kenneth K. The dawn of chinese pure land buddhism. Ching-ying hui-yüan's commentary on the visualization sutra. SUNY (1990) xxiv + 304 p, tsl of comm, app, notes, gloss, bibliog, index.

Thich, Nhat Hanh & Peter Levitt. The heart of understanding: commentaries on the prajnaparamita heart sutra. Berkeley calif (1989) 54 p.

Tucci, Guiseppe (tsl) Pre-dignaga buddhist texts on logic from chinese sources. Baroda (1929) Repr san francisco (1976) 2nd ed, madras (1981) xxx + 91 p, indices.

Willemen, Charles (tsl) The chinese hevajratantra. The scriptural text of the ritual of the great king of the teaching, the adamantine one, with great compassion and knowledge of the void. Leuven (1983) 208 p.

Yamamoto, Kosho. The mahayana mahaparinirvanasutra. Ubeshi, 3 vol: (1973, 1974, 1975) Complete tsl of "southern recension" fr chin into engl. Text is taisho no 375, vol X, 605ff.

III.4 Studies of Texts and Terms

Aitken, Robert (tsl & comm). Wu-men-kuan, case II, chao-chou and the hermits. EB n.s.22.2 (autumn 1989) 78-84.

Bagchi, P. C. Buddhist studies in japan and the taisho edition of the chinese tripitaka. New asia 1.1 (1939) 16-20.

Baruch, Willy. Beiträge zum saddharmapundarika-sutra. Leiden (1938). See ii teil: Die chinesischen übersetzungen des saddharmapundarikasutra, 29-47; also anhang: Der stupasamdarsana- und der devadattaparivarta des saddharmapundarikasutras in der übersetzung des dharmavaksa und des kumarajiva und das sa-t'an-fen-t'o-li king, 49-100.

Beal, Samuel. Abstract of four lectures on buddhist literature in china, delivered at university college, london. London (1882) xvi + 185 p, 5 pl. Repr india (1988)

Berling, Judith. Bringing the buddha down to earth: notes on the emergence of yü-lu as a buddhist genre. HR 27.1 (aug 1987) 56-88.

Boltz, Judith & Richard Salomon. A new fragment of the kathinavastu of the sarvastivadinaya. JAOS 108.4 (oct-dec 1988) 539-544.

Buswell, Robert E. jr (ed). Chinese buddhist apocrypha. Univ hawaii (1990) 342 p, genl index, index of texts. Indiv art sep listed in this bibliog; abbrev CBA.

Buswell, Robert E. jr. The formation of ch'an ideology in china and korea: the vajrasamadhi-sutra, a buddhist apocryphon. Princeton univ (1989) 315 p, illus, gloss, works cited, index. Study and tsl.

Buswell, Robert E. jr. Prolegomenon to the study of buddhist apocryphal scriptures. In CBA (1990) 1-30.

Chang, Aloysius. Ten powers of the wu liang yi ching. CC 28.2 (june 1987) 59-67. Re budd text.

Cheng, Hsueh-li (tsl & comm) Nagarjuna's twelve gate treatise. Dordrecht etc (1982) xv + 151 p, bibliog, notes, index. Text exists only in chin as shih-er-men lun.

Chi, Richard See Yee. Buddhist formal logic. Part 1: A study of dignaga's 'hetucakra' and k'uei-chi's 'great commentary on the nyayapravesa' London (1969) 222 p, illus. See rev by Jacques May in TP 59 (1973) 346-351; by Douglas D. Daye in PEW 23.4 (oct 1973) 525-535.

Coblin, W. South. Notes on the dialect of the han buddhist transcriptions. ProcICS, Language and writing vol (1981) 121-183.

Davidson, Ronald M. An introduction to the standards of scriptural authenticity in indian buddhism. In CBA (1990) 291-325. Background for chin budd apocrypha.

Enomoto, Fumio. On the formation of the original texts of the chinese agamas. BSR 3.1 (1986) 19-30.

Franke, Herbert. Zu einem apokryphen dharani-sutra aus china. ZDMG 134.2 (1984) 318-336.

Freeman, Robert R. The importance of spurious texts in early chinese buddhism with special reference to the "ta-ch'eng ch'i-hsin lun" Proc31stICHS, tokyo, vol 1 (1984) 176-177. Abstr.

Fujita, Kotatsu. Tsl by Kenneth K. Tanaka. The textual origins of the kuan wu-liang-shou ching: a canonical scripture of pure land buddhism. In CBA (1990) 149-173.

Fung, Ch'êng-chün. Les moines chinois et étranger qui ont contribué à la formation du tripitaka chinois. Shanghai (1931)

Griffiths, Paul J., Noriaki Hakamaya, John P. Keenan & Paul L. Swanson (tsl and notes). The realm of awakening: a translation and study of the tenth chapter of asanga's mahayanasangraha. Oxford univ (1989) xix + 399 p. Intro by Keenan. Incl tsl of chin comm.

Groner, Paul. The fan-wang ching and monastic discipline in japanese tendai: a study of annen's futsu jubosatsukai koshaku. In CBA (1990) 251-290.

Grosnick, William. The categories of t'i, hsiang, and yung: evidence that paramartha composed the awakening of faith. JIABS 12.1 (1989) 65-92.

Gupta, R. D. The chinese version of the story of ghozaka. In M. Hendrickx-Baudot et al, Orientalia lovaniensia periodica 3 (1972) 163-177.

Hahn, M. & H. Schmidt-Glintzer. Die legende von dardara und upadardara in der fassung des tsa-pao-tsang-ching. MS 34 (1979-80) 219-262. Chin tsl of tsa-pao-tsang-ching (T.203) 472 c.e.

Held, Axel. Enthält tao-an's vorwort in CSTCC 8.1, wirklich "leitsätze für die übersetzer"? NachrDGNVO 127/128 (1980) 111-119. Abbrev is ref to ch'u-san-tsang chi-chi, earliest extant catalog, comp by seng-yu (445-518)

Hirakawa, Akira. Tsl by Paul Groner. Buddhist literature: a survey of texts. EncyRel 2 (1987) 509b-526b.

Hsüan-hua. A general explanation of the buddha speaks the sutra in forty-two section. BTTSoc (1979) 97 p.

Huntington, John C. Note on a chinese text demonstrating the earliness of tantra. JIABS 10.2 (1987) 88-98. Text is chin version of suvarna-prabhasa sutra, tsl early 5th c.

Iyanaga, Nobumi. Récits de la soumission de mahesvara par trailokyavijay—d'après les sources chinoises et japonaises. In T&TStudies 3 (1985) 633-745.

Kajiyama, Yuichi. Stupas, the mother of buddhas, and dharma-body. In NPBR (1985) 9-16. Re astasahasrika-prajnaparamita sutra.

Kajiyama, Yuichi. Women in buddhism. EB n.s.15.1 (spring 1982) 53-70. Historically and acc to budd texts.

Kanakura, Yensho (ed) Hokekyo no seiritsu to tenkai (the lotus sutra and the development of buddhist thought. Kyoto (1970) Text in jap, with 33 p. engl summ.

Katsura, Shoryu. Chinese translation of buddhist texts on logic. Proc31stICHS, tokyo, vol 1 (1984) 199-200. Abstr.

Keenan, John P. Asanga's understanding of madhyamika: notes on the shung[sic]-chung-lun. JIABS 12.1 (1989) 93-107. Title also romanized as hsun-chung lun.

Kim, Young-ho (tsl & annot) Tao-sheng's commentary on the lotus sutra. A study and translation. SUNY (1990) xix + 374 p, abbrev, gloss, bibliog, index.

King, Sallie B. The buddha nature: true self as action. RS 20 (june 1984) 255-267. Per text of fo hsing lun.

King, Sallie B. Buddha nature. SUNY (1990) 205 p, notes, gloss, index. Study of fo hsing lun attributed to vasubandhu, chin tsl by paramartha, 6th c.

Kudara, Kogi & Peter Zieme. Chinesisch-alttürkische fragmente des "schwitzbad-sutras" Altorientalische forschungen 15.1 (1988) 189-191.

Lahiri, Latika. Dhammapada in chinese. BuddSt 7 (mar 1983) 58-65.

Lahiri, Latika. Interpretation of buddhist terminology at the background of chinese traditional thoughts. BuddSt (1974) 57-67.

Lai, Whalen. Before the prajna schools: the earliest known chinese commentary on the astasahasrika. JIABS 6.1 (1983) 91-108.

Lai, Whalen. The buddhist "prodigal son"; a story of misperceptions. JIABS 4.2 (1981) 91-98.

Lai, Whalen. The chan-ch'a ching: religion and magic in medieval china. In CBA (1990) 175-206.

Lai, Whalen. A clue to the authorship of the awakening of faith: "siskananda's" redaction of the word "nien" JIABS 3.1 (1980) 34-53.

Lai, Whalen W. The earliest folk buddhist religion in china: t'i-wei po-li ching and its historical significance. In BTS-II (1987) 11-35.

Lai, Whalen. The mahaparinirvana-sutra and its earliest interpreters in china: two prefaces by tao-lang and tao-sheng. JAOS 102 (1982) 99-105.

Lai, Whalen. The predocetic "finite buddhakaya" in the lotus sutra: in search of the elusive dharmakaya therein. JAAR 49.3 (sept 1981) 447-469.

Liu, Ming-wood. The lotus sutra and garland sutra according to the t'ien-t'ai and hua-yen schools in chinese buddhism. TP 74.1-3 (1988) 47-80.

Magnin, P. Une copie amidique du t'ien-t'ai tche-tchö ta che fa-yuan wen (une étude sur le manuscrit p.3183) In CETH (1979) 99-114.

Magnin, Paul. Dépassement de l'expérience noétique selon trois courts traités de madhyamika chinois. Une étude du manuscrit p.3357Vo. CETH 3 (1984) 263-303, 10 pl.

Magnin, Paul. Un traité de bouddhisme chinois: sens des deux extrêmes de tous les dharma du grand véhicle (dacheng zhufa erbian yi) EOEO 6 (1985) 109-111. Présentation et trad.

Makita, Tairyo. Tsl by Antonino Forte, who also supplied ftnotes. The ching-tu san mei ching and the tun-huang manuscripts. E&W n.s.21.3/4 (sep-dec 1971) 351-361.

Maruyama, Takao. Chinese theory of the three ages after the buddha's decease—chinese lotus sutra commentaries. Proc31stICHS, todkyo, vol 1 (1984) 159-160. Abstr.

Mather, Richard. The impact of the nirvana sutra in china. In LB (1981) 155-173.

Matsuda, Yuko. Chinese versions of the buddha's biography. JIBS37.1 (dec 1988) 24-33.

Matsumura, Hisashi. A lexical note on the vinaya literature: stupa in the saiksa rules. Wiener zeitschrift für die kunde sud und ostasiens und archiv für indische philosophie 33 (1989) 45-91. Re chin text.

McRae, John R. Ch'an commentaries on the heart sutra: preliminary inferences on the permutation of chinese buddhism. JIABS 11.2 (1988) 85-115.

Meisig, Konrad (heraus) Das sramanyaphala-sutra. Synoptische übersetzung und glossar der chinesischen fassungen verglichen mit dem sanskrit und pali. Wiesbaden (1987) 625 p, parallel chin and sanskrit and pali texts, gloss, engl summ.

Meisig, Konrad. Das sutra von der vier ständen. Das agganna-sutra im licht seiner chinesischen parallelen. Wiesbaden (1988) 249 p, parallel chin and sanskrit and pali texts, gloss.

Mizuno, Kogen. Tsl by M. Takanashi, K. Yoshida, T. Matsumura, K. Osaka. Adapted by Rebecca M. Davis. Buddhist sutras. Origin, development, transmission. Tokyo (1982) 220 p, app, gloss-index, map.

Nakamura, H[ajime]. The astamahasthana-caityastotra and the chinese and tibetan versions of a text similar to it. In I&B (1980) 259-265.

Pak, Song-bae. On the canonization standard in east asian buddhism. Korea journal 21.8 (aug 1981) 49-54.

Paul, Diana Y. (tsl & ed) Philosophy of mind in sixth-century china. Paramartha's "evolution of consciousness" Stanford univ (1984) 266 p, intro, tsl, app of ref materials.

Pedersen, K. Priscilla. Notes on the ratnakuta collection. JIABS 3.2 (1980) 60-66.

Raguin, Yves. Terminologie raisonnée du bouddhisme chinois. Taipei (1985) 480 p.

Richardson, Hugh E. "The dharma that came down from heaven": a tun-huang fragment. In BT&AC (1977) 219-230.

Robert, Jean-Noël. Sutra des quarante-deux articles. ACF 80 (1979-80) 159-160.

Röhrborn, Klaus. Zur rezeption der chinesisch-buddhistischen terminologie im alttürkischen. WZKM 30 (1986) 179-187.

Saigusa, Mitsuyoshi. Bhavanakrama. ZDMG 115.2 (1965) 309-319. Uses chin text to correct tsl of t 30 no 1664.

Sakurabe, H. On the wu-t'ing-hsin-kuan. In I&B (1980) 307-312.

Schlütter, Morten. A study in the genealogy of the platform sutra. SCEAR 2 (1989) 53-114.

Schmidt-Glintzer, Helwig. Das budddhistische gewand des manichäismus: zur buddhistischen terminologie in den chinesischen manichaica. In Walter Heissig & Joachim Klimkeit (ed) Synkretismus in den religionen zentralasiens, wiesbaden (1987) 76-90.

Schuster, Nancy. The bodhisattva figure in the ugrahariprccha. In NPBR (1985) 26-56.

142

Shih, R. La préface du ta tche che louen par seng-jouei. In I&B (1980) 313-328. Same title in ProcICS (1981) History and archaeology vol 2, 735-750, in engl.

Stein, R. A. Etude du monde chinois: institutions et concepts. ACF 81 (1981) 533-560. See 1, Sutras apocryphes en chine et au tibet.

Stein, R. A. Sudden illumination or simultaneous comprehension: remarks on chinese and tibetan terminology. In S&G (1987) 41-65.

Stein, R. A. Tibetica antiqua I. Les deux vocabulaires des traductions indo-tibétaine et sino-tibétaine dans les manuscrits de touen-houang. BEFEO 72 (1983) 149-236.

Strickmann, Michel. The consecration sutra: a buddhist book of spells. In CBA (1990) 75-118.

Sueki, Fumihiko. Some problems of the kuan-wu-liang-shou-ching. JIBS 31.1 (dec 1982) 21-24.

Sueki, Fumihiko. The tragedy of rajagrha in the guan-wu-liang-shou-jing. Proc31stICHS, tokyo, vol 1 (1984) 212. Abstr.

Suganuma, Akira. The five dharmas (pancadharma) in the lankavatarasutra. JIBS 15.2 (mar 1967) 32-39. Fr earliest chin tsl.

Takasaki, J. Analysis of the lankavatara. In search of its original form. In I&B (1980) 339-352.

Tanaka, Kenneth K. The dawn of chinese pure land buddhism. Ching-ying hui-yüan's commentary on the visualization sutra. SUNY (1990) xxiv + 304 p, tsl of comm, app, notes, gloss, bibliog, index.

Teiser, Stephen F. The ghost festival in medieval china. Princeton univ (1988) xvii + 275 p, char gloss, bibliog, index.

Thich, Thien Chau. The literature of the pudgalavadins. JIABS 7.1 (1984) 7-16. As preserved in 4 chin texts of their opponents.

Tillemans, Tom J. F. Some reflections on R. S. Y

Chi's Buddhist formal logic. JIABS 11.1 (1988) 155-171.

Tokuno, Kyoko. The evaluation of indigenous scriptures in chinese buddhist bibliographical catalogues. In CBA (1990) 31-74.

Watanabe, Fumimaro. A study of the first chapter in the abhidharma-sarasastra. In NPBR (1985) 119-134. Fr chin text.

Willemen, Charles (tsl) The chinese hevajratantra. The scriptural text of the ritual of the great king of the teaching, the adamantine one, with great compassion and knowledge of the void. Leuven (1983) 208 p.

Willemen, Charles. The chinese hevajratantra (t.892). More than a faultive (sic) translation? Proc31stICHS, tokyo, vol 1 (1984) 211-212. Abstr. Re northern sung tsl of esoteric texts.

Willemen, Charles. Tripitaka shan wu-wei's name: a chinese translation from prakrit. TP 67.3-5 (1981) 362-365.

Yeh, Ah-yueh. A study on the theories of yavad-bhavikata and yathavad-bhavikata in the abhidharma samuccaya. Proc31stICHS, tokyo, vol 1 (1984) 181-183. Chin: chin so yu hsing and ru so yu hsing. Abstr.

Zürcher, Erik. Late han vernacular elements in the earliest buddhist translations. JCLTA 12.3 (1977) 177-203.

Zürcher, E. "Prince moonlight." Messianism and eschatology in early medieval chinese buddhism. TP 68.1/3 (1982) 1-59. Incl facsimile of chin text.

III.5 Theory and Doctrine

Bugault, Guy. Les paradoxes de la vajracchedika: une connexion qui opère une coupure. CEC 8 (1989) 45-63.

Cabezon, Jose I. The concepts of truth and meaning in the buddhist scriptures. JIABS 4 (1981) 7-23.

Ch'ien, Edward T. The conception of language and the use of paradox in buddhism and taoism. JCP 11 (dec 1984) 375-399.

Chappell, David W. Hermeneutical phases in chinese buddhism. In BHerm (1988) 175-205.

Cheng, Hsüeh-li. Chi-tsang's treatment of metaphysical issues. JCP 8.3 (sept 1981) 371-389. Comm of chi-tsang (549-623) a san-lun master on madhyamika scriptures.

Cheng, Hsüeh-li. Empty logic: madhyamaka buddhism from chinese sources. NY (1984) 220p.

Cheng, Hsüeh-li. Nagarjuna, kant and wittgenstein: the san lun madhyamika exposition of emptiness. RS 17.1 (mar 1981) 67-85.

Cheng, Hsüeh-li. Truth and logic in san-lun madhyamika buddhism. IPQ 21.3 (sept 1981) 261-276.

Cheng, Hsüeh-li. Zen and san-lun madhyamika thought: exploring the theoretical foundation of zen teachings and practice. RS 15 (sept 1979) 343-363.

Eoyang, Eugene. "Vacuity," "vapor," and "vanity": some perspectives on the void. TR 16.1 (fall 1985) 51-65.

Faure, Bernard. La volonté d'orthodoxie dans le bouddhisme chinois. Paris (1988) 320 p.

Fu, Charles Wei-hsun. Chinese buddhism as an existential phenomenology. In Anna-Teresa Tymieniecka (ed) Phenomenology of life in a dialogue between chinese and occidental philosophy, dordrecht (1984) 229-251.

Fujita, Kotatsu. Tsl by Kenneth K. Tanaka. Pure and impure lands. EncyRel 12 (1987) 90a-91b.

Ganguly, Swati. Paramartha and hsuan-tsang on the tathagatagarbha and alayavijnana causation: a perspective of the buddhist idealism in china. BuddSt 8 (mar 1984) 7-12.

Gernet, Jacques. Sur le corps et l'esprit chez les chinois. In Poikilia: études offerts à jean-pierre

vernant, paris (1987) 369-377. Incl tsl of fan chen's essay, shen mieh lun.

Gomez, Luis O. Buddhist literature: exegesis and hermeneutics. EncyRel 2 (1987) 529b-540a.

Gomez, Luis O. From the extraordinary to the ordinary: images of the bodhisattva. In Donald S. Lopez jr & Steven C. Rockefeller (ed) The christ and the bodhisattva, SUNY (1987) chap 5, 141-191.

Gomez, Luis O. Purifying gold: the metaphor of effort and intuition in buddhist thought and practice. In S&G (1987) 67-165.

Gregory, Peter N. The problem of theodicy in the "awakening of faith" RS 22.1 (1986) 63-78.

Gregory, Peter N. Sudden and gradual: approaches to enlightenment in chinese thought. Honolulu (1987) 474 p, index. Art sep listed in this bibliog; abbrev S&G.

Gregory, Peter N (rapporteur). The sudden/gradual polarity: a recurrent theme in chinese thought. JCP 9.4 (1982) 471-486. Report of a conference held in may 1981.

Grosnick, William. Cittaprakrti and ayonisomanaskara in the ratnagotravibhasa: a precedent for the hsin-nien distinction of the awakening of faith. JIABS 6.2 (1983) 35-47.

Hurvitz, Leon. The mind of the early chinese buddhist. In Roy C. Amore (ed) Developments in buddhist thought, wilfrid laurier univ (1979) 477-485.

Ichimura, Shohei. A determining factor that differentiated indian and chinese madhyamika methods of dialectic as reductio-ad-absurdum and paradoxical argument respectively. JIBS 33.2 (mar 1985) 29-36.

Ichimura, Shohei. On the dialectical meaning of instantiation in terms of mayadrstanta in the indian and chinese madhyamikas. JIBS 36.2 (mar 1988) 9-15.

Iida, Shotaro. Who best can re-turn the dharmacakra?—A controversy between wonch'uk (632-696) and k'uei-chi (632-682) JIBS 34.2 (mar 1986) 11-18.

Jan, Yün-hua. The bodhisattva idea in chinese literature: typology and significance. In Leslie S. Kawamura (ed) The bodhisattva doctrine in buddhism, wilfrid laurier univ (1981) 125-152.

Jan, Yün-hua. The chinese buddhist wheel of existence and deliverance. MexICHS 2: China (1976) 127-140.

Jan, Yün-hua. The chinese understanding and assimilation of karma doctrine. In Ronald W. Neufeld (ed) Karma and rebirth: post classical developments, SUNY (1986) 145-168.

Jan, Yün-hua. A comparative study of 'no-thought' (wu-nien) in some indian and chinese buddhist texts. JCP 16.1 (1989) 37-58.

Jan, Yün-hua. Patterns of chinese assimilation of buddhist thought: a comparative study of no-thought (wu-nien) in indian and chinese texts. JOS 24.1 (1986) 21-36.

Jan, Yün-hua. Rajadharma ideal in yogacara buddhism. In Prasabanand Jash (ed) Religion and society in ancient india, calcutta (1984) 221-234. Utilizes wang-fa cheng-li lun, chin tsl of rajadharma-nyaya-sastra.

Jong, J. W. de. Lamotte on the doctrine of non-self. CEA 3 (1987) 151-153.

Kanakura, Yensho (ed) Hokekyo no seiritsu to tenkai (the lotus sutra and the development of buddhist thought. Kyoto (1970) Text in jap, with 33 p. engl summ.

Kasulis, Thomas P. Buddhist existentialism. EB n.s. 17.2 (fall 1984) 131-141.

Kasulis, Thomas P. Nirvana. EncyRel 10 (1987) 448a-456a.

King, Sallie B. Buddha nature and the concept of person. PEW 39.2 (apr 1989) 151-170.

King, Sallie B. The buddha nature: true self as

action. RS 20 (june 1984) 255-267. Per text of fo hsing lun.

Kiyota, Minoru. Tathagatha thought: a basis of buddhist devotionalism in east asia. JJRS 12.2-3 (june-sept 1985) 207-231.

Kloetzli, W. Randolph. Buddhist cosmology. EncyRel 4 (1987) 113a-119b.

Ko, Wing Siu. The buddhist concept of karma. CF 29.1 (mar 1986) 14-15. Reply to d. w. mitchell.

Koseki, Aaron. Chi-tsang's sheng-man pao-k'u: the true dharma doctrine and the bodhisattva ideal. PEW 34.1 (jan 1984) 67-83.

Koseki, Aaron K. The concept of practice in san lun thought: chi-tsang and the "concurrent insight" of the two-truths. PEW 31.4 (oct 1981) 449-466.

Lai, Whalen. The buddhist "prodigal son"; a story of misperceptions. JIABS 4.2 (1981) 91-98.

Lai, Whalen. Chou yang vs chang jung (on sunyata): the pen-mo yu-wu controversy in fifth century china. JIABS 1.1 (1978) 23-44. Re 2 5th c scholars.

Lai, Whalen. The defeat of vijnaptimatrata in china: fa-tsang on fa-hsing and fa-hsiang. JCP 13.1 (mar 1986) 1-19.

Lai, Whalen. A different religious language: the tian-tai idea of the triple truth. CF 25.2 (june 1982) 67-78.

Lai, Whalen. The early chinese buddhist understanding of the psyche: chen hui's commentary on the yin chih ju ching. JIASBS 9.1 (1986) 85-103.

Lai, Whalen. Emperor wu of liang on the immortal soul, shen pu mieh. JAOS 101.2 (apr-june 1981) 167-175.

Lai, Whalen. From sakyamuni to amitabha: the logic behind pure land devotion. CF 24 (1981) 156-174.

Lai, Whalen. Hu-jan nien-ch'i: (suddenly a thought

rose): chinese understanding of mind and consciousness. JIABS 3.2 (1980) 42-59.

Lai, Whalen. The humanity of the buddha: is mahayana "docetic"? CF 24.2 (june 1981) 97-107.

Lai, Whalen. Non-duality of the two truths in sinitic madhyamika: origin of the 'third truth' JIABS 2.2 (1979) 45-65.

Lai, Whalen. Once more on the two truths: what does chi-tsang mean by two truths or "yueh-chiao"? RS 19.4 (1983) 505-521.

Lai, Whalen. The predocetic "finite buddhakaya" in the lotus sutra: in search of the elusive dharmakaya therein. JAAR 49.3 (sept 1981) 447-469.

Lai, Whalen. The pure and the impure: the mencian problematic in chinese buddhism. In ECCT (1983) 299-326.

Lai, Whalen. Sinitic speculations on buddhanature: the nirvana school. PEW 32.2 (apr 1982) 135-149.

Lai, Whalen. Some notes on perceptions of pratitya-samutpada in chinese from kumarajiva to fa-yao. JCP 8.4 (dec 1981) 427-435.

Lai, Whalen. Wonhyo (yüan hsiao) on the nirvana school: summation under the "one mind" doctrine. JIABS 8.2 (1985) 75-83. Tsl of nieh-p'an tsung-yao.

Lai, Whalen. Yao hsing's discourse on mahayana: buddhist controversy in early fifth-century china. RTrad 4 (1981) 35-58.

Lancaster, Lewis R. The bodhisattva concept: a study of the chinese buddhist canon. In Leslie S. Kawamura (ed) The bodhisattva doctrine in buddhism, wilfrid laurier univ (1981) 153-164.

Liu, Ming-wood. The advent of the practice of p'an-chiao in chinese buddhism. JOS 26.1 (1988) 1-27. Term p'an-chiao means "dividing doctrine," a six dyn attempt to categorize indian budd thought.

Liu, Ming-wood. The early development of the buddha-nature doctrine in china. JCP 16.1 (mar 1989) 1-36.

Liu, Ming-wood. Fan chen's treatise on the destructibility of the spirit and its buddhist critics. PEW 35.4 (oct 1987) 402-428.

Liu, Ming-wood. The problem of the icchantika in the mahayana mahaparinirvana sutra. JIABS 7.1 (1984) 57-81.

Liu, Ming-wood. The three-nature doctrine and its interpretation in hua-yen buddhism. TP 68.4/5 (1982) 181-220.

Long, J. Bruce. Cosmic law. EncyRel 4 (1987) 90a-91b.

Magnin, Paul. Le discours de libération de l'homme: quelques traits caracteristiques de l'évolution du bouddhisme au sein de la tradition chinoise,—nirvana, nature de bouddha et culte d'amitaba. EOEO 6 (1985) 95-102. Theme of this issue: "Une civilisation sans théologie?"

Maruyama, Takao. Chinese theory of the three ages after the buddha's decease—chinese lotus sutra commentaries. Proc31stICHS, tokyo, vol 1 (1984) 159-160. Abstr.

Mather, Richard. The impact of the nirvana sutra in china. In LB (1981) 155-173.

Meier, Franz Josef. Die mythologie des chinesischen buddhismus. Sec 23-24 in Egidius Schmalzried & Hans Wilhelm Haussig (heraus) Wörterbuch der mythologie, augsburg (1988) 441-735, illus, chin char.

Nakasone, Ronald. Sagamudra samadhi, the rationale for hua-yen thought. TPW 1.3 (spring 1984) 25-27.

Nishi, Giyu. The bodhisattva: his vows and practices. TUAS 2 (1964) 31-50.

Pachow, W. The controversy over the immortality of the soul in chinese buddhism. MexICH 2: China (1976) 95-126. Same title in JOS 16.1/2 (1978) 21-38; repr in ChBudd (1980) 117-162.

146

Pachow, W. A hermeneutical approach to the supernatural phenomena in buddhist history. CC 27 (1986) 73-100.

Pas, Julian. Six daily periods of worship: symbolic meaning in buddhist liturgy and eschatology. MS 37 (1986/87) 49-82.

Paul, Diana Y. (tsl & ed) Philosophy of mind in sixth-century china. Paramartha's "evolution of consciousness" Stanford univ (1984) 266 p, intro, tsl, app of ref materials.

Pye, Michael. Skilful means; a concept in mahayana buddhism. London (1978) 211 p, app, bibliog, index. See passim.

Rawlinson, Andrew. The ambiguity of the buddha-nature concept in india and china. In ECCT (1983) 259-279.

Schuster, Nancy. The bodhisattva figure in the ugrahariprccha. In NPBR (1985) 26-56.

Schuster, Nancy. Changing the female body: wise women and the bodhisattva career in some maharatnakuta sutras. JIABS 4.1 (1981) 24-69.

Seidel, Anna. Daigo (la sagesse du bouddha, la nature du bouddha, la meillure doctrine) In Hobogirin, 6e fasc (1983) 640b-651b.

Shih, Joseph. l'Eschatologie dans le monde chinois. SM 32 (1983) 181-194.

Tu, Wei-ming. Afterword: thinking of "enlightenment" religiously. In S&G (1987) 447-456.

Tucker, John Allen. Nagarjuna's influence on early hua-yen and ch'an thought. CC 25.2 (june 1984) 43-61.

Unno, Taitetsu. The buddhata theory of fa-tsang. Trans 8th ICfO Japan (1963) 34-41.

Williams, Paul. Mahayana buddhism: the doctrinal foundation. London & NY (1989) See for chin budd, passim, esp relevant sec so identified.

Yü. Chün-fang. Chinese buddhist responses to contemporary problems. JD 10.1 (jan-mar 1985) 60-74.

Zürcher, E. Eschatology and messianism in early chinese buddhism. In LSS (1981) 34-56.

Zürcher, E. "Prince moonlight." Messianism and eschatology in early medieval chinese buddhism. TP 68.1/3 (1982) 1-59 Incl facsimile of chin text.

III.6 Buddhism and History

Aubert-Chen, R.-y. C. (Ch'en Jui-yü). Han yü and the confucianists' anti-buddhism in t'ang china. CC 29.1 (1988) 75-92.

Barnes, Nancy Schuster. Striking a balance: women and images of women in early chinese buddhism. In Yvonne Yazbeck Haddad & Ellison Banks Findly (ed) Women, religion, and social change, SUNY (1985) 87-112.

Berling, Judith. Bringing the buddha down to earth: notes on the emergence of yü-lu as a buddhist genre. HR 27.1 (aug 1987) 56-88.

Berval, René de. Présence du bouddhisme. This is overall title for France-asie 16 (1959) New ed, paris (1987) engl essays all tsl into french.

Bokshchanin, A. A. Sino-indian relations from ancient times to the sixteenth century. In S. L. Tikhvinsky & L. S. Perelomov (ed) China and her neighbors from ancient times to the middle ages: a collection of essays, moscow (1981) 105-138.

Bras, Gabriel le. Quelques problèmes sociologiques de l'histoire du bouddhisme. ASR 11.21 (jan-juin 1966) 119-124.

Chan, Sin-wai. Buddhism and the late ch'ing intellectuals. JICS:CUHK 16 (l985) 97-109.

Chan, Sin-wai. Buddhism and the major concepts in an exposition of benevolence by t'an ssu-t'ung. New asia academic bulletin 2 (1979) 179-202.

Chan, Sin-wai. Buddhism in late ch'ing political thought. Chin univ of HK (1985) 192 p.

Chandra, Lokesh. The role of tantras in the defence strategy of t'ang china. In Surathi: Sreekrishna sarma felicitation volume, tirupati (1983) 31-44.

Chang, Aloysius. Four historical chinese temples in nagasaki. CC 30.2 (june 1989) 51-60.

Chang, Sheng-yen. Four great thinkers in the history of modern chinese buddhism. In SHB (1980) 283-294.

Chappell, David W. Early forebodings of the death of buddhism. Numen 27 (1980) 122-154.

Char, S. V. R. Dharmaraksha—a short biography. CC 23.2 (sept 1982) 57-65. Re 3rd c missionary-translator.

Cheung, Frederick Hok-Ming. Religion and politics in early t'ang china: taoism and buddhism in the reigns of kao-tsu and t'ai-tsung. JICS:CUHK 18 (1987) 265-276.

Covell, Ralph R. Confucius, the buddha, and christ. Maryknoll, NY (1986) See chap 7, Buddhism in china—the contextualization of a foreign faith, 133-149.

Dalia, Albert A. The "political career" of the buddhist historian tsan-ning. In BTS-II (1987) 146-180. Tsan-ning's dates are 919-1001.

Davidson, J. LeRoy. Indian influences on china. In A. Basham (ed) A cultural history of india, oxford univ (1975) 455-460.

Demiéville, Paul. Le concile de lhasa. Une controverse sur le quiétisme entre bouddhistes de l'inde et de la chine au VIIIième siècle de l'ère chrétien. Paris (1952) viii + 398 p. Repr (1987)

Demiéville, Paul. l'Iconoclasme anti-bouddhique en chine. In A. Bareau (ed) Mélanges d'histoire des religions offerts à henri-charles puech, paris (1974) 17-25. Mostly on t'ang period.

Demiéville, Paul. l'Introduction au tibet du bouddhisme sinisé d'après les manuscrits de touen-houang. (Analyse de récents travaux japonais) CETH 1 (1979) 1-16.

Demiéville, Paul. Philosophy and religion from han to sui. In CHC vol 1: The ch'in and han empires, 221 b.c.-a.d. 220 (1986) Sec 16: 808-872.

Enomoto, Fumio. The formation and development of the sarvastivada scriptures. Proc31stICHS, tokyo, vol 1 (1984) 197-198. Abstr.

Faure, Bernard. La volonté d'orthodoxie dans le bouddhisme chinois. Paris (1988) 320 p.

Forte, Antonino. The activities in china of the tantric master manicintana (pao-ssu-wei: ? - 721 c.e.) from kashmir and of his northern indian collaborators. E&W 34 (1984) 301-345.

Forte, Antonino. Hui-chih (fl 676-703 a.d.) a brahmin born in china. Instituto universitario orientale annali [napoli] 45 (1986) 105-134. Hui-chih became a budd monk.

Forte, Antonino. Mingtang and buddhist utopias in the history of the astronomical clock; the tower, statue and armillary sphere constructed by empress wu. Rome & paris (1988) 333 p, app, bibliog, illus, genl index. Discusses inter-connections of history, science, and relig.

Forte, Antonino. Political propaganda and ideology in china at the end of the seventh century; inquiry into the nature, authors and function of the tunhuang document s.6502 followed by an annotated translation. Napoli, instituto universitario oriental. (1976) 312 p. Text composed by a group of budd monks to legitimate ascension to throne of empress wu chao (r.683-707) See rev by M. Strickmann in EB n.s.10.1 (may 1977) 156-160.

Forte, Antonino. The relativity of the concept of orthodoxy in chinese buddhism: chih-sheng's indictment of shih-li and the proscription of the dharma mirror sutra. In CBA (1990) 239-249.

Franke, Herbert. Sha-lo-pa (1259-1314), a tangut buddhist monk in yuan china. In RPO-A (1985)

148

201-222. He tsl budd texts into chin.

Franz, Rainer von. Die unbearbeiten peking-inschriften der franke-laufer sammlung. Wiesbaden (1984) 259 s. Re budd temples in north china dating to 17th and 18th c.

Fujieda, Akira. The tun-huang manuscripts. In Donald D. Leslie, Colin Mackerras & Wang Gungwu (ed) Essays on the sources for chinese history, australian natl univ (1973) 120-128. Book also publ by univ of south carolina (1975)

Fung, Ch'êng-chün. Les moines chinois et étranger qui ont contribué à la formation du tripitaka chinois. Shanghai (1931)

Gimello, Robert M. Imperial patronage of buddhism during the northern sung. ProcC&S (1987) 71-85.

Gong, Shaoying. A discussion of the anti-buddhism struggle in china before the mid-tang dynasty and the path of buddhist development. CSP 14.4 (summer 1983) 3-102. This art occupies entire issue.

Grison, P. Le rôle des langues dans la diffusion du bouddhisme. EtTrad 82, no 472 (1981) 86-92. Re taoist contribution to zen.

Groner, Paul. Saicho. The establishment of the japanese tendai school. Berkeley calif (1984) See chap 4, Voyage to china, 38-64; also passim.

Guisso, R. W. L. Wu tse-t'ien and the politics of legitimation in t'ang china. Western washington univ (1978) xiii + 335 p. See chap 4, The empress wu and the creation of state ideology, 26-50.

Hirakawa, Akira. Tsl by Paul Groner. Buddhist literature: a survey of texts. EncyRel 2 (1987) 509b-526b.

Hori, Toshikazu. Tsl by P. A. Herbert. Social change in tun-huang from the latter half of the t'ang dynasty. ActaA 55 (nov 1988) 48-74.

Huntington, John C. Note on a chinese text demonstrating the earliness of tantra. JIABS 10.2 (1987) 88-98.

Hurvitz, Leon. The mind of the early chinese buddhist. In DBT (1979) 114-161. Re sinicization of budd, with bibliog.

Ikeda, Daisaku. Tsl by Burton Watson. The flower of chinese buddhism. NY & tokyo (1986) 193 p, maps, chin names, budd texts, brief engl bibliog. Hist of intro and early development (to mid 9th c) of budd in china.

Jagchid, Sechin. Chinese buddhism and taoism during the mongolian rule of china. Mongolian studies 6 (1980) 61-98.

Jagchid, Sechin. The mongol khans and chinese buddhism and taoism. JIABS 2.1 (1979) 7-28.

Jan, Yün-hua. Chinese buddhism in ta-tu: the new situation and new problems. In YT (1982) 375-417.

Jenner, William John Francis. Memories of loyang. Yang hsüan-chih and the lost capital (493-534) Oxford univ (1981) xii + 310 p, 3 maps, app, bibliog, index. See rev by Andrew C. H. Jones in JCR 10 (1983) 162-169.

Jinananda, B. Early routes between china and india. Journal of the bihar univ 4.1 (nov 1958) 82-91. Re arrival of budd in china.

Jorgensen, John. The 'imperial' lineage of ch'an buddhism: the role of confucian ritual and ancestor worship in ch'an's search for legitimation in the mid-t'ang dynasty. PFEH 35 (mar 1987) 89-133.

Kajiyama, Yuichi. Women in buddhism. EB n.s. 15.1 (spring 1982) 53-70. Historically and acc to budd texts.

Khare, Brij B. Church state relations and the legacy of buddhism in china. ProcC&S (1987) 47-54.

Kudara, Kogi. Chinese buddhist manuscripts from central asia in the mannerheim collection [helsinki] Proc31stICHS, tokyo, 2 (1984) 995-997. Abstr.

Lahiri, Latika (tsl). Chinese monks in india. Delhi etc (1986) xxvii + 160 p, chin text, bibliog, index.

Tsl of i-ching's (635-713) Ta t'ang hsi yü ch'iu fa kao seng chuan.

Lai, Whalen W. The earliest folk buddhist religion in china: t'i-wei po-li ching and its historical significance. In BTS-II (1987) 11-35.

Lai, Whalen. Emperor wu of liang on the immortal soul, shen pu mieh. JAOS 101.2 (apr-june 1981) 167-175.

Lai, Whalen. Kang yuwei and buddhism: from [formless] enlightenment to [concretized confucian] sagehood. CF 26.1 (apr 1983) 14-34.

Lai, Whalen. Society and the sacred in the secular city: temple legends of the lo-yang ch'ieh-lan-chi. Chap 8 in Albert E. Dien (ed) State and society in early medieval china, stanford univ (1990) 229-268.

Lai, Whalen. Why the lotus sutra?—On the historic significance of tendai. JJRS 14.2-3 (junc-sept 1987) 71-81.

Lai, Whalen. Yao hsing's discourse on mahayana: buddhist controversy in early fifth-century china. RTrad 4.2 (oct-nov 1981) 35-59. Yao hsing was later ch'in ruler 383-415.

Lancaster, Lewis R. Buddhist literature: canonization. EncyRel 2 (1987) 504b-509b.

Landry-Deron, Isabelle. The clouds terrace: esoteric buddhist monument at chu-yung pass. AofA 19.4 (july-aug 1989) 99-108. Located northwest of peking.

Lee, Lily Hsiao Hung. The emergence of buddhist nuns in china and its social ramifications. JOSA 18-19 (1986-87) 82-100.

Lewis, Mark Edward. The suppression of the three stages sect: apocrypha as a political issue. In CBA (1990) 207-238.

Li, Jung-hsi (tsl) Engl text revised by Christopher Cullen. Biographies of buddhist nuns: pao-chang's pi-ch'iu-ni chuan. Osaka (1981) 144 p, index. Text is early 6th c composition; see rev art by Kathryn Tsai in CEA 1 (1985) 87-101.

Li, Thomas Shiyu & Susan Naquin. The baoming temple: religion and the throne in ming and ching china. HJAS 48.1 (june 1988) 131-188. Re temple near peking, a "small buddhist nunnery"

Liu, Xinru. Ancient india and ancient china. Trade and religious exchanges a.d. 1-600. Oxford univ (1988) See pt III, 139-182; bibliog incl chin lit.

Liu, Xinru. Buddhist institutions in the lower yangtze during the sung dynasty. BSYS 21 (1989) 31-51.

Mather, Richard. The impact of the nirvana sutra in china. In LB (1981) 155-173.

Miyakawa, Hisayuki. Liang wu-ti. EncyRel 8 (1987) 536b-537a.

Miyakawa, Hisayuki. T'an-yao. EncyRel 14 (1987) 280b-282a.

Mizuno, Kogen. Tsl by M. Takanashi, K. Yoshida, T. Matsumura, K. Osaka. Adapted by Rebecca M. Davis. Buddhist sutras. Origin, development, transmission. Tokyo (1982) 220 p, app, gloss-index, map.

Nakamura, Kikunoshin. Tun-huang document s.4644—its diplomatic significance. Proc31stICHS, tokyo, vol 2 (1984) 984-986. Abstr.

Nehru, Shri Jawaharlal. It was buddhism that fostered indo-chinese relations. The young buddhist (1986) 37-40.

Ocho, Enichi. Tsl by Robert F. Rhodes. The beginnings of tenet classification in china. EB n.s. 14.1 (autumn 1981) 71-94.

Pachow, W. A hermeneutical approach to the supernatural phenomena in buddhist history. CC 27.1; 27.2 (mar 1986; june 1986) 15-36; 73-100.

Pachow, W. The sino-indian buddhist debate in eighth century tibet: some questions and answers. The lotus [bulletin of the singapore polytechnic buddhist society] 18 (1984)

150

Paul, Diana. Portraits of the feminine: buddhist and confucian historical perspectives. In SHB (1980) 209-221.

Powell, Andrew. Photos by Graham Harrison. Living buddhism. NY (1989) See sec 5, Decline and destruction; the fate of buddhism in china and tibet, 144-179.

Raguin, Yves. Buddhism: origins and evolution. Areopagus (fall 1987) 38-40.

Rawlinson, Andrew. Mahayana buddhism in china, t'ang-sung. In EncyWF (1987) 245a-249a.

Sankrityayan, Rahul. Selected essays of rahul sankrityayan. New delhi (1984) See, Ancient relations between china and india, 160-178.

Schipper, K. M. Millenarismes et messianismes dans la chine ancienne. In Understanding modern china; proceedings of the 26th conference of chinese studies, european association of chinese studies, rome (1979) 31-49.

Schmidt-Glintzer, Helwig. Die identität der buddhistischen schulen und die kompilation buddhistischer universalgeschichten in china. Ein beitrag zur geistesgeschichten der sung-zeit. Wiesbaden (1982) viii + 190 s.

Schuster, Nancy. Yoga-master dharmamitra and clerical misogyny in fifth century china. TibJ 9 (1984) 33-46.

Seah, Ingram S. Nestorian christianity and pure land buddhism in t'ang china. TJT 6 (1984) 75-92.

Seidel, Anna. Le sutra merveilleux du ling-pao suprême, traitant de lao tseu qui convertit les barbares (le manuscrit s.2081) Contribution à l'étude du bouddho-taoïsme des six dynasties. CETH (1984) 305-352, sec of pl.

Seiwert, Hubert. Hochkultur und fremde religion: buddhismus und katholizimus in china. In Michael Pye (ed) Religion in fremder kultur, saarbrücken-scheidt (1987) 55-76.

Shinohara, Koichi. Two sources of chinese buddhist biographies: stupa inscriptions and miracle stories. In M&M (1988) 119-228.

Singhal, D. P. Buddhism in east asia. New delhi (1984) See chap 2, China, 38-138, notes and refs, biblio.

Strickmann, Michel. India in the chinese looking-glass. In SR/DP (1982) 52-63.

Sun, George C. H. A summit meeting in metaphysics, religion, and philosophical anthropology: the chinese-indian-western encounter on creativity. ProcICS, Thought & philosophy vol 1 (1981) 117-182.

T'ien, Ju-k'ang. The decadence of buddhist temples in fukien in late ming and early ch'ing. In FukienD&D (1990) 83-100.

Tanaka, Ryosho. Relations between the buddhist sects in the t'ang dynasty. JA 269 (1981) 163-169.

Tang, Yijie. A perspective on the meaning of comparative philosophy and comparative religious studies: the case of the intro of indian buddhism into china. CSP 15.2 (winter 1983-84) 39-106.

Tang, Yijie. The relationships between traditional and imported thought and culture in china: from the standpoint of the importation of buddhism. JCP 15.4 (dec 1988) 415-424.

Tang, Yijie. The significance of comparative philosophy and comparative religion: a view from the introduction of indian buddhism into china. CSP 18.4 (summer 1987) 3-63.

Tatz, Mark. T'ang dynasty influences on the early spread of buddhism in tibet. TibJ 3.2 (summer 1978) 3-32.

Todaro, Dale. Kumarajiva. EncyRel 8 (1987) 398b-400b.

Tonami, Mamoru. Tsl by P. A. Herbert. Policy toward the buddhist church in the reign of t'ang hsüan-tsung. ActaA 55 (nov 1988) 27-47.

Tschen, Yuan. Adam schall von bell und der bonze mu tschen-wen. MS 5 (1940) 316-328.

Tsukamoto, Zenryu. Tsl and annot by Leon Hurvitz. A history of early chinese buddhism from its introduction to the death of hui-yuan. Tokyo, NY & san francisco (1985) 2 vol: 1, xxii to p.652; 2, 657-1305. Tsl of author's Chugoku bukkyo tsushi (1979) Tsl provides 21 app, notes, bibliog, gloss, index. No chin char in text.

Vandermeersch, Léon. Bouddhisme et pouvoir dans la chine confucianiste. In BetSA (1990) 31-39.

Waldschmidt, Ernst. Die legende vom leben des buddha. In auszügen aus den heiligen texten aus dem sanskrit, pali und chinesischen übersetzt und eingeführt. Graz, austria (1982) 270 s.

Wang, Yi-t'ung (tsl) A record of buddhist monasteries in lo-yang by yang hsüan-chih. Princeton univ (1984) xxii + 310 p, maps, illus, gloss, official titles, bibliog, index. Tsl of Lo-yang ch'ieh-lan chi.

Weinstein, Stanley. Buddhism under the t'ang. Cambridge univ (1987) 236 p, notes, gloss, bibliog, index.

Yen, Chüan-ying. The tower of seven jewels and empress wu. NPMB 22.1 (mar-apr 1987) 1-18. The ch'i-pao-t'ai in ch'ang-an and its 32 extant sculptures.

Yü, Chün-fang. The renewal of buddhism in china. Chu-hung and the late ming synthesis. Columbia univ (1981) xvi + 328 p, bibliog.

Yü, Chün-fang. Chu-hung. EncyRel 3 (1987) 472a-473a.

Yü, Chün-fang. Chung-feng ming-pen and ch'an buddhism in the yüan. In YT (1982) 419-477.

Yü, Chün-fang. Some ming buddhists' responses to neo-confucianism. JCP 15.4 (1988) 371-413.

Yuan, Heh-hsiang. Introduction of buddhism into china: from religion to philosophy. ACQ 15.4 (winter 1987) 1-18.

Zdún, Genowefa. Matériaux pour l'étude de la culture chinoise du moyen age: le lo-yang k'ie ki.

Warszawa (1982) 160 p, 10 fig, 2 folding plans, bibliog, index.

Zürcher, Erik. Buddhism in a pre-modern bureaucratic empire: the chinese experience. In SHB (1980) 401-411.

Zürcher, Erik. Eschatology and messianism in early chinese buddhism. In LSS (1981) 34-56.

Zürcher, Erik. Maha-cina: la réinterpretation bouddhique de l'histoire de la chine. CRAIBL (juil-oct 1985) 477-492.

Zürcher, Erik. Buddhism: buddhism in china. EncyRel 2 (1987) 414a-421a.

Zürcher, Erik. Missions: buddhist missions. EncyRel 9 (1987) 570a-573b.

Zürcher, Erik. Bouddhisme, christianisme et société chinoise. Paris (1990) 95 p.

Zürcher, Erik. Han buddhism and the western region. In T&L (1990) 158-182.

III.7 Schools and Individuals

N.B. Sections III.7 and III.8 of 1985 bibliography have been subdivided and all items placed in new categories.

III.7 (A) General

Blofeld, John. Beyond the gods. Buddhist and taoist mysticism. London & NY (1974) 164 p, short gloss.

Blofeld, John Calthorpe. Lamaism and its influence on chinese buddhism. THM 7.2 (1938) 151-160, photos.

Chuan, T. K. Some notes on kao seng chuan. THM 7 (1938) 452-468.

Demiéville, Paul. l'Origine des sectes bouddhiques d'après paramartha. MCB 1 (1931-32) 15-64. Repr in CEB (1973)

Dutt, S. The ten schools of chinese buddhism. In HPEW 1 (1952) 590-595.

Hackmann, Heinrich. Die schulen des chinesischen buddhismus. MSOS 14.1 (1912) 232-266.

Harlez, Charles d'. The buddhist schools. Dublin review no 105, 3rd ser, vol 22 (july 1889) 47-71. See also author's art: Les écoles bouddhistes, in Science catholique 5 (mai-juil 1890)

Julien, Stanislas. Listes diverses des noms des dix-huit écoles schismatiques qui sont sorties du bouddhisme. JA 5e sér 14 (1859) 327-361.

Li, Jung-hsi (tsl) Engl text revised by Christopher Cullen. Biographies of buddhist nuns: pao-chang's pi-ch'iu-ni chuan. Osaka (1981) 144 p, index. Text is early 6th c composition; see rev art by Kathryn Tsai in CEA 1 (1985) 87-101.

Lu, K'uan-yü (Charles Luk) The secrets of chinese meditation. Self-cultivation by mind control as taught in the ch'an, mahayana and taoist schools in china. London (1964) 240 p, gloss, illus, index. Repr london (1984) German tsl by H.-U. Rieker, Geheimnisse der chinesischen meditation, zürich & stuttgart (1967)

Ocho, Enichi. Tsl by Robert F. Rhodes. The beginnings of tenet classification in china. EB n.s. 14.2 (autumn 1981) 71-94.

Rousselle, Erwin. Die typen der meditation in china. CDA (1932) 20-46.

Schmidt-Glintzer, Helwig. Die identität der buddhistischen schulen und die kompilation buddhistischer universalgeschichten in china. Ein beitrag zur geistesgeschichten der sung-zeit. Wiesbaden (1982) viii + 190 s.

Shih, Robert (tsl). Hui-chiao. Biographies des moines éminents de houei-kiao. Kao seng tchouan, 1 partie. Biographies des premiers traducteurs. Louvain (1968) xi + 177 p, chin text with french tsl.

Shinohara, Koichi. Two sources of chinese buddhist biographies: stupa inscriptions and miracle stories. In M&M (1988) 119-228.

Sino-american budd assoc. Vajra bodhi sea. A monthly journal of orthodox buddhism. City of ten thousand buddhas—talmage, calif. See passim.

Weinstein, Stanley. Buddhism, schools of: chinese buddhism. EncyRel 2 (1987) 482a-487b.

Wright, A. F. Biography and hagiography. Hui-chiao's lives of eminent monks. In SJV (1954) 383-432.

III.7 (B) Lü (Vinaya)

Bush, Susan H. & Victor Mair. Some buddhist portraits and images of the lü and ch'an sects in twelfth- and thirteenth-century china. AAA 31 (1977-78) 32-51, illus.

Chen, Gerald. Jian zhen comes home. EH 19.6 (june 1980) 11-16, illus. "Visit" of lacquer statue of monk chien-chen fr toshodaiji, nara, to yangchou and peking.

Tamura, Kwansei. Ganjin (chien-chen), transmitter of buddhist precepts to japan. YE n.s.6.4 (autumn 1980) 4-6.

III.7 (C) Hua-yen

Chang, Garma C. C. The buddhist teaching of totality. The philosophy of hwa yen buddhism. Penn state univ (1971) xxv + 270 p, list of chin terms, gloss, index.

Cook, Francis. Causation in the chinese hua-yen tradition. JCP 6.4 (1979) 367-385.

Cook, Francis H. The dialogue between hua-yen and process thought. EB n.s. 17.2 (autumn 1984) 12-29.

Cook, Francis H. Hua-yen buddhism. The jewel net of indra. Penn state univ (1977) xiv + 146 p, notes, gloss, index.

Cook, Francis H. The meaning of vairocana in huayen buddhism. PEW 22.4 (1972) 403-415.

Gimello, Robert M. The doctrine of "natural origination" in early hua-yen buddhism. MexICHS 2: China (1976) 8-36.

Gimello, Robert M. Early hua-yen, meditation, and early ch'an: some preliminary considerations. In ECCT (1983) 149-164.

Gimello, Robert M. Hua-yen. EncyRel 6 (1987) 485b-489b.

Gimello, Robert M. Li t'ung-hsüan and the practical dimensions of hua-yen. In SCHY (1983) 321-387.

Gimello, Robert M. & Peter N. Gregory (ed) Studies in ch'an and hua-yen. Univ hawaii (1983) Art sep listed in this bibliog; abbrev SCHY.

Gregory, Peter N. Chinese buddhist hermeneutics: the case of hua-yen. JAAR 51.2 (june 1983) 231-249.

Gregory, Peter N. The place of the sudden teaching within the hua-yen tradition: an investigation of the process of doctrinal change. JIABS 6.1 (1983) 31-60.

Gregory, Peter N. Sudden enlightenment followed by gradual cultivation: tsung-mi's analysis of mind. In S&G (1987) 279-320.

Gregory, Peter N. Tsung-mi. EncyRel 15 (1987) 75a-b.

Gregory, Peter N. Tsung-mi and the single word 'awareness' (chih) PEW 35.3 (1985) 249-269.

Gregory, Peter N. What happened to the "perfect teaching"? Another look at hua-yen buddhist hermeneutics. In BHerm (1988) 207-320.

Izutsu, Toshihiko. The nexus of ontological events: a buddhist view of reality. EJ 49 (1980) 357-392. The budd view ref to is that of hua-yen.

Jan, Yün-hua. A buddhist critique of the classical chinese tradition. JCP 7.4 (dec 1980) 301-318. Re Tsung-mi (780-841)

Jan, Yün-hua. Conflict and harmony in ch'an and buddhism. JCP 4.3 (oct 1977) 287-302. Re Tsung-mi (780-841)

Jan, Yün-hua. Mind, existence and liberation: religious philosophy of tsung-mi. In N. H. Samtini & H. S. Prasad (ed) Amala prajna: aspects of buddhist studies, delhi (1989) 413-421.

Jan, Yün-hua. Portrait and self-portrait: a case study of biographical and autobiographical records of tsung-mi [780-841] In M&M (1988) 229-248.

Jan, Yün-hua. Tsung-mi's questions regarding the confucian absolute. PEW 30.4 (oct 1980) 495-504.

Kimura, Kiyotaka. Chih-yen. EncyRel 3 (1987) 242a-243b.

Kimura, Kiyotaka. Fa-tsang. EncyRel 5 (1987) 299a-300a.

King, Winston L. Hua-yen mutual interpenetrative identity and whitehead organic relation. JCP 6.4 (dec 1979) 387-410.

Lai, Whalen. The defeat of vijnaptimatrata in china: fa-tsang on fa-hsing and fa-hsiang. JCP 13.1 (mar 1986) 1-19.

Lai, Whalen. The i-ching and the formation of the hua-yen philosophy. JCP 7.3 (sept 1980) 245-258.

Liu, Ming-wood. The harmonious universe of fa-tsang and leibnitz: a comparative study. PEW 32.1 (jan 1982) 61-76.

Liu, Ming-wood. The lotus sutra and garland sutra according to the t'ien-t'ai and hua-yen schools in chinese buddhism. TP 74.1-3 (1988) 47-80.

Liu, Ming-wood. The p'an-chiao system of the hua-yen school in chinese buddhism. TP 67.1-2 (1981) 10-47.

Liu, Ming-wood. The three-nature doctrine and its interpretation in hua-yen buddhism. TP 68.4/5 (1982) 181-220.

154

Miyuki, Mokusen. Chinese response to buddhism: the case of hua-yen buddhism. In StAs (1975) 221-260.

Nakamura, Hajime. The kegon sect of buddhism and its influence on asian cultures. East 11.1 (jan 1975) 15-18.

Nakasone, Ronald. Sagamudra samadhi, the rationale for hua-yen thought. TPW 1.3 (spring 1984) 25-27.

Odin, Steve. A metaphysics of cumulative penetration: process theory and hua-yen buddhism. Process studies (claremont calif) 11.2 (1981) 65-82.

Odin, Steve. Process metaphysics and hua-yen buddhism. A critical study of cumulative penetration vs interpenetration. SUNY (1982) 242 p, app, notes, gloss, indexes.

Oh, Kang-nam. Dharmadhatu—an introduction to hua-yen buddhism. EB n.s.12.2 (oct 1979) 72-91.

Okakura, Kakuzo (tsl) Prefactory note by William Sturgis Bigelow. Chi ki (sic) i.e. founder of japanese tendai: chisho daishi: on the method of practising concentration and contemplation. HTR 16.2 (1923) 109-141.

Prince, A. J. The hua-yen vision of enlightenment. JOSA 15-16 (1983-84) 137-160.

Shim, Joe-ryong. A critique of fa-tsang (643-712) by li t'ung-hsüan (646-740) In BTS-II (1987) 109-124.

Thurman, Robert A. F. Voidnesses and totalities: madhyamika and hua yen. In SHB (1980) 343-348

Tucker, John Allen. Nagarjuna's influence on early hua-yen and ch'an thought. CC 25.2 (june 1984) 43-61.

Unno, Taitetsu. The buddhata theory of fa-tsang. Trans 8th ICfO Japan (1963) 34-41.

Wright, Dale S. Language and truth in hua-yen buddhism. JCP 13.1 (mar 1986) 1-19.

Wright, Dale S. The significance of paradoxical language in hua-yen buddhism. PEW 32 (1982) 325-338.

Yashizu, Yoshihide. A study of hua-yen-ch'an. Proc31stICHS, tokyo, 1 (1984) 160-161. Re tsung-mi (780-841) Abstr.

III.7 (D) T'ien-t'ai

Armstrong, R. C. The doctrine of the tendai school. EB 3 (1924) 32-54.

Chappell, David W. Introduction to the t'ien-t'ai ssu-chiao-i. EB n.s. 9 (may 1976) 72-86.

Chappell, David W. & M. Ichishima (comp) T'ien-t'ai buddhism. An outline of the fourfold teachings. Tokyo (1983) 191 p. Text recorded by chegwan (d.?971) Tsl by budd tsl seminar of hawaii.

Donner, Neal. Chih-i. EncyRel 3 (1987) 240b-242a.

Donner, Neal. Chih-i's meditation on evil. In BTS-II (1987) 49-64.

Donner, Neal. Sudden and gradual intimately conjoined: chih-i's t'ien-t'ai view. In S&G (1987) 201-226.

Groner, Paul. Saicho. The establishment of the japanese tendai school. Berkeley calif (1984) See chap 4, Voyage to china, 38-64; also passim.

Hackmann, Heinrich. Ein heiliger des chinesischen buddhismus und seine spüren im heutigen china (tsi k'ae) ZMK 18 (1903) 65. Re Chih-k'ai.

Hurvitz, Leon. Chih-i (538-597) An introduction to the life and ideas of a chinese buddhist monk. Comprises MCB 12 (1962) 372 p.

Kawakatsu, Yoshio. A propos de la pensée de huisi. BEFEO 69 (1981) 97-105.

Lai, Whalen. A different religious language: the tian-tai idea of the triple truth. CF 25.2 (june 1982) 67-78.

Lai, Whalen. Faith and wisdom in the t'ien-t'ai buddhist tradition: a letter by ssu-ming chih-li. JD 6.3 (1981) 281-298.

Lai, Whalen. Why the lotus sutra?—On the historic significance of tendai. JJRS 14.2-3 (june-sept 1987) 71-81.

Liu, Ming-wood. The lotus sutra and garland sutra according to the t'ien-t'ai and hua-yen schools in chinese buddhism. TP 74.1-3 (1988) 47-80.

Magnin, P. La vie et l'oeuvre de huisi (515-577) (Les origines de la sect bouddhique chinoise du tiantai) Paris (1979) 289 p, 15 pl, bibliog.

Petzold, Bruno. The chinese tendai teachings. EB 4 (1927-28) 299-347.

Petzold, Bruno. Heraus von Horst Hammitzch. Die quintessenz der t'ien-t'ai-(tendai)lehre; eine komparative untersuchung. Wiesbaden (1982) xv + 619 s, bemerkungen zur herausgezogenen literatur, erganzende bibliographische angaben zu arbeiten von Bruno Petzold, zeichen glossar wesentlicher chinesischer und japanischer, termini und namen. Contains extensive discussion of relationships with taoism.

Petzold, Bruno. Tendai buddhism as modern world-view (chinese tendai) YE 4 (oct 1929) 281-304.

Pruden, Leo M. T'ien-t'ai. EncyRel 14 (1987) 510a-519a.

Robert, Jean-Noël. La secte boudhique ten-dai (t'ien-t'ai) Samadhi 6.2 (apr-june 1972) 56-74.

Stevenson, Daniel B. The four kinds of samadhi in early t'ien-t'ai buddhism. In TradMed (1986) 45-97.

Swanson, Paul L. Chih-i's interpretation of jneyavarana: an application of the threefold truth concept. In Annual memoirs of the otani univer-

sity shin buddhist comprehensive research institute 1 (1983) 51-72. Same title in Proc31stICHS, tokyo, 1 (1984) 158-159 (abstr)

Swanson, Paul L. Foundations of t'ien-t'ai philosophy: the flowering of the two truths theory in chinese buddhism. Berkeley calif (1989) xii + 399 p. Focuses on chih-i (538-597) and his thought.

Swanson, Paul L. T'ien-t'ai studies in japan. CEA 2 (1986) 219-232.

Tamaki, Koshiro. The way of bodhisattvahood as viewed in t'ien-t'ai teaching. TBMRD 30 (1972) 35-53.

III.7 (E) Chên-yen (Esoteric)

Astley-Kristensen, Ian. An example of vajrasattva in the sino-japanese tantric buddhist tradition. SCEAR 1 (1988) 67-87.

Chou, Yi-liang. Tantrism in china. HJAS 8 (1945) 241-332.

Forte, Antonino. The activities in china of the tantric master manicintana (pao-ssu-wei: ? - 721 c.e.) from kashmir and of his northern indian collaborators. E&W 34 (1984) 301-345.

Hakeda, Yoshito S. (tsl). Kukai: major works; translated, with an account of his life and a study of his thought. Columbia univ (1972) See chap 4, Encounter with master hui-kuo, 29-33; also part 3, Major works of kukai, passim.

Hall, David A. The question of the 'left hand' path in china and japan. YE n.s.4.1 (winter 1978) 19-29. Re tantrism.

Howard, Angela. Planet worship: some evidence, mainly textual, in chinese esoteric buddhism. AS 37.2 (1983) 103-119.

Huntington, John C. Note on a chinese text demonstrating the earliness of tantra. JIABS 10.2 (1987) 88-98. Text is chin version of suvarnaprabhasa sutra, tsl in early 5th c.

156

Landry-Deron, Isabelle. The clouds terrace: eso-teric buddhist monument at chu-yung pass. AofA 19.4 (july-aug 1989) 99-108. Located northwest of peking.

Lin, Li-kouang. Punyodaya (na-t'i), un propagateur due tantrisme en chine et au camboge à l'époque de hiuan tsang. JA 227 (1935) 83-100.

Matsunaga, Yukei. A history of tantric buddhism in india with reference to chinese translations. In BT&AC (1977) 167-181.

Meissig, Marion (tr). Die "china-lehre" des saktismus: mahacinacara-tantra. Wiesbaden (1988) 225 s.

Orlando, Raffaelo. The last will of amoghavajra. Instituto orientale di napoli, Annali 40. n.s. 30 (1980) 89-113.

Orzech, Charles D. Amoghavajra. EncyRel 1 (1987) 238a-239a.

Orzech, Charles D. Chen-yen. EncyRel 3 (1987) 233b-238a.

Orzech, Charles D. Seeing chen-yen buddhism: traditional scholarship and the vajrayana in china. HR 29.2 (nov 1989) 87-114.

Orzech, Charles D. Subhakarasimha. EncyRel 14 (1987) 96a-97b.

Schuster, Nancy. Yoga-master dharmamitra and clerical misogyny in fifth century china. TibJ 9 (1984) 33-46.

Stein, Rolf A. Nouveaux problèmes du tantrisme sino-japonais. ACF 75e ann (1975) 481-488.

Stein, Rolf A. Quelques problèmes du tantrisme chinois. ACF 74e ann (1974) 499-508.

Strickmann, Michel. Homa in east asia. In Frits Staal (ed) Agni. The vedic ritual of the fire altar, univ calif (1983) vol 2, 418-455.

Strickmann, Michel. India in the chinese looking-glass. In SR/DP (1982) 52-63.

Strickmann, MIchel (ed) Tantric and taoist stud-ies in honour of r. a. stein. Being MCB 20, 21, 22 (1981-83-85) Art sep listed in this bibliog; abbrev T&TStudies.

The book of tao. A brief outline of the esoteric schools of buddhist (sic) and tao in china. Adyar, theosophical publ house (1933) 24 p.

Whitfield, Roderick. Esoteric buddhist elements in the famensi reliquary deposit. AS 44.2 (1990) 247-266. Near sian; cache made in 874.

III.7 (F) Ching-t'u (Pure Land)

Andrews, Allan A. Nembutsu in the chinese pure land tradition. EB n.s.3.2 (oct 1970) 20-45.

Andrews, Allan A. Genshin's "essentials of pure land rebirth" and the transmission of pure land buddhism to japan. Part 1, The first and second phases of transmission . . .the nara period and the early heian period. Part II, The third phase of transmission: a quantitative survey of the resources utilized by genshin. PW n.s.5; ibid n.s.6. (fall 1989; fall 1990) 20-32; 1-15.

Bando, Shojun. Shinran's indebtedness to t'an-luan. EB n.s.4.1 (may 1971) 72-87. Same title in SCR 5.4 (autumn 1971) 221-234.

Bloom, Alfred. Shinran's gospel of pure grace. Univ arizona (1965) On chin pure land patriarchs see 7-17.

Chappell, David W. Ching-t'u. EncyRel 3 (1987) 329a-333b.

Chappell, David W. From dispute to dual cultiva-tion: pure land responses to ch'an critics. In S&G (1987) 163-197.

Chappell, David W. Tao-ch'o. EncyRel 14 (1987) 286b-287a.

Corless, Roger J. The brilliance of emptiness: t'an-luan as a mystic of light. PW n.s.5 (fall 1989) 13-19.

Corless, Roger J. Monotheistic elements in early pure land buddhism. Religion 6.2 (1976) 176-189.

Corless, Roger J. T'an-luan. EncyRel 14 (1987) 270a-271b.

Eilert, Hakan. A brief outline of pure land buddhism in india and china. Japanese religions (kyoto) 14.1 (1985) 1-12.

Eracle, J. La doctrine bouddhique de la terre pure. Introduction à trois sutras bouddhiques. Paris (1973) 117 p.

Fujita, Kotatsu. Pure land buddhism and the lotus sutra. In I&B (1980) 117-130.

Fujiwara, Ryosetsu. The conception of the nembutsu in shan-tao's pure land buddhism. RDR 394 (dec 1970) 69-94.

Fujiwara, Ryosetsu. The nembutsu. Its origin and development. RDR 383 (mar 1967) 28-54.

Fujiwara, Ryosetsu. Shan-tao. EncyRel 13 (1987) 224a-225b.

Fujiwara, Ryosetsu. Shan-tao's influence on later pure land buddhism. RDR 400/401 (mar 1973) 12-33.

Heng-ching. Yung-ming's syncretism of pure land and ch'an. JIABS 10.1 (1987) 117-134. Re yung-ming yen-shou (904-975)

Hsüan-hua. BTTSoc (tsl) Buddha root farm. San francisco (1976) 72 p. Meditation by recitation of name of amitabha.

Hsüan-hua. BTTSoc (tsl) Listen to yourself think it over. San francisco (1978) Meditation instructions on name of kuan-yin and ch'an.

Hsüan-hua. BTTSoc (tsl) Pure land and ch'an dharma talks. San francisco (1972) 72 p.

Hurvitz, Leon. Chu-hung's one mind of pure land and ch'an buddhism. In SSMT (1970) 451-482.

Inglis, James W. The vows of amida. A comparative study. JNCBRAS 48 (1917) 1-11.

Ingram, Paul O. The dharma of faith: an introduction to classical pure land buddhism. Lanham, md (1977) See chap 2, The chinese tradition, 22-44.

Ingram, Paul O. The symbolism of light and pure land buddhist soteriology. JJRS 1.4 (dec 1974) 331-344.

Makita, Tairyo. Tsl by Philip Yampolsky. Hui-yüan—his life and times. Zinbun 6 (1962) 1-28.

Matsumoto, Shoji. The modern relevance of donran's pure land buddhist thought. PW n.s.2 (fall 1986) 36-41.

Mochizuki, Shinko. Tsl by Leo Pruden. Development of chinese pure land buddhism. PW: pt I, 1.2; pt II, 1.3 (spring 1983-84) 6-9, 13; 5-9.

Ono, Gemmyo. A note on tz'u-min's works and some points of his religious teachings. PIAJ 2.8 (1926) 361-363.

Ono, Gemmyo. On the pure land doctrine of tz'u-min. EB 5 (1930) 200-213.

Pas, Julian. Dimensions in the life and thought of shan-tao. In BTS-II (1987) 65-84.

Pas, Julian F. Shan-tao's interpretation of the meditative vision of buddha amitayus. HR 14 (nov 1974) 96-116.

Paul, Diana. Kuan-yin: savior and savioress in chinese pure land buddhism. Chap 12 in Carl Olson (ed) The book of the goddess: past and present, NY (1983) 161-175.

Re, Arundel del. Amidism and christianity. Marco polo 3 (apr 1941) 68-81.

Sasaki, G. What is the true sect of the pure land? EB 1 (1921) 167-179.

Seah, Ingram S. Nestorian christianity and pure land buddhism in t'ang china. TJT 6 (1984) 75-92.

Shih, Joseph. l'Eschatologie dans le monde chinois. SM 32 (1983) 181-194.

Steadman, James D. Pure land buddhism in the buddhist historical tradition. RS 23 (sept 1987) 407-421.

Suzuki, D. T. The development of the pure land doctrine. EB 3 (1924) 285-327.

Tamaki, Koshiro. The ultimate enlightenment of hui-yüan in lu-shan. JIBS 12.2 (1964) 1-12.

Tanaka, Kenneth K. Bibliography of english-language works on pure land buddhism: primarily 1983-1989. PW n.s.5 (fall 1989) 85-99. Classified by topic.

Tanaka, Kenneth K. The dawn of chinese pure land buddhism. Ching-ying hui-yüan's commentary on the visualization sutra. SUNY (1990) xxiv + 304 p, tsl of comm, app, notes gloss, bibliog, index.

Tanaka, Kenneth K. Earliest usage of "ta-ching" (daikyo) and "wang-shêng lun" (ojoron) by a non-orthodox pure land buddhist: its implication for chinese pure land buddhism. PW n.s.2 (fall 1986) 63-74. The "non-orthodox pure land buddhist" is hui-yüan (523-592)

Tanaka, Kenneth K. Hui-yüan. EncyRel 6 (1987) 497b-498b.

Tanaka, Kenneth K. Where is the pure land? Controversy in chinese buddhism on the nature of pure land. PW n.s.3 (fall 1987) 36-45.

Tokunaga, Michio. A view of tariki in tan-luan's ronchu. JIBS 22.2 (mar 1974) 22-27.

Wagner, Rudolf G. The original structure of the correspondence between shih hui-yüan and kumarajiva. HJAS 31 (1971) 28-48. Re taisho tripitaka no 1856.

Wei, Francis C. M. The doctrine of salvation by faith as taught by the buddhist pure land sect and its alleged relation to christianity. ChRec 51.6; 51.7 (june & july 1920) 395-401; 485-491.

Wieger, Léon. Amidisme chinois et japonais. Hien-hien (1928) 51 p, illus.

III.7 (G) Ch'an (Zen)

N.B. Many works on zen in japan or son in korea contain ref to ch'an, with chin names in transliteration.

Addiss, Stephen. Blake, taoism and zen. In SpF (1982) 281-287. "Parallel passages" showing "similar visions"

Aitken, Robert. The body of the buddha. Parabola 10.3 (1985) 26-31. Zen teachings.

Aitken, Robert. The cloud of unknowing and the mumonkan: christian and buddhist meditation methods. BCS 1 (1981) 87-91.

Aitken, Robert (tsl) The gateless barrier: the wu-men kuan (mumonkan) San francisco (1990) 332 p, notes, bibliog, app, gloss, index.

Aitken, Robert (tsl & comm) Wu-men-kuan, case 11, "chao-chou and the hermits" EB n.s. 22.2 (autumn 1989) 78-84.

Anonymous. Zen. Bratislava, CAD press, vol 1 (1986) 375p; vol 2 (1988) 365p; vol 3 (1989) 355 p; 2nd ed (1990, 1991).

App, Urs. Chan/zen's greatest encyclopaedist, mujaku dochu. CEA 3 (1987) 155-174. Edo monk (1653-1744).

Augustine, Morris J. Zen and benedictine monks as mythopoeic models of nonegocentered worldviews and lifestyles. BDS 6 (1986) 23-49.

Barnet, Sylvan & William Burto. Zen ink paintings. Tokyo (1982) 94 p, 32 reproductions, suggestions for further reading.

Berthier, Annie & François Berthier. Le thème chinois des "quatre dormants" et sa résurgence dans le monde musulman. ArtsAs 42 (1987) 59-64. Re ch'an theme that appears on a small painting in topkapi museum.

Bielefeldt, Carl. Ch'ang-lu tsung-tse's tso-ch'an i and the "secret" of zen meditation. In TradMed (1986) 129-161.

Bielefeldt, Carl. Dogen's manuals of zen meditation. Univ calif (1988) 259 p, gloss, works cited. See passim for chin ch'an.

Blofeld, John (tsl) The path to sudden attainment. A treatise of the ch'an (zen) school of chinese buddhism by hui hai of the t'ang dynasty. London (1948) 51 p. 2nd ed, titled The zen teaching of hui hai on sudden illumination, london (1962) 160 p; 3rd rev ed, 130 p (1987)

Blofeld, John (tsl) The zen teaching of huang po on the transmission of mind. Being the teaching of the zen master huang po as recorded by the scholar p'ei hsiu of the t'ang dynasty. NY (1959) 136 p, index. This is rev and enl ed of tsl titled The huang po doctrine . . . q.v. under Chu Ch'an. Rev and partly retsl german version, Der geist des zen, münchen (1988)

Brinker, Helmut. Religiöse metaphorik in vogeldarstellungen zen-buddhistischer malermönche. In FW/CG (1985) 25-42. See passim.

Brinker, Helmut. Some secular aspects of ch'an buddhist painting during the sung and yüan dynasties. In MA (1972) 86-95.

Brinker, Helmut, R. P. Kramers & C. Ouwehand (ed) Zen in china, japan, east asian art. Berne etc (1985) Symposium papers fr conference at zurich univ; indiv papers sep listed in this bibliog; abbrev ZCJEAA.

Brun, Pierre (tsl.) Meister linji—begegnungen und reden. Zürich (1986) First german tsl of lin-chi lu.

Bundy, Les. The last bull: a journey through buddhist thought to christianity. Areopagus (christmas 1990, 4.1) 5-7. "Last bull" ref to ox-herding pictures.

Burckhardt, Titus. Tsl by Lord Northbourne. Sacred art in east and west. Bedfont, middlesex, engl (1967). Tsl fr french version , Principes et méthodes de l'art sacré, lyon (1958) See chap 6, Landscape in far eastern art, 134-142; mostly on zen painting.

Burr, Ronald L. Lin-chi on "language dependence," an interpretive analysis. In ECCT (1983) 207-227.

Bush, Susan H. & Victor Mair. Some buddhist portraits and images of the lü and ch'an sects in twelfth- and thirteenth-century china. AAA 31 (1977-78) 32-51, illus.

Buswell, Robert jr. Ch'an hermeneutics: a korean view. In BHerm (1988) 231-256.

Buswell, Robert E. jr. Chinul's systemization of chinese meditative techniques and korean son buddhism. In TradMed (1986) 199-242. Chinul's dates are 1158-1210.

Buswell, Robert E. jr. The formation of ch'an ideology in china and korea: the vajrasamadhi-sutra, a buddhist apocryphon. Princeton univ (1989) 315 p, illus, gloss, works cited, index. Study and tsl.

Buswell, Robert E. jr. The "short-cut" approach of k'an-hua meditation: the evolution of a practical subitism in chinese ch'an buddhism. In S&G (1987) 321-377.

Chang, Chen-chi. The practice of zen. London (1960) 256 p, notes, bibliog, app, index. German tsl, Die praxis des zen, freiburg im breisgan (1982)

Chang, Sheng-yen. Ch'an at the end of the ming dynasty. Proc31stICHS, tokyo, 1 (1984) 169. Abstr.

Chappell, David W. From dispute to dual cultivation: pure land responses to ch'an critics. In S&G (1987) 163-197.

Chappell, David W. The teachings of the fourth ch'an patriarch tao-hsin (580-651) In ECCT (1983) 89-129.

Chen, T. H. Chinese dhyana slokas. Kalakshetra qtly [madras] 5.3 (1983) 3-8. Poems by chin buddhists.

Cheng, Hsüeh-li. Psychology, ontology and zen soteriology. RS 22.3/4 (sept/dec 1986) 459-472.

Cheng, Hsüeh-li. Zen and san-lun madhyamika thought: exploring the theoretical foundation of zen teachings and practices. RS 15.3 (sept 1979) 343-363. Republ as The roots of zen buddhism in JCP 8 (1981) 451-478.

Cheng, Hsüeh-li. Zen, wittgenstein and neo-orthodox theology: the problem of communicating truth in zen buddhism. RS 18.2 (june 1982) 133-149. Same title in TJT 12 (mar 1990) 99-119.

Chu, Ch'an (pseud for John Blofeld) The huang po doctrine of universal mind, being the teaching of dhyana master hsi yün as recorded by p'ei hsiu, a noted scholar of the t'ang dynasty. London (1947) 136p. French tsl by Y. Laurence: Le mental cosmique selon la doctrine de huang po... Adyar (1954) 144 p. See, for rev & enl engl version: Blofeld, John, The zen teaching of huang po.

Clasper, Paul D. Eastern paths and the christian way. Maryknoll NY (1982) See chap 4, Zen: the pathless path to authentic living, 48-61.

Clasper, Paul & Janet. The ox-herder pictures: zen buddhism's version of "the pilgrim's progress" CF 28.2-3 (1984) 115-136. Repr as book in HK (n.d.) 32 p.

Cleary, J. C. (tsl) A time beyond the clouds; zen teachings from old china. Berkeley, calif (1990) 123 p.

Cleary, J. C. (tsl) Zen dawn. Early zen texts from tun huang. Boston (1986) 135 p, gloss.

Cleary, J. C. Zibo, the last great zen master of china. Fremont calif (1989) 155 p. Re zibo zhanke (1543-1604)

Cleary, Thomas (tsl) The book of serenity; one hundred zen dialogues. NY (1990) 463 p, notes, gloss. Kung-an with comm.

Cleary, Thomas. Lin-chi. EncyRel 8 (1987) 555b-556b.

Cleary, Thomas (tsl and ed) Zen essence. The science of freedom. Boston (1990) 136 p. Passages fr chin masters of t'ang and sung.

Cleary, Thomas (tsl). Zen lessons; the art of leadership. Boston ??? 160 p. Based on sung texts.

Collcutt, Martin. The early ch'an monastic rule: ch'ing-kuei and the shaping of ch'an community life. In ECCT (1983) 165-184.

Copleston, Frederick. Religion and the one; philosophers east and west. NY (1982) See chap 3, The one in taoism and buddhism 40-67.

Demiéville, Paul. Tsl by Neal Donner. The mirror of the mind. In S&G (1987) 13-40.

Despeux, Catherine. Le chemin de l'éveil. Illustré par le dressage du buffle dans le bouddhisme chan, le dressage du cheval dans le taoïsme, le dressage de l'éléphant dans le bouddhisme tibétaine. Paris (1981) 139 p.

Dieuer, Michael S. Zen. In The encyclopedia of eastern philosophy and religion, boston (1988) Tsl of Lexicon der östlichen weisheitlehren, bern & munich (1986). For chin ch'an, see this art passim.

Dumoulin, Heinrich. Tsl by James W. Heisig. Ch'an. EncyRel 3 (1987) 184b-192b.

Dumoulin, Heinrich. The encounter between zen buddhism and christianity. JCS 7 (1970) 53-63.

Dumoulin, Heinrich. Tsl by James W. Heisig & Paul Knitter. Zen buddhism: a history. Vol I, India and china. NY & london (1988) See pt 2, Origins and blossoming in china, 63-349.

Epping, Franz M. von Ordnung und ritual: zu den "chan-regulationen" der sung- und ming-zeit. Saeculum 36.2-3 (1985) 175-186.

Fabian, Ludwig & Peter Lengsfeld (heraus) Die torlose schranke—mumonkan—zen-meister mumons koan-sammlung. München (1989) Tsl of Yamada Koun's tsl of Gateless Gate.

Faure, Bernard. Bodhidharma. EncyRel 2 (1987) 263a-265b.

Faure, Bernard. Bodhidharma as textual and religious paradigm. HR 25.3 (feb 1986) 187-198.

Faure, Bernard. Le bouddhisme ch'an en mal d'histoire: genèse d'une tradition religieuse dans la chine des t'ang. Paris (1989) 245 p, index, lexique, bibliog sélective, annexe: chronologie sommaire de la période 645-845.

Faure, Bernard. The concept of one-practice samadhi in early ch'an. In TradMed (1986) 99-128.

Faure, Bernard. The daruma-shu, dogen, and soto zen. MN 42.1 (spring 1987) 25-55.

Faure, Bernard. Le maître de dhyana chih-ta et le "subitisme" de l'école du nord. CEA 2 (1986) 123-132. Engl summ 132.

Faure, Bernard. Shen-hsiu et l'avatamsaka-sutra. Zinbun 19 (1983) 1-15.

Faure, Bernard. Space and place in chinese religious traditions. HR 26.4 (may 1987) 337-356.

Faure, Bernard. Le traité de bodhidharma: la première anthologie du bouddhisme tchan. Paris (1986)

Faure, Bernard. La volonté d'orthodoxie; genealogy and doctrine of northern-school ch'an buddhism. Paris (1988) 318 p.

Feng, Youlan [Fung Yu-lan] On the chan sect. CSP 20.2 (winter 1988-89) 3-38.

Fisher, John F. Analysis of the koans in the mu mon kwan. Numen 25 (apr 1978) 65-76.

Franck, Frederick. Notes on the koan. Parabola 13 (fall 1988) 33-39.

Fukunaga, Mitsuji. 'No-mind' in chuang-tzu and in ch'an buddhism. Zinbun 12 (1969) 9-45.

Fung, Yu-lan. Ch'anism, the philosophy of silence. Chap 22 in author's A short history of chinese philosophy, ed by Derk Bodde, NY (1948) 255-265.

Fung, Yu-lan. Tsl by Derk Bodde. A history of chinese philosophy. Vol II, The period of classical learning. Princeton univ (1953) See The ch'an school, 386-406.

Gardner, James L. Zen buddhism: a classified bibliography of western-language publications through 1990. Salt lake city (1991) 412 p, author and subj indexes.

Garner, Richard T. The deconstruction of the mirror and other heresies: ch'an and taoism as abnormal discourse. JCP 12.2 (1985) 155-168.

Gelburd, Gail & Geri De Paoli. Asian philosophy in recent american art. Univ penn for hofstra museum (1990) 124 p, ll col and b-&-w illus.

Gimello, Robert M. Early hua-yen, meditation, and early ch'an: some preliminary considerations. In ECCT (1983) 149-164.

Gimello, Robert M. & Peter N. Gregory (ed) Studies in ch'an and hua-yen. Univ hawaii (1983) Essays sep listed in this bibliog; abbrev SCHY.

Glum, Peter. The two-faced budai. ArtsAs 40 (1985) 107-116. Re famous painting attributed to liang k'ai.

Gomez, Luis O. The direct and gradual approaches of zen master mahayana: fragments of the teachings of mo-ho-yen. In SCHY (1983) 69-167.

Gomez, Luis O. Purifying gold: the metaphor of effort and intuition in buddhist thought and practice. In S&G (1987) 67-165.

Grégory, Claude. Chan. In EncyUniv 5 (1990) 326c-336c.

Gregory, Peter N. The integration of ch'an/son and their teachings (chiao/kyo) in tsung-mi and chinul. JIABS 12.2 (1989) 7-19.

Gregory, Peter N. Introduction. In S&G (1987) 1-9.

Gregory, Peter N. (ed) Sudden and gradual: approaches to enlightenment in chinese thought. Univ hawaii (1987) Art sep listed in this bibliog; abbrev S&G.

Gregory, Peter N. Sudden enlightenment followed by gradual cultivation: tsung-mi's analysis of mind. In S&G (1987) 279-320.

Gregory, Peter N. Tsung-mi. EncyRel 15 (1987) 75a-b.

Gregory, Peter N. Tsung-mi and the single word 'awareness' (chih) PEW 35.3 (1985) 249-269.

Gundert, Wilhelm. Das zweite kapitel des pi-yan-lu. OE 2 (1955) 22-38.

Gundert, Wilhelm (tsl) Die nonne liu bei we-schan; das 24. kapitel des bi-yän-lu, eingeleitet, übersetzt und erläutert. In Asiatica (1954) 184-197.

Gundert, W. (tsl) Meister yüan-wu's niederschrift von der smaragdenen felswand. München (1960; 1981) First vol incl chap 1-33; second vol incl chap 34-50.

Ham, Wol. The study of living words in zen buddhism. JD 7.3 (july-sept 1982) 331-336.

Han, Ki-doo. On the sudden awakening of ch'an school in dharma teaching of the mind ground. Won buddhism 4.4 (1987-88) 22-29.

Hanson-Barber, A. W. "No-thought" in pao-t'ang ch'an and early ati-yoga. JIABS 8.2 (1985) 61-73.

Hart, Patrick. The zen insight of shen hui. Merton annual 1 (1988) 4-15.

Heine, S. Does the koan have buddha-nature? The zen koan as religious symbol. JAAR 58.3 (1990) 357-387. Comparison of ta-hui and dogen.

Heng-ching. Ch'an (zen) buddhism in china, its history and method. In Sidney Ratner (ed) Vision and action: essays in honor of horace m. kallen on his 70th birthday, rutgers univ (1953) 223-250.

Heng-ching. Yung-ming's syncretism of pure land and ch'an. JIABS 10.1 (1987) 117-134. Yung-ming yen-shou's dates are 904-975.

Herbert, Edward (pseud for Edward H. Kenney)

Bodhidharma; the patriarch of the way of non-sense. MW 41.4 (feb 1967) 170-175.

Hirai, Shun'ei. Tsl by Silvio Vita. The school of mount niu-t'ou and the school of the pao-t'ang monastery. E&W n.s. 37.1-4 (1987) 337-372.

Hisamatsu, Shin'ichi. Tsl by Ohashi Ryosuke & Hans Brockard. Die fünf stände von zen-meister tosan ryokai. Strukturanalyse des erwachens. Pfullingen (1980) 94 p. Tosan ryokai is tung-shan liang-chieh (807-869)

Hisamatsu, Shin'ichi. Tsl by Tokiwa Gishin & Christopher A. Ives. On the record of rinzai. EB n.s. 14.1 (spring 1981) 1-12; 14.2 (autumn 1981) 11-21; 15.1 (spring 1982) 74-88; 17.2 (autumn 1984) 75-92; 18.2 (autumn 1985) 65-78; 20.1 (spring 1987) 120-135. Rinzai is Lin-chi i-hsüan (d. 867).

Hoffman, Yoel (tsl) Radical zen: the sayings of joshu. Brookline mass (1978) Joshu is chao-lun (788-897).

Hsu, Sung-peng. A buddhist leader in ming china: the life and thought of han-shan te-ching 1546-1623. Penn state univ (1979) 409 p.

Hsu, Sung-peng. Han-shan te-ching: a buddhist interpretation of taoism. JCP 2.4 (sept 1975) 418-427.

Xu Yun (Hsü yün). Tsl by Charles Luk. Rev and ed, with intro, by Richard Hunn. Empty cloud. The autobiography of the chinese zen master xu-yün. Longmead, shaftesbury, dorset engl (1988) 244p, app, gloss, bibliog, photos. Orig ed publ 1980.

Hsüan-hua. BTTSoc (tsl) Listen to yourself think it over. San francisco (1978) Meditation instructions on name of kuan-yin and ch'an.

Hsüan-hua. BTTSoc (tsl) Pure land and ch'an dharma talks. San francisco (1972) 72 p.

Hsüan-hua. Water mirror reflecting heaven. Collected writings of tripitaka master hua. Dharma realm univ, talmage calif (1982) 77 p.

Hu, Shih. "A history of chinese philosophy" and its subsequent researches, particularly on ch'an buddhism. CSH 14.3 (spring 1981) 88-101.

Hurvitz, Leon. Chu-hung's one mind of pure land and ch'an buddhism. In SSMT (1970) 451-482.

Inada, Kenneth. Zen and taoism: common and uncommon grounds of discourse. JCP 15.1 (1988) 51-65.

Izutsu, Toshihiko. The interior and exterior in zen buddhism. EJ (1975) 581-618. Repr in TPZB; repr as book, delhi (1984) 36 p. Mostly taken fr chin sources.

Jan, Yün-hua. Conflict and harmony in ch'an and buddhism. JCP 4.3 (oct 1977) 287-302. Re Tsung-mi (780-841)

Jan, Yün-hua. The mind as the buddha-nature: the concept of the absolute in ch'an buddhism. PEW 31.4 (oct 1981) 467-477.

Jan, Yün-hua. Portrait and self-portrait: a case study of biographical and autobiographical records of tsung-mi [780-841] In M&M (1988) 229-248.

Jan, Yün-hua. Seng-chou's method of dhyana. In ECCT (1983) 51-63.

Jarand, Ursula (tsl) Hui-neng: das sutra des sechten patriarchen. München (1989) Tsl of text and morinaga soko's comm.

Johnson, Willard L. Riding the ox home. A history of meditation from shamanism to science. London (1982) 261 p, sel bibliog, index. See passim.

Jorgensen, John. The 'imperial' lineage of ch'an buddhism: the role of confucian ritual and ancestor worship in ch'an's search for legitimation in the mid-t'ang dynasty. PFEH 35 (mar 1987) 89-133.

Kadowaki, J. K. (tsl) Zen and the bible. A priest's experience. London (1980) 180 p. Tsl of a jap bk orig publ in tokyo (1977) Author is a jesuit priest.

Kao, Mu-sen. Mu ch'i's schematization versus the literati's lyricism—dharma versus samadhi. NPMB; in 3 parts: 23.4 (sept-oct 1988) 1-17; 23.5 (nov-dec 1988) 1-17; 23.6 (jan-feb 1989) 1-21.

Kawakatsu, Yoshio. A propos de la pensée de huisi. BEFEO 69 (1981) 97-105. Re ch'an master hui ssu, 515-577.

Knaul, Livia. Chuang tzu and the chinese ancestry of ch'an. JCP 13 (1986) 411-428.

Kodera, Takashi James. Ta-hui tsung-kao (1089-1163) and his "introspecting-the-kung-an ch'an" (koan zen) Ohio journal of religious studies 6 (apr 1978) 45-60.

Lai, Robert Sheng-yu. Blake and zen buddhism: a study in the uses of orthodox religion. TR 18.1-4 (aut 1987-sum 1988) 351-369.

Lai, Whalen. After mcrae, whither hui-neng? JCR 17 (1989) 117-127. Rev art.

Lai, Whalen. The formless mind verse of shen-hsiu; reconstructing the northern ch'an position. JOS 22.1 (1984) 13-24.

Lai, Whalen. Ma-tsu tao-i and the unfolding of southern zen. JJRS 12.2-3 (june-sept 1985) 173-192.

Lai, Whalen. Sinitic mandalas: the wu-wei-t'u of ts'ao-shan. In ECCT (1983) 229-257.

Lai, Whalen. T'an-ch'ien and the early ch'an tradition: translation and analysis of the essay "wang-shih-fei-lun" In ECCT (1983) 65-87.

Lai, Whalen. The transmission verses of the ch'an patriarchs: an analysis of the genre's evolution. HHYC:CS (dec 1983) 593-623.

Lancaster, Lewis & Whalen Lai (ed) Early ch'an in china and tibet. Berkeley calif (1983) Relevant art sep listed in this bibliog; abbrev ECCT.

Laycock, Steven W. Hui-neng and the transcendental standpoint. JCP 12.2 (1985) 205-211.

Laycock, Steven W. Sartre and a chinese theory of no-self: the mirroring of mind. BCS 9 (1989) 25-42. The theory is that of hui-neng.

164

Lee, Cyrus. Thomas merton and zen buddhism. CC 13.2 (june 1972) 35-48.

Lee, Cyrus. Life, death and reincarnation—a comparative study on hanshan tzu and thomas merton. CC 22.4 (dec 1981) 111-120.

Levering, Miriam L. The dragon girl and the abbess of mo-shan: gender and status in the ch'an buddhist tradition. JIABS 4.2 (1982) 19-35.

Levering, Miriam. Ta-hui and lay buddhists: ch'an sermons on death. In BTS-II (1987) 181-206.

Liao, Ping-hui. Image, power, zen discourse. TR 18.1-4 (aut 1987-sum 1988) 371-378.

Liebenthal, Walter (übers) Wu-men hui-k'ai. Ch'an-tsung wu-men kuan. Zutritt nur durch die wand. Übersetzt und mit einleitung und anmerkungen versehen. (1977) 142 s.

Lievens, Bavo. Tsl fr dutch by Julian F. Pas. The recorded sayings of matsu. NY (1987) 140 p, bibliog, index.

Linssen, R. l'Eveil suprême. Base théoretique et pratique du bouddhisme ch'an, du zen du taoïsme et des enseignements de krishnamurti. Bruxelles (1970) 160 p.

Lipski, Alexander. Thomas merton and asia: his quest for utopia. Kalamazoo mich (1983) See chap 2, Merton and zen buddhism, 21-36.

Lu, K'uan-yü (Charles Luk). The secrets of chinese meditation. Self-cultivation by mind control as taught in the ch'an, mahayana and taoist schools in china. London (1964) 240 p, gloss, illus, index. Repr london (1984) German tsl by H.-U. Rieker, Geheimnisse der chinesischen meditation, zürich & stuttgart (1967)

Luk, Charles (Lu K'uan-yü) The 30th patriarch: great master seng-ts'an. MB 67 (1959) 22-23. Seng-ts'an d.606.

Luk Charles (tsl) Yung chia's song of enlightenment. MW 36.1; 36.2 (may 1961; aug 1961) 27-30; 77-80. See tsl's Ch'an and zen teaching, third

series (1962) 105-145, for much extended treatment.

Lynn, Richard John. The sudden and gradual in chinese poetry criticism: an examination of the ch'an poetry analogy. In S&G (1987) 381-427.

Maraldo, John C. Is there historical consciousness within ch'an? JJRS 12.2-3 (june-sept 1985) 141-172.

Maraldo, John C. Das studium des zen und zen als studium. In FW/CG (1985) 177-195. See passim.

McRae, John R. Ch'an commentaries on the heart sutra: preliminary inferences on the permutation of chinese buddhism. JIABS 11.2 (1988) 85-115.

McRae, John R. The northern school and the formation of early ch'an buddhism. Univ hawaii (1986) 393 p + chin texts of hsiu-hsin yao lun and yuan-ming lun.

McRae, John R. The ox-head school of chinese ch'an buddhism: from early ch'an to the golden age. In SCHY (1983) 169-252.

McRae, John R. The platform sutra in religious and cultural perspective. EB n.s. 22.2 (autumn 1989) 130-135. Report on "Fo kuang shan intl conference on ch'an buddhism" held in kaohsiung in jan 1989.

McRae, John R. Shen-hui and the teaching of sudden enlightenment in early ch'an buddhism. In S&G (1987) 227-278.

McRae, John R. The story of early ch'an. In Kenneth L. Kraft (ed) Zen in tradition and transition, NY (1988) 125-139.

Merton, Thomas. A christian looks at zen. Intro to John C. H. Wu, The golden age of zen, taipei (1967) 1-28.

Merton, Thomas. Patrick Hart (ed) The zen insight of shen hui. Merton annual 1 (1988) 4-15. Posthumous publ.

Monastic community and transmission of zen: india-china-korea. Spring wind [toronto] (summer 1984) 3-24.

Mörth, Robert Christian. Das lin-chi lu des ch'an-meister lin chi yi-hsüan (gest 866): der versuch einer systematisierung des lin-chi lu. MDGNVO 106 (1987) 231 p. Intro and tsl.

Nagashima, Takayuki Shono. Truths and fabrications in religion: an investigation from documents of the zen (ch'an) sect. London (1978) 394 p.

Nakajima, Kumakichi (tsl) Hekigan-roku: the pi-yen-lu, a collection of koan of zen buddhism in the sung period. Tokyo (1954) 2 vol, 555 p.

Nakamura, Hajime. Ch'an and mysticism in later times. JJRS 12.4 (dec 1985) 299-317.

Nakamura, Hajime. The non-logical character of zen. JCP 12.2 (june 1985) 105-115.

Nan, Huai-chih. Tsl by Margaret Yuan & Janis Walker. Grass mountain; a seven-day intensive in ch'an training. York beach, maine (1986) 134 p, brief bibliog, chin sources.

Odier, Daniel. Nirvana tao: techniques de méditation. Paris (1974) See for ch'an, 149-169.

Ogata, Shohaku (tsl) Paul F. Schmitt (ed) The transmission of the lamp: early masters. Compiled by tao yuan. Wolfeboro new hampshire (1990) xxiv + 401 p, index. Fasc 1-10 of 30 fr ching-te ch'uan-teng lu, comp 1004.

Olson, Carl. Beatings, shouts and finger raising: a study of zen language. Journal of religious studies 10.2 (1983) 45-50.

Pa, Hu-t'ien. Tsl by Whalen Lai & Joseph Wu with assistance of Mary Smith. Looking through the ch'an public cases (kung an) CC 25.2 (june 1984) 63-70.

Pa, Hu-t'ien. Tsl by Whalen Lai & Joseph Wu with assistance of Mary Smith. On ch'an dialectics: principle and structure of kung-an (koan) CC 25.3 (sept 1984) 43-52.

Pachow, W. Chinese ch'an: a transformation of indian dhyana. CC 26 (1985) 45-58.

Powell, William F. (tsl) The record of tung-shan.

Univ hawaii (1986) 99 p, notes, index of persons, bibliog. Tung-shan liang-chieh's dates are 807-869.

Red pine (tsl) The zen teaching of bodhidharma. San francisco (1989) 125 p, notes. Bi-lingual text.

Ren, Jiyu. A brief discussion of the philosophical thought of chan buddhism. CSP 15.4 (summer 1984) 3-69.

Ren, Jiyu. On hu shih's mistakes in his study of the history of the chan sect. CSP 15.4 (summer 1984) 70-98.

Rousselle, Erwin. Das leben des patriarchen huineng. Sinica 5 (1930) 174-191.

Sayama, Mike K. Samadhi. Self-development in zen, swordsmanship, and psychotherapy. SUNY (1986) 160 p, illus.

Schlütter, Morten. A study in the genealogy of the platform sutra. SCEAR 2 (1989) 53-114.

Schmidt-Glintzer, Helwig. Eine ehrenrettung für den suden. Pao-chih (418/25-514) und fu hsi (497-569)—zwei heilige aus dem unteren yangtse-tal. In RPO-A (1985) 247-265.

Schnorr, Adam. Ch'an rhetoric and ming dynasty poetry and painting criticism. JAC 13 (1989) 17-41.

Seckel, Dietrich. Zen art. In ZCJEAA (1985) 99-113.

Seidl, Achim. Das weisheit des zen: koans aus dem bi-yän-lu. München/wien (1988) Reduction of Gundert's german tsl (q.v.) to about a fourth of the original.

Sheng-yen. Faith in mind. Elmhurst NY (1987) 139 p. Comm on poem traditionally attributed to seng-ts'an (d.606)

Sheng-yen. Getting the buddha mind: on the practice of ch'an retreat. Elmhurst NY (1982 rev ed 1989) 147 and 227 p respectively.

Sheng-yen. The infinite mirror: ts'ao-tung ch'an;

166

commentaries on Inquiry into matching halves, and Song of the precious mirror samadhi. Elmhurst NY (1990) 123 p.

Sheng-yen. Ox herding at morgan's bay. Elmhurst NY (1988) 47 p, illus.

Sheng-yen (tsl). The poetry of enlightenment. Poems by ancient ch'an masters. Elmhurst NY (1987) 3 + 94 p. Tsl and comm by a contemporary ch'an master.

Sheng-yen (tsl & comm) The sword of wisdom. Lectures on The song of enlightenment. Elmhurst NY (1990) 237 p, gloss. Tsl and comm on text by yung-chia (665-713)

Sheng-yen. Zen meditation. In Kenneth L. Kraft (ed) Zen; tradition and transition, NY (1988) 30-43.

Shimizu, Yoshiaki. Six narrative paintings by yin t'o-lo: their symbolic content. AAA 33 (1980) 6-37. Re fragments of narrative scroll paintings and their ch'an iconography.

Shimizu, Yoshiaki. Zen art? In ZCJEAA (1985) 73-98.

Sorensen, Henrik H. The "hsin-ming" attributed to nin-t'ou fa-jung. JCP 13.1 (1986) 101-119.

Sorensen, Henrik H. The life and times of the ch'an master yün-men wen-yen. AO 49 (1988) 105-131. He died 949.

Sorensen, Henrik H. Observations on the characteristics of the chinese ch'an manuscripts from dunhuang. SCEAR 2 (1989) 115-140.

Stein, Rolf A. Sudden illumination and simultaneous comprehension: remarks on chinese and tibetan terminology. In S&G (1987) 41-65.

Stroud, Michael. The root-heritage of ch'an buddhism—1500 years later. FCR 32.10 (oct 1982) 31-36, col photos. Re nongchan temple in peitou, and master sheng-yen and students.

Stryk, L & T. Ikemoto (tsl) Zen poems, prayers, sermons, anecdotes, interviews. ?NY (2nd ed 1981) xlvi + 160 p.

[Suzuki, Daisetz T.]. EB 2.1 (aug 1967) Entire issue is in memoriam.

Suzuki, Daisetz T. Koan. Der sprung ins grenzenlose. München (1988) Tsl of first essay of author's Essays in zen buddhism, first ser.

Suzuki, Daisetz T. Satori. Der zen-weg zur befeiung. München (1989) Tsl of essays 1, 2, 3, 5 of author's Essays in zen buddhism, first ser.

Suzuki, D. T., William Segal (ed) [Kuo-an's] The ten oxherding pictures. Parabola 15 (fall 1990) 92-95, illus.

Suzuki, Daisetz T. Zazen. Die übung des zen. München (1988) Essays 4, 6, 7, 8 of author's Essays in zen buddhism, first ser.

Tanaka, Ryosho. A historical outline of japanese research on the chinese chan writings from dunhuang. SCEAR 2 (1989) 141-170.

Toda, Teisuke. Figure painting and ch'an-priest painters in the late yüan. In Proc of the intl symposium on chin painting, taipei, natl palace museum (1972) 391-416.

Tokiwa, Gishin. Chan (zen) view of suffering. BCS 5 (1985) 103-129.

Tsuneki, Nishiwaki. Das bewusstein buddhistischer geschichtschreiben am beispiel der autobiographie des hui-hung (1071-1128) In Helwig Schmidt-Glintzer (heraus) Lebenswelt und weltanschauung im frühzeitlichen china, wiesbaden (1990) 223-237.

Tu, Wei-ming. Ch'an in china: a reflective interpretation. In ZCJEAA (1985) 9-27.

Tucker, John Allen. Nagarjuna's influence on early hua-yen and ch'an thought. CC 25.2 (june 1984) 43-61.

Ueyama, Daishun. A chronological stratification of the tun-huang ch'an manuscripts. Proc31stICHS, tokyo, 2 (1984) 975-976. Abstr.

Ueyama, Daishun. Tsl by K. W. Eastman & Kyoko Tokuno. The study of tibetan ch'an manuscripts recovered from tun-huang: a review of the field and its prospects. In ECCT (1983) 327-349.

Visvader, John & William C. Doub. The problem of desire and emotions in taoism and ch'an. In ECCT (1983) 281-197.

Vos, Fritz. Tsl by T. Westow. The discovery of the special nature of the buddha: sudden enlightenment in zen. In C. Geffré (ed) Buddhism and christianity (1979) 31-39.

Waldberg, Michael. Un zeste de zen. Paris (1984) 181 p.

Wang, Chester C. I. Master yung-ming yen-shou (904-975) and his tsung-ching lu. Proc31stICHS, tokyo, 1 (1984) 169-171. Abstr.

Welter, Albert. The contextual study of chinese buddhist biographies: the example of yung-ming yen-shou (904-975) In M&M (1988) 247-268.

Whitehill, James. Is there a zen ethic? EB n.s. 20.1 (spring 1987) 9-33.

Wienpahl, Paul. Ch'an buddhism, western thought, and the concept of substance. Inquiry 14.1/2 (1971) 84-101. Comparisons with spinoza.

Wong, Mou-lam (tsl) Sutra spoken by the sixth patriarch, wei lang [hui neng] . . . Shanghai (preface 1930) 76 p. New ed rev by Christmas Humphreys, The sutra of wei lang (or hui neng) london (1944) further rev ed (1953) 128 p; repr westport, conn (1973); HK (1982)

Wu, Ching-hsiung (John C. H. Wu) Zen (ch'an): its origin and its modern significance. ACQ 8.4 (winter 1980) 1-11. Same title in ProcICS (1981) Thought and philosophy vol 2, 497-508.

Wu, Yi. On chinese ch'an in relation to taoism. JCP 12 (1985) 131-154.

Wydler, Agatha. Der 6. patriarch kommt nach manhattan: sokei-ans kommentar zum platform sutra des zen-meisters hui-neng. Küsnacht (1988)

Xu Yun (Hsü-yün) Tsl by Charles Luk. Rev and ed , with intro, by Richard Hunn. Empty cloud. The autobiography of the chinese zen master xu-yün. Longmead, shaftesbury, dorset engl (1988) 244 p, app, gloss, bibliog, photos. Orig ed publ 1980.

Yamada, Koun (tsl) Gateless gate. Los angeles (1979) xxiii + 283 + 10 p, 4 app incl gloss and lineage charts. Tsl and comm on Wu-men kuan; 2nd rev ed, univ arizona (1991) german version, Die torlose schranke mumonkan; zen-meister mumons koan sammlung, münchen (1989) 319 p.

Yampolsky, Philip. Hui-neng. EncyRel 6 (1987) 495a-496b.

Yampolsky, Philip. New japanese studies in early ch'an history. In ECCT (1983) 1-11.

Yanagida, Seizan. Tsl by Carl Bielefeldt. The li-tai fa-pao and the ch'an doctrine of sudden awakening. In ECCT (1983) 13-49.

Yanagida, Seizan. Tsl by John R. McRae. The "recorded sayings" texts of chinese ch'an buddhism. In ECCT (1983) 185-205.

Yorke, Gerald J. Ch'an buddhism. MW 35 (1960) 9-13.

Yü, Chün-fang. Buddha-invocation (nien-fo) as koan. JD 2 (apr 1977) 189-203.

Yü, Chün-fang. Ch'an education in the sung: ideals and procedures. In NCEduc (1989) 57-104.

Yü, Chün-fang. Chung-feng ming-pen and ch'an buddhism in the yüan. In YT (1982) 419-477.

Zeuschner, Robert B. Awakening in northern ch'an. In BTS-II (1987) 85-108.

Zeuschner, Robert B. The concept of li nien ("being free from thinking") in the northern line of ch'an buddhism. In ECCT (1983) 131-148.

Zeuschner, Robert. The understanding of karma in early ch'an buddhism. JCP 8.4 (dec 1981) 399-425.

Zürcher, Erik. Chinese ch'an and confucianism. In ZCJEAA (1985) 29-46.

III.7 (H) Other

Broomhall, Marshall. In quest of god. The life story of pastors chang and ch'u, buddhist priest and chinese scholar. London etc (preface 1921) xiii + 190 p.

BTTSoc (tsl) Records of the life of the venerable master hsüan hua. San francisco, 2 vol (1973 & 1975) 96 p; 229 p. Vol 1 is on his life in china; vol 2 is on his life in HK; a further vol is forthcoming.

Callahan, Paul E. T'ai hsü and the new buddhist movement. Harvard univ Papers on china 6 (1952) 149-188.

Chan, Hok-lam. Liu pin-chung (1216-1274), a buddhist-taoist statesman at the court of khubilai khan. TP 53.1/3 (1967) 98-146.

Chang, Sheng-yen. Four great thinkers in the history of modern chinese buddhism. In SHB (1980) 283-294. They are: Ou-i chih-hsü (1599-1655) t'ai-hsü wei-hsin (1889-1947) ou-yang ching-wu (1872-1944) yin-shun sheng-chang (1906-)

Char, S. V. R. Dharmaraksha—a short biography. CC 23.3 (sept 1982) 57-65. Re a 3rd c missionary-tsl.

Chavannes, Edouard. Seng-houei . . . + 280 p.c. TP 10 (mai 1909) 199-212.

Chen, Gerald. Jian zhen comes home. EH 19.6 (june 1980) 11-16, illus. "Visit" of lacquer statue of monk chien-chen fr toshodaiji, nara, to yangchou and peking.

Chen, Tsu-lung. La vie et les oeuvres de wou-tchen (816-895): contribution à l'histoire culturelle de touen-houang. Paris (1966) 165 p, app, bibliog, pl, cartes, index générale, index des termes chinois.

Chen-hua. Tsl by Denis Mair. Ed by Chün-fang Yü. Random talks about my mendicant life. CSA: 1, 13.1; 2, 13.4; 2, 14.3. (fall 1980; summer 1981; spring 1983) each installment occupies entire issue of journal. Sel fr book publ in kaohsiung (1965) about author's life on mainland during mid 1940s.

Cheng, Hsüeh-li. Chi-tsang's treatment of metaphysical issues. JCP 8.3 (sept 1981) 371-389. San-lun master chi-tsang's (549-623) comm on madhyamika scriptures.

Cheng, Hsüeh-li. Empty logic: madhymika buddhism from chinese sources. NY (1984) 220 p, gloss, chin terms, bibliog.

Cheng, Hsüeh-li. Truth and logic in san-lun madhyamika buddhism. IPQ 21.3 (sept 1981) 261-276.

Cheng, Hsüeh-li. Zen and san-lun madhyamika thought: exploring the theoretical foundation of zen teachings and practices. RS 15 (apr 1979) 343-363.

Chou, Hsiang-kuang. T'ai hsü. His life and teachings. Allahabad (1957) 74 p.

Chu, Pao-tang. Venerable tai-hsu and his buddhist reformation in modern china. CC 13.3 (sept 1972) 78-118.

Cummings, Mark D. Tao-an. EncyRel 14 (1987) 282a-283b.

Cummings, Mark D. Tao-sheng. EncyRel 14 (1987) 333a-335a.

Dien, Albert E. Yen chih-t'ui (531-591+): a buddho-confucian. In CP (1962) 43-64.

Edkins, Joseph. Notice of the wu-wei-kiau . . . a reformed buddhist sect. Trans China Branch RAS 6 (1858) 63-69. Otherwise called lo chiao, an eclectic sect of ming and ch'ing.

Fang, Li-t'ien. A tentative treatise on the buddhist philosophical thought of hui-yüan. CSP 4.3 (spring 1973) 36-76.

Franke, Herbert. Zur biographie des pa-ta-shan-jen. In Asiatica (1954) 119-130.

Friese, Heinz. Der mönch yao kuang-hsiao...und seine zeit. OE 7.2 (1960) 158-184.

Gundert, W. Die nonne liu bei we-schan. In Asiatica (1954) 184-197.

Haas, Hans. Ein wenig bekannter buddhisticher autor des alten china und sein werk. Orientalisches archiv 1 (1910-11) 25-33.

Hamilton, C. H. An hour with t'ai shu (sic), master of the law. OC 42 (mar 1928) 162-169.

Hamilton, C. H. Hsüan chuang and the wei shih philosophy. JAOS 51 (1931) 291-308.

Held, Axel. Der buddhistische mönch yen-tsung (557-610) und seine übersetsungstheories. Univ köln (1972) 150 p.

Hubbard, James B. Notes on the epigraphical remains of the san-chieh-chiao. Proc31stICHS, tokyo, 1 (1984) 175-176. Abstr.

Hurvitz, Leon. Hsüan-tsang and the heart scripture. In PRS (1977) 103-121.

Jan, Yün-hua. Hui-ch'ao and his works: a reassessment. IAC 12 (1964).

Jan, Yün-hua. Nagarjuna, one or more? A new interpretation of buddhist hagiography. HR 10.2 (aug 1970) 139-155.

Johnston, Reginald. A poet monk of modern china (su man-shu) JNCBRAS 63 (1932) 14-30.

Koseki, Aaron. Chi-tsang. EncyRel 3 (1987) 335a-336b.

Koseki, Aaron K. Chi-tsang's sheng-man pao-k'u: the true dharma doctrine and the bodhisattva ideal. PEW 34.1 (jan 1984) 67-83.

Koseki, Aaron K. The concept of practice in san lun thought: chi-tsang and the "concurrent insight" of the two-truths. PEW 31.4 (oct 1981) 449-466.

Koseki, Aaron K. Later madhymika in chinese: some current perspectives on the history of chinese prajnaparamita thought. JIABS 5 (1982) 53-62.

Koseki, Aaron K. Prajnaparamita and the buddhahood of the non-sentient world: the san-lun assimilation of buddha-nature and middle path doctrine. JIABS 3.1 (1980) 16-33.

Koseki, Aaron K. Seng-chao. EncyRel 13 (1987) 172b-173b.

Lai, Whalen. Chou yung vs chang jung. JIABS 1.1 (1978) 23-46. Re 2 5th c scholars.

Lai, Whalen. The early prajna schools, especially "hsin-wu," reconsidered. PEW 33.1 (jan 1983) 61-77.

Lai, Whalen. Non-duality of the two truths in sinitic madhyamika: origin of the 'third truth' JIABS 2.2 (1979) 45-65.

Lai, Whalen. Once more on the two truths: what does chi-tsang mean by two truths or "yueh-chiao"? RS 19.4 (dec 1983) 505-521.

Lai, Whalen. Sinitic speculations on buddha-nature: the nirvana school. PEW 32.2 (apr 1982) 135-149.

Lai, Whalen. Tao-sheng's theory of sudden enlightenment re-examined. In S&G (1987) 169-200.

Lai, Whalen (tsl). Wonhyo (yüan hsiao) on the nirvana school: summation under the "one mind" doctrine. JIABS 8.2 (1985) 75-83. Tsl of nieh-p'an tsung-yao.

Laufer, Berthold. Zum bildnis des pilges hsüan tsang. Globus 88 (1905) 257-258.

Lee, Peter H. Fa-tsang and uisang. JAOS 82.1 (1962) 56-59 + chin text 60-62.

Li, Jung-hsi (tsl) Engl text rev by Christopher Cullen. Biographies of buddhist nuns: pao-chang's pi-ch'iu-ni chuan. Osaka (1981) 144 p, index. See rev art by Kathryn Tsai in CEA 1 (1985) 87-101. Text is early 6th c composition.

170

Liebenthal, Walter. A biography of chu tao-sheng. MN 11.3 (1955) 64-96.

Liebenthal, Walter. Shih hui-yüan's buddhism as set forth in his writings. JAOS 70 (1950) 243-259.

Liebenthal, Walter. The world conception of chu tao-sheng. MN 12.1/2; 12.3/4 (1956 & 1957) 65-104; 241-268.

Link, Arthur (tsl) Biography of tao an. TP 46 (1958) 1-48.

Link, Arthur E. Hui-chiao's 'critical essay on the exegetes of the doctrine' in the kao seng chuan (lives of eminent monks) In NCELYY (1970) 51-80.

Link, Arthur E. Remarks on shih seng-yu's ch'u san tsang chi-chi as a source for hui-chiao's kao-seng chuan as evidenced in two versions of the biography of tao-an. Oriens 10.2 (1957) 292-295.

Liu, Ts'un-yan. Lu Hsi-hsing: a confucian scholar, taoist priest and buddhist devotee of the sixteenth century. AS 18/19 (1965) 115-142. Repr in LTY:SP (1976)

Liu, Wu-chi. Su man-shu. NY (1972) 173 p.

Liu, Ming-wood. The mind-only teaching of ching-ying hui-yüan: an early interpretation of yogacara thought in china. PEW 35.4 (oct 1985) 351-376.

Liu, Ming-wood. The yogacara and madhyamika interpretations of the buddha-nature concept in chinese buddhism. PEW 35.2 (apr 1985) 171-193.

Lo, Hsiang-lin. Transmission of the she-lun school of buddhism. JOS 1 (1954) 313-326.

Magnin, Paul. Dépassement de l'expérience noétique selon trois courts traités de madhyamika chinois. Une étude de manuscrit p.3357Vo. CETH 3 (1984) 263-303, 10 pl.

Makita, Tairyo. Tsl by Philip Yampolsky. Hui-yüan—his life and times. Zinbun 6 (1962) 1-28.

McAleavy, Henry. Su man-shu, a sino-japanese genius. London (1960) 51 p.

Millican, Frank R. Buddhism in the light of modern thought as interpreted by the monk t'ai hsü. ChRec 57.2 (feb 1926) 91-94.

Miyakawa, Hisayuki. Hsin-hsing. EncyRel 6 (1987) 478b-479b.

Miyakawa, Hisayuki. Paramartha. EncyRel 11 (1987) 195b-196b.

Monestier, Alphonse. The monk lu cheng-hsiang. BCUP 5 (1930) 11-21.

Nagao, Gadjin. Tsl by John P. Keenan. The foundational standpoint of madhyamika philosophy. SUNY (1989) xi + 183, notes, gloss, textual refs.

Niset, J. Bhiksu shih tao-an, la doctrine du bouddha et les droits de l'homme. RDH 10.1/2 (1977) 5-13.

Paul, Diana. Empress wu and the historians: a tyrant and a saint of classical china. In VW (1980) 191-206.

Paul, Diana Y. The life and times of paramartha (499-569) JIABS 5.1 (1982) 37-69.

Paul, Diana Y. (tsl & ed) Philosophy of mind in sixth-century china. Paramartha's "evolution of consciousness" Stanford univ (1984) 266 p, intro, tsl, app, ref materials.

Rachewiltz, Igor de. Yeh-lü ch'u-ts'ai (1189-1243): buddhist idealist and confucian statesman. In CP (1962) 189-216.

Robinson, Richard H. Early madhyamika in india and china. Univ wisconsin (1967) 347 p, documents, notes, bibliog, index.

Robinson, Richard H. Mysticism and logic in seng-chao's thought. PEW 8 (1958-59) 99-120.

Sargent, Galen E. (tsl) The sramana superintendent t'an-yao and his times. MS 16 (1957) 363-

396. A chap fr Tsukamoto Zenryu's book, Shina bukkyoshi kenkyu hokugi-ken, tokyo (1942).

Sasaki, Genjun H. Hinayana schools in china and japan. FA:BPB (1959) 499-514.

Schuster, Nancy. Yoga-master dharmamitra and clerical misogyny in fifth century china. TibJ 9 (1984) 33-46.

Shig (sic) Jen-hua. The prajna state in the master hui-ssu's 'samadhi without strife' Proc31stICHS, tokyo, 1 (1984) 187. Abstr.

Shih, Robert. Fa-ho, a great buddhist monk of the fourth century. MexICHS 2: China (1976) 92-94. Subj was a disciple of tao-an.

Soymié, Michel. Biographie de chan tao-k'ai. MIHEC 1 (1957) 415-422.

Sponberg, Alan. Hsüan-tsang. EncyRel 6 (1987) 480b-482b.

Sponberg, Alan. K'uei-chi. EncyRel 8 (1987) 394a-395a.

Sponberg, Alan. Meditation in fa-hsiang buddhism. In TradMed (1986) 15-43.

Su, Ying-hui. A study of the identity of monk wu (wu ho-shang) in the tunhuang manuscripts p.2913, p.4660 and s.1947v. CC 15.4 (dec 1974) 89-98.

Suzuki, Daisetz T. The madhyamika school in china. Journal of the buddhist text society of india 20.6 (1898) 23-30.

T'ai hsü. Tsl by Frank Rawlinson. The meaning of buddhism. ChRec 65.11 (nov 1934) 689-695.

T'ai-hsü. Tsl by Frank Rawlinson. Buddhism and the modern mind. ChRec 657 (july 1934) 435-440.

Takakusu, Junjiro. K'uei-chi's version of a controversy between the buddhist and the samkhya philosophers.—An appendix to the translation of paramartha's 'life of vasubandhu" TP 2e sér 5 (1904) 461-466.

Takakusu, Junjiro (tsl). The life of vasu-bandhu by paramartha (a.d.499-569) TP 2e sér 5 (1904) 269-296.

Takakusu, Junjiro (tsl). Le voyage de kanshin en orient, 742-754, par aomi-no mabito kankai, 779. BEFEO 28; 29 (1928 & 1929) 1-41, 441-472; 47-62.

Tamaki, Koshiro. The ultimate enlightenment of hui-yüan in lu-shan. JIBS 12.2 (1964) 1-12.

Tamura, Kwansei. Ganjin (chien-chen), transmitter of buddhist precepts to japan. YE n.s.6.4 (autumn 1980) 4-6.

Thurman, Robert A. F. Voidness and totalities: madhyamika and hua-yen. In SHB (1980) 343-348.

Todaro, Dale. Kumarajiva. EncyRel 8 (1987) 398b-400b.

Tschen, Yin-ko. Buddhistischer in den biographien von tsan tschung und hua to im san guo dschi. TJ 6 (1930) 17-20.

Tsukamoto, Zenryu. Tsl by Leon Hurvitz. The dates of kumarajiva ... and seng-chao ... reexamined. In SJV (1954) 568-584.

Ui, Hakuju. Maitreya as an historical personage. In Indian studies in honor of charles rockwell lanman, cambridge, mass (1929) 95-101.

Wagner, Rudolf G. The original structure of the correspondence between shih hui-yüan and kumarajiva. HJAS 31 (1971) 28-48. Re taisho tripitaka no 1856.

Walleser, Max. The life of nagarjuna from tibetan and chinese sources. In AMHAV (1923) 421-455. Repr as book, delhi (1979) 43 p.

Weinstein, Stanley. A biographical study of tz'u-en. MN 15.1/2 (1959) 119-149.

Wilhelm, Richard. Der grossabt schi tai hü. Sinica 4 (1929) 16.

Wright, Arthur F. Biography of the nun an-ling-shou. HJAS 15 (1952) 192-196.

Wright, Arthur F. Fo t'u teng . . . a biography. HJAS 11 (1948) 322-370.

Wright, Arthur F. Seng-jui alias hui-jui: a biographical bisection in the kao-seng chuan. SIS 5.3/4 (Liebenthal festschrift) (1957) 272-294.

Yin-shun. Tsl by Douglas Lancashire. How i came to choose buddhism. In CERF (1981) 53-76.

Yoon, Yee-heum. Two forms of religious understanding of man from a comparative study of buddhist and christian thinkers, chi-tsang and h. richard niebuhr. Journal of east west studies [seoul] 10.2 (oct 1981) 91-127.

Yü, David C. Skill in means and the buddhism of tao-sheng: a study of a chinese reaction to mahayana of the fifth century. PEW 24.4 (oct 1974) 413-427.

Yü, Chün-fang. Chu-hung. EncyRel 3 (1987) 472a-473a.

Yü, Chün-fang. The renewal of buddhism in china. Chu-hung and the late ming synthesis. Columbia univ (1981) xvi + 328 p, bibliog.

III.8 Sangha - Monachism - Monasteries

Augustine, Morris J. Zen and benedictine monks as mythopoeic models of nonegocentered worldviews and lifestyles. BCS 6 (1986) 23-49.

Bechert, Heinz. Samgha: an overview. EncyRel 13 (1987) 36-40.

Buddhist monasteries of taiwan. I. Kuan-yin hill and lin-yün buddhist temple; II. Yuan tung shih, a nunnery. New force 2.4 (feb 1951) 20-25, illus photos.

Collcutt, Martin. The early ch'an monastic rule:

ch'ing-kuei and the shaping of ch'an community life. In ECCT (1983) 165-184.

Collcutt, Martin. Monasticism: buddhist monasticism. EncyRel 10 (1987) 41a-44b.

Goodrich, G. Nuns of north china. Asia 37 (1937) 90-93.

Groot, J. J. M. de. Le code du mahayana en chine, son influence sur la vie monacale et sur le monde laïque. Amsterdam (1893) 271 p. Incl tsl of the 58 vows of the fan wang ching. Repr NY & london (1980)

Hahn, Thomas H. New developments concerning buddhist and taoist monasteries. In TT:RCT (1989) 79-101.

Hase, P. H. Cheung shan kou tsz (chiang shan ku ssu), an old buddhist nunnery in the new territories, and its place in local society. JHKBRAS 29 (1989) 121-157.

Lee, Lily Hsiao Hung. The emergence of buddhist nuns in china and its social ramifications. JOSA 18-19 (1986-87) 82-100.

Li, Jung-hsi (tsl) Engl text rev by Christopher Cullen. Biographies of buddhist nuns: pao-chang's pi-ch'iu-ni chuan. Osaka (1981) 144 p, index. See rev art by Kathryn Tsai in CEA 1 (1985) 87-101. Text is early 6th c composition.

Mather, Richard B. The bonze's begging bowl: eating practices in buddhist monasteries of medieval india and china. JAOS 101.4 (9ct-dec 1981) 417-424.

Miller, Alan L. The buddhist monastery as a total institution. Cleveland state univ, Journal of religious studies 7.2 (fall 1979) 15-29.

Monastic community and transmission of zen: india-china-korea. Spring wind [toronto] (summer 1984) 3-24.

Nagao, Gadjin. The architectural tradition in buddhist monasticism. In SHB (1980) 189-208.

Nan, Huai-chih. Tsl by Huang Fu. Dhyana monastic system and chinese society. Taipei (1964) Bilingual text: chin 58 p, engl 126 p.

Page, William. Notes on a chinese monastery. Prabuddha bharata [calcutta] 85.10; 85.11 (oct & nov 1980) 416-420; 457-462.

Prip-Moller, Johannes. Chinese buddhist monasteries. Their plan and its function as a setting for buddhist monastic life. Copenhagen & oxford univ (1937) 396 p, sketches, plans, elevations, photos, chin char throughout, index. Repr univ HK (1967) repr univ washington (1983)

Schopen, Gregory. Filial piety and the monk in the practice of indian buddhism: a question of 'sinicization' viewed from the other side. TP 70.1-3 (1984) 110-126.

Schuster, Nancy. Yoga-master dharmamitra and clerical misogyny in fifth century china. TibJ 9 (1984) 33-46.

Sorensen, Henrik H. Ennin's account of a korean buddhist monastery, 839-840 a.d. AO 47 (1986) 141-155. Korean monastery in china, very close to t'ien-t'ai.

Tsai, Kathryn A. The chinese buddhist monastic order for women: the first two centuries. In Richard W. Guisso & Stanley Johannesen (ed) Women in china, youngstown NY (1981) 1-20. Same title in Historical reflections/reflexions historiques 8.3 (fall 1981) 1-20.

Tsui, Bartholomew P. M. The self-perception of buddhist monks in hong kong today. JHKBRAS 23 (1983) 23-40.

Welch, Holmes. The buddhist revival in china. Harvard univ (1968) 385 p, app, notes, bibliog, illus, gloss-index. Sec of photos by Henri Cartier-Bresson: A buddhist festival [photos taken in 1949]

Welch, Holmes. The practice of chinese buddhism, 1900-1950. Harvard univ (1967) 568 p, notes, bibliog, illus, gloss-index.

Yü, Chün-fang. Ch'an education in the sung: ideals and procedures. In NCEduc (1989) 57-105.

Zieme, Peter. Uigurische steuerbefreiungs-urkunden für buddhistische klöster. Schriften zur geschichte und kultur des alten orients 8 (1981) 237-263.

Zürcher, Erik. Beyond the jade gate: buddhism in china, vietnam and korea. In Heinz Bechert & Richard Gombrich (ed) The world of buddhism: buddhist monks and nuns in society and culture, london (1984) 193-211.

Zürcher, Erik. Bouddhisme, christianisme et société chinoise. Paris (1990) 95 p.

Zürcher, Erik. Buddhism and education in t'ang times. In NCEduc (1989) 19-56.

III.9 Pilgrims

Bareau, André. Aspects du bouddhisme indien décrits par les pèlerins chinoise. ACF 93 (1984-85) 649-653.

Birnbaum, Raoul. Translator as pilgrim. Humanities 8 (sept-oct 1987) 29-31.

Fuchs, Walter. Huei-ch'ao pilgerreise durch nordwest-indien und zentral-asien um 726. Sitzungsberichte der preussischen akademie der wissenschaften, phil-hist kl, 30 (1938) 456-457.

Hoshino, Eiki. Pilgrimage: buddhist pilgrimage in east asia. EncyRel 11 (1987) 349b-351b.

Jan, Yün-hua. Fa-hsien. EncyRel 5 (1987) 245a-246b.

Jan, Yün-hua. I-ching. EncyRel 6 (1987) 574b-575b.

Kudara Kogi & Peter Zwieme. Fragmente zweier unbekannter handschriften der uigurischen xuanzang-biographie. Altorientalische forschungen 11.1 (1984) 136-148.

Kuwayama, Shoshin. Kapisi and gandhara according to chinese buddhist sources. Orient [tokyo] 18 (1982) 133-139. Re pilgrim itineraries during 4th and 5th c.

174

Lahiri, Latika (tsl). Chinese monks in india. Delhi etc (1986) xxvii + 160 p, chin text, bibliog, index. Tsl of I-ching's (635-713) Ta t'ang hsi yü ch'iu fa kao seng chuan.

Magnin, Paul. Le pèlerinage dans la tradition bouddhique chinoise. In Jean Chelini & Henry Branthomme (ed) Histoire des pèlerinages non chrétien . . . paris (1987) 278-310.

Mair, Victor H. The origins of an iconographical form of the pilgrim hsüan-tsang. TS 4 (1986) 29-42. Re tun-huang painting.

Röhrborn, Klaus. Zur 'werktreue' der alttürkischen übersetzung der hsüan-tsang-biographie. In Jens P. Laut & Klaus Röhrborn (ed) Buddhistische erzählliteratur und hagiographie in türkischer überlieferung, wiesbaden (1990) 67-73.

Schneider, Richard. Un moine indien au wou-t'ai chan—relation d'un pèlerinage— CEA 3 (1987) 27-40, illus.

Sponberg, Alan. Hsüan-tsang. EncyRel 6 (1987) 480b-482b.

Stevens, Keith G. The pilgrimage of the chinese buddhist monk hsüan-tsang. ArtsAs 12.3 (may-june 1982) 84-89.

Twitchett, Denis C. Hsüan-tsang. CHC vol 3, 1 (1979) Chap 7.

Wriggins, Sally. A buddhist pilgrimage along the silk route. Archaeology 40.5 (1987) 34-41.

Yu, Anthony C. Two literary examples of religious pilgrimage: the commedia and the journey to the west. HR 22 (1983) 202-230.

III.10 Rites - Cults - Praxis

Blofeld, John. Kuan yin and tara: embodiments of wisdom-compassion void. TibJ 4.3 (autumn 1979) 28-36. Re meditation.

Despeux, Catherine. Le chemin de l'éveil. Illustré par le dressage du buffle dans le bouddhisme chan, le dressage du cheval dans le taoïsme, le dressage de l'éléphant dans le bouddhisme tibétaine. Paris (1981) 139 p.

Duquenne, Robert. Ganapati [i.e. ganesa] rituals in chinese. BEFEO 77 (1988) 321-354. Chin texts incl; the "rituals" are marginally budd.

Eliasberg, Danielle. Quelques aspects de l'exorcisme no à touen-houang. In PM&MD (1984) 49-51.

Eliasberg, Danielle. Quelques aspects du grand exorcisme no à touen-houang. CETH 3 (1984) 237-253, 4 pl.

Fujiwara, Ryosetsu. Nien-fo. EncyRel 10 (1987) 435a-438a.

Gregory, Peter N. (ed) Traditions of meditation in chinese buddhism. Honolulu (1986) Art sep listed in this bibliog; abbrev TradMed.

Heng-ching. The yu-chia yen-k'ou ritual in the chinese buddhist tradition. D&A 4.1 (spring 1990) 105-117.

Hou, Ching-lang. Le cérémonie du yin-cha-fo d'après les manuscrits de touen-houang. CETH 3 (1984) 205-235, 6 pl.

Howard, Angela. Planet worship: some evidence, mainly textual, in chinese esoteric buddhism. AS 37.2 (1983) 103-119.

Jan, Yün-hua. The power of recitation: an unstudied aspect of chinese buddhism. Studi storico-religiosi 1.2 (1977) 289-299.

Jan, Yün-hua. Tsung-mi's theory of the "comparative understanding" (ho-hui) of buddhism. In MS/CA (1977) 181-186.

King, Winston L. Meditation: buddhist meditation. EncyRel 9 (1987) 331b-336b.

Mukhopadhyaya, Sujitkumar. An outline of the principal methods of meditation. Santiniketan (1972) Tsl fr chin version of kumarajiva, Ssu wei yao lüeh fa, of ten kinds of meditation acc to sanskrit texts. Orig publ in VBQ 3 (1950)

Pas, Julian. Six daily periods of worship: symbolic meaning in buddhist liturgy and eschatology. MS 37 (1986/87) 49-82.

Seidel, Anna. Dabi (crémation) Hobogirin 6 (1983) 573-585.

Soymié, Michel. Les dix jours de jeûne de ksitigarbha. CETH 1 (1979) 135-159.

Sponberg, Alan. Meditation in fa-hsiang buddhism. In TradMed (1986) 15-43.

Unno, Taitetsu. Worship and cultic life: buddhist cultic life in east asia. EncyRel 15 (1987) 467b-472a.

Yü, Chün-fang. Buddha-invocation (nien-fo) as koan. JD 2 (apr 1977) 189-203.

Yun, Eugenia. Photos by Chen Min-jeng. Wooden fish. FCR 40.5 (may 1990) 56-61, col photos. Re instrument used to accompany chanting.

III.11 Art and Iconography

III.11 (A) General

Buddhist art in china.   Taipei, natl museum of history (1978) bi-lingual text; 142 b-&-w & col pl.

Fossati, Gildo (text) Tsl by Bruce Penman. The monuments of civilisation: china. Engl ed sevenoaks, kent, engl (1983) many col illus. See esp, The signs of the buddha, 65-124; pagodas, temples, palaces, 125-182, passim.

Getty, Alice. The gods of northern buddhism. Oxford univ 1st ed (1914) 2nd ed (1928) liv + 220 p, bibliog, 67 pl, index. Repr of 2nd ed (1962) Dover paperback repr (1988) See rev by Kanaoka Shuyu in CRJ 5.3 (sept 1964) 207-220.

Gillman, Derek. Chinese buddhist art. Apollo 122.2 (nov 1985) 328-331. Re certain items in exhibit at british museum: Buddhism, art and faith, shown in 1985.

Goepper, Roger. Der priester kukai und die kunst. In RPO-A (1985) 223-232.

Minamoto, H. Tsl by R. Linossier; tsl completed by E. J. Lévy & M. S. Elisséev. l'Iconographie de la 'descente' d'amida. In EORL (1932) 99-130.

Moss, Paul. Between heaven and earth. Secular and divine figural images in chinese paintings and objects. London (1988) no pagination; 66 col illus of paintings & objects, with comments; char index, bibliog, map. Catalog.

Pal, Pratapaditya & Julia Meech-Pekarik. Buddhist book illuminations. NY etc (1988) See chap 6, China and korea, 225-268; also see chap 7, japan, passim.

Seckel, Dietrich. Tsl by Ulrich Mammitzsch. Buddhist art of east asia. Western washington univ (1989) 411 p, bibliog, 169 pl, index. Tsl of Buddhistische kunst ostasiens, q.v.

Sugimura, Toh. The encounter of persia with china. Research into cultural contacts based on fifteenth century persian pictorial materials. SES no 18 (1986) See chap 2, Religious themes, 17-66.

Yen, Chüan-ying. The beauty in tang buddhist art. ChPen 48 (1990) 39-48, illus.

Zwalf, W. Buddhism. Art of faith. NY (1985) See China, 197-234, incl many illus. "A display of artworks"

III.11 (B) Iconography and Motifs

Covell, Jon C. Angels in flight: india through china to korea and japan. APQCSA (spring 1983) 52-64.

Cummings, Mary. The lives of the buddha in the art and literature of asia. Univ of michigan, center for south and southeast asian studies (1982)

Edwards, Richard. Pu-tai-maitreya and a reintroduction to hangchou's fei-lai-feng. ArsO 14 (1984) 5-50, 51 fig.

176

Fong, Wen. Buddha on earth and in heaven. RMHA-PU 13 (1954) 38-61, illus.

Gaulier, Simone & Robert Jera-Bezard. Tsl by Ina Baghdiantz. Iconography: buddhist iconography. EncyRel 7 (1987) 45a-50a.

Ho, Judy C. The perpetuation of an ancient model. AAA 41 (1988) 32-46. Traces theme of vimalakirti-nirdesa sutra ill fr rubbing of stone engraving in sickman collection, kansas, to carving at pei shan in ta-tsu, ssuchuan.

Howard, Angela Falco. Heavenly mounts—horses and elephants—in chinese buddhist art. OA n.s. 28.4 (winter 1982/83) 368-381. Illus with photos fr yunkang and tunhuang.

Howard, Angela Falco. The imagery of the cosmological buddha. Leiden (1986) xviii + 194 p, 60 pl, 6 fig. Fr extant chin examples, 6 dyn to sung.

James, Jean M. Some iconographic problems in early daoist-buddhist sculptures in china. AAA 42 (1989) 71-76.

Karetzky, Patricia Eichenbaum. Post-enlightenment miracles of the buddha. Orientations 21.1 (jan 1990) 71-77.

Karetzky, Patricia Eichenbaum. A scene of the parinirvana on a recently excavated reliquary of the tang dynasty. E&W 38.1-4 (dec 1988) 215-230.

Kuwayama, George. The buddha image in china. In Light of asia. Buddha sakyamuni in asian art, los angeles (1984) 165-174. Catalog of exhibition at los angeles county museum of art.

Lee, Yu-min. Ketumati maitreya and tusita maitreya in early china. NPMB; pt 1, Intro and literary survey, 19.4; pt 2, Iconographic study, 19.5 (sept-oct 1984; nov-dec 1984) 1-13; 1-13.

Manabe, Shunsho. The mandalas at chü-yung-kuan. Coming into existence and the idea. JIBS 32.1 (dec 1983) 22-26.

Manabe, Shunsho. The mandalas of touen-houang. JIBS 33.2 (mar 1985) 37-42.

Manabe, Shunsho. On the mandala carved on boards in t'ang period china. JIBS 31.2 (mar 1983) 19-24.

Martin, Charmian. Honoring the buddha. FCR 38.8 (aug 1988) 48-57. Exhibition at natl palace museum.

Mukherjee, B. N. An illustration of iconographic contact between karttikey and manjusri in china. BuddIcon (1989) 138-141. Re a brahmanical deity in yün-kang caves.

Murray, J. K. Representations of hariti, the mother of demons, and the theme of "raising the almsbowl" in chinese painting. AA 43.4 (1981-82) 253-285.

Oort, H. A. van. The iconography of chinese buddhism in traditional china. Leiden (1986) 1. Han to liao, xii + 30p, 48 pl. 2. Sung to ch'ing, viii + 27p, 48 pl.

Riddell, Sheila. The kuan-yin image in post-t'ang china. In MA (1972) 17-24.

Saunders, E. Dale. Mudra. EncyRel 10 (1987) 134b-137b.

Schumann, Hans Wolfgang. Buddhistische bilderwelt; ein ikonographisches handbuch des mahayana- und tantrayana buddhismus. Köln (1986) 381 s, literatur, register. See passim.

Snodgrass, Adrian. The symbolism of the stupa. Cornell univ (1985) 469 p, copious illus. For china see passim.

Watson, William. Styles of mahayanist iconography in china. In MA (1972) 1-9.

Whitfield, Roderick. The lohan in china. In MA (1972) 96-101.

Yen, Chüan-ying. The double tree motif in chinese buddhist iconography. NPMB pt 1, 14.5; pt 2, 14.6. (nov-dec 1979; jan-feb 1980) 1-14; 1-13.

III.11 (C) Specific Temples

Chayet, Anne. Récouverture du wenshu yuan de chengdu. ArtsAs 37 (1982) 47-52.

Hsing, Lawrence Fu-ch'üan. Taiwanese buddhism and buddhist temples. Taipei (1983) 351 p, app, bibliog, chin names and titles, illus 127 fig and pl.

Raguin, Yves. La montagne de la tête du lion. Taipei (1983) Guidebook to budd temples.

Sirén, Osvald. A chinese temple and its plastic decoration of the 12th century. In EORL vol 2 (1932) 499-505, pl lvi-lxiv. Temple in ta-t'ung, shanhsi, dating fr chin dyn (hsia-hua-yin ssu)

Steinhardt, Nancy Shatzman. The yuan dynasty main hall: guangsheng si lower monastery and youngle gong. In CTA (1984) 127-137, illus. In southern shanxi.

Tseng, Yung-li. Photos by Shen Yi. Spirit of a temple. FCR 36.2 (feb 1986) 50-57. Re taipei's lung-shan ssu.

Whitfield, Roderick. Esoteric buddhist elements in the famensi reliquary deposit. AS 44.2 (1990) 247-266. Near sian.

III.11 (D) Architecture (except Pagodas)

Liu, Laurence G. Chinese architecture. NY (1989) 297 p, notes, gloss, bibliog, profusely illus, index. See passim, esp chap 4, Religious buildings, 55-160; chap 7, Funeral and ceremonial buildings, 219-246.

Meister, Michael W. & Nancy Shatzman Steinhardt. Temple: buddhist temple compounds. EncyRel 14 (1987) See sec, Expansion into east asia, 376a-380a.

Nagao, Gadjin. The architectural tradition in buddhist monasticism. In SHB (1980) 189-208.

Steinhardt, Nancy Shatzman. Nanchan si main

hall. In CTA (1984) 101-107. On wu-t'ai shan; constructed originally between 618 and 782; "the oldest wooden structure in china"

III.11 (E) Pagodas

Durt, H., K. Riboud, Lai Tung-hung. A propos de "stupa minatures" votifs du Ve siècle découverts à tourfan et au gansu. ArtsAs 40 (1985) 92-106.

Iida, Shotaro. The three stupas of ch'ang an. Papers of the 1st internatl conference of korean studies, 1979, seongnam-si, kyeonggi-do (1980) 484-497.

Ledderose, Lothar. Chinese prototypes of the pagoda. In Stupa (1980) 238-248.

Matics, K. I. A chinese pagoda in new york. APQCSA 15.3 (aug 1983) 1-21.

Seckel, Dietrich. Stupa elements surviving in east asian pagodas. In Stupa (1980) 249-259.

Shig (sic) Jen-hua. The symbolism and meaning of buddhist pagodas. Proc31stICHS, tokyo, 1 (1984) 186-187. Abstr.

Snodgrass, Adrian. The symbolism of the stupa. Cornell univ (1985) 469 p, copiously illus. For china see passim.

Steinhardt, Nancy Shatzman. Ying xian timber pagoda. In CTA (1984) 109-119. In north shanxi province; "the tallest timber structure in china"

Swart, Paula & Barry Till. The diamond seat pagoda, an example of indian architectural influences in china. Orientations 16.2 (feb 1985) 28-39. Pagoda in peking suburb.

Swart, Paula & Barry Till. The xiuding temple pagoda; a buddhist architectural masterpiece unveiled. Orientations 21.5 (may 1990) 64-76. At mt qinliang near anyang, honan; it dates to 6th c.

Till, Barry. Balizhuang ta: a forgotten pagoda of the ming dynasty. Orientations 12.7 (july 1981) 33-35. In western suburbs of peking.

178

Yang, Baoshun & Li Linhe. A hidden tang pagoda at anyang. RDChArch (1984) 81-82.

Yang, Hongxun. A wooden pagoda more than 900 years old. In Ancient china's technology and science, beijing (1983) 471-478.

III.11 (F) Sculpture

Ancient chinese buddhist sculpture: the c. k. chan collection ?Taipei. Album of 80 col pl; chin text; identifications in chin and engl, fig in b-&-w.

Chinese buddhist sculpture from the wei through the t'ang dynasties. Taipei, natl hist museum (1983) 206 p, text in chin & engl, illus in col and b-&-w. Catalog of 42 pieces fr various caves.

Croissant, Doris. Der unsterbliche leib. Ahneneffigies und reliquienporträt in der porträtplastik chinas und japans. In M. Kratz (ed) Das bildnis in der kunst des Orients. Abhandlungen für die kunde des morgenlandes 50.1 (1990) 235-268, illus.

Edwards, Richard. Pu-tai-maitreya and a reintroduction to hangchou's fei-lai-feng. ArsO 14 (1984) 5-50, 51 fig.

Gillman, Derek. A new image in chinese buddhist sculpture of the tenth to the thirteenth century. TOCS 47 (1982-83) 32-44.

H. H. S. [Henrik H. Sorensen]. On recent publications and field-work related to religious sculptures in the province of sichuan. SCEAR 2 (1989) 176-178.

Hall, Dickson. Sculpture at kongwangshan. Orientations 13.3 (mar 1982) 50-55. In north chiangsu; shows both budd and taoist influence; dated 160-180 c.e.

Hanselaar, Marcelle. Photos by Barry Crisp(?) Images of guan-yin from yunnan province, s.w. china. MW 65.1 (may 1990) 33-34. Descr— supposedly accompanied by photos, but there are no photos in art.

Hanselaar, Marcelle. Photos by Barry Crisp. The rock sculptures of dazu, s.w. china. MW 65.3 (nov 1990) 160-162, 7 photos.

Hawkins, R. B. A statue of kuan-yin: a problem in sung sculpture. RMHA-PU 12 (1953) 1-36, illus.

Ho, Judy C. The perpetuation of an ancient model. AAA 41 (1988) 32-46. Traces theme of vimalakirti-nirdesa sutra illus fr rubbing of stone engraving in sickman collection, kansas, to carving at pei shan in ta-tsu, ssuchuan.

Howard, Angela Falco. Buddhist sculpture of pujiang, sichuan: a mirror of the direct link between southwest china and india in high tang. AAA 42 (1989) 49-61.

Howard, Angela Falco. Buddhist sculptures of the liao dynasty: a reassessment of osvald siren's study. BMFEA 56 (1984) 1-95, 56 photo-pl.

Howard, Angela Falco. The monumental "cosmological buddha" in the freer gallery of art: chronology and style. ArsO 14 (1984) 53-73, 22 fig. Re sui dyn stone sculpture.

Howard, Angela Falco. Royal patronage of buddhist art in tenth century wu yueh; the bronze kuan-yin in the virginia museum of fine arts, richmond. BMFEA 57 (1985) 1-60, 22 photo-pl.

Howard, Angela F. T'ang and song images of guanyin from sichuan. Orientations 21.1 (jan 1990) 49-57. Sculptures.

Howard, Angela Falco. T'ang buddhist sculptures of sichuan: unknown and forgotten. BMFEA 60 (1988) 1-164, 143 photo-pl.

Hu, Wenhe. Tsl & adapted by Anna Elisabeth Gronvald. The nirvana scene in the buddhist cliff carvings in sichuan. SCEAR 3 (1990) 60-80. Re various cave temples.

James, Jean M. Some iconographic problems in early daoist-buddhist sculptures in china. AAA 42 (1989) 71-76.

Karetzky, Patricia Eichenbaum. A scene of the parinirvana on a recently excavated reliquary of the tang dynasty. E&W 38.1-4 (dec 1988) 215-230.

Klein-Bednay, Ildikó. Gewand und schmuck des bodhisattva in der frühen chinesischen plastik. Bonn (1983)

Larson, John & Rose Kerr. Guanyin; a masterpiece revealed. London (1985) 79 p, 86 illus, bibliog, index. Re sung wooden polychrome fig in victoria and albert museum.

Leidy, D. P. The ssu-wei figure in sixth-century chinese buddhist sculpture. AAA 45 (1990) 126-127. What author calls "pensive figure," seated, with hand to cheek.

Linrothe, Rob. Provincial or providential: reassessment of an esoteric buddhist "treasure" MS 37 (1986/87) 197-225. Re stone sculpture of esoteric deity acala in chicago's field museum.

Liu, Hongshi. Tsl by Rui An. Early chinese buddhist stone carvings. CL (apr 1982) 130-135, photo illus. Carvings fr kongwang mt, lianyungang, jiangsu, the earliest dating fr jin dyn, 4th c.

Munsterberg, Hugo. Chinese buddhist bronzes. Rutland, vt (1967) 192 p, illus, bibliog, index. Repr NY (1988)

Pontynen, Arthur. Philosophia perennis ars orientalis. A buddhist-taoist icon in the freer gallery of art. OA n.s.28.4; 29.2 (winter 1982/83; summer 1983) 359-367; 143-158. Re a gilt-bronze sculpture.

Rhie, Marylin M. Late sui buddhist sculpture: a chronology and regional analysis. AAA 35 (1982) 27-54.

Robinson, James. Object of the month: sixth-century chinese bronze buddha. Orientations 14.3 (mar 1983) 22-24.

Rousselle, Erwin. Buddhistische studien. Die typischen bildwerke des buddhistischen tempels in china. Sinica 7; 8; 9; 10 (1932, 33, ,34, 35) 62-71, 106-116; 62-77; 203-217; 120-165. Publ sep as, Von sinn der buddhistischen bildwerke in china, darmstadt (1958)

Soper, A. C. Chinese, korean and japanese bronzes. A catalogue of the anriti collection . . . preserved in the museo nazionale d'arte in rome. Leiden (1966) xli + 80 p, 118 pl. Incl wei, sung, and t'ang buddhistic bronzes.

Sorensen, Henrik H. A survey of the religious sculptures of anyue. Univ copenhagen (1989) Anyue county is in ssuchuan province; bk deals with budd and taoist sculptures.

Spiro, Audrey. Forty years on: art history, methodology, and how a great scholar came to make a small error. OA n.s.36.3 (autumn 1990) 130-137. Re lung-men sculptures.

Swart, Paula. Buddhist sculpture at fei lai feng; a confrontation of two traditions. Orientations 18.12 (dec 1987) 54-61. Located at peak near hangchou, showing tibetan as well as chin influences.

Wang, Betty. Buddhist images are shaped of emotion: the return of shao lai-cheng. FCR 34.8 (aug 1983) 66-71, illus.

Wang, Betty. Heritage of the cave temples. FCR 34.5 (sic) (may 1983) 67-74, col photos. Re exhibition of chin budd sculpture fr northern wei through t'ang, at natl museum of history in taipei.

Yen, Chüan-ying. The tower of seven jewels and empress wu. NPMB 22.1 (mar-apr 1987) 1-18. The ch'i-pao-t'ai in ch'ang-an and its 32 extant sculptures.

Zhang, Jiaqi. The splendour of the grotto arts of the later period in china. The sculptures of dazu. OA n.s.35.1 (spring 1989) 7-21.

III.11 (G) Stelae

Tonami, Mamoru. Tsl by P. A. Herbert. The shaolin monatery stele on mount song. Epigraphical series, No. 1, Italian school of east asian studies. Kyoto (1990) 61 p, 14 pl.

III.11 (H) Painting (including Woodcuts and Frescoes)

Barnet, Sylvan & William Burto. Zen ink paintings. Tokyo (1982) 94 p, 32 reproductions, suggestions for further reading.

Brinker, H. Some secular aspects of ch'an buddhist painting during the sung and yüan dynasties. In MA (1972) 86-95.

Burckhardt, Titus. Tsl by Lord Northbourne. Sacred art in east and west. Bedfont, middlesex, engl (1967). Tsl fr french version, Principes et méthodes de l'art sacré, lyon (1958) See chap 6, Landscape in far eastern art, 134-142; mostly on zen painting.

Bush, Susan. Tsung ping's essay on painting landscape and the "landscape buddhism" of mount lu. In TAC (1983) 132-164.

Cahill, James. Tung ch'i-ch'ang's "southern and northern schools" in the history and theory of painting: a reconsideration. In S&G (1987) 429-456.

Chen, Yuyin. Pictures of the four demon kings. CL (summer 1987) 182-184, 4 col pl. Discovered in ruigang pagoda in suzhou; they date fr 1013.

Glum, Peter. The two-faced budai. ArtsAs 40 (1985) 107-116. Re famous painting attributed to liang k'ai.

Kao, Mu-sen. Mu ch'i's schematization versus the literati's lyricism—dharma versus samadhi. NPMB, pt 1, 23.4; pt 2, 23.5; pt 3, 23.6 (sept-oct, nov-dec 1988; jan-feb 1989) 1-17; 1-17; 1-21. "The question is, can ch'an be intelligently approached and ch'an painting be iconographically studied?"

Larre, Claude. l'Esprit taoïste de peintures bouddhiques chinoises. In MA (1972) 82-85.

Mu, Jiaqi. Tsl by Rui An. The pilu temple murals. CL (june 1982) 90-95, photo illus. In vairocana temple, shangjing village, just northwest of shijiazhuang, hebei. Temple founded in t'ien-pao period of t'ang dyn.

Oates, L. R. Buddhist thought as reflected in east asian landscape art. In Purusottama Bilimoria & Peter Fenner (ed) Religious and comparative thought . . . delhi (1988) 71-86.

Shaw, Miranda. Buddhist and taoist influences on chinese landscape painting. JHI 49 (apr-june 1988) 183-206.

Shimizu, Yoshiaki. Six narrative paintings by yin t'o-lo: their symbolic content. AAA 33 (1980) 6-37. Re fragments of narrative scroll paintings and their ch'an iconography.

Toda, Teisuke. Figure painting and ch'an-priest painters in the late yüan. In Proc of the intl symposium on chinese painting, taipei, natl palace museum (1972) 391-416.

Vandier-Nicolas, Nicole. Tsl by Janet Seligman. Chinese painting; an expression of a civilization. London & NY (1983) 250 p, 200 illus. French title, Peinture chinoise et tradition lettrée, fribourg (1983) See Contents and passim (mostly budd examples)

Watson, William (ed). Mahayanist art after a.d. 900: proceedings of a colloquy held 28 june-1 july 1971 at the percival david foundation of chinese art. London (1972) 5 + 104 p, 19 pl. Indiv art sep listed in this bibliog; abbrev MA.

III.11 (I) Historical Emphasis

Durt, H., Krishna Riboud et Lai Tung-hung. A propos de "stupa miniatures" votifs du Ve siècle découvertes à tourfan et au gansu. ArtsAs 40 (1985) 92-106. Re 12 votive stupas of early 5th c with similar iconography and the same sutra.

Howard, Angela Falco. Royal patronage of buddhist art in tenth century wu yueh. BMFEA 57 (1985) 1-60.

Mu, Jiaqi. Tsl by Rui An. The pilu temple murals. CL (june 1982) 90-95. In t'ang dyn vairocana temple just north of shih-chia-chuang, hopei.

Whitfield, Roderick. The significance of the famensi deposit. Orientations 21.5 (may 1990) 84-85.

Wu, Hung. Buddhist elements in early chinese art (2nd and 3rd centuries a.d.) AA 47.3-4 (1986) 263-316, 86 pl.

Wu, Hung. From temple to tomb: ancient chinese art and religion in transition. EC 13 (1988) 78-115, architectural renderings.

Zhu, Qixin. Buddhist treasures from famensi; the recent excavation of a tang underground palace. Orientations 21.5 (may 1990) 77-83. 6th c temple near sian.

III.11 (J) Miscellaneous

Ang, John. The crucible of compassion and wisdom: buddhist bronzes from the nitta group collection at the national palace museum, taiwan, republic of china. AofA 18.4 (july-aug 1988) 91-103.

Chinese paper cutting patterns of gods and buddhas (shen fo chien chih) Taipei (1983) 112 p.

Le trésor du famensi. ArtsAs 44 (1989) 127-128. Summ of lecture by mme wang yarong re cache buried under pagoda of temple near sian in 874.

Seckel, Dietrich. Zen art. In ZCJEAA (1985) 99-113.

Smithies, Richard. The search for the lohans of i-chou (yixian) OA n.s.30.3 (autumn 1984) 260-274. Ceramic fig in cave in hopei province.

Stein, Marc Aurel. Specimens from a collection of ancient buddhist pictures and embroideries discovered at tun-huang. Journal of indian art and industries n.s.15 (1912) 60-66, 4 pl.

Wang, Zhao-lin & Xiong Lei. Discovery of rare buddhist relics. OA n.s.35.1 (spring 1989) 61-65. Re cache discovered under pagoda of fa-men ssu near sian, dating to 874.

Whitfield, Roderick. The art of central asia. The stein collection in the british museum. Vol 3, Textiles, sculpture and other arts. Tokyo & NY (1985) Intro, 340 p, 200 col pl, 64 b-&-w pl, notes, maps, gloss, concordance, bibliog.

Whitfield, Roderick. Esoteric buddhist elements in the famensi reliquary deposit. AS 44.2 (1990) 247-266. Cache dates to 874; temple and pagoda near sian.

Yoshiaki, Shimizu. Zen art? In ZCJEAA (1988) 73-98.

III.12 Specific Deities

Birnbaum, Raoul. Seeking longevity in chinese buddhism: long life deities and their symbolism. JCR 13/14 (1985/86) 143-176.

Boyer, Martha. An essay on the eleven-headed avalokitesvara. In AnHaf (1988) 19-28.

Edwards, Richard. Pu-tai-maitreya and a reintroduction to hangchou's fei-lai-feng. ArsO 14 (1984) 5-50, 51 fig. Fei-lai-feng is a hill west of west lake near hangchou; art deals with sculptures.

Gomez, Luis O. From the extraordinary to the ordinary: images of the bodhisattva in east asia. In Donald S. Lopez jr & Steven C. Rockefeller (ed) The christ and the bodhisattva, SUNY (1989) 141-191.

Howard, Angela. Planet worship: some evidence, mainly textual, in chinese esoteric buddhism. AS 37.2 (1983) 103-119.

Hummel, Siegbert. Der dickbauchbuddha. AO 48 (1987) 157-167.

Kinsley, David R. The goddesses' mirror; visions of the divine from east and west. SUNY (1989) See chap 2, Kuan-yin, the chinese goddess of mercy, 25-57.

Lahiri, Latika. Avalokiteshvara in chinese buddhism. TibRev 19.4 (apr 1984) 8-11.

Lahiri, Latika. Kuan-shih-yin, avalokitesvara in chinese buddhism. In BuddIcon (1989) 142-148.

182

Lancaster, Lewis R. Maitreya. EncyRel 9 (1987) 136b-141b.

Larson, John & Rose Kerr. Guanyin; a masterpiece revealed. London (1985) 79 p, 86 illus, bibliog, index. Re sung wooden polychrome fig in victoria and albert museum.

Lee, Yu-min. Ketumati maitreya and tusita maitreya in early china. NPMB, pt 1, Intro and literary survey, 19.4; part 2, Iconographic study, 19.5 (sept-oct 1984; nov-dec 1984) 1-13; 1-13.

Levering, Miriam. Ksitigarbha. EncyRel 8 (1987) 392a-393b.

Matsuda, Yuko. Chinese versions of the buddha's biography. JIBS 37.1 (dec 1988) 24-33.

Orzech, Charles D. Mahavairocana. EncyRel 9 (1987) 126a-128b.

Overmyer, Daniel. Messenger, savior, and revolutionary: maitreya in chinese popular religious literature of the sixteenth and seventeenth centuries. In Alan Sponberg & Helen Hardacre (ed) Maitreya, the future buddha, cambridge univ (1988) 110-134.

Pachow, W. The omnipresence of avalokitsevara bodhisattva in east asia. CC 28.4 (dec 1987) 67-84.

Paul, Diana. Kuan-yin: savior and savioress in chinese pure land buddhism. Chap 12 in Carl Olson (ed) The book of the goddess past and present, NY (1983) 161-175.

Riddell, Sheila. The kuan-yin image in post-t'ang china. In MA (1972) 17-24.

Stein, Rolf A. Avalokitesvara/kouan-yin, un exemple de transformation d'un dieu en déesse. CEA 2 (1986) 17-80; engl summ 78-80.

Strong, John S. The legend of the lion-roarer: a study of the buddhist arhat pindola bharadraja. Numen 26 (june 1979) 50-88. Legend and cult in india and china.

Tay, C. N. Kuan-yin: the cult of half asia. Taipei (1984) 179 p.

Visser, M. D. de. Engl "adaptation" by Sushama Lohia fr german original. The goddess mahamayuri in china and japan. Studies in indo-asian art & culture [new delhi] 6 (1980) 193-209.

Waldschmidt, Ernst. Die legende vom leben des buddha. In auszügen aus den heiligen texten aus dem sanskrit, pali und chinesischen übersetzt und eingeführt. Graz, austria (1982) 270 p.

Whitfield, Roderick. The lohan in china. In MA (1972) 96-101.

Yü, Chün-fang. Feminine images of kuan-yin in post-t'ang china. JCR 18 (1990) 61-89, illus.

Yü, Chün-fang. Images of kuan-yin in chinese folk literature. HHYC:CS 8.1, vol 1 (june 1990) 221-285.

Zürcher, Erik. Amitabha. EncyRel 1 (1987) 235a-237b.

III.13 Caves and Mountains

III.13 (A) General

Birnbaum, Raoul. Thoughts on t'ang buddhist mountain traditions and their context. TS 2 (winter 1984) 5-24.

Juliano, Annette L. Buddhism in china [a rare look at the kuyang, pinyang and yunkang cave complexes]. Archaeology 33.3 (may-june 1980) 23-30.

Qin, Mongxiao. Ascent to buddhism: chinese mountain temples. San francisco (1988) 287 p, illus.

Wang, Betty. Heritage of the cave temples. FCR 34.5 (sic) (may 1983) 67-74. Re exhibition of chin budd sculpture fr northern wei through t'ang, at natl museum of history.

III.13 (B) Yün-kang

Caswell, James O. Written and unwritten. A new history of the buddhist caves at yungang. Univ british columbia (1988) 277 p, 62 b-&-w and 4 col photos.

Huntington, John C. The iconography and iconology of the "tan yao" caves at yungang. OA n.s.32.2 (summer 1986) 142-160.

Juliano, Annette L. New discoveries at the yungang caves. In CTA (1984) 78-89, illus.

Knauer, Elfriede Regina. The fifth century a.d. buddhist cave temples at yün-kang, north china: a look at their western connections. Expedition 25.4 (sum 1983) 27-46.

Meyer, Jeffrey F. The buddhism of the yün-kang caves. Visible religion 3 (1984) 131-158, illus.

Mukherjee, B. N. An illustration of iconographic contact between karttikey and manjusri in china. In BuddIcon (1989) 138-141. Re a brahmanical deity in yün-kang caves.

III.13 (C) Lung-mên

Spiro, Audrey. Forty years on: art history, methodology, and how a great scholar came to make a small error. OA n.s. 36.3 (autumn 1990) 130-137. Re lung-men sculptures.

III.13 (D) T'ien-lung Shan

III.13 (E) O-mei Shan

III.13 (F) Wu-t'ai Shan

Birnbaum, Raoul. The manifestation of a monastery: shen-ying's experiences on mount wu-t'ai in t'ang context. JAOS 106.1 (jan-mar 1986) 119-137.

Birnbaum, Raoul. Secret halls of the mountain lords: the caves of wu-t'ai shan. CEA 5 (1989-90) 115-140. Sacred geography in texts.

Schneider, Richard. Un moine indien au wou-t'ai chan—relation d'un pèlinerage— CEA 3 (1987) 27-40, illus.

Steinhardt, Nancy Shatzman. Nanchan si main hall. In CTA (1984) 101-107, illus. Re a temple on wu t'ai shan.

Zheng, Xin & Wei Lingwen (text) Ding Yunyan & Zhao Yunqing (photos) Engl tsl by He Fei. Wutaishan. Peiching (1984) 113 p, chin & engl text, 198 col pl, sketch map. Ed by dept of commerce, shanxi province, and tourist supply co.

III.13 (G) P'u-t'o Shan

III.13 (H) Tun-huang

N. B. Tun-huang items have been categorized under 3 headings, III.13 (H-1, 2, 3) and all relevant items from 1985 bibliography have also been incorporated.

III.13 (H-1) Tun-huang Texts

Bischoff, F. A. (ed, tsl, comm) Arya mahabalanama-mahayanasutra. Tibétain (mss de touen-houang) et chinois. Contribution à l'étude des divinités mineures du bouddhisme tantrique. Paris (1956 138 p, 4 facsimiles.

Catalogue des manuscrits chinois de touen-houan. Fonds pelliot chinois de la bibliothèque nationale, vol III, no 3001-3500. Paris (1983) xx + 482 p. Sec 1, Bouddhisme; sec 2, Taoïsme; sec 3, Textes divers; sec 4, Particularités diverses.

Cerbu, A. Zigmund. A tun-huang version of the asrayaparavrtti. Adyar library bulletin 25 (1961) 40-48.

Chen, Tieh-fan. The sources of four tun-huang mss of the tso-chuan. TP 57.5 (1971) 302-204, photos of texts.

184

Chen, Tsu-lung. Liste alphabétique des impressions de sceaux sur certains manuscrits retrouvés à touen-houang et dans les régions avoisinantes. MIHEC 2 (1960) 5-14.

Cleary, J. C. (tsl) Zen dawn. Early zen texts from tun huang. Boston (1986) 135 p, gloss.

Csongor, B. Some chinese texts in tibetan script from tun-huang. Acta orientalia academiae scientiarum hungaricae 10 (1960) 97-140.

Demiéville, Paul (adapte et trad). Mission paul pelliot. Documents conservés à bibliothèque nationale, II: Airs de touen-houang (touen-houang k'iu) Textes à chanter des VIIIe-Xe siècles. Manuscrits reproduits en facsimile, avec une introduction en chinois par Jao Tsong-yi. Adaptes en francais avec la traduction de quelques textes d'air, par P. Demiéville. Paris (1971) 370 p, 58 pl.

Demiéville, Paul. Deux documents de touen-houang sur le dhyana chinois. In EZT (1961) 1-27. Repr in CEB (1973)

Demiéville, Paul. Manuscrits chinois de touen-houang à leningrad. TP 51.4/5 (1964) 355-376.

Demiéville, Paul. l'Oeuvre de wang le zélateur (wang fan-tche) suivi des "instructions domestiques de l'aïeul" (t'ai-kong kia-kiao). Poèmes populaires des t'ang (viiie - xe siècles), édités, traduits et commentés d'après de manuscrits de touen-houang. Paris (1983) 890 p.

Drège, Jean-Pierre. A propos de quelques collections "nouvelles" de manuscrits de dunhuang. CEA 3 (1987) 113-150, 7 reproductions.

Drège, J.-P. Clefs des songes de touen-houang. In NCET (1981) 205-249.

Drège, Jean-Pierre. Etude formelle des manuscrits de tunhuang conservés à taipei: datation et authenticité. BEFEO 74 (1985) 477-484.

Drège, Jean-Pierre. Note sur les couleurs des papiers des manuscrits de dunhuang. CEA 3 (1987) 147-150, illus.

Drège, Jean-Pierre. Notes codicologiques sur les manuscrits de dunhuang et de turfan. BEFEO 74 (1985) 485-504.

Dzo, Ching-chuan. La composition du dongyuan shenzhou jing. In PM&MD (1984) 79-87.

Dzo, Ching-chuan. Un fragmente du fo chou cheng king. In NCET (1981) 129-136, pl.

Eliasberg, Danielle. l'Expression eul-lang wei dans certains manuscrits de touen-houang. In NCET (1981) 261-271.

Eliasberg, Danielle. Quelques aspects de l'exorcisme no à touen-houang. In PM&MD (1984) 49-51. Same title in CETH 3 (1984) 237-253.

Eliasberg, Danielle. Les signatures en forme d'oiseau dans les manuscrits chinois de touen-houang. CETH 1 (1979) 29-44, 8 pl.

Forte, Antonino. Political propaganda and ideology in china at the end of the seventh century: inquiry into the nature, authors, and function of the tunhuang document s.6502, followed by an annotated translation. Napoli, instituto universitario oriental (1976) 312 p. Re text composed by a group of budd monks to legitimate ascension to throne of empress wu chao (r.683-707) See rev by M. Strickmann in EB n.s. 10.1 (may 1977) 156-160.

Fuchs, Walter. Eine buddhistische tun-huang-rolle v.j.673. In Asiatica (1954) 155-160, illus.

Fujieda, Akira. The tun-huang manuscripts. In ESCH (1973) 120-128.

Fujieda, Akira. The tun-huang manuscripts. In Donald D. Leslie, Colin Mackerras & Wang Gungwu (ed) Essays on the sources for chinese history, australian natl univ (1973) 120-128. Book also publ by univ of south carolina (1975)

Fujieda, Akira. The tunhuang manuscripts: a general description. Zinbun 9 & 10 (1966; 1969) 1-32; 17-39.

Gauthiot, R. et P. Pelliot (tsl) Le sutra des causes et des effets, texte sogdien de touen-houang, publié en facsimilé, avec transcription, traduction et commentaire par r. gauthiot, accompagné du facsimilé et de la traduction de la version chinoise par p. pelliot, et un glossaire sogdien-francais-chinois par r. gauthiot et p. pelliot. Paris (1914-23) Mission pelliot en asie centrale, série linguistique, t.1.

Giles, Lionel. Dated chinese manuscripts in the stein collection: I. Fifth and sixth century a.d. II.Seventh century a.d. III. Eighth century a.d. IV. Ninth century a.d. BSOAS 7.4; 8.1; 9.1; 9.4 (1935, 36, 37, 39) 809-836; 1-26; 1-25; 1023-1046.

Giles, Lionel. Descriptive catalogue of the chinese manuscripts from tun-huang in the british museum. London (1957) xxv + 334 p.

Giles, Lionel. Six centuries at tun-huang. A short account of the stein collection of chinese mss in the british museum. London (1955) 50 p, facs.

Guignard, Marie-Roberte (ed) Catalogue des manuscrits chinois de touen-houang. Paris, vol 1 (1970) xxix + 407 p, 24 pl. Incl items no 2001-2500.

Hou, Ching-lang. La cérémonie du yin-cha-fo d'après les manuscrits de touen-houang. CETH 3 (1984) 205-235, 6 pl.

Hou, Ching-lang. La cérémonie du yin-cha-fo et les estampes de mille buddha. In PM&MD (1984) 45-48.

Hou, Ching-lang. Physiognomonie d'après le teint sous la dynastie des t'ang. CETH 1 (1979) 55-66, illus.

Hubbard, James B. Notes on the epigraphical remains of the san-chieh-chiao. Proc31stICHS, tokyo, 1 (1984) 175-176. Abstr.

Imaeda, Y. Documents tibétains de touen-houang concernant le concile du tibet. JA 263.1/2 (1975) 125-146.

Imaeda, Y. Histoire du cycle de la naissance et de la mort. Hautes études orientales 15 (1981) 96 p text, 49 pl. Ed of a tun-huang ms.

Inokuchi, Taijun. The translation of buddhist texts at tun-huang. JA 269 (1981) 99-100.

Jao, Tsong-yi. Le "voeu de la capital de l'est" de l'empereur wu des liang. CETH 3 (1984) 143-154, 1 pl.

Kaltenmark, Max. Notes sur le pen-tsi king (personnages figurant dans le sutra) CETH 1 (1979) 91-98.

Kanaoka, Shoko. On the word "pien" TUAS 1 (1961) 15-24. Re tun-huang mss.

Kawaguchi, Hisao. The legend of 'the prince and a starving tigress'—on the manuscript of hung tzu no. 62 from tunhuang possessed in the beijing national library. Proc31stICHS, tokyo, 2 (1984) 980-983. Abstr.

Kuo, Li-ying. Un texte ancien de voeux et de confession: p.2189, le "voeu de la capitale de l'est." In PM&MD (1984) 111-119.

Kyodo, Jiko. A study of the buddhist manuscripts of dunhuang—classification and method. Proc31stICHS, tokyo, 2 (1984) 974-975. Abstr.

Lagerwey, John. Wu-shang pi-yao: somme taoïste du VIe siècle. Paris (1981) 290 p, chin char used throughout, listes des ouvrages cités, notes bibliog, bibliog, index. Intro and "traduction" de la table des matières complète retrouvée à tun-huang; résumé du texte . . .

Magnin, Paul. l'Ancienne version du fo-fa tong-lieou tchouan. In NCET (1981) 57-127, pl.

Magnin, Paul. Une copie amidique du t'ien-t'ai tche-tchö ta-che fa-yuan wen. CETH 1 (1979) 99-114.

Magnin, Paul. Dépassement de l'expérience noétique selon trois courts traités de madhyamika chinois. Une étude du manuscrit p.3357Vo. CETH (1984) 263-303, 10 pl.

186

Magnin, Paul. Un exemple de catéchèse bouddhique. In PM&MD (1984) 103-109.

Magnin, Paul. Pratique religieuse et manuscrits datés. CEA 3 (1987) 131-141. Re tun-huang mss.

Mair, Victor. Lay students and the making of written vernacular narrative: an inventory of tun-huang manuscripts. Chinoperl 10 (1980) 5-96, app.

Mair, Victor H. Parallels between some tun-huang manuscripts and the 17th chapter of the kozanji journey to the west. CEA 3 (1987) 41-53.

Mair, Victor H. Tun-huang popular narratives. Cambridge univ (1983) 329 p, intro, notes, ref, index.

Mair, Victor. Tun-huang popular narratives. AsFS 46.2 (1987) 273-286. Rev art on kanaoka shoko's work.

Makita, Tairyo. Tsl by Antonino Forte, who also supplied ftnotes. The ching-tu san mei ching and the tun-huang manuscripts. E&W n.s.21.3/4 (sep-dec 1971) 351-361.

Morgan, Carole. La divination d'après les croassements des corbeaux dans les manuscrits de tunhuang. CEA 3 (1987) 55-76.

Morgan, Carole. Dog divination from a dunhuang manuscript. JHKBRAS 23 (1983) 184-193.

Morgan, Carole. l'Ecole des cinq noms dans les manuscrits de touen-houang. CETH 3 (1984) 255-261. Same title in PM&MD (1984) 121-122.

Morgan, Carole. Les "neuf palais" dans les manuscrits de touen-houang. In NCET (1981) 251-260.

Musée Guimet (comp) Manuscrits et peintures de touen-houang: mission pelliot 1906-1909. Collections de la bibliothèque nationale et du musée guimet. Paris (1947) 41 p, map.

Overmyer, Daniel L. Buddhism in the trenches: attitudes toward popular religion in chinese scriptures found at tun-huang. HJAS 50.1 (1990) 197-222.

Pachow, W. (tsl) A buddhist discourse on meditation from tun huang. Univ of ceylon review 21.1 (apr 1963) 47-62. Repr in author's ChBuddh (1980) Tsl of discourse of hung-jen.

Pelliot, Paul. Arthur waley: a catalogue of paintings recovered from tun-huang (etc) TP 28 (1931) 383-413. Rev art.

Pelliot, Paul. Nicole Vandier-Nicolas (avant-propos) Mme Maillard (notes préliminaires) Grottes de touen-houang. Carnet de notes de paul pelliot. Inscriptions et peintures murales. Paris, 3 vol (1983; 1983; 1986) II, Grottes 31 à 72; III, Grottes 73 à 111a; V, Grottes 120 à 146.

Petersen, Jens O. The dunhuang manuscripts in the royal library in copenhagen. In AnHaf (1988) 112-117.

Research soc of central asian culture (ed) Monumenta serindica: Vol I: Chinese buddhist texts from tunhuang. Kyoto (1958)

Richardson, Hugh E. "The dharma that came down from heaven": a tun-huang fragment. In BT&AC (1977) 219-230.

Schipper, Kristofer M. Taoist ordination ranks in the tunhuang manuscripts. RPO-A (1985) 127-148.

Seidel, Anna. Le sutra merveilleux du ling-pao suprême, traitant de lao tseu qui convertit les barbares (le manuscrit s.2081) Contribution à l'étude du bouddho-taoïsme des six dynasties. CETH (1984) 305-352.

Sorensen, Henrik H. Observations on the characteristics of the chinese chan manuscripts from dunhuang. SCEAR 2 (1989) 115-140.

Soymié, Michel. Catalogue des manuscrits chinois de touen-houang. Fonds pelliot chinois de la bibliothèque nationale. Vol III. Paris (1983) xx + 482 p.

Soymié, Michel. Les dix jours de jeûne de ksitigarbha. CETH 1 (1979) 135-159. Same title in Mélanges yoshioka, tokyo (1977) 1-21.

Soymié, Michel. Les manuscrits de dunhuang. Courrier de centre national de la recherche scientifique 48 (1982) 70-73.

Soymié, Michel. Les peintures murales et les manuscrits de dunhuang. Colloque franco-chinois organisé par la fondation singer-polignac (21-23 février 1983) Paris (1984) 180 p, 28 pl. Indiv art sep listed in this bibliog; abbrev PM&MD

Soymié, Michel. Un recueil d'inscriptions sur peintures: le manuscrit p.3304 verso. In NCET (1981) 169-204, pl.

Stein, R. A. Tibética antiqua I. Les deux vocabulaires des traductions indo-tibétaine dans les manuscrits de touen-houang. BEFEO 72 (1983) 149-236.

Strassberg, Richard E. Buddhist storytelling texts from tun-huang. Chinoperl 8 (1978) 39-99, transcriptions, bibliog.

Su, Ying-hui. The analytical study of the tunhuang manuscripts with regard to their urbane or popular tastes. CC 27.2 (june 1986) 101-102.

Su, Ying-hui. The dancing guidebook of tunhuang. APQCSA 12.1 (spring 1980) 47-49. A text fr 2 mss.

Su, Ying-hui. A study of the identity of monk wu (wu ho-shang) in the tunhuang manuscripts p.2913, p.4660, and s.1947v. CC 15.4 (dec 1974) 89-98.

Tanaka, Ryosho. A historical outline of japanese research on the chinese chan writings from dunhuang. SCEAR 2 (1989) 141-170.

Tanaka, Ryosho. Relations between the buddhist sects in the t'ang dynasty, through the ms p.3913. JA 269 (1981) 163-169.

Ueyama, Daishun. A chronological stratification of the tun-huang ch'an manuscripts. Proc31stICHS, tokyo, 2 (1984) 975-976. Abstr.

Ueyama, Daishun. Tsl by K. W. Eastman & Kyoko Tokuno. The study of tibetan ch'an manuscripts recovered from tun-huang: a review of the field and its prospects. In ECCT (1983) 327-349.

Vandier-Nicolas, Nicole. Sariputra et les six maîtres d'erreur; facsimilé du manuscrit chinois 4524 de la bibliothèque nationale, présenté par nicole vandier-nicolas avec traduction et commentaire du texte. Paris (1954) 3, 1, 32 p. Collection mission pelliot en asie centrale.

Waley, Arthur (comp & tsl). Ballads and stories from tun-huang: an anthology. London (1960) See 10, The buddhist pieces, 202-215; 11, Mu-lien rescues his mother, 216-235.

Yoke, Ho Peng. A long lost astrological work: the dunhuang ms of the zhan yungi shu. Journal of asian history 19.1 (1985) 1-7.

III.13 (H-2) Tun-huang Art

Abe, Stanley K. Art and practice in a fifth-century chinese buddhist cave temple. ArsO 20 (1990) 1-32. ". . . relationship between buddhist art and practice in cave 254 . . . from the mogao cave site near dunhuang"

Agnew, Neville H. & Inee Yang Slaughter. Mogao grottoes project: the getty conservation institute. Orientations 20.3 (mar 1989) 76-77, illus.

Alexandrian, Sarane. Ex-voto pour bouddha. Connaissance des arts 253 (mar 1973) 60-67, col pl. Re tun-huang banners in paris.

Allag, C. Les peintures bouddhiques de dunhuang. Archéologia/préhistoire et archéologia ancient 171 (1982) 41-50.

Chang, Cornelius P. Kuan-yin paintings from tun-huang: water-moon kuan-yin. JOS 15.2 (1977) 140-160, 5 pl.

Chang, Dai-chien. Tun-huang frescoes and i. APQCSA 8.2 (autumn 1976) 43-45.

Chang, Shuhong. The art treasures of tunhuang. China pictorial 1 (jan 1956) 19-21, illus.

Chang, Shuhong. Art in the mogao caves at dunhuang. In RDChArch (1984) 45-48.

188

Chang, Shuhong & Li Chengxian. Photos by Wang Miao. The flying devis of dunhuang. Peking (1980) 200 pl, 190 in col. Col illus and detailed descriptions of 98 frescoes.

Chou, Shao-miao & Wu Mi-feng (copyists) Intro by Wang Hsun. Designs from the tunhuang caves. Peking (1956) 20 leaves in portfolio.

Denés, Francoise. Catalogue raisonné des objets en bois provenant de dunhuang et conservés au musée guimet. Paris (1976) 81 p.

Duan, Wenjie. Recherches sur le style et le contenu iconographique de la grotte 249 de mogaogu. In PM&MD (1984) 137-147.

Dunhuang institute for cultural relics (comp) The art treasures of dunhuang. Ten centuries of chinese art from the mogao grottoes. NY (1981) 254 p, 200 col illus.

Fengère, Laure. The pelliot collection. Orientations 20.3 (mar 1989) 41-52.

Fong, Wen. Ao-t'u-hua or "receding-and-protruding painting" at tun huang. ProcICS, Art history vol (1981) 73-94, pl.

Foreign languages press (comp) Murals from the tun-huang caves. Peking (1956) 20 pl in portfolio.

Fourcade, Francois. Le peinture murale de touen-houang. Paris (1962) 134 p, illus, maps, plans, table.

Gray, Basil. Photos by J. B. Vincent; preface by Arthur Waley. Buddhist cave paintings at tun-huang. Univ chicago (1959) 83 p, 70 pl, notes on pl, bibliog.

Hadl, R. Langdon warner's buddhist wall paintings. AA 9 (1946) 160-164.

Hambis, L. Bannières et peintures de touen-houang conservées au musée guimet. Planches. Paris (1976) 133 p. Complement to Vandier-Nicolas catalogue, q.v. Reproductions of 220 paintings.

Jao, Tsung-i. The vedas and the murals of dunhuang. Orientations 20.3 (mar 1989) 71-76, illus.

Jera-Bezard, Robert. Six triangles sur soie inédits de la collection paul pelliot. La revue du louvre et de musées de france 28.4 (1978) 230-235, illus.

Karetzky, Patricia Eichenbaum. A chinese illustration of the guoqu xianzai yingguo jing at dunhuang. JCR 16 (1988) 54-72, illus.

Kwon, Young-pil. The otani collection. Orientations 20.3 (mar 1989) 53-63, illus.

Lang, Shaojun. Tsl by Wu Ling. Early dunhuang murals. CL (spring 1988) 129-135, 6 col pl.

Lao, Kan. Tsl by Ho Chien. The art of tunhuang. CC 1 (oct 1957) 47-74.

Mair, Victor H. The origins of an iconographical form of the pilgrim hsüan-tsang. TS 4 (1986) 29-42. Re tun-huang painting.

March, Benjamin. A tun-huang buddhist painting. BDetIA 10 (may 1929) 109-111.

Marchand, Ernesta. Monument of the western regions. OA n.s.29.1 (spring 1983) 49-58. Study of detail of mural, tun-huang cave 217.

Matsumoto, Yeiichi. On some amulet pictures from tun-huang. Kokka 482, 488 (1931) 3-6; 249-254.

Mizuno, S. Wall paintings of tun-huang. Tokyo (1958)

Musée Cernuschi. Relevés de touen-houang et peintures anciennes de la collection tchang ta-ts'ien. Paris (1956) 25 p, 29 pl.

Pelliot, Paul. Arthur waley: a catalogue of paintings recovered from tun-huang (etc) TP 28 (1931) 383-413. Rev art.

Pelliot, Paul. Une bibliothèque médiévale retrouvé au kan-sou. BEFEO 8 (1908) 501-529.

Pelliot, Paul. Les fresques de touen-houang et les fresques de m. eumorfopoulos. RAA 5 (1928) 143-163, 193-214, illus.

Pelliot, Paul. Mission pelliot en asie centrale: les grottes de touen houang. Paris, 6 vol (1914-24) All pl, no text.

Pelliot, Paul. Nicole Vandier-Nicolas (avant-propos) Mme Maillard (notes préliminaires) Grottes de touen-houang. Carnet de notes de paul pelliot. Inscriptions et peintures murales. Paris, 3 vol (1983; 1983; 1986) II, Grottes 31 à 72; III, Grottes 73 à 111a; V, Grottes 120 à 146.

Petrucci, R. Les peintures bouddhiques de touen-houang (mission stein) AMG (1916) 115-140, illus.

Research group for the tunhuang cultural relics (comp) Tunhuang painted sculptures. ?Peking (1978) 86 col pl. Text in chin with engl tsl.

Riboud, Mme Krishna & Gabriel Vial, avec le concourse de Mlle M. Hallade. Tissus de touen-houang, conservés au musée guimet et à la bibliothèque nationale. Paris (1970) 443 p, 103 pl, charts. (Mission paul pelliot no 13)

Sasaguchi, Rei. A dated painting from tun-huang in the fogg museum. AAA 26 (1972) 26-49. Painting of maitreya's paradise.

Ségny, Marie-Rose. Images xylographiques conservées dans les collections de touen-houang de la bibliothèque nationale. CETH 1 (1979) 119-133, 6 pl.

Shen, I-chang; Sun Yu & Ronald J. Dickson (tsl) Chang dai-ch'ien's copies of the tun-huang cave paintings. NPMB 12.3 (july-aug 1977) 1-21.

Shih, Hsio-yen. New problems in the tun-huang studies. ProcICS, History of arts vol (1981) 211-246, pl.

Silva-Vigrier, Anil de. Chinese landscape painting in the caves of tun-huang. London (1967) 240 p, maps tables, illus.

Soper, Alexander C. Representations of famous images at tun-huang. AA 27 (1965) 349-364, pl.

Soymié, Michel. Notes d'iconographie bouddhique—des vidyaraja et vajradhara de touen-houang— CEA 3 (1987) 9-26, illus.

Soymié, Michel. Les peintures murales et les manuscrits de dunhuang. Colloque franco-chinois organisé par la fondation singer-polignac (21-23 février 1983) Paris (1984) 180 p, 28 pl. Indiv art sep listed in this bibliog; abbrev PM&MD.

Soymié, Michel. Quelques représentations de statues miraculeuses dans les grottes de touen-houang. CETH 3 (1984) 77-102.

Soymié, Michel. Un recueil d'inscriptions sur peintures: le manuscrit p.3304 verso. In NCET (1981) 169-204, pl.

Stein, Marc Aurel. Specimens from a collection of ancient buddhist pictures and embroideries discovered at tun-huang. Journal of indian art and industries n.s.15 (1912) 60-66, 4 pl.

Stein, Aurel. The thousand buddhas: ancient buddhist paintings from the cave-temples of tun-huang on the western frontier of china. London, 3 vol pl (1921) Facs ed NY (?1980)

Su, Ying-hui. The buddhist art of the tunhuang caves in china. APQCSA 2.3 (winter 1970) 28-33.

Su, Ying-hui. The buddhist art of wei, tsin, and southern and northern dynasties at tunhuang in china. CC 11.2 (june 1970) 55-61.

Su, Ying-hui. A comparative study on the contour techniques of wall-paintings found in tunhuang, ajanta, sigiriya and polonnaruwa. APQCSA 7.1 (summer 1975) 10-12.

Tomita, Kojiro. A dated buddhist painting from tun-huang. BMFA 25 (1927)

Tomita, Kojiro. Two more dated buddhist paintings from tun-huang. BMFA 26 (1928) 11.

Tunhuang painted sculptures. Peiching (1978) 85 col pl, with chin & engl text.

Vandier-Nicolas, N. avec le concours de Mmes Gaulier, Leblond et Maillard, et M. Jera-Bezard. Bannières et peintures de touen-houang conservés au musée guimet. Paris (1974) xiii + 435 p, pl. A second vol with same title plus Planches, paris (1976) 252 p, 134 pl. Mission paul pelliot vol 14-15.

Waley, Arthur. A catalogue of paintings recovered from tun-huang by sir aurel stein, k.c.i.e., preserved in the british museum and in the museum of central asian antiquities, delhi. London (1931) lii + 328 p, diagr. Rev art by Paul Pelliot in TP 28 (1931) 383-413.

Wang, Hsün (intro) Designs copied by Chou Shao-miao & Wu Mi-feng. Designs from the tun-huang caves. Peking (1956) 4p, 20 pl.

Warner, Langdon. Buddhist wall-paintings. A study of a ninth-century grotto at wan fo hsia. Harvard univ (1938) xv + 33 p, map, pl.

Whitfield, Roderick. The art of central asia. The stein collection in the british museum. Vol 1, Paintings from dunhuang. Tokyo & NY (1982) 344 p, 66 col pl, 113 monochrome fig, notes, bibliog.

Whitfield, Roderick. The art of central asia. The stein collection in the british museum. Vol 2, Paintings from dunhuang. Tokyo & NY (1983) 340 p, intro, 200 col pl, 64 b-&-w pl, notes, concordance, bibliog.

Whitfield, Roderick. An art treasury of china and mankind: some recent studies on the dunhuang caves. Orientations 20.3 (mar 1989) 34-40, illus.

Whitfield, Roderick. Buddhist paintings from dunhuang in the aurel stein collection. Orientations 14.5 (may 1983) 14-28.

Whitfield, Roderick. The monk liu sahe and the dunhuang paintings. Orientations 20.3 (mar 1989) 64-70.

Whitfield, Roderick. Visions of the buddha world: paintings from dunhuang. Apollo 220 no 269 (1984) 14-17.

Whitfield, Roderick and Anne Ferrar. The caves of the thousand buddhas: chinese art from the silk route. NY (1990) 208 p, 155 col pl, 75 b-&-w illus.

Wright, Harrison K. The thousand buddhas of the tun-huang caves. NCR 4 (oct 1922) 401-407.

III.13 (H-3) Tun-huang Miscellaneous

Bohlin, B. Newly visited western caves at tun-huang. HJAS 1 (1935) 163-166.

Bonin, Charles-Eudes. Les grottes de mille bouddhas. CRAIBL pt 1 (mar-avr 1901) 209-217.

Chavannes, Edouard. Présentation du touen-houang che chi yi chou. CRAIBL (juin 1910) 245-246.

Chen, Tsu-lung. Eloges de personnages éminents de touen-houang sous les t'ang et les cinq dynasties. Paris (1970)

Chen, Tsu-lung. Notes on the weddding ceremonies and customs observed in tun-huang in the second half of the ninth century. E&W n.s.22.3/4 (sep-dec 1972) 313-327.

Chen, Tsu-lung. Table de concordance des numérotages des grottes de touen-houang. JA 250.2 (1962) 257-276.

Chen, Tsu-lung. La vie et les oeuvres de wou-tchen (816-895): contribution à l'histoire culturelle de touen-houang. Paris (1966) 165 p, app, bibliog, pl, cartes, index générale, index des termes chinois.

Chêng, Tê-k'un. Tun-huang studies in china. Chengtu (1947) 14 p.

Demiéville, Paul. Récents travaux sur touen-houang. Apercu bibliographique et notes critiques. TP 56.1/3 (1970) 1-95.

Demiéville, Paul. l'Introduction au tibet du bouddhisme sinisé d'après les manuscrits de touen-houang. (Analyse de récents travaux japonais.) CETH 1 (1979) 1-16.

Drège, Jean-Pierre. Les accordéons de dunhuang. CETH 3 (1984) 195-204, 7 pl. Re format of texts.

Drège, Jean-Pierre. l'Analyse fibreuse des papiers et la datation des manuscrits de dunhuang. JA 274.3-4 (1986) 403-415.

Drège, Jean-Pierre. Les cahiers des manuscrits de touen-houang. CETH 1 (1979) 17-28, 9 pl.

Excavation and protection of relics in tunhuang cave-temples. Economic reporter 2 (apr-june 1972) 26-28.

Friend, Robert. The caves of the thousand buddhas—tunhuang and the old silk road. EH 17.8 (aug 1978) 22-24, illus.

Fujieda, Akira. Recent trends of dunhuang and turfan studies. Proc31stICHS, tokyo, 2 (1984) 1000-1002. Abstr.

Hejzlar, Josef. Recollections of tunhuang. NO 5 (feb 1966) 15-16, 4 p. illus.

Hori, Toshikazu. Tsl by P. A. Herbert. Social change in tun-huang from the latter half of the t'ang dynasty. ActaA 55 (nov 1988) 48-74.

Hou, Ching-lang. Le cérémonie du yin-cha-fo et les estampes de mille buddha. In PM&MD (1984) 45-48.

Hou, Ching-lang. Trésors du monastère long-hing à touen-houang: une étude sur le manuscrit p.3432. In NCET (1981) 149-168.

Huntington, John C. A note on dunhuang cave 17, "the library," or hong bian's reliquary chamber. ArsO 16 (1986) 93-101.

Jackson, David. A group of young tun-huang scholars in the kyoto-osaka area. CEA 3 (1987) 143-145.

Kanaoka, Shoko. Les études sur touen-houang au japon. JA 269 (1981) 21-24.

King, Yung-hua. Some current tun huang projects in taiwan and hongkong. CC 21.1 (mar 1980) 91-92.

Mair, Victor H. Dunhuang as a funnel for central asian nomads into china. In Ec&Emp (1989) 143-163.

Mibu, Taishun & Hirai Yuhkei. Present state of the mo-kau-ku cave temples at tunhuang. JIBS 28.2 (mar 1980) 1-12.

Musée Guimet. Manuscrits et peintures de touen-houang: mission pelliot 1906-1909. Collections de la bibliothèque nationale et du musée guimet. Paris (1947) 41 p, map.

Nakamura, Kikunoshin. Tun-huang document s.4644—its diplomatic significance. Proc31stICHS, tokyo, 2 (1984) 984-986. Abstr.

Pekarik, Andrew J. The cave temples of dunhuang. Archaeology 36.1 (jan-feb 1983) 20-27.

Pelliot, Paul. Une bibliothèque médiévale retrouvé au kan-sou. BEFEO 8 (1908) 501-529.

Pelliot, Paul. Les grottes des mille bouddhas. JRAS (1914) 421-426.

Pelliot, Paul. Mission pelliot en asie centrale: les grottes de touen houang. Paris, 6 vol (1914-24) All pl, no text.

Plumer, James M. Tun huang: vision of buddhist glory as seen in irene vincent's photographs. AQ 14 (spring 1951) 56-57, illus.

Shih, Kuang-ch'ing. Achievements in china's tun-huang studies. AofA 19.1 (jan-feb 1989) 158-159. Re new discoveries and studies.

Shor, Franc & Jean. The caves of the thousand buddhas. NGM (mar 1951) 383-415, illus.

Soymié, Michel (ed). Contributions aux études de touen-houang. Vol 3. Sous la direction de michel soymié. Paris (1984) 352 p. Art sep listed in this bibliog; abbrev CETH.

Soymié, Michel (ed). Nouvelles contributions aux études de touenhouang. Genève (1981) Essays sep listed in this bibliog; abbrev NCET.

Stein, Aurel. Serindia: detailed report of explorations in central asia and westernmost china. Oxford univ, 5 vol (1921)

Strickmann, Michel. India in the chinese looking-glass. In SR/DP (1982) 52-63.

Su, Ying-hui. A collection of articles on tunhuang. Taipei (1969) 80 p. Most art in chin; 3 art in engl, with abstr of others.

Su, Ying-hui. On the tunhuang science. West and east 9.6; 9.7 (june & july 1964) 7-10; 5-7; illus.

Su, Ying-hui. On the tunhuang studies. CC 17.1 (mar 1976) Rev art. Same title in APQCSA (spring 1974) 34-55.

Su, Ying-hui. A study of the identity of monk wu in the tun-huang manuscripts. In MS/CA (1977) 305-318.

Su, Ying-hui. The tun huang stone cave and the thousand buddha caves. CC 5.2 (oct 1963) 32-46, illus.

Takata, Tokio. Note sur le dialecte chinois de région du hexi aux IXe-Xe siècles. CEA 3 (1987) 93-102.

Tunhuang, Kansu, National Art Institute. The sacred grottoes of tunhuang. China magazine 19 (jan 1949) 28-42, illus.

Vetch, Hélène. Lieou sa-ho et les grottes de mokao. In NCET (1981) 137-148.

Vetch, Hélène. Liu sahe: traditions et iconographie. In PM&MD (1984) 61-78.

Vincent, Irene Vongehr. The sacred oasis. Caves of the thousand buddhas. London (1953) 114 p, map, bibliog, photos, index.

Waite, Arthur E. The shrine of a thousand buddhas. Occult review 15 (1912) 195-203.

Waley, Arthur. A legend about the caves of the myriad buddhas. SIS 5.3/4 (liebenthal festschrift) (1957) 241-242.

Warner, Langdon. The long old road in china. Descriptive of a journey into the far west of china to discover and bring back famous buddhist frescoes and statuary. NY (1926) 176 p, illus.

Xi, Yongnian & Zhao Hong. Devotees' inscriptions give clues to dunhuang mystery. OA n.s.36.1 (spring 1990) 47-48. Re dating of caves and contents.

III.13 (I) Others

Bai, Ziran (ed) Tsl by W. C. Chau. Dazu grottoes. Beijing (1984) 11 p.

Murray, Julia K. Tientai shan: a chinese buddhist centre. Orientations 19.12 (dec 1988) 60-64.

Raguin, Yves. La montagne de la tête du lion. Taipei (1983) Guidebook to budd temples.

Swart, Paula. Imperial cave-chapels of the northern wei dynasty. The buddhist caves at gongxian—an interpretive description. Orientations 20.10 (oct 1989) 56-66.

Wu Chi-yü. Le séjour de kouan-hieou [kuan-hsiu, 832-912] au houa chan et le titre du recueil de ses poèmes. Mélanges publié par l'institut des hautes études chinoises 2 (1969) 158-178.

Zhang, Jiaqi. The splendor of the grotto arts of the later period in china. The sculptures of dazu. OA n.s.35.1 (spring 1989) 7-21. Re dazu in ssuchuan, with budd and other sculpture.

III.14 Popular Buddhism - Buddhism in Stories

Blantly, Francisca Cho. Buddhist allegory in the journey to the west. JAS 48.3 (1989) 512-524.

Brandenauer, Frederick. Violence and buddhist idealism in the xiyou novels. In VC (1990) 115-148.

Chang, Ching-erh. The structure and theme of the hsi-yu chi. TR 11.2 (winter 1980) 169-188.

Chang, Ching-erh. The monkey hero in hsi-yu chi. HHYC:CS, pt 1, 1.1; pt 2, 1.2 (june & dec 1983) 191-216; 537-591.

Fu, James S. Mythic and comic aspects of the quest: hsi yu chi as seen through don quixote and huckleberry finn. Singapore univ (1977) 125 p, bibliog, index.

Gjertson, Donald E. Miraculous retribution; a study and translation of t'ang lin's ming-pao chi. Univ calif (1989) 305 p, notes, bibliog, index.

Han, Sherman. The satire of religion in hsi-yu chi. JCLTA 19.1 (feb 1984) 45-65.

Hermanová-Novotná, Zdenka. An attempt at linguistic analysis of the text of ta t'ang ch'ü ching shih-hua. ArchOr 39 (1971) 167-189. Re text preserved in japan and ed by lo chen-yü in 1916, narrating story of hsi yu chi.

Idema, W. L. Chasing shadows. TP 76.4-5 (1990) 299-310. Rev art on 3 works by Victor Mair: T'ang transformation texts; Painting and performance; Contribution of t'ang and five dynasties transformation texts, qq.v.

Jan, Yün-hua. Buddhist literature. In ICTCL (1986) Part 1: Essays: 1-12. Incl texts and popular literature.

Luo, Tzong-tao. Au sujet de terme bian: les procédés d'adaptation des textes bouddhiques aux bianwen. JA 269 (1981) 151-157.

Mair, Victor H. The contribution of t'ang and five dynasties transformation texts (pien-wen) to later chinese popular literature. Sino-platonic papers, no 12, dept of oriental studies, univ penn (1989) 71 p.

Mair, Victor H. Notes on the maudgalyayana legend in east asia. MS 37 (1986/87) 83-93.

Mair, Victor H. Parallels between some tun-huang manuscripts and the 17th chapter of the kozanji journey to the west. CEA 3 (1987) 41-53.

Mair, Victor H. Records of transformation tableaux (pien-hsiang) TP 72 (1986) 3-43.

Mair, Victor H. T'ang transformation texts. A study of the buddhist contribution to the rise of vernacular fiction and drama in china. Harvard univ (1989) xxi + 286 p, abbrev, notes, bibliog, index.

Mair, Victor H. & Maxine Belmont Weinstein. Popular literature. In ICTCL (1986) Part 1: Essays: 75-82. Much of this popular literature is relevant to relig.

Overmyer, Daniel L. Messenger, savior, and revolutionary: maitreya in chinese popular religious literature of the sixteenth and seventeenth centuries. In Alan Sponberg & Helen Haracre (ed) Maitreya, the future buddha, cambridge univ (1988) 110-134.

Pai, Hua-wen. Tsl by Victor H. Mair. What is pien-wen? HJAS 44.2 (dec 1984) 493-514.

Pan, Yihong. A true account of the rebirth in paradise of the venerable master pinxing. By dharma master shixing and zhu shanshuo. BCAR 2 (1988) 169-173. Chin budd miracle biog.

Plaks, Andrew H. The four masterworks of the ming novel. Princeton univ (1987) See chap 3, Hsi-yu chi: transcendence of emptiness, 183-276.

Ptak, Roderich. Hsi-yang chi—an interpretation and some comparisons with hsi-yu chi. ChLit 7.1-2 (july 1985) 117-141.

Roth, Robert Paul. Chinese stories and religion. Areopagus (christmas 1990, 4.1) 14-20. Both budd and other.

Seaman, Gary. The divine authorship of pei-yu chi [journey to the north] JAS 45.3 (may 1986) 483-497.

Seaman, Gary. Journey to the north. An ethnohistorical analysis and annotated translation of the chinese folk novel pei-yu chi. Univ calif (1987) 236 p, intro, map, gloss to intro, bibliog, char index.

194

Teiser, Stephen F. The ghost festival in medieval china. Princeton univ (1988) xvii + 275 p, char gloss, bibliog, index.

Teiser, Stephen F. "Having died and returned to life": representations of hell in medieval china. HJAS 48.2 (dec 1988) 433-464.

Yu, Anthony C. Liu i-ming on how to read the hsi-yu chi (the journey to the west) Chap 6 in David L. Rolston (ed) How to read the chinese novel, princeton univ (1990) 295-315.

Yu, Anthony C. The quest of brother amor: buddhist intimations in the story of the stone. HJAS 49.1 (1989) 55-92.

Yu, Anthony C. Two literary examples of religious pilgrimage: the commedia and the journey to the west. HR 22 (1983) 202-230.

Yü, Chün-fang. Images of kuan-yin in chinese folk literature. HHYC:CS 8.1, vol 1 (june 1990) 221-285.

III.15 Buddhism and Chinese Culture

Birnbaum, Raoul. Buddhist meditation teachings and the birth of 'pure' landscape painting in china. SSCRB 9 (1981) 42-58.

Chu, Fei. Influence of buddhist culture in chinese culture. In CBWCC (1983) 91-94. Same title in Ananda W. P. Guruge & D. C. Ahir (ed) Buddhist contributions to the world culture and civilization, new delhi (n.d.) 106-109.

Gard, Richard A. Buddhist contributions to asian cultural arts. In Ananda W. P. Guruge & D. C. Ahir (ed) Buddhist contributions to world culture and civilization, new delhi (n.d.) 135-157.

Henricks, Robert G. The poetry of han-shan. A complete, annotated translation of cold mountain. SUNY (1990) 475 p, 4 app, bibliog, index.

Hodous, Lewis. Awakening of buddhism and some of the results. MRW 49 (may 1926) 339-

343. Re modern buddhist "revival" and mission of karl reichelt to the buddhists.

Hurvitz, Leon. The mind of the early chinese buddhist. In Roy C. Amore (ed) Developments in buddhist thought, wilfrid laurier univ (1979) 477-485.

Lancaster, Lewis R. Buddhism and family in east asia. SES 11 (1984) 139-154. Repr in RFEA (1986) 87-95.

Liu, Ts'un-yan. Buddhist sources of the novel feng-shen yen-i. JHKBRAS 1 (1960/61) 68-97.

Mair, Victor H. T'ang transformation texts. A study of the buddhist contribution to the rise of vernacular fiction and drama in china. Harvard univ (1989) xxi + 286 p, abbrev, notes, bibliog, index.

Mather, Richard B. The life of the buddha and the buddhist life: wang jung's (468-93) "songs of religious joy" (fa-le-tz'u) JAOS 107.1 (jan-mar 1987) 31-38. Wang jung was a lay devotee.

Ren, Jiyu. Buddhism and chinese culture. Beijing review 27.52 (dec 24, 1984) 20-22.

Sanford, J. H. The nine faces of death: su tung-po's kuzo-shih. EB n.w.21.2 (1988) 54-77. Budd ideas in lit, text attributed to chin poet.

Strong, John S. Filial piety and buddhism: the indian antecedents to a "chinese problem" In Peter Slater & Donald Wiebe (ed) Traditions in contact and change, wilfrid laurier univ (1983) 171-186.

Teiser, Stephen F. The ghost festival in medieval china. Princeton univ (1988) xvii + 275 p, char gloss, bibliog, index.

Teiser, Stephen F. Ghosts and ancestors in medieval chinese religion: the yü-lan-p'en festival as mortuary ritual. HR 26.1 (aug 1986) 47-67.

Tong, Fung-wan (Tung Fang-yüan) Tsl by G. G. Caldwell. Understanding of the social ethical dimensions of buddhism and christianity. TJT 7 (mar 1985) 151-165.

Unschuld, Paul U. Medicine in china. A history of ideas. Univ of calif (1985) See chap 6, Buddhism and indian medicine, 132-153.

Watson, Burton. Buddhism in the poetry of po chü-i. EB n.s.21 (spring 1988) 1-22.

Yü, Chün-fang. Ch'an education in the sung: ideals and procedures. In NCEduc (1989) 57-104.

Zürcher, Erik. Buddhism and education in t'ang times. In NCEduc (1989) 19-56.

III.16 Modern (Pre-1949) Buddhism

Blofeld, John. The wheel of life. The autobiography of a western buddhist. London (1959) 263 p, illus, index. Repr (1988) with foreword by Huston Smith; author's "Farewell letter"

Welch, Holmes. The buddhist revival in china. Harvard univ (1968) 385 p, notes, bibliog, gloss-index. Sec of photos by Henri Cartier-Bresson, taken in 1949, titled A buddhist festival.

Welch, Holmes. The practice of chinese buddhism, 1900-1950. Harvard univ (1967) 568 p, notes, bibliog, gloss-index, app, illus.

III.17 Buddhism Under Communism

Welch, Holmes. Buddhism under mao. Harvard univ (1972) 666 p, app, notes, bibliog, gloss, index, illus.

III.18 Taiwan - Hong Kong - Overseas

Matics, K. I. A chinese pagoda in new york. APQCSA 15.3 (aug 1983) 1-21.

Nan, Huai-chih. Tsl by Margaret Yuan & Janis Walker. Grass mountain; a seven-day intensive in ch'an training. York beach, maine (1986) 134 p, brief bibliog, chin sources.

Raguin, Yves. La montagne de la tête du lion. Taipei (1983) Guidebook to budd temples.

Tsui, Bartholomew P. M. The self-perception of buddhist monks in hong kong today. JHKBRAS 23 (1983) 23-40.

Wee, V. Buddhism in singapore. In R. Hassan (ed) Singapore: country in transition, kuala lumpur (1976)

Welch, Holmes. Buddhism under mao. Harvard univ (1972) 666p, app, notes, bibliog, gloss, illus, index. See passim.

III.19 Comparisons - Interactions

Aitken, Robert. The cloud of unknowing and the mumonkan: christian and buddhist meditation methods. BCS 1 (1981) 87-91.

Augustine, Morris J. Zen and benedictine monks as mythopoeic models of nonegocentered worldviews and lifestyles. BCS 6 (1986) 23-49.

Blofeld, John Calthorpe. Lamaism and its influence on chinese buddhism. THM 7.2 (1938) 151-160, photos.

Blofeld, John. Kuan yin and tara: embodiments of wisdom-compassion void. TibJ 4.3 (autumn 1979) 28-36. Re meditation.

Bokshchanin, A. A. Sino-indian relations from ancient times to the sixteenth century. In S. L. Tikhvinsky & L. S. Perelomov (ed) China and her neighbors from ancient times to the middle ages: a collection of essays, moscow (1981) 105-138.

Broomhall, Marshall. In quest of god. The life story of pastors chang and ch'u, buddhist priest and chinese scholar. London etc (preface 1921) xiii + 190 p.

Bundy, Les. The last bull: a journey through buddhist thought to christianity. Areopagus (christmas 1990, 4.1) 5-7. "Last bull" ref to ox-herding pics.

Buswell, Robert jr. Ch'an hermeneutics: a korean view. In BHerm (1988) 231-256.

Buswell, Robert E. jr. Chinul's systemization of chinese meditative techniques and korean son buddhism. In TradMed (1986) 199-242. Chinul's dates are 1158-1210.

Buswell, Robert E. jr. The formation of ch'an ideology in china and korea: the vajrasamadhi-sutra, a buddhist apocryphon. Princeton univ (1989) 315 p, illus, gloss, works cited, index. Study and tsl.

Chappell, David W. From dispute to dual cultiva-tion: pure land responses to ch'an critics. In S&G (1987) 163-197.

Cheng, Hsüeh-li. Zen and san-lun madhyamika thought: exploring the theoretical foundation of zen teachings and practices. RS 15 (sept 1979) 343-363. Republ in JCP 8 (1981) 451-478, titled The roots of zen buddhism.

Cheng, Hsüeh-li. Zen, wittgenstein and neo-or-thodox theology: the problem of communicating truth in zen buddhism. RS 18.2 (june 1982) 133-149. Same title in TJT 12 (mar 1990) 99-119.

Despeux, Catherine. Le chemin de l'éveil. Illustré par le dressage du buffle dans le bouddhisme chan, le dressage du cheval dans le taoïsme, le dressage de l'éléphant dans le bouddhisme tibétaine. Paris (1981) 139 p.

Etiemble, René. Le bouddhisme chinois vu par les jésuites confucéens. In L. Lanciotti (ed) Sviluppi scientifici prospettive, ?rome (1975) 103-114.

Gimello, Robert M. Early hua-yen, meditation, and early ch'an: some preliminary considerations. In ECCT (1983) 149-164.

Gimello, Robert M. & Peter N. Gregory (ed) Studies in ch'an and hua-yen. Univ hawaii (1983) Essays sep listed in this bibliog; abbrev SCHY.

Gregory, Peter N. The integration of ch'an/son and their teachings (chiao/kyo) in tsung-mi and chinul. JIABS 12.2 (1989) 7-19.

Heine, S. Does the koan have buddha-nature? The zen koan as religious symbol. JAAR 58.3 (1990) 357-387. Comparison of ta-hui and dogen.

Hodous, Lewis. Awakening of buddhism and some of the results. MRW 49 (may 1926) 339-343. Re modern buddhist "revival" and mission of karl reichelt to the buddhists.

Inada, Kenneth. Zen and taoism: common and uncommon grounds of discourse. JCP 15.1 (1988) 51-65.

Jinananda, B. Early routes between china and india. Journal of the bihar univ 4.1 (nov 1958) 82-91. Re arrival of budd in china.

King, Winston L. Hua-yen mutual interpenetrative identity and whitehead organic relation. JCP 6.4 (dec 1979) 387-410.

Knauer, Elfriede Regina. The fifth century a.d. buddhist cave temples at yün-kang, north china: a look at their western connections. Expedition 25.4 (sum 1983) 27-46.

Knaul, Livia. Chuang tzu and the chinese ancestry of ch'an. JCP 13 (1986) 411-428.

Lai, Whalen. The buddhist-christian dialogue in china. In RIID (1989) 613-631.

Laycock, Steven W. Sartre and a chinese theory of no-self: the mirroring of mind. BCS 9 (1989) 25-42. The theory is that of hui-neng.

Lee, Cyrus. Life, death and reincarnation—a comparative study on hanshan tzu and thomas merton. CC 22.4 (dec 1981) 111-120.

Lee, Peter H. Fa-tsang and uisang. JAOS 82.1 (1962) 56-59 + chin text 60-62.

Liu, Ming-wood. The harmonious universe of fa-tsang and leibnitz: a comparative study. PEW 32.1 (jan 1982) 61-76.

Mukherjee, B. N. An illustration of iconographic contact between karttikey and manjusri in china. In BuddIcon (1989) 138-141. Re a brahmanical deity in yün-kang caves.

Pachow, W. The sino-indian buddhist debate in eighth century tibet: some questions and answers. The lotus [bulletin of the singapore polytechnic buddhist society] 18 (1984)

Petzold, Bruno. Heraus von Horst Hammitzch. Die quintessenz der t'ien-t'ai-(tendai)lehre; eine komparative untersuchung. Wiesbaden (1982) xv + 619 s, bemerkungen zur herausgezogenen literatur, erganzende bibliographische angaben zu arbeiten von Bruno Petzold, zeichen glossar wesentlicher chinesischer und japanischer, termini und namen. Contains extensive discussion of relationships with taoism.

Schopen, Gregory. Filial piety and the monk in the practice of indian buddhism: a question of 'sinicization' viewed from the other side. TP 70.1-3 (1984) 110-126.

Seah, Ingram S. Nestorian christianity and pure land buddhism in t'ang china. TJT 6 (1984) 75-92.

Seiwert, Hubert. Hochkultur und fremde religion: buddhismus und katholizismus in china. In Michael Pye (ed) Religion in fremder kultur, saarbrückenscheidt (1987) 55-76.

Su, Ying-hui. A comparative study on the contour techniques of wall-paintings found in tunhuang, ajanta, sigiriya and polonnaruwa. ACQCSA 7.1 (summer 1975) 10-12.

Tatz, Mark. T'ang dynasty influences on the early spread of buddhism in tibet. TibJ 3.2 (summer 1978) 3-32.

Tong, Fung-wan (Tung Fang-yüan) Tsl by G. G. Caldwell. Understanding of the social ethical dimensions of buddhism and christianity. TJT 7 (mar 1985) 151-165.

Tschen, Yin-ko. Buddhistischer in den biographien von tsan tschung und hua to im san guo dschi. TJ 6 (1930) 17-20.

Tschen, Yuan. Adam schall von bell und der bonze mu tschen-wen. MS 5 (1940) 316-328.

Unschuld, Paul U. Medicine in china. A history of ideas. Univ of calif (1985) See chap 6, Buddhism and indian medicine, 132-153.

Vandermeersch, Léon. Bouddhisme et pouvoir dans la chine confucianiste. In BetSA (1990) 31-39.

Wagner, Rudolf G. The original structure of the correspondence between shih hui-yüan and kumarajiva. HJAS 31 (1971) 28-48. Re taisho tripitaka no 1856.

Wei, Francis C. M. The doctrine of salvation by faith as taught by the buddhist pure land sect and its alleged relation to christianity. ChRec 51.6; 51.7 (june & july 1920) 395-401; 485-491.

Wu, Yi. On chinese ch'an in relation to taoism. JCP 12 (1985) 131-154.

Yoon, Yee-heum. Two forms of religious understanding of man from a comparative study of buddhist and christian thinkers, chi-tsang and h. richard niebuhr. Journal of east west studies [seoul] 10.2 (oct 1981) 91-127.

Zürcher, Erik. Bouddhisme, christianisme et société chinoise. Paris (1990) 95 p.

III.20 Miscellaneous

Birnbaum, Raoul. Chinese buddhist traditions of healing and the life cycle. In Lawrence E. Sullivan (ed) Healing and restoring: health and medicine in the world's religious traditions, ? place of publ (1989) 33-57.

Goodrich, L. Carrington. A note on unrecorded buddhist scriptures in ta-t'ung. Ming St 16 (spring 1983) 30. Re 2 sets of tripitaka in hua-yen ssu.

McDermott, Robert A. (ed). Focus on buddhism; a guide to audio-visual resources for teaching religion. Chambersburg, penn (1981) See 5, China, 78-83.

Part Four

Indices

Details Concerning Serial Sources

The following list assembles publication data for most of the serials named in the bibliography. Reference is made to our abbreviations in the left-hand column. Because it was not possible in many cases to determine date of termination, the absence of such an indication should not be taken as implying that the serial continued publication through 1990. Where we do not have sufficient information to be useful, the serial has been omitted from this list.

ASBIE-----Academia sinica. The institute of ethnology. Taipei. **Bulletin,** 1, march 1956-.

ASBIHP-----Academia sinica. The institute of history and philology. Peking and taipei. **Bulletin** 1, october 1928-.

Académie des inscriptions et belles-lettres. Paris. Publ the following five ser:

CRAIBL-----**Comptes-rendus des séances.** 1,1857-.

Histoire et mémoires. 1-51, 1666/1710-1784/93. Publ 1736-1843. Individual numbers with **Mémoires de littérature tirés des registres.** See below.

MAIBL-----**Mémoires.** 1, 1803-. Publ 1815-. May be listed as new ser.

Memoires concernant l'asie orientale, inde, asie centrale, extrême-orient. 1-3, 1913-1919.

MAI-----**Mémoires de littérature tirés des registres.** 1-81, 1666/1710-1773/1776. Reprfrom vol 1-41 of the **Histoire.**

Académie des sciences. Paris. **Comptes-rendus hebdomadaires des séances,** 1, 1835-.

Académie impériale des sciences. St.Petersburg. **Bulletin.** See Akademiia nauk. SSSR, Leningrad.

Académie royale de belgique. Classe des lettres et des sciences morales et politiques. **Bulletin.** See académie royale des sciences .. brussels.

Académie royale des sciences, des lettres et beaux-arts de belgique, brussels. **Bulletin,** 1,1832-98. Classe des lettres et des sciences morales et politiques, **Bulletin,** 1899-. Also publ:

MCAM-----**Memoires couronnés et autre memoires,** 1840-1904. Title varies as **Mémoires couronnés mémoires des savants étrangers.**

Academy-----**Academy and literature.** London. 1, 1869-. Title varies.

ActaA-----**Acta asiatica.** Tokyo. 1,1960-.

ActaOr-----**Acta orientalia** academiae scientiarum hungaricae. See Magyar tudomanyos. Akademia.

AO-----**Acta orientalia.** Copenhagen. 1,1922-.

Acts of various congresses, institutions, etc. are listed by name or title of congress or institution.

Adyar library bulletin. Madras. 1, february 1937.

Akademie der wissenschaften (Royal Prussian Academy of Science) Berlin. See also under Institut für orientforschung. **Abhandlungen.** 1804-1907 in one volume a year including publications of various klasses. 1908- as **Abhandlungen** under Philosophisch-historische and physikalisch-mathematische klasse.

AWGN-----Akademie der wissenschaft in göttingen,. philologisch-historischeklasse. **Nachrichten.**

Akademie der wissenschaften. Leipzig. The name of the institute varies as Königlich sächsische gesellschaft der wissenschaften; Sächsische akademie der wissenschaften. **Berichte über die verhandlungen,** 1846-48. Philologisch-historische klasse, **Berichte..** 1.1849-.

SAWW-----Akademie der wissenschaften. Vienna. Philosophisch-historische klasse,

Sitzungsberichte. 1,1848-.

Akademiia nauk. SSSR, Leningrad. **Bulletin.** Ser 3, 1, 1860-. Previously divided by class. **Izvestiia** Ser 7, 1928-. Earlier titled **Bulletin.**

All the year round. London. April 30, 1859-95.

AMZ-----**Allgemeine missions-zeitschrift.** Berlin. 1-50,1874-1923. Superseded by **Neue allgemeine missions-zeitschrift.**

Ambix. Society for the study of alchemy and early chemistry. London. 1, May 1937-.

PAAAS-----American academy of arts and sciences. **Proceedings.** See **Daedalus.**

American anthropologist. Washington, NY., pa. 1,1888-.

American antiquarian and oriental journal. n.p. 1, 1878-.

AmEth-----**American Ethnologist.** American **ethnological society. 1, 1974-.**

AJCM-----**American journal of chinese medicine.** Grant city, n.j. 1.1, jan 1973. With 5.2,1977, title changed to

CME&W-----**Comparative medicine east and west.**

American journal of economics and sociology. Lancaster, pa. 1, 1941-.

JR-----**American journal of theology.** Baltimore. 1-15, 1880-95. Chicago. 1-24, 1897-1920, united with **Biblical world** to form **Journal of religion.**

American magazine of art. See **Magazine of art.**

JAOS-----**American oriental society.** New haven, conn. **Journal.** 1.1843-.

AUFS-----American university field staff. Reports service: **East**

Asian series. NY. August 1952-.

Anatomical record. Wistar institute of anatomy and biology. Baltimore; philadelphia. Nov 1906-.

Dergisi. Ankara, Turkey. Université. Dil ve tarih-cografya fakultesi. 1,1942-. Title page in french, Université d'ankara, **Revue de la faculté de langues, d'histoire et de géographie.**

Annales, annuals, annuairie, etc. of institutions, societies, etc, see under the name or location of the organization.

ACP-----**Annales de chimie et de physique.** Paris. 1,1789-.

Annales d'hygiène et de médecine coloniales. See **Annales de médecine et de pharmacie coloniales.**

AEO-----**Annales de l'extrême-orient et de l'afrique.** Paris. 1,1878-91. 1-3 as **Annales de l'extrême-orient; bulletin de la société académique indochinoise.**

Annales de médecine et de pharmacie coloniales. Paris. 1,1898-. 1-17 titled **Annales d'hygiène de médecine coloniales.**

Annales de philosophie chr´étienne. Paris. 1-166,1830-1913.

APC-----**Annales des voyages de la géographie, de l'histoire et de l'archéologie.** Paris. 1-188, 1819-70. 1819-65 as **Nouvelles annales des voyages.**

AL-----**Annali lateranensi.** (Rome lateran. Museo lateranense. Pontificio museo missionario ethnologico) 1, 1937-.

AMH-----**Annals of medical history.** NY. 1, 1917-.

Année sociologique. Paris. Ann 1-12,1896/97-1909/12; n.s. 1-2 1923-25; 3e sér 1940/48-. 1934-42 superseded by **Annales sociologique.**

Antaios. Athens. 1, 1945-.

Anthropological institute. **Journal.** See Royal anthropological institute of great britain and ireland and/or the ethnological society of london.

Anthropological quarterly. Washington, d.c. 1, 1928.

Anthropologie. Paris. 1, 1890-/ Suspended 1941-46.

Anthropos; ephemeris internationales ethnologica et linguistic. Salzburg, vienna, fribourg. 1, 1906-.

Antiquity; a quarterly review of archaeology. Gloucester. 1, 1927-.

Apollo; journal of the arts. London. 1, 1925-.

Archaeologia, or miscellaneous tracts relating to antiquity. London. 1, 1770-.

Archaeology. Cambridge, mass. 1,1948-.

Archiv für geschichte der philosophie. Berlin. 1, 1888-. Vol 37-39 (1925-30) as **Archiv für geschichte der philosophie und soziologie:** vol 8-39 (1895-1930) as n.s. vol 1-32.

ARW-----Archiv für religionswissenschaft. Heidelberger akademie der wissenschaften. Leipzig, etc. 1-37, 1898-1942.

AV-----Archiv für völkerkunde. Museum für völkerkunde. Vienna. 1, 1946-.

ArchOr-----Archiv orientální. Prague. Oriental institute, czechoslovak academy of sciences. 1,1929-.

Archives d'anthropologie criminelle, de médecine légale et de psychologie normale et pathologique. Paris. 1-29, 1886-1914. 1886-92 as **Archives de l'anthropologie criminelle et des sciences pénales.**

ASSR-----Archives de sciences sociales des religions. Succeeded ASR. T. 18,1973-.

ASR-----Archives de sociologie des religions. Paris. C. N. R. S., Groupe de sociologie des

religions et groupe religions et développement. 1, 1956-. Title changed with t 18, 1973 to **ASSR.**

Archives suisses d'anthropologie générale. Genève. 1, 1914.

AAA-----Archives of asian art. See Chinese art society of america.

AGP-----Archives of general psychiatry. Chicago American medical association. With july 1960- continues **A.M.A. archives of general psychiatry.**

ACASA-----Archives of the Chinese art society of america. See Chinese art society of america.

Ateopagus-----Tao xong shan christian centre, HK. Continues vol 11 of Update. Fall 1987. Aristotelian society for the systematic study of philosophy. **Proceedings.** London. 1,1887-; n.s. 1,1900-.

Ars islamica. Michigan university research seminar in islamic art; Detroit institute of arts. Ann arbor.1-15/16,1934-51. Superseded by **Ars orientalis.**

ArsO-----Ars orientalis. the arts of islam and the east. Washington, d.c., freer gallery, smithsonian institution, & univ of michigan dept of fine art. 1, 1954-.

AArch-----Art and archaeology. Archaeological institute of america. Baltimore/washington, d.c 1-35, 1914-34.

Art and letters; india and pakistan. London, 1,1925-26; n.s. 1, 1927+1925-47 as **Indian art and letters.**

AB-----Art bulletin. College art association of america. NY. 1913-.

Art in america. NY. 1,1913-.

ANA-----Art news (annual) NY. 1,1902-.

AQ-----Art quarterly. See Detroit institute of arts of the city of detroit.

Art studies; medieval, renaissance and modern. Ed members of the departments of fine arts at harvard and princeton universities. 1-8,1923-31. Note also that these were issued as extra numbers of the American journal of archaeology in 1923,1925-28.

Artes; monuments et memoires. Copenhagen. 1-8,1932-40.

AA-----Artibus asiae; quarterly of asian art and archaeology for scholars and connoisseurs. Ascona,
switzerland. 1925- There is also a ser of Supplementa issued from 1937.

ArtsAs-----Arts asiatiques. Annales du musée guimet et du musée cernuschi. Paris. 1, 1954-.

AofA-----Arts of asia. HK (Kowloon) 1.1 jan/feb 1971-. Issued bimonthly.

AP-----Aryan path. Bombay. 1,1930-.

Asia. NY. See Asia and the americas. From march 1917 to october 1942 title was simply Asia.

Asia. Asia society, NY. 1, spring 1964-.

CMBA-----Asia. Shanghai and HK. 1, 1948-. Title varies as follows: jan 1948-june 1949, China missionary; sep 1949-july 1953, China missionary bulletin; sep 1953-dec 1959, Mission bulletin.

Asia; asian quarterly of culture and synthesis. Saigon. 1-4,1951-55.

Asia-----Asia and the americas. NY. 1-46,1898-1946. Title varies as follows: 1898-Jan 1917, Journal of the american asiatic association; mar 1917-oct 1942, Asia.

Asia journal of theology. Singapore. 1.1, apr 1987.

AM-----Asia major. London, Leipzig. 1-10, 1924-34/35;1944; n.s.London 1,1949-1975 3rd ser 1.-, Princeton univ. 1988..

AMHAV-----Asia major; Hirth anniversary volume. Oct 1922. The introductory issue, not included in vol numbering.

APQCSA-----Asian and pacific quarterly of cultural and social affairs. Seoul. Asian and pacific cultural and social centre for the asian and pacific region. 1. 1, summer 1969-.

ACQ-----Asian culture quarterly. Taipei Asian cultural center, asian parliamentarians union 1. 1,. autumn1973-.

AsFS-----Asian folklore studies. Nagoya. Nanzan univ. Succeeded FS in 1963.

AH-----Asian horizon. London 1-3, spring 1948-winter 1950/51.

AQR-----Asian review. London etc. 1, 1886-. Title varies. as follows: AR follows: 1886-90,1913. Asiatic quarterly review;1891-1912, Imperial and asiatic quarterly review; or Oriental and colonial record; 1914-52, Asiatic review.

AsSur-----Asian survey. Berkeley 1,1961-. Supersedes Far eastern survey.

ATS-----Asian thought and society: an international review. Oneonta. State univ of ny. Dept of political science. 1.1. apr 1976-.

Asiatic journal. See Asiatic journal and monthly review.

Asiatic journal and monthly register. See Asiatic journal and monthly review.

Asiatic journal and monthly review. London. 1816-45 Title varies as follows: ser 1-2, Asiatic journal and monthly register, ser 3, Asiatic journal and monthly miscellany. United with Colonial magazine and East india review to form Colonial and asiatic review.

AQR-----Asiatic quarterly review. See Asian review. London.

AR-----Asiatic review. See Asian review. London.

JRASB-----Asiatic society of bengal, calcutta. 1936- as Royal asiatic society of bengal. **Asiatic researches**; or **Transactions** of the society. Calcutta. 1-20, 1778-1839. Superseded by **Journal**. Title varies. **Journal**. 1-33, 1832-64. Continued in the following: **Journal and proceedings**, n.s. 1-30, 1905-34; ser 3,1,1935-. **Proceedings**. 1865-1904. Continued in preceding title.

JBBRAS-----Asiatic society of bombay. 1804-27, Literary society of bombay; 1827-1955, Royal asiatic society of great britain and ireland, bombay branch. **Journal**. 1841-1922/23; n.s. 1925-. Proc incl. **Transactions**. 1-3, 1804/5-1819-21.

Asiatic society of great britain and ireland. See Royal asiatic society of great britain and ireland.

TASJ-----Asiatic society of japan. **Transactions**. 1, 1872/73-. Various series.

AS-----**Asiatische studien; études asiatiques. Zeitschrift der schweitzerischen gesellschaft für asienkunde; review de la société d'études asiatiques.** Bern. 1, 1947-.

Asiatisches magazin. Weimar. 1-2, 1802.

BAF-----**Asie française; bulletin mensuel.** Paris, Comité de l'asie française. 1, 1901-,1901-10 as **Bulletin** de la comité.

Asien. Berlin. 1-16,1901-19. Superseded by **Ostasiatische rundschau.**

BAAFC-----Association amicale franco-chinoise. **Bulletin**. See **Revue franco-chinoise.**

Association françoise des amis de l'orient. **Bulletin**.Paris.No1-6, 1921-23; n.s.no 1-11.mar 1925-déc1927; no 77, oct 1929. N.s. in **Revue des arts asiatiques** q.v. Nothing publ in 1924,1928.

AAAG-----Association of american geographers. n.p. **Annals**. 1, 1911-.

Athenaeum; journal of literature, science, the fine arts, music and the drama. London. 1828-1921.

Atlantic monthly. Boston. 1, nov 1857-.

Ausland. Stuttgart. 1-66, 1828-93. Merged into **Globus**.

Aussenpolitik. Stuttgart. 1, 1950-.

PFEH-----Australian national univ. **Papers in far eastern history**. Canberra, 1-, 19

BCAR-----**B.c. asian review**. Dept of asian studies, univ british columbia. Grad students publ. 1, 1987-.

BOR-----**Babylon and oriental record.** London.1-9,1886-1901.

Baessler-archiv; beiträge zur völkerkunde. Leipzig, berlin. 1-25,1910-43; n.s. 1,1952-.

Basavangudi, bangalore. Indian institute of culture. **Transactions**. See Indian institute of world culture.

Belgrade. Institut imeni N. P. Kondakova. **Annaly**. 1-11, 1927-40. 1927-36 as **Sbornik statei po arkheologii i vizantinoiedieniiu seminarium kondakovianum.**

Berichte der K -Sach. ges. d. wiss. phil-hist. cl. see Akademie der wissenschaften. Leipzig. **Berichte**.

Berichte des rheinischen missionsgesellschaft. See Rheinische missionsgesellschaft.

Berlin. Staatliche museen. Ethnologische abtheilung. **Mitteilungen**. 1,1885-86.

Berlin. Staatliche museen. Museum für völkerkunde. **Veröffentlichungen**, 1-12, 1889-1919. Vol 11 not publ. 12 publ in 1907.

MSOS-----Berlin. Universität Ausland-hochschule. Through 1935, this organization was the university's seminar für orientalische sprachen. **Mitteilungen**. 1, 1898-.

Berliner gesellschaft für anthropologie, ethnologie und urgeschichte. **Verhandlungen**. 1869-1902. May be bound with **Zeitschrift für ethnologie**.

Berliner museum (museen) Amtliche berichte aus den preussischen kunstsammlungen. Berlin. 1-64, 1880-1943.

Biblical world. Chicago. 1, 1882-1920. United with the **American journal of theology** to form the **Journal of religion.**

Bibliotheca sacra; a theological quarterly. Oberlin 1, 1844-.

Bibliothèque d'école hautes. See Paris. École pratique des hautes études.

BVAMG-----Bibliothèque de vulgarisation des annales du musée guimet. See Paris. Musée guimet.

BTLVK-----Bijdragen tot de taal-, land- en volkskunde von nederlandsche-indie. The hague. 1, 1853-.

Biologie médicale. Paris. 1,1903-.

BIM-----Blackwood's magazine. Edinburgh, london. 1,1817-. 1817-1905 as **Blackwood's edinburgh magazine.**

Bombay. University. **Journal** 1, july 1932-. Also numbered in various sub-ser.

BMFA-----Boston. Museum of fine arts. **Bulletin.** 1, 1903-.

British academy for the promotion of historical, philosophical and philological studies. London. **Proceedings.** 1, 1903-.

BJP-----British journal of psychiatry. London. Publ by authority of the royal medico-psychological association. Continues **Journal of mental science** and **Asylum journal of mental science** with vol 109,1963-.

BJS-----British journal of sociology. London. 1,1950-.

BMQ-----British museum quarterly. London. 1,1926-.

AIPHO-----Brussels Université libre. Institut de philologie et d'histoire orientales et slaves. **Annuaire.** 1, 1932/33-.

Buddhism in england. See **Middle way.**

The buddhist annual. Colombo. 1,1964-.

BCS-----Buddhist-christian studies. Honolulu. East-west center. Annual. 1, 1981-.

BuddSt-----Journal of the dept of buddhist studies, univ of delhi. Annual.

BSR-----Buddhist studies review. Bi-annual journal of institut de recherche bouddhique linh-so'n & pali buddhist union, london. 1, 1984-.

Buddhist text society. Calcutta. **Journal.** 1-7, 1893-1906. The name of the organization varies and is superseded by the Indian research society.

BTTSoc-----Buddhist text translation society. Affiliate of sino-american buddhist association, san francisco.

Buecherei (bücherei) der kultur und geschichte. Bonn, leipzig. 1-30,1919-23?

BAF-----Bulletin asie-française. See **Asie française.**

Bulletin de géographie historique et descriptive. See under France. Comité des travaux historiques et scientifiques.

Bulletin de l'académie impériale des sciences de st. petersburg. See Akademiia nauk, SSSR; Leningrad.

BAAFC-----Bulletin de l'association amicale franco-chinoise See **Revue franco-chinoise.**

BMFJ-----Bulletin de la maison franco-japonaise. See under Tokyo. Maison franco-japonaise.

Bulletin de la société saint-jean-baptiste. See **Information nationale.**

Bulletin des missions. Bruges 1,1899-. Title varies.

BAAFC-----Bulletin franco-chinoise. See **Revue franco-chinoise.**

Bulletin médical franco-chinois. Peking. 1,1920-.

BEA-----**Bulletin of eastern art.** Tokyo. No 1-19/20,1940-41.

BSYS-----**Bulletin of sung and yuan studies.** Ithaca, ny. Cornell univ. Dept. of history. Through vol 13, 1977, titled **Sung studies newsletter.** 1, may 1970-.with vol 22 (1990-1992) titled **Journal of sung yuan studies.**

BHM-----**Bulletin of the history of medicine.** Johns hopkins univ. Institute of the history of medicine. 1, 1933-. From 1933-38 as Bulletin of the institute of the history of medicine.

Bulletin of the john herron institute. See under indianapolis. Art association of indianapolis. John herron art institute.

Bulletins of other societies, libraries, museums, etc. are listed by name or place of the institution.

BM-----**Burlington magazine.** London. 1,1903-.

CEA-----**Cahiers d'extrême-asie.** Revue de l'école francaise d'extrême-orient, sec de kyoto. Bilingual, french and engl. Annual. Paris. 1, 1985-.

CHM-----**Cahiers d'histoire mondiale; journal of world history.** Superseded by **Cultures.** Paris 1,1953-1972.

CalR-----**Calcutta review.** Calcutta 1,1844-.

CFQ-----**California folklore quarterly.** Berkeley. Univ california 1, jan 1942-.

Canadian magazine of politics, science, art and literature. Toronto. 1-91, 1893-1939. 1925-7 titled **Canadian.**

Canadian review of sociology and anthropology. 1, 1964-.

BCUP-----Catholic universiy of peking. **Bulletin.** See under Peking.

CW-----**Catholic world; monthly magazine of general literature and science.** NY. 1, apr 1865-.

Central asiatic journal. The hague. 1, 1955-.

Century, a popular quarterly. N.Y. 1-120,1870-1930. Title varies as follows. 1870-81 as **Scribner's monthly**; 1881-1925 as **Century Illustrated magazine**; 1925-29 as **Century monthly magazine.** United with **Forum** to form **Forum and century.**

Century illustrated magazine. See **Century, a popular quarterly**.

Century magazine. See **Century, a popular quarterly.**

BAIC-----Chicago Art institute. **Bulletin.** 1, 1907-1-45 as **Bulletin** and now **Quarterly.**

China analysen. Frankfurt-am-main. 1,1962-.

CCY-----China Christian yearbook. Shanghai. 1910-35. 1910-25 as **China mission yearbook.**

ChFor-----China forum. Taipei 1.1, jan 1974-. Publ semiannually.

China informatie. Delft. 1,1967-.

China institute bulletin. China institute in america. N.Y. 1936-47,1949-.

CJ-----China journal. Shanghai 1-35, 1923-41. 1-5 as **China journal of science and arts.**

China magazine. Hankow. chungking, NY.1-19, 1938-49-. 1-15 as **China at war.**

China magazine. NY. 1, 1924-. 1-10 as **China.**

China mail. HK.

CMH-----China mission hand-book. Shanghai 1,1896. Only one vol published.

China mission year book. See **China christian yearbook.**

CMBA-----China missionary or **China missionary bulletin.** See **Asia.** Shanghai; HK.

China monthly; the truth about china. NY. 1-11,1931-50.

CWR-----China monthly review. Shanghai. 1-24,1917-53. Title varies as follows: 1917-21, **Millard's review;** 1921-23, **Weekly review of** the far east; 1923-50, **China weekly review.**

CNA-----China news analysis. HK. 1,1953-.

CN-----China notes. NY. The china committee, far eastern office, division of foreign missions, national council of churches of christ/usa. 1.1, sept 1962-.

China pictorial. Peking. 1951-.

CQ-----China quarterly. London. 1,1960-.

China quarterly. Shanghai. 1-6,1935-41.

CRecon-----China reconstructs. Peking. 1,1952-.

ChRev-----China review. HK. 1-25,1872-1901.

China review. London. 1-5,1931-38.

ACSS-----China society. Singapore. **Annual.** 1948-(Chung-kuo hsüeh-hui)

JCS-----China society. Taipei. **Journal.** 1,1961- Alternate listing under Chung-kuo hsüeh-hui, taipei.

China society occasional papers. London. N.s. 1,1942-.

China today. NY. 1937-42.

China today. Taipei 1958-.

CWR-----China weekly review. See **China monthly review.**

La chine; revue bi-mensuelle illustrée. Peking. 1-73,1921-25.

Chine et sibérie. Brussels. 1-2 (no 1-40), 1900-01.

Chinese and japanese repository of facts and events in science, history, and art, relating to eastern asia. London. 1-2 (no 1-29) 1863-65.

ACASA-----Chinese art society of america NY.

Archives. 1, 1945/46

AAA-----. With vol 20, 1966/67, changed to **Archives of asian art.**

Chinese buddhist. pure karma buddhist association. Shanghai 1-2,1930-31(?)

CC-----**Chinese culture.** Taipei 1,1957-.

CEd-----**Chinese education.** White plains, NY. 1, spring 1968-.
A journal of translations.

CLG-----**Chinese law and government.** White plains, NY. 1, spring 1968-. A journal of translations.

CL-----**Chinese literature.** Peking. Foreign languages press. 1, autumn 1951-. Monthly, each year numbered vol 1 through 12 with 1984 changed to quarterly.

ChLit-----**Chinese literature: essays, article, reviews.** Madison. Univ wisconsin. 1, jan 1979-
.

CMJ-----**Chinese medical journal.** Shanghai 1, 1887-.

ChPen-----**The chinese pen.** Taipei.

ChRec-----**Chinese recorder.** Shanghai 1-72, 1868-1941. Supersedes **Missionary recorder.**

ChRep-----**Chinese repository.** Canton 1-20,1832-51.

Chinese review. London 1-4,1914.

ChSci-----**Chinese Science.** Publ irregularly in USA.. 1, 1975-.

CSPSR-----**Chinese social and political science review.** Peking 1-24,1916-41.

CSA-----**Chinese sociology and anthropology.** White plains, NY. 1, fall 1968-. A journal of translations.

CSH-----**Chinese Studies in history.** White plains, NY. 1, a journal of translations.

CSM-----**Chinese students' monthly.** Baltimore. 1-26,1905-30.

CSP-----**Chinese studies in philosophy.** White plains, NY. 1, fall 1969-. A journal of translations..

Chinese year book. Shanghai. 1-7, 1935/36-1944/45.

CDA-----**Chinesische-deutscher almanach.** Frankfurt-am-main. China-institut 19-; probably 1926.

Chinesische blätter für wissenschaft und kunst. 1,1925/27. Superseded by **Sinica.**

CF-----**Ching feng.** HK. 1957-. 1-7 has title Quarterly

QNCCR-----**notes on christianity and chinese religion and culture.**

Ch'ing hua hsüeh-pao. See **Tsinghua journal of chinese studies.**

Ch'ing-shih wen-t'i. New haven. 1, 1965-. Title changes to **Late Imperial China**, with 6.1 (june 1985) abbrev **LIC.**

Chinoperl China with 6.1, june 1985

ChrCent-----**Christian century.** Chicago. 1,1884-.

Christliche welt. Marburg. 1,1886-.

CCJ-----**Chung chi journal.** HK 1,. July, 1961-1976.

Chung-kuo hsüeh-hui. See China society, taipei, or China society, singapore.

Chung mei yüeh-k'an. Taipei 1, 1956-. **West and east** is the engl title of this journaL

CMI-----**Church missionary intelligencer.** See **Church missionary review.**

Church missionary review. London. 1-78,1849-1927. From 1849-1906 as **Church missionary intelligencer.**

Church missionary society. London. **Annual report of the committee of the church missionary society for africa and the east.** 1,1801-. Title varies as **Proceedings** of the society for missions to africa and the east, or **Proceedings** of the church missionary society.

Ciba symposia. New jersey. 1-11, 1939-51. Engl companion vol to **Ciba zeitschrift.**

Ciba zeitschrift. Basel. 1-11, 1933-52. See also **Ciba symposia.**

Cina. Rome. Istituto italiano per il medio estremo oriente. 1-8, 1956-64.

Claremont quarterly. Claremont, california. 1-11, 1956/57-64.

BCMA-----Cleveland. Museum of art. **Bulletin.** 1, 1914-.

Club alpin français. Paris. **Annuaire.** 1-30,1874-1903.

Colonial and asiatic review. See **Asiatic journal and monthly review.**

Comité japonais des sciences historiques. A section of the Xle Congrès international des sciences historiques. Stockholm, 1960.

Comité sinico-japonais. See Société sinico-japonaise. Paris.

Common cause. Chicago. 1-4, 1947-51.

Common cause. London, n.y. 1,1944-.

CME&W-----**Comparative medicine east and west.** NY. Neale watson academic publications. Continues **AJCM**(1973-77) Publ for the Institute for advanced research in asian science and medicine.

CSSH-----**Comparative studies in society and history, an international quarterly.** The hague. 1, 1958-.

Comptes rendus. See under name of institution or organization.

Concilium; internationale zeitschrift für theologie. Zürich, mainz, etc. 1, 1965-.

CMG-----**Conférences faites au musée guimet.** See under Paris. Musée guimet.

Conferenze tenute all' istituto italiano per il medio ed estremo orlente. See under Istituto italiano per il medio ed estremo oriente.

CIHR-----Congrès international d'histoire des religions. (Société ernest renan) Paris, 1923. **Actes,** Paris, 1925, 2 vol. See also International congress for the history of religions.

Congrès international des sciences anthropologiques et ethnologiques. See International congress of anthropological and ethnological sciences.

ICO/ICHS-----Congrès international d'orientalistes. See International congress of orientalists.

CPOL-----Congrès provincial des orientalistes français. Lyon, paris. **Compte rendu.** 1-3, 1875-78.

Congrès scientifique international des catholiques. 1888-. 4e congrès, Fribourg, 1897. **Compte rendu.** Fribourg. 1898, 11 vol in 3 vol.

CRJ-----**Contemporary religions in japan.** Tokyo. 1,1960-70 with mar 1974, 1.1, title becomes **Japanese Journal of Religious Studies,** JJRS .

CR-----**Contemporary review.** London. 1, 1866-.

La controverse et la contemporain. Paris. 1,1845-89.

Cornhill magazine. London. 1,1860-.

CM&P-----**Culture, medicine, and psychiatry.** Dordrecht. 1, 1977-.

CB-----**Current background.** HK. American

consulate general. 1, 1950-.

Current science; science in the making. Bangalore, india. 1, july 1932-.

The cycle; a political and literary review. Shanghai. 1st ser may 1870-june 1981. All publ in 1871.

Daedalus. American academy of arts and sciences. Cambridge, mass. 1.1, may 1846-. The Academy's Pro**ceedings.**

Dan viet nam. École française d'extrême-orient. Hanoi. No 1-3, 1948-49.

BDetlA-----Detroit institute of arts of the city of detroit. **Art quarterly.** 1, winter 1938-. **Bulletin.** 1,1904-; n.s. 1919-. A.k.a. following entry.

AQ -----Detroit institute of arts of the city of detroit. **Art quarterly.** 1, winter 1938-. **Bulletin.** 1,1904-; n.s. 1919-.

DGNVO-----Deutsche gesellschaft für natur- und völkerkunde ostasiens. See under Gesellschaft für natur-und völkerkunde ostasiens.

ZDMG-----Deutsche morgenländische gesellschaft. Leipzig. **Zeitschrift.** 1,1847-.

Deutsche rundschau für geographie. Vienna, leipzig. 1-37, 1878-1915. 1-32 titled **Deutsche rundschau für geographie und statistik.**

D&A-----**Dialogue and alliance.** Qtly. NY. 1.1 spring 1987-.

Diogène. Paris. 1,1952-. French edition of **Diogenes.**

Diogenes: an international review of philosophy and humanistic studies. NY. 1, 1952-.

Discovery; a popular journal of knowledge. London, cambridge. 1,1920-.

Les documents du progrès. Paris. 1, 1909-. See following item. **Dokumente des fortschritte; internationale revue.** Berlin. 1-11, 1907-18. Affiliated with **Documents du progrès.** Paris.

Occasionally art are duplicated. **Records of progress** is the american ed.

Dublin review. London. 1, 1836-.

EC-----**Early china.** Berkeley. Univ of california. Institute of east asian studies. Publ for Society for the study of early china. 1, fall 1975-. Publ annually.

E&W-----**East and west.** Rome. 1, 1950-.

EAJT-----**East asia journal of theology.** Singapore. 1.1, 1983-.

EA-----**East of asia; an illustrated quarterly.** Shanghai 1-5, 1902-06. This is engl ed of **Ferne osten**, q.v.

EWCR-----**East-west center review.** Honolulu. 1-4, 1964-68.

EArt-----**Eastern art.** College art association of america. Philadelphia 1-3, 1928-31.

EB-----**Eastern buddhist.** Kyoto. Otani univ. 1,1921-1937; n.s. 1,1965-.

EH-----**Eastern horizon.** HK. 1,1960-.

EW-----**Eastern world.** London. 1,1947-.

Eclectic magazine of foreign literature. NY. boston. 1-148, 1844-1907.

École des hautes études. See Paris. École pratique des hautes études.

BEFEO-----École française d'extrême-orient. Hanoi. **Bulletin.** 1,1901-.

École pratique des hautes études. See under Paris.

Education. France. Haut-commissariat de france pour l'indochine. Saigon. 1, 1948.

Eine heilige kirche. Munich. 1-22 no 2,1919-41-. Vol 1-15 as **Hochkirche.** Superseded by **Ökumenische einheit.**

Encounter. London. 1,1953-.

Endeavour; revue trimestrielle, publiée en cinq langues et destlnée à tenir registre du progrès des sciences au service du genre humain. Imperial chemical industries. London. vol 1,1942-.

EJ-----Eranos-jahrbuch. Zürich. 1933.

Etc; a review of general semantics. Chicago. 1, 1943-.

Ethics. Chicago. 1, 1890. Vol 1-48, 1890-1938 titled **International journal of ethics.**

Ethnographie. Paris. 1-22,1860-1903. N.s. no 1, oct 1913-. Vol 1-2 as **Comptes rendus** of Société d'ethnographie; vol 3-8 as **Actes** of the society. Vol 1-22 also numbered in ser.

Ethnological society of london. **Journal.** 1848-71. 1861-69 as **Transactions.** This society united with the anthropological society of london to form the Royal anthropological institute of great britain and ireland.

Ethnologisches notizblatt. Königliche museum für völkerkunde. Königliche museum, berlin. 1-3, 1894-1904.

Ethnos. Staten etnogtafiska museum. Stockholm. 1,1936-.

AS-----Études asiatiques. See **Asiatische studien.**

EtCh-----Etudes chinoises. Paris. 1, 1982-.

Études sociales. Paris, 1,1881-. 1881-1930 as **La reforme sociale.**

Études-----Études des pères de la compagnie de jésus. Paris. 1,1856-. Title varies as follows: 1856-61 as **Études de théologie, de philosophie et d'histoire;** 1862-94 as **Études religieuses, philosophiques et historiques.**

ER-----Études religieuses. See **Études des péres....**

EtTrad-----Études tradionnelles. Paris.

Evangelischen missionen, illustriertes

familienblatt. Güterslah. 1, 1898-.

EMM-----Evangelisches missions-magazin. Basel. 1816-1939. In 1940 merged with **NAM. ZM,** and **Orient** (Potsdam?) to form **Evangelische missionszeitschrift.** Stuttgart 1, 1940-.

Évidences. Paris. No 1,1949-. Preceded in mar 1949 by one unnumbered issue.

l'Explorateur: Journal géographique et commercial. Paris. 1-4,1875-76.

ET-----Expository times. Edinburgh 1, oct 1889-

EOEO-----Extrême-orient extrême occident. Cahier de recherches comparatives. Paris. 1,1982-.

FE-----The far east. Shanghai? 1, no 1-12,1905-06.

FEER-----Far eastern economic review. HK. 1,1946-.

FEQ-----Far eastern quarterly. See **Journal of asian studies.**

Far eastern review. Shanghai 1-38, 1904-41.

FO-----Ferne osten. Shanghai 1-3,1902-05. See also **East of asia.**

Fogg museum of art. See Harvard University. William H. Fogg art museum.

Folk-lore; quarterly review of myth, tradition, institution and custom. London. 1, 1890-

FLJ-----Folklore journal. London. 1-7,1883-89.

FS-----Folklore studies. Catholic university. Museum of oriental ethnology. Peking, nagoya 1,1942-.

AsFS-----1963, title changed to Asian **folklore** studies.

FF-----Forschungen und fortschritte; korrespondenzblatt der deutschen wissenschaft und tecknik. Berlin. 1-41? 1925-67(?)

Fortnightly. London. 1-182,1865-1954. From 1865-1934 titled **Fortnightly review.**

France. Comité des travaux historiques et scientifiques. Section de géographie. **Bulletin.** 1, 1886-. From1886-1912 titled **Bulletin de géographie historique et descriptive.**

FA-----France-asie; revue de culture et de synthèse franco-asiatique. Saigon. 1,1946-.

Frankfurter hefte. Stadtisches völkermuseum. Frankfurter universität. 1-39,1915-31. N.s. 1946-.1,1946.

Fraser's Magazine. London. 1, 1869-82.

FCR-----Free China review. Taipei. 1, 1951-.

Freer gallery of art, Washington, d.c. **Occasional papers.** 1, 1947-.

GBA-----Gazette des beaux-arts. Paris. 1,1859-1939. American ed NY. Ser 6, vol 22,1942-.

Geist des ostens. Munich. 1-2, 1913-15.

Geisteswissenschaften. Leipzig. No 1-39, 1913-14.

Geisteswissenschaftliche forschungen. Stuttgart. 1,1936-.

Gentleman's magazine. London. 1-303,1731-1907.

Geographical journal. Royal geographical society of london. London. 1,1893-. Supersedes the society's **Proceedings.**

GM-----Geographical magazine. London. 1-5,1874-78. Superseded by the Royal geographical society of london, **Proceedings.**

Geographical magazine. London. 1,1935-.

Géographie. Paris. 1-72, no 3,1900-39. Supersedes **Bulletin** of the Société de géographie (Paris) See also listing under the Société.

MDGNVO-----Gesellschaft für natur- und völkerkunde ostasiens. Tokyo to 1945. Deutsche gesellschaft für natur- ... is an earlier name of the institution. **Mitteilungen.** 1-32E, 1873/76-1943. Continued after 1945.

DGNVO -----Nachrichten. Tokyo, wiesbaden. No 1,1926-. No 1-Nachr-----70,1926-45 as **Nachrichten aus dergesellschaft.**

Globus. Hildburghausen, brunswick 1-98,1861-1910. Merged into **Petermanns geographische mitteilungen.**

Goldthwaite's geographical magazine. N Y. 1-7,1891-95.

Gregorianum Rome. 1, 1920-.

Gutenberg jarbuch. Mainz 1,1926-.

Han-hiue. Paris Université. Centre d'études sinologiques de Pékin. 1-3.4,1941-49. Vol 1 titled **Bulletin** de la centre.

HHYC:CS-----Han-hsüeh yen-chiu; chinese studies. Taipei. Resource and information center for chinese studies. Publ june and dec. 1.1,1983-.

HZ-----Hansei Zasshi See Orient. Tokyo.

Harper's magazine. NY. 1, 1850-, 1-101 as **Harper's new monthly magazine;** 102-28 as **Harper's monthly magazine.**

Harper's weekly. NY., 1-62, 1857-.

Harvard divinity bulletin. Harvard university. Divnity school. Cambridge, mass. 1,1935/36-. Title varies as follow: **Harvard divinity school annual; Harvard divinity school bulletin; Harvard divinity school.**

HJAS-----Harvard journal of asiatic studies. Cambridge, mass. 1, 1936-

HTR-----Harvard theological review. Harvard University. Theological school. 1,1908-.

Harvard university. Center for east-asian studies. **Papers on China.** 1, 1947-.

BFog:MA-----Harvard university. William H Fogg art museum. **Bulletin.** 1,1931-.

Hermès; recherches sur l'expérience spirituelle. Paris. 1,1963-.

HJ-----Hibbert journal; quarterly review of religion, theology and philosophy. London, boston. 1, 1902-.

HM-----Histoire de la médecine. Paris. 1,1951-

HR-----History of religions. Chicago. 1,1961-

History today. London. 1,1951-.

Hitotsubashi academy annals. Tokyo. **Annals.** 1-10,1950-59. In 1960, vol 1 of the Hitotsubashi **journal of arts and sciences** partially superseded the **Annals.** May also be listed under Tokyo. Hitotsubashi Daigaku.

Hobbies; the magazine for collectors. N.p. Begins with vol 36, 1931-.

Hochland; monatschrift für alle gebiete des wissens, der literatur und kunst. Munich; kempton. 1, 1903-.

l'Homme. Revue française d'anthropologie. Paris. École des hautes études en sciences sociales avec le concours du centre nationale de la recherche scientifique. 1,1961-.

Honolulu academy of arts. **Special Studies.** 1,1947-. Supersedes its **Annual bulletin.** 1-3, 1939-41(?)

HRAF-----Human relations area files inc. County survey series. New haven. 1, 1956-.

Illustrated london news. London. 1, 1842-.

Illustration. Paris 1-102,1843-1944.

PIAJ-----Imperial academy of japan. **Proceedings.** See Japan academy. Tokyo. **Proceedings.**

IAQR-----Imperial and asiatic quarterly review. See **Asian review.** London.

IA-----Indian antiquary. Bombay. 1-62,1872-1933. Superseded by **New indian antiquary.**

Indian art and letters. See **Art and letters: India and pakistan.**

Indian culture. Calcutta. 1.1934-.

IHQ-----Indian Historical quarterly. Calcutta. 1,1925-.

Indian institute of culture. See Indian institute of world culture.

Indian institute of world culture. Basavangudi, bangalore. **Transactions.** No 1,1948-.

Indian journal of social research. Baraut, india. 1960-.

Indian journal of (the) history of medicine. Madras. 1, 1956-.

JISOA-----Indian society of oriental art. Calcutta. **Journal.** 1-19,1933-52/53. Superseded by **Rupam.**

Indianapolis. Art association of indianapolis. John herron art institute. **Bulletin;** 1,1911-.

IAC-----Indo-asian culture, New delhi. 1,1952-

ICG-----Indo-chinese gleaner. Malacca. 1-3 (no 1-20)1817-22.

Information nationale. Montreal. 1953-. Vol 1-10 as **Bulletin** de la société saint-jean-baptiste de montreal.

AIPHO-----Institut de philologie et d'histoire orientales. See under Brussels. Université.

MIOF-----Institut für orientforschunq. Deutsche akademie der wissenschaften. Berlin. **Mitteilungen.** 1953-.

JICS-----Institute of chinese studies, chin univ of HK. **Journal.** Replaced by **JICS:CUHK.**

Institute of pacific research. China academy. Taipei. **Journal** or **Bulletin.** 1, 1967-.

IAE-----**International archives of ethnography.** Leiden. 1, 1888-. Title varies as **Internationales archiv für ethnographie; Archives internationales d'ethnographie**, etc.

PIAHA-----International association of historians of asia. **Conference proceedings.** 1st biennial conference. Manila 1960.
2nd biennial conference. Taipei. 1962.

ICfO-----International conference of orientalists in japan. **Transactions.** 1956.

ICHR-----International congress for the history of religions. Proceedings title varies with host country. 1900-. 2nd congress Basel (1904) **Verhandlungen.** Basel (1905) 382p. 3rd congress. Oxford (1908) **Transactions.** Oxford (1908) 2 vol. 7th congress. Amsterdam (1950) **Proceedings.** Amsterdam (1951) 196p. 11th congress. Claremont, calif (1965) **Proceedings.** Leiden (1968?) 3 vol. See also under Congrès international d'histoire des religions, paris, 1923, for data on a congress which is not one of this ser.

International congress of anthropological and ethnological sciences. 1st congress. London. 1934. **Proceedings.** 2nd congress. Copenhagen. 1938. **Proceedings.** 6th congress. Paris. 1960. 3 vol **Proceedings.**

ICO/ICHS-----International congress of orientalists with 1976, title of organization changed to International congress of human sciences in asia and north africa.. Transactions. Title varies with host country. 2nd congress. London (1874) **Transactions.** 1876. 4th congress. Florence (1878) **Atti.** 2 vol 1880-81. 6th congress. Leiden (1883) **Actes.** 4 vol 1884-85. 9th congress. London (1892) **Transactions.** 2 vol 1893. 10th congress. Genève (1894) **Actes.** 3 vol (Leide)

1895-97. 11th congress. Paris (1897) **Actes.** 5 vol 1898-99. 13th congress. Hamburg (1902) **Verhandlungen** (Leiden)1904. 14th congress. Algiers (1905) **Actes.** 3 vol in 4 (Paris) 1906-8. 18th congress. Leiden (1931) **Actes.** 1932. 21st congress. Paris (1948) **Actes.** 1949. 26th congress. New delhi (1964) **Daily Bulletins. Proc 31st ICHS, tokyo (aug-sept** 1983) 2 vol. Tokyo, 1984.

International journal of ethics. See **Ethics**

IJSP-----**International journal of social psychiatry.** London. 1, 1955-.

IPQ-----**IPQ: International philosophical quarterly.** NY. 1,1961-.

IRM-----**International review of missions.** Edinburgh. 1,1912-.

IAF-----**Internationales asien forum.** München. 1, jan 1970-.

Ipek; jahrbuch für prähistorische und ethnographische kunst. Berlin. 1-2,1925-69.

IQB-----**Iqbal review.** Karachi, pakistan. 1960-. Alternately in engl and urdu.

Isis, international review devoted to the history of science and civilization. Brussels, bern. 1,1913-.

I&S-----**Issues and studies.** Taipei. Institute of international relations. 1, oct 1964-.

IsMEO-----Istituto italiano per il medio el'estremo oriente. Conferenze tenute all'is (tituto italiano per il) M(edio el') e(stremo)o(riente) 1952-.

Izvestiya (izvestiia) akademiya nauk. See under Akademiia nauk, SSSR Leningrad. **Izvestia.**

JAK-----**Jahrbuch der asiatischen kunst.** Leipzig. 1-2. 1924-25.

JSMVL-----**Jahrbuch der städtliches museum für völkerkunde.** See under Leipzig.

Jahrbuch für psychologie, psychotherapie und medizinische anthropologie. Munich, etc. 1,1952/53-. Title varies. Vol 1-6 (1952-59) as Jahrbuch für psychologie und psychotherapie.

Jahresberichte der geschichtswissenschaft. Berlin. 1-36,1878-1913.

Jahrbuch für prähistorische ethnographische kunst. See Ipek.

Janus; revue internationale de l'histoire des sciences, de la médecine. de la pharmacie et de la technique. Leiden. 1,1896-.-----

PIAJ-----Japan academy. Tokyo. Proceedings. 1,1912-. From 1912-47 listed as published by the imperial academy of japan.

Japan quarterly. Tokyo. 1,1954-.

JSR:HS-----Japan science review: humanistic studies. Tokyo.

JSR:LPH-----1,1950-. Vol 1-9, 1950-58 as Japan science review: literature, philosophy and history.

JSR:LPH-----Japan science review: literature, philosophy and history. See Japan science review: humanistic studies.

TPJS-----Japan society, London. Transactions and Proceedings 1,1892-.

JJRS-----Japanese journal of religious studies. 1.1, mar 1974. From 1960-70 known as Contemporary religions in japan (abbrev CRJ)

Japanese studies in the history of science. (Nippon kagakusi gakkai)Tokyo. 1,1962-.

John herron institute. See under Indianapolis. Art association.

JRLB-----John rylands library. Manchester, england. Bulletin. 1,1903-.

JA-----Journal asiatique. Paris. 1,1822-. 1828-35 as NouvJAu-----Nouveau journal asiatique.

Journal des savans. Paris. 1665-1792. Superseded by Journal des savants.

Journal des savants. Académie des inscriptions et belles-lettres. Paris. No1-12,1797; sér2,1,1816-

Journal d'hygiéne. Paris. 1-40,1875-1914.

JSSR-----Journal for the scientific study of religion. Washington, d.c. 1, oct 1961-. Official journal of the society for the scientific study of religion.

JEAC-----Journal of aesthetics and art criticism. NY. 1, 1941-.

JAFL-----Journal of american folklore. Boston, lancaster. 1,1888-.

JAAS-----Journal of asian and african studies. Leiden. 1,1966-.

JAC-----Journal of asian culture. Los angeles. Univ california. Dept of oriental languages. 1,1977-. Publ annually by graduate students of the dept.

JAS-----Journal of asian studies. Ann arbor. 1, 1941-. Years 1941-56 titled Far eastern quarterly.

JCE-----Journal of chemical engineering, China. Chinese institute of chemical engineers. Tientsin. 1,1934-.

JCP-----Journal of chinese philosophy. Dordrecht & boston. 1.1 dec 1973-.

JD-----Journal of dharma. Bangalore. Dharmaram college. Dharma research association, center for the study of world religions. 1,1975-.

JHP-----Journal of humanistic psychology. Brandeis univ. 1, spring 1961-.

JIBS-----Journal of indian and buddhist studies (Indogaku bukkyogaku kenkyu) Tokyo. 1,1952-.

Journal of indian art and industries. London. 1-17,1884-1916.

JIC-----Journal of intercultural studies. Hirakawa city, Kansai univ of foreign studies. Intercultural research institute. 1, 1974-. Publ annually.

JOR-----Journal of oriental research. See under university of madras. **Annals of oriental research.**

Journal of oriental research. Kuppuswami sastri research institute. Madras. 1,1927-.

JOS-----Journal of oriental studies. HK univ. Centre of asian studies. 1,1954-.

JR-----Journal of religion. Chicago. 1,1921-.

JRE-----Journal of religious ethics. Waterloo, ont. 1, fall 1973. Published for the american academy of religion.

JRH-----Journal of religious history. University of Australia. Sydney. 1, 1960.

Journal of religious psychology including its anthropological and sociological aspects. Worcester, mass. 1-7. 1904-15.

JRS-----Journal of ritual studies. Univ pittsburgh.

JSS-----Journal of social science. National taiwan university. College of law. 1, 1956-. May be catalogued by chin title: **She-hui k'o-hsüeh lun-ts'ung.**

JSEAS-----Journal of southeast asian studies. Singapore & NY. 1, mar 1970-.

JAOS-----Journal of the American oriental society. 1, 1842-

JCLTA-----Journal of the chinese language teachers association. Univ pennsylvania. 1, fall 1966-.

JIABS-----Journal of the international association of buddhist studies. 1.1,1978-.

JOSA-----Journal of the oriental society of **australia.**

JSiamSoc-----Journal of the Siam Society. Bangkok. 1,1904-.

JTP-----Journal of transpersonal psychology. Palo alto, calif. American transpersonal association. 1, spring 1969-.

Journal of unified science. Leipzig, the hague. 1,1930-. Supersedes **Annalen der philosophie und philosophischen kritik** (1-8 no 9/10, 1919-apr 1930). Vol 1-7 no 5/6,1930- april 1939, as **Erkenntniss.**

Journal société finno-ougrienne. See under Suomalais-ugrilainen seura. Helsingfors.

JHI-----Journal of the history of ideas. NY, lancaster. 1,1940-.

JHMAS-----Journal of the history of medicine and allied sciences. NY. 1, 1946-.

JIA-----Journal of the indian archipelago and eastern asia. Singapore. 1, 1847-. superseded by **Journal eastern asia.** Singapore. 1, 1875-.

Journals of societies and institutions are sometimes listed under the name or locations of their respective organizations.

Kairos; religionswissenschaftliche studien. Salzburg. 1,1964-.

Kairos; zeitschrift für religionswissenschaft und theologie. Salzburg. 1, 1959.

Die katholischen missionen. Freiberg i.b; st. Louis, mo.; aachen, etc. 1, July 1873-. Numbering .irregular.

KT:OS-----Keleti tanu/manyok. Oriental studies. Budapest 1,1977-.

Kokka, an illustrated monthly journal of the fine and applied arts of Japan and other eastern countries. 1,1889-. Subtitle varies.

Königlichen museum für völkerkunde. See under Berlin. Staatliche museem.

Koloniale rundschau. Berlin, leipzig. 1-34,1909-

43. May have the title **Kolonialdeutsche, wissenschaftliche beihefte.**

TransKBRAS Korea branch, royal asiatic society. **Transactions.** Seoul. New series begins with vol 32, 1951-.

KdeO-----Kunst des orients. Wiesbaden. 1,1950-.

KGUAS-----Kwansei gakuin university. Nishinomiya, japan. **Annual studies.** 1,1953-.

Lancet. London, 1823-.

LIC-----Late imperial China. Supersedes Ch'ing-shih wen-t'i with vol 6.1, june 1985.

Laval théologique et philosophique. Quebec. 1, 1945-.

JSMVL-----Leipzig. Städtisches museum für völkerkunde. **Jahrbuch.** 1-9,1906-22/ 25;10,1926/51-. **Mitteilungen.** No 1-17,1960-64;1965-.

Leipzig. Universität. **Wissenschaftliche zeitschrift. Gesellschafts und sprachwissenschaftliche reihe.** 1951/52.

Life. NY. 1936-72.

LD-----Light of dharma. San francisco. 1-6, 1901-07.

Littell's living age. Boston. 1844-1941.

Litterae orientales. Leipzig, wiesbaden. 1-84, ?-1939; n.s. no 1-44,1953-1958.

BSOAS-----London. University. School of oriental and african studies. **Bulletin.** 1,1917-.

London. University. Warburg Institute. **Journal of the warburg and courtauld institutes.** 1, 1937-.

London and china express. London. 1-73, 1858-1931. Title varies.

Lotus. See under Société sinico-japonais. Paris.

Lyons. Université. **Annales.** 1-9,1891-98; n.s. 1, **Sciences, médecine,** no 1-50,1899-1934; n.s. 2, **Droit, lettres,** no 148, 1899-1934; Both superseded by n.s.3, **Science,** 1936-.

MacMillan's magazine. London, etc. 1,1859-1907.

Magasin littéraire. Paris. 1-15, 1884-98. 1884-93 as **Magasin littéraire et scientifique.**

MLA-----Magazin; monatschrift für literatur, kunst und kultur. Berlin. 1832-1915. Title varies as follows 1832-80, **Magazin für die literatur des auslandes,** 1881-90, **Magazin für die literatur des in- und auslandes;** 1890-1904, **Magazin für literatur;** 1904-05, **Neue magazin;** 1906-07, **Magazin für literatur des in- und auslandes.**

Magazine of art. Washington, NY. 146 no 5, nov 1909- may 1953. 1909-15 as **Art and progress;** 1916-36 as **American magazine of art.**

ActaOr-----Magyar tudomanyos akademia. Budapest. **Acta orientalia.** 1, 1950-.

Maharaja sayajirao university of baroda. **Journal.** 1, 1952-.

MB-----Maha Bodhi; a monthly journal of international buddhist brotherhood. Calcutta. 1, 1892-. Title varies as follow: 1892-1901. **Journal of the Maha Bodhi society;** 1901-23, **Mahabodhi and the united buddhist world.**

Main currents in modern thought. NY. 1, 1940-.

BMFJ-----Maison franco-japonaise. See under Tokyo.

Man. Royal anthropological institute of great britain and ireland. London 1,1901-.

JMGS-----Manchester geographical society. Manchester, england. **Journal.** 1, 1885-.

Marco polo. Shanghai 1, 1939-.

Mariner's mirror. London 1,1911-.

MCB-----Mélanges chinois et bouddhiques. Louvain. 1, 1932-. Monographic ser, issued irregularly

MIHEC-----Mélanges,Paris universitaire, institut des hautes études chinoise. See under Paris. Université.

Mélanges sinologiques. Centre d'études sinologiques. Peking 1951-.

Mémoires concernant l'asie orientale, inde, asie-centrale, extrême-orient. See Académie des inscriptions et belles-lettres.

MCLC-----Mémoires concernant l'histoire, les sciences, les arts, les moeurs, les usages etc. des chinois; par les missionnaires de pékin. Ed C, Batteux, L. G. Oudert, Feudrix de Brequigny, J. de Guignes, and A. J. Silvestresle Sacy. Paris 1-16, 1776-1804.

MCAM-----Mémoires couronnés et autre mémoires. See under Académie royale des sciences, des lettres beaux-arts de belgique.

MAIBL-----Mémoires de l'académie des inscriptions et belles-lettres. See under Académie des inscriptions. . .

MAI-----Mémories de littérature tirés des registres de l'académie des inscriptions. See under Académie des inscriptions et belles-lettres.

Mémories de la societe d'emulation de roubaix. See under société d'émulation. . . .

Merkur; deutsche zeitung für europäisches denken. Stuttgart, baden-baden 1,1947-.

WMM-----Methodist magazine. London 1,1778-. Title varies as follows: 1778-97, Arminian magazine; 1798-1821, Methodist magazine; 1822-1912, Wesleyan methodist magazine; 1914-26, Magazine of the wesleyan methodist church.

Methodist review. NY.1-114, 1818-1931. Title varies as follows: 1818-28, Methodist magazine;1830-40, Methodist magazine and quarterly review; 1841-84, Methodist quarterly review.

MexICHS-----30th intl congress of human sciences in asia and north africa (formerly ICO) El colegio de méxico. Proceedings. 1976. See vol 2, china.

BMMA-----Metropolitan museum of art. Bulletin. See under New York.

MW-----Middle way. London. 1, 1926-. Vol 1-17 as Buddhism in england.

MingSt-----Ming studies. 1, 1975-.

Ministry; a quarterly theological review for east and south africa. Moriji, basutoland. 1, 1960-.

Minneapolis institute of art. Minneapolis. Bulletin. 1,1905-.

Missiology. Continuation of PrAnthro beginning with vol 19,1973..

Mission bulletin. Shanghai, HK. See Asia.

Missionary recorder. Foochow 1, no 1-2, 1867. Superseded by Chinese recorder.

Missionary research library. New York Bulletin. 1,1928-. This publication coincides with dating of Occasional bulletin.

MRW-----Missionary review of the world. London, etc 1-62, 1878-1939. 1878-87 as Missionary review.

MC-----Missions catholiques. Paris 1, 1868-.

Mitteilungen aus der ethnologischen abteilung der königl- museen zu berlin. See Berlin. Staatliche museen. Ethnologische abteilung.

MSGFOK-----Mitteilungen der schweizerischen gesellschaft der freunde ostasiatische kultur. See schweizerische gesellschaft für asien-kunde.

Mitteilungen des instituts für orientforschung. East berlin. Deutsche akademie der wissenschaften zu berlin, institut für orientforschung. 1, 1953-.

MSOS-----Mitteilungen des seminars für

218

orientalische sprachen. See under Berlin. Universität. Ausland-hochschule.

MIOF-----Mitteilungen deutsche preussiche akademie der wissenschaften zu berlin. See Institut für orientforschung.

MDGNVO-----Mitteilungen der deutsche gesellschaft für natur- und völkerkunde ostasiens, tokyo. See Gesellschaft für natur-und völkerkunde.

ModCh-----Modern china; an international quarterly of history and social science. Beverly hills, calif & london. Sage publications. 1, 1975-.

Moderne welt. Cologne. 1, 1959-.

Monde moderne et la femme d'aujourdhui. Paris. 1-28,1895-1908. 1895-1905 as Monde moderne. Merged into Revue hebdomadaire.

Monist, a quarterly magazine devoted to the philosophy of science. Chicago. 1-46, 1890-1936.

Moniteur universel: Journal officiel. Paris. 1789-1868.

MN-----Monumenta nipponica. Tokyo. 1,1938-

MS-----Monumenta serica. Peking, nagoya, los angeles, st. augustin (germany) 1,1935/36-.

Muséon. Société des lettres et des sciences. Paris, louvain. 1, 1882-.

Museum; tijdschrift woor filologie geschiedenis. Groningen, leyden. 1-64, 1893-1959?

Museum journal. See under Pennsylvania. Universiy. University museum.

BMFEA-----Museum of far eastern antiquities. Bulletin. See under Stockholm.

BMFA-----Museum of finé arts (Boston) Bulletin. See under Boston.

NachrDGNVO-----Nachrichten der deutsche gesellschaft für natur- und völkerkunde ostasiens. See Gesellschaft für natur- und völkerkunde ostasiens.

NGM-----National geographic magazine. Washington, d.c. 1,1888-.

National medical journal. London. 1,1914-.

National medical journal of china. Shanghai. 1915-.

NPMB-----National palace museum bulletin. Taipei. 1,1966-. May be catalogued under Kuo-li ku-kung po-wu-yüan.

NRJ-----National reconstruction journal. NY. 1-8,1942-47.

National review. Shanghai. 1-20, ?-1916.

NH-----Natural history. NY. American museum of natural history. 1, apr 1900-.

NLIP-----Natural law institute proceedings. Notre dame university. Law school (college of law) 1-15,1947-51. Superseded by Natural law forum.

Nature. London. 1, 1869.

Nature. Paris. l, 1873-.

Neue orient. Berlin 1-17, 1917-43.

Neue orient; abhandlungen zür geographie, kultur und wirtschaft der länden des ostens. Halle-a-saale. 1-13, 1905-18.

Neue schweizer rundschau. Zürich. 1-41, 1907-33; n. s. 1-22, 1933-55. 1907 as Wissen und leben.

NZM-----Neue zeitschrift für missionwissenschaft. Beckenreid, switz. 1,1945-

New age. Communist party of india. New delhi. 1, sep 1952-? n.s. 1, apr 1964-.

New asia; an organ of oriental culture and thought. Calcutta. 1-2, 1939-40?

New century review. London. 1-8,1897-1900.

NCR-----New china review. Shanghai. 1-4, 1919-22.

NewIA-----New indian antiquary; a monthly journal of oriental research in archaeology. art, epigraphy. Bombay 1, 1938-. Supersedes Indian antiquary. See also New Indian antiquary. Extra series.

NewIA-----New indian antiquary. Extra Series. Bombay 1, 1939-.

New orient. NY. 1-3, 1923-27. Vol 1 as Orient; an international magazine of art and culture. Superseded by Oriental magazine.

NO-----New orient. Prague 1, 1960-68.

New world; a quarterly review of religion, ethics and theology. Boston 1-9.1892-1900.

BMMA-----New York Metropolitan museum of art. Bulletin. 1, 1905-.

New zealand institute. See Royal society of new zealand.

NC-----Nineteenth century. See Twentieth century. London.

Nineteenth century and after. See Twentieth century. London.

North american review. NY, boston. 1,1815-.

NCH-----North China herald. Shanghai. 1850-?

NQ-----Notes and queries on china and japan. HK. 14,1867-70.

NouvJA-----Nouveau journal asiatique. See Journal asiatique.

NouvClio-----Nouvelle clio. Brussels. 1,1949-.

NR-----Nouvelle revue. Paris. 1, 1879-.

Nouvelle revue française. Paris. 1-31, 1909-43. N.s. 1,1953-. Title varies as La nouvelle revue.

Nouvelles annales des voyages. See Annales des voyages, de la géographie, de l'histoire et de l'archeologie.

Nucleus. American chemical society. Boston. 1,1924-.

Numen; international review for the history of religions. Leyden, 1,1954-.

Numismatic and antiquarian society of philadelphia. Proceedings. Philadelphia 1,1865/66-.

Occult review. See Rider's review. London.

Occult review. Boston. 1888-97.

Okurayama oriental research institute. Proceedings. 1,1954-.
Engl title of Okurayama gakuin. Yokohama. Okurayama Gakuin Kiyo.

OC-----Open court, a quarterly magazine. Chicago. 1-1887-.

Oriens. Leiden. 1,1948-.

OE-----Oriens extremus. Wiesbaden. 1, 1954-.

Orient. HK. 1-6, 1950-56.

HZ-----Orient. Tokyo, 1-16, ?-1901. Vol 1-13 titled Hanzei zasshi.

Orient et occident. Geneva. 1-2,1934-36.

OA-----Oriental art. London. 1-3,1948-51; n.s. 1-1955-.

TOCS-----Oriental ceramic society. London. Transactions. 1,1921-.

JOSA-----Oriental society of australia. Sydney. Journal. 1,1960-.

Orientalia suecana. Uppsala. 1,1952-.

Orientalische archiv. Leipzig. 1-3, 1910-13.

OL-----Orientalistische literatur tung. Berlin, leipzig. zei 1,1898-.

Orientations. HK Pacific communications ltd. monthly. 1.1, jan 1970-.

Oriente poliana. Istituto italiano per il medio e l'estremo oriente. Rome.

OstL-----Ostasiatische lloyd. Shanghai. 1-31, 1866-1917.

Ostasiatische rundschau. Berlin. 1-25,1920-44.

OZ-----Ostasiatische zeitschrift. Berlin.1,1912-42/43.

Österreichische monatschrift für den orient. Vienna. 1-44, 1875-1918.

Our missions. London. 1-24, 1894-1917.

Outlook, a weekly review of politics, art, literature and finance. London. 1-61,1898-1928.

OM-----Overland monthly & out west magazine. San francisco. 1, 1868-.

PA-----Pacific affairs. Honolulu, NY. 1, 1926-.

PW-----Pacific world. Berkeley. 1-4,1925-28. n.s. 1, 1985-.

Paideuma; mitteilungen zur kulturkunde. Bamberg. 1,1938-.

Pakistan journal of science. See **Pakistan journal of scientific research.**

Pakistan journal of scientific research. Pakistan association for the advancement of science. Lahore. 1, 1949-.

Pakistan philosophical journal. Lahore. 1, 1957-.

JPTS-----Pali text society. London. **Journal.** 1882-1924/27.

Pantheon; international zeitschrift für kunst. Munich. 1, 1928-.

PFEH-----Papers on far eastern history. Canberra.

Australian national univ. 1

ACF-----Paris. Collège de france. **Annuaire.** 1,1901-.

Paris. École pratique des hautes études. Bibliothèque. **Sciences religieuses.** 1, 1889-.

AMG-----Paris. Musée guimet. **Annales.** 1-51,1880-1935? **BVAMG-----Bibliotheque de vulgarisation.** 1,1889-.

CMG-----Conférences faites au musée guimet. 1898/99-1914; 1902-16.

MIHEC-----Paris. Université. Institut des hautes études chinoises. **Mélanges.** 1, 1957-.

Parnassus. NY. 1-13.1929-41.

BCUP-----Peking. Catholic university. **Bulletin.** 1-9,1926-34.

JPOS-----Peking oriental society. **Journal.** 1-4, 1885-98.

UPUMB-----Pennsylvania. State university. University museum. **Museum journal.** 1-24,1910-35. **Museum bulletin,** 1-22, 1930-55.

Pennsylvania museum bulletin. See **Philadelphia museum bulletin.**

La pensée; revue du (bon) rationalisme moderne. Paris. 1939-; n.s. 1, oct/dec 1944-.

PC-----People's china. Peking. 1,1950-57.

PT-----People's tribune. Peking. 1,1931-1941 (?)

Petermanns geographische mitteilungen. Gotha. 1,1855-. Title varies.

Pharmazeutische industrie. Aulendorf. 1,1933-.

PTP-----Phi theta papers. Berkeley. 1, 1950-. 1950,1954-55 titled **Phi theta annual.**

PMB-----Philadelphia museum bulletin. Philadelphia. 1,1903-, From 1920-38 titled **Pennsylvania museum bulletin.**

Philosophical magazine. London. 1, 1798-. Ser varies.

Philosophical quarterly. Calcutta 1, 1925-.

Philosophical studies of japan. Comp by the Japanese national commission for UNESC0. Tokyo 1,1959-.

Philosophisches jahrbuch der görresgesellschaft. Munich, etc 1,1888-. Suspended 1943-45 and1952.

PEW-----Philosophy east and west. Honolulu. 1,1951-.

PS-----Popular science monthly. NY. 1,1872-.

PrAnthro-----Practical anthropology. Tarrytown, NY, 1953-72. Continued with vol 19, 1973, by **Missiology.**

Praxis der psychotherapie. Munich. 1,1956-. 1-3 (1956-58) as **Psychotherapie.**

Proceedings of various societies and institutions are sometimes listed under the name or location of the organization in question.

Psyche. Heidelberg, stuttgart. 1,1947-.

Psychoanalysis and the psychoanalytic review. NY. 1, 1913-. 1913-57, titled **Psychoanalytic review.**

Psychoanalytic review. See **Psychoanalysis and the psychoanalytic review.**

Psychologia; international journal of psychology in the orient. Kyoto univ. 1, june 1957-.

Psychotherapie. See **Praxis der psychotherapie.**

QJCA-----Quarterly journal of current acquisitions. See under United States. Library of Congress.

QNCCR-----Quarterly notes on christianity and

chinese religion. See **Ching feng.**

Quarterly review. London 1, 1809.

Quest. London. 1-21,1909-30.

Quiver. London 1,1861-. NY. 1-39, 1884-1926 is american ed of london publ.

Race. London. 1,1959-.

RechScRelig-----Recherches de science religieuse. Paris. 1,1910-.

RMHA-PU-----Record of the museum of historic art, princeton university.

Records of progress. See **Dokumente des fortschritte.**

Reforme sociale. See **Études sociales.**

RC-----Relations de chine (Kiang-nan) Paris. 1,1903-27 (?)

Religion. A journal of religion and religions. London etc. 1, spring 1971-.

RCDA-----Religion in communist dominated areas.

Religion in life; a christian quarterly. NY. 1,1932-.

Religion und geisteskult. Göttingen. 1-8,1907-14.

Religions. London No 1-77, 1931-53.

RelEduc-----Religious education. New Haven, conn. 1,1906-.

RH-----Religious humanism. Yellow springs, ohio. Fellowship of religious humanists. 1, winter 1967-.

RS-----Religious studies. London 1,1965-.

RTrad-----Religious traditions. Publ in australia. With vol 11 publ by mcGill univ and univ sydney. With vol 4.1 (may-june 1981) incorporates **Journal of studies in mysticism.**

RSR-----Religious studies review. Waterloo, ont. Council on the study of religion. 1, sept 1975-.

Rencontre orient-occident. Geneva 1,1954-.

Renditions. A chinese-english translation magazine. Univ HK. Translation centre. 1, autumn 1973-.

RofR-----Review of religion. NY. 1-22,1936-58.

Review of religions. Punjab. 1, 1902-.

La revue. (Ancient revue des revues) Paris. 1, ? Vol 46, pt 3, 1903-. Title changes to **La revue mondiale.**

La revue; littérature, histoire, arts et sciences des deux mondes. Paris. 1948-. Supersedes **Revue des deux mondes.**

La revue; littéraire et artistique. Paris. 1, 1882-.

Revue anthropologique. Paris 1-50,1891-1942;1955-.

Revue apologétique. Paris. 1-68,1905-39.

Revue apologétique. Brussels. 1-13,1900-12.

RA-----Revue archéologique. Paris. 1944-.

Revue blanche. Paris. 1-30,1891-1903.

Revue bleu, politique et littéraire. Paris. 1863-1939. Title varies.

Revue britannique. Paris 1-77,1825-1901.

Revue catholique. Université catholique. Louvain. 1-61, 1843-98.

Revue critique. Paris. 1866-1935.

RE-----Revue d'ethnographie. Paris 1-8, 1882-91.
Revue d'ethnographie et des traditions populaires. Paris 1-10, 1920-29. Supersedes Re-

vue des traditions populaires.

Revue d'europe et d'amerique. Paris. 1-20, 1898-1908. Title varies.

Revue de l'art ancien et moderne. Paris. 1-71,1897-1937.

REO-----Revue de l'extreme-orient. Paris. 1882-87.

Revue de la faculté de langues, d'histoire et de géographie. See under Ankara. Université.

RHR-----Revue de l'histoire des religions. Musée guimet. Paris 1,1880-.

ROA-----Revue de l'orient et de l'algérie et des colonies. Paris. 1843-65.

RMM-----Revue de métaphysique et de morale. Paris. 1,1893-.

Revue de paris. Paris 1, 1894-.

Revue de théologie et de philosophie. Genève 1868-1911; 1913-.

RAA-----Revue des arts asiatiques. Paris 1-13,1924-42. Superseded by **Arts asiatiques.** See also Association française des amis de l'orient, **Bulletin.**

RDM-----Revue des deux mondes. Paris 1829-1948.

Revue des études ethnographiques et sociologiques. Paris. 1-2, 1908-09. Superseded by **Revue.**

Revue des questions historiques. Paris 1866-.

RR-----Revue des religions. Paris. 1-8, 1889-96.

Revue des revues. Paris. 1-50,1876-1925.

Revue des traditions populaires. Paris. 1-34, 1886-1919. Superseded by **Revue d'ethnographie et des traditions populaires.**

Revue du clergé français. Paris. 1-103,1895-1920.

Revue du monde catholique. Paris. 1-64,1861-1925.

Revue du sud-est asiatique et de l'extrême-orient. Brussels. 1961-.

Revue encyclopédique. See Revue universelle. Paris.

Revue française de l'étranger et des colonies. Paris. 1885-1914.

Revue franco-chinoise. Association amicale franco-chinoise. Paris. 1, 1907-. 1907-15 as the association's Bulletin.

Revue de géographie commerciale. See Société de géographie commerciale de bordeaux.

RGI-----Revue géographique internationale. Paris. 1-28, no 1-326,1876-1903.

Revue hebdomadaire. Paris. 1892-1939.

RIC-----Revue indochinoise. Hanoi. 1,1893-.

Revue maritime et coloniale. Paris. no 1-202, 1861-1914; n.s. no 1-236, 1920-39.

Revue nationale chinoise. Shanghai. 1, 1929-. Suspended jan-june 1938.

Revue orientale et américaine. Paris. 1859-99. Title and ser vary.

Revue politique et parlementaire. Paris. 1,1894-

Revue scientifique. Paris. 1863-1954-.

Revue universelle. Paris. 1891-1905. To 1900 as Revue encyclopédique.

Rheinische missionsgesellschaft. Barmen, germany. Berichte. 1,1828/30-. Vol 1-8 (1829/30-36/37) as Jahresbericht.

R-WAW-----Rheinisch-Westfälische akademie der wissenschaften.

Rider's review. London. 1, 1905-. Title varies as

follows: 1-58.2 and 63-75.5 as Occult review; 58.3-62 London Forum.

RSO-----Revista degli studi orientali. Roma. 1, 1907-.

Rocznik orjentalistyczny. Krakow. 1,1914/15-.

Rome Pontifica universita gregoriana. Studia missionalia. 1, 1943-.

Royal anthropological institute of great britain and ireland. London. Journal. 1, 1871-. Proceedings. 1965-.

Royal geographical society. London. Proceedings. 1-22,1855/57-77/78; n s. 1-14, 1879-92. See also Geographical magazine and Geographical journal publ by the society.

JRASB-----Royal asiatic society of bengal. See Asiatic society of bengal.

JRAS-----Royal asiatic society of great britain and ireland. Journal. London. 1-20, 1834-63; n.s. 1-21, 1864-89; 1889-. Transactions. London. 1-3, 1827-33. Superseded by Journal. Publications of branches o the RAS are as follows:

JBBRAS-----Bombay branch. See under Asiatic society of bombay.

China branch. Shanghai. Transactions. 1-6,1847-59. Journal, see North China branch.

JHKBRAS-----HK branch. HK. Journal. 1,1960/61-.

JMBRAS -----Malayan branch. Singapore. Journal. 1, 1923-. Supersedes the Straits branch.

JNCBRAS-----North China Branch. Shanghai. Journal. 1-2, 1858-60; n.s. 1, 1864-. Vol 1 as Shanghai literary and scientific society journal. 1886-95 as the China branch, Journal.

JSBRAS-----Straits branch. Singapore. Journal. 1-86, 1878-1922. Superseded by the Malayan branch.

BROMA-----Royal ontario museum of archaeol-

224

ogy. See under Toronto. Royal ontario museum.

Royal society of new zealand. Wellington. **Transactions and proceedings.** 1,1868-.

Rupam. Calcutta. 1920-30. Superseded by the Indian society of oriental art. **Journal.**

Rythmes du monde. Lyons. April, 1946-.

RDR-----Ryukoku daigaku ronshu; the journal of ryukoku univ.

S.E.T.; structure et évolution des techniques. Association pour l'étude des techniques. .Paris. 1, 1949-.

Saeculum; jahrbuch für universal geschichte. Freiburg, 1, 1950-.

Saturday review of literature. NY. 1925-1973.

SSP-----**Schafer sinological papers.** Berkeley, calif. Numbered ser. Appeared irregularly. By Edward H. Schafer.

Schweitzerische gesellschaft der freunde ostasiatische kultur. See Schweitzerische gesellschaft für aisenkunde.

MSGFOK-----Schweitzeriche gesellschaft für asienkunde. Founded 1939 as above and changed to asienkunde in1947. **Mitteilungen.** St. gall. 1-8,1937-46. Superseded by Asi**atische studien.**

Science catholique. Paris. 1-20,1886-1906.

Sciences religieuses. See under Paris. École pratique des hautes études.

SR/SR-----Sciences religieux/studies in religion. Waterloo, ont. Wilfrid laurier univ. 1,1971-.

'Scientia,' revista di scienza. Bologna. 1,1907-.

Scientifiic monthly. Washington, etc. 1-85,1915-1957. Merged into **Science.**

SCCM-----**Selections from china mainland magazines.** HK. No 1,1955-.

SPRCM-----**Selections from peoples republic of china magazines.** HK American consulate general. Publ quarterly. jan/mar 1974-sept 1977.

Seminarium kondakovianum. See under Belgrade.

Seminars für orientalische sprachen. See under Berlin. Universität.

SES-----**Senri ethnological studies.** Natl museum of ethnology, senri, expo park, suita, osaka. Appear irregularly.

Shanghae almanac for 1854 (1855) and miscellany. Shanghai. 1851-62. Subtitle varies. See also **Shanghai miscellany.**

Shanghai literary and scientific society. **Journal.** 1, 1858. First vol of the **Journal** of the North china branch of the royal asiatic society.

Shanghai miscellany. 1-2, 1834-57. 1853-56 included in **Shanghae almanac.** 1857 publ sep.

Siam respository. Bangkok 1-6, 1869-74.

Siam society. Bangkok. **Journal.** 1,1904-.

BUA-----Shanghai. Université de l'aurore. **Bulletin.** 1909-.

SJ-----**Silliman journal.** Dumaguete city. Silliman univ. 1, jan 1954-.

Sinica; zeitschrift für chinakunde und china forschung. Frankfurt 1-17, 1926-42. Suppl to **Chinesischer blätter für wissenschaft und kunst.**

Sinica-sonderausgabe. Frankfurt a.m., 1934.

SAR-----**Sino-american relations.** Taipei. College of chinese culture. Publ quarterly. 1, spring 1975-.

SIJ-----**Sino-indian journal.** Santiniketan, bengal. 1,1947-.

SIS-----**Sino-indian studies.** Santiniketan, bengal. 1,1944-.

Sino-indica. Calcutta university. Paris 1, 1927-

Sinologica. Basel. 1,1947-.

SAWW-----Sitzungsberichte der akademie der wissenschaften in wien. See Akademie der wissenschaften. Vienna.

Social action. Boston, chicago. 1,1935-.

SSM-----Social science and medicine. Oxford. 1, apr 1967-.

Société d'acupuncture. Paris. **Bulletin.** 1, 1950-

BMSAP-----Société d'anthropologie de paris. **Bulletin et mémoires.** 1860-.

Société d'émulation de roubaix. **Mémoires.** 1868-1931.

Société d'ethnographie. **Actes.** See **Ethnographie.**

BSEIS-----Société des études indochinoises de saigon. **Bulletin.** 1-71, 1883-1923; n.s. l, 1926-.

Société de géographie. Paris. **Comptes rendus.** 1882-99. Continued in **Géographie.**

Société de géographie commerciale de bordeaux. **Bulletin.** 1874-1939. Title varies as **Revue de géographie commerciale.**

Société de géographie de l'est. Paris. **Bulletin.** 1-35,1879-1914.

Société des études japonaises, chinois, tartares et indo-chinois. See Société sinico-japonaise. Paris.

Société finno-ougrienne. See Suomalais-ugrilanen seura.

Société française d'histoire de la médecine. Paris. **Bulletin,** 1902-42. Superseded by **Histoire de la médecine.**

BSAB-----Société royale belge d'anthropologie et de préhistoire de bruxelles. **Bulletin.** 1, 1882-.

ASAB-----Société royale d'archéologie de bruxelles. **Annales.** 1,1887-.

Société sinico-japonaise. Paris. 1877 -? as a section of the société d'ethnographie, Paris; also as Société des études japonaises, chinoises, tartares et indo-chinoises and Société sinico-japonaise et océanienne. Sometimes cited as Comité sinico-japonaise. **Annuaire.** 1873-. **Mémoires.** 1-10, 1873-91; n.s. 1-22,1892-1901? Vol 5-9 of the first ser has title of **Lotus.**

SSCRB-----Society for the study of chinese religions. **Bulletin.** Boulder. Univ of colorado. Dept of religious studies. First 3 issues titled SSCR **Newsletter** (1 mar 1976, 2 july 1976, 3 feb 1977). With vol 10 (fall 1982) title changed again, to **Journal of chinese religions,** abbrev **JCR** with vol 13/14 (1985/86) publ was relocated at Saskatoon. Univ of Saskatchewan.

Sociological bulletin. Bombay, delhi. 1, 1952-.

Sources orientales. Publisher's series. Paris. 1, 1959-. Irregularly publ; each vol has its own title.

Southeast asia; an international quarterly. Carbondale. Southern illinois univ. Center for vietnamese studies. 1.1/2, winter-spring 1971-.

SEAJT-----South east asia journal of theology. Singapore. 1, 1959-.

SEAJSOCSCI-----Southeast asian journal of social science. Singapore, univ of Singapore, 1, 1972-.

SWJA-----Southwestern journal of anthropology. Albuquerque. 1,1945-.

BMFEA-----Stockholm. Ostasiatiska samlingama (Museum of far eastern antiquities) **Bulletin.** 1,1929-.

Structure et évolution des techniques. See **S.E.T.**

Studi e materiali di storia delle religioni. Rome universati. Rome. 1,1925-.

SM-----Studia missionalia. See under Rome.

SS-----Studia serica. West china union university. Chinese cultural studies research institute. 1,1940-. See also **Monograph** ser A, no 1, 1947- ; B, no 1,1942-.

226

Studia taiwanica. Taipei. 1, 1956-. Catalogued under T'ai-wan yen-chiu.

Studien zur frühchinesischen kulturgeschichte. Antwerp. 1-2,1941-43.

SCEAR-----Studies in central and east asian religions. Journal of the seminar for buddhist studies, copenhagen and aarhus univ. Annual. 1,1988-.

SCR-----Studies in comparative religion. Bedfont, engl. 1. winter 1967-. Publ quarterly.

Studies on buddhism in japan. International buddhist society. Tokyo. 1-3,1939-41.

Studio; an illustrated magzine of fine and applied art. London. 1, 1893-. **London Studio.** NY.1931-3. american ed.

Studium generale; zeitschrift für die einheit der wissenschaften zusammenhang ihrer begriftsbildungen und forschungs methoden. Berlin 1,1947-.

Sunday at home. London. 1854-1940.

Suomalais-ugrilainen seura. Helsingfors. **Aika kau skirja (Journal)** 1,1886-.

SCMM-----Survey of China mainland magazines. See **Selections from china. . .**

SCMP-----Survey of china mainland press. HK. American consulate general. 1, nov 1,1950-.

Symbolon; jahrbuch für symbolforschung. Basel 1, 1960-.

Synthesis; the undergraduate journal in the history and philosophy of science. Boston. 1. 1., winter 1972.

TJT-----Taiwan journal of theology. Taiwan theological college, taipei. 1, mar 1974-.

Tamkang journal. See **Tan-chiang hsüeh-pao.**

TR-----Tamkang review. Taipei. Tamkang college of arts and sciences .Graduate institute of western languages and literature. 1. 1, apr 1970-.

Tan-chiang hsüeh-pao. Taipei. 1958-. English title **Tamkang journal.**

TS-----T'ang studies. 1,1983-.

TaoRes-----Taoist resources. Annual. 1.1 and 1.2,1988, peralta, new mex. With 2.1, june 1990, relocated to indiana univ.

Technology review. MIT boston. 1,1899-.

TJR-----Tenri journal of religion. Research institute for religion. Tenri, japan. 1, 1955-.

TheE&TheW-----The east and the west. A quarterly review for the study of missions. Westminster, s. w. engl. Publ by Society for the propagation of the faith in foreign parts. 1-25,1903-27.

Theologische literaturzeitung. Leipzig, berlin. 1, 1876-.

Theosophical forum. NY, point loma, calif. 1-70, 1889-95; ser 2,1,1929-.

Theosophical path; illustrated monthly. Point loma, calif. 1-45,1911-1935. Merged into **Theosophical forum.**

THM-----T'ien hsia monthly. Shanghai. 1-12,1935-41.

Tohogaku ronshu. Tokyo. 1,1954-.

BMFJ-----Tokyo. Maison franco-japonaise. Bulletin. 1-15, 1927/29-47; n.s. 1, 1951-. 1-5, titled **Bulletin seri-française.**

TBMRD-----Tokyo. Toyo bunko (oriental library). Research department. Memoirs. No. 1,1926-.

BROMA-----Toronto. Royal ontario museum. Art and archaeology division. Bulletin. No 1-27,1923-58. Supersedes the Royal ontario museum of archaeology which publ no 1-23.

TP-----T'oung pao. Leiden. 1-10,1890-99; ser 2,1, 1900-.

TBMRD-----Toyo bunko, memoirs of the research department. See under Tokyo.

Toyo gakuho. Tokyo. 1, 1911-.

TUAS-----Toyo university asian studies. Tokyo. 1,1961; 2,1964.

Transactions. See under the name or location of the organization.

Travel. NY. 1,1901-. Title varies. Combined with Holiday in 1931.

TM-----A travers le monde. Paris. 1-20, 1895-1914.

Tri-quarterly. Evanston, illinois. 1-6,1958-64; n.s. no 1,1964-.

Tribus; veroeffentlichungen des linden-museum. (Stuttgart. Museum für laend- und völkerkunde) Heidelberg. N.f. 1, 1951-. Vol 1 issue as Jahrbuch des linden museum.

TJ-----Tsinghua journal of chinese studies. Peking, taipei. 1-12, 1924-37; n.s. 1,1956-. Supersedes Tsing-hua journal. Pekinq. 14,1919-? Chinese title, Ch'ing-hua hsüeh-pao.

NC-----Twentieth century. London. 1, 1877-. Title varies as follows: 1877-1900 as Nineteenth century; a monthly review; 1901-50 as Nineteenth century and after.

Unitas. Quarterly review of the arts and sciences. Manila. Univ of santo tomas. 1, 1922-.

United asia; international magazine of asian affairs. Bombay. 1, 1948-.

QJCA-----United States. Library of congress. Quarterly journal of current acquisitions. 1,1943-.

United States. National museum. Bulletin. 1,1875-. Proceedings. 1,1878-.

United states. National museum. Smithsonian institution. Annual report of the board of regents. 1,1846-. From 1884, there are two ann vol, the second of which is Report of the u.s. national museum.

USJPRS-----United states joint publications research service.

Universitas; zeitschrift für wissenschaft, kunst und literatur. Stuttgart. 1, 1946-.

University of ceylon review. Colombo. 1,1943-.

JOR-----University of madras. Madras. Journal. 1-14, 1928-42. Continued in two sections as follows: A-Humanities. 15-18,1943-46; B-Science. 15, 1943-. Annals of oriental research. 1, 1936- Vol 1 as Journal of Oriental research.

UPUMB-----University of Pennsylvania museum bulletin.
See under Pennsylvania. State University. University museum.

VBS-----Vajra bodhi sea. Monthly publication of the orthodox buddha dharma in america. San francisco, sino-american buddhist association. 1.1, apr 1970-

Variétés sinologiques. Shanghai, taipei. 1-66, 1892-1938.

Verhandlungen. See under the name of the institution, organization, congress, etc.

Veröffentlichungen aus dem königlichen museum für völkerkunde. See under Berlin, Staatliche museem.

VBA-----Visva-bharati annals. Santiniketan, india. No. 1,1945-

Visva-bharati bulletin. Calcutta. 1, 1924-.

VBQ-----Visva-bharati quarterly. Calcutta. 1-8,1923-32; n.s. 1,1935-.

Voice of Buddhism. Buddhist missionary society. Kuala lumpur. 1, 1964?-.

Le voile d'isis. Paris. 1-?,1890-?, 2e sér, 2, (?) 3e sér, 3, no 1-56, 1910-14.

Walters art gallery. Baltimore. **Journal.** 1, 1938-

Warburg and courtauld institutes. **Journal.** See under London. University.

Welt des orients: wissenschaftliche beiträge zur kunde des morgenländes. Wuppertal. 1, 1947-

Die weisse fahne. Pfullingen. 1-16, 1920-35;?-.

Der weltkreis. Berlin. 1-3, 1929-33.

Der wendepunkt im leben und im leiden. Zürich, Leipzig. 1, 1923- Vol 1 lacks date.

WMM-----Wesleyan Methodist magazine. See **Methodist magazine.**

West and East. Taipei 1, 1956- Also listed under chinese title **Chung mei yüeh-k'an.**

JWCBorderReS-----West china border research society. Chengtu. **Journal.** 16, 1922/23-45. 12-16 issued in two series, General and natural sciences, A and B respectively.

West china missionary news. Chengtu. 1, 1899-.

WBKKGA-----**Wiener beiträge zur kunst- und kulturgeschichte asiens.** Verein der freunde asiatischen kunst und kultur in wien. Vienna. 1-11, 1926-37?

Wiener völkerkundliche mitteilungen. Vienna 1, 1953-. Issuing agent varies.

WZKM-----**Weiner zeitschrift für die kunde des morgenländes.** Wien. Orientalisches institut. ,1 1887-. Suspended 1919-23; 1942-47.

Wiener zertschrift für die kunde sud- und ostasiens und archiv für indische philosophie. Indologische institut, univeritaet wien. Vienna, 1, 1957-.

Wirkendes wort. Paedagogischen verlag schwann. Duesseldorf. 1, 1966-.

Wissen und leben. See **Neue schweizer rundschau.**

Wissenschaftliche annalen der gesammten heilkunde. Berlin. 1-30, 1825-34. 1-24 (1825-32) as **Litterarische annalen der gesammten heilkunde.** Superseded by the **Neue wissenschaftliche. . .**

Die woche, modern illustrierte zeitschrift. Berlin. 1, 1899-.

Worcester, mass. Art museum. **Annual.** 1, 1935/36.

World mission. London 1966-.

Worldmission. NY. 1, 1950-.

World's chinese students' journal. Shanghai. 1-8, 1906-14.

Yana. Zeitschrift für buddhismus und religiöse kultur auf buddhistischen grundlage. München; utting am ammersee.

Yoga; international journal on the science of yoga. Bulsar, india. 1, 1933-.

Yoga; internationale zeitschrift für wissenschaftliche yoga-forschung. Harburg-wilhelmsburg 1, 1931-?

Yoga series. Madanapalli, india. 1, 1956-.

YE-----**Young East.** Tokyo. 1-8, 1925-41. Superseded by **Young east; Japanese buddhist quarterly.**

Young East. Tokyo. 1-15, 1952-66.

Zalmoxis, revue des études religieuses. Paris. 1, 1938.

Zeitschrift. See also the names or locations of issuing organizations.

Zeitschrift für bauwesen. Berlin. 1-81, 1851-1931.

ZBK-----**Zeitschrift für bildende kunst.** Leipzig. 1-65, 1866-1932.

Zeitschrift für buddhismus. Half-title for the following item: **Zeitschrift für buddhismus und vervandt gebiete.** Munich. 1 -9,1914-31.

Zeitschrift fur die historische theologie. Leipzig. 1-45, 1831-75.

ZE-----Zeitschrift für ethnologie. Berliner gesellschaft für anthropologie, ethnologie und urgeschichte. Berlin. 1, 1869-. May include **Verhandlungen** of the society.

Zeitschrift für geopolitik in gemeinschaft und politik. Bad godesberg, etc. 1, 1924-. 1924-1955 as **Zeitschrift für geopolitik.**

Zeitschrift für menschenkunde und zentralblatt für graphologie. Heidelberg, vienna, etc. 1, may 1925-. Title varies. Cited in text as **Zeitschrift für menschenkunde.**

ZMK-----Zeitschrift für missionskunde and religionswissenschaft. Allgemeiner evangelisch-protestantischen missionsverein. Berlin. 1-54, 1886-1939.

ZMR-----Zeitschrift für missionswissenschaft und religionswissenschaft. Institut für missionswissenschaftlich forschungen. Munster 1, 1911-. Title varies.

Zeitschrift für religionspsychologie. Güterslah. 1-11, 1928-37.

Zeitschrift für religions-psychologie. Leipzig. 1-6, 1907-13.

ZRGG-----Zeitschrift für religious- und geistes-geschichte. Marburg. 1, 1948-.

Zeitschrift für systematische theologie. Berlin 1, 1923-.

Zeitschrift für theologie und kirche. Tübingen. 1891-1917; 1920-38; 1950-.

Zeitwende; die neue furche. Hamburg, etc. 1,1925-.

Zinbun. Memoire of the research institute for humanistic studies, kyoto university, kyoto. Publ annually in english, each issue containing usually 1 or 2 art and tsl. Postwar ser, 1, 1957-.

Zygon

Index of Authors, Editors, Compilers, Translators, Photographers, Illustrators as cited in the 1985 bibliography, Publications through 1980

A

Abe, Masao 217R, 263R
Abegg, Emil 228L, 254L
Abel, Karl 4R, 232L
Abel, M. 154L
Abel-Rémusat, J.P. 83R, 88R, 137R, 182L, 192R, 201R, 204R, 228L, 229R, 230L, 231R
Abraham, A. 236L, 238L
Adam, Maurice 117L, 247R
Adams, Charles J. 2R, 4L
Adams, P.R. 239L
Addison, James Thayer 68L, 164R
Addiss, Stephen 217R, 243R
Adolph, Paul E. 112R
Ahern, Emily M. (also Martin, Emily) 68R, 105R, 125L, 133R, 155R, 164R, 172R, 173R, 174R, 175L
Aigran, René 24L
Aijmer, Göran 68R, 73L, 108L, 117L, 125L, 155R
Aiyaswamisastri, N. 201R
Akanuma, Chizen 180L
Akatsuka, Kiyoshi 19R
Akiyama, Satoko 217R
Akiyama, Terukazu 247L
Alabaster, Chaloner 143L
Albrecht, Ardon 155R
Aldington, Richard 28L
Ales, A. d' 14R
Alexander, Edwin 83R, 137R, 164R
Alexander, Frances 28R
Alexander, G.G. 83R
Alexander, Mary 28R
Alexandre, Noël 125L, 164R
Alexandrian, Sarane 246L, 251L
Alexéiev, Basil M. 112R
Allan, C. Wilfrid 67L, 228L, 255R
Allan, Sarah 19R, 105R
Allen, C.F.R. 38L, 121R
Allen, G.W. 117L
Allen, Herbert J. 38L, 49R, 94L, 204R
Allen, Rodney F. 150L, 155R
Allen, William Dangaix 246R
Alley, Rewi 121R, 123R, 238L, 247R, 249R
Almeder, Robert 63R

Amberley, Viscount John Russell 49R, 84L
Amélineau, E. 68R, 164R
American Theological Library Association 2L
Ames, Delano 28L
Amicus 74R, 111R
Amiot [Amyot] J.J.M. 11L, 94L, 99R
Amore, Roy C. 268R
Ampère, J.J. 79L, 182L, 204R
Amritananda, Bhikku 261L
Andersen, Poul 88R, 99R
Anderson, A.E. 84L
Anderson, Eugene N. jr 73L, 105R, 108L, 112R, 117L, 133R, 160L, 175L
Anderson, J.N.D. 50L
Anderson, Marja L. 73L, 105R, 108L, 133R, 160L, 175L
Anderson, Mary 99R, 112R, 117L, 155R
Anderson, Norman 57L
Andersson, John Gunnar 19R, 29L, 121R, 131R
Andrews, Allan A. 201R, 213L
Andrews, F.H. 243R
Anesaki, Masaharu 180L, 192R, 264L
Anon. 56R, 125R, 204R, 265R
Ansari, Zafar Ishaq 57R, 81R
Ansley, Delight 5L
Antonini, P. 42L
Arai, S. 217R
Archer, John C. 5L
Arène, Jules 250L
Arlington, L.C. 25L, 49R, 68R, 74R, 125L, 127R, 133R, 164R, 236L
Armstrong, Alexander 49R
Armstrong, E.A. 125L
Armstrong, R.C. 213R
Arthaud, Claude 78L, 234R, 242R, 247R
Ashen, Ruth Nanda 65R
Ashmore, William 49R, 63R
Ashton, Leigh 239L
Asmussen, J.P. 10R
Association for Asian Studies 2L
Atkins, Gaius G. 49R
Atkinson, F.M. 27R, 106R, 115L
Atkinson, R.W. 34L

Benton, Warren G. 182R
Benz, Ernst 2L, 164R, 259L, 261L
Bergen, Paul D. 50L, 121R
Bergeron, Marie-lna 50L, 99R
Bergesen, Albert James 150L, 172R, 174L
Berk, William R. 101L, 134L
Berkowitz, M.J. 2L, 160R, I75L
Berle, A.A. 5L
Berling, Judith A. 42L, 62L, 100L, I64R, 263R
Bernard, Henri (see Bernard-Maître, Henri) 165L
Bernard-Maître, Henri 2L, 5R, 18L, 125L, 125R, 165L, 263R
Berndt, Manfred 165L, 175L
Berry, Gerald L. 5R
Berthier, Brigitte 91L, 175L
Bertholet, Alfred 7R, 13L
Bertholet, René 42L, 64L, 201R
Berthrong, John 62L, 165L, 263R
Bertolucci, Guiliano 99L, 121R
Berval, René de 205L
Besse, J. 84L
Bester, John 243R
Bettelheim, P. 13L
Beurdeley, M. 100L
Beyerhaus, Peter 68R, 165L
Beylié, L. de 237L
Bhattacharya, D.M. 194R
Bhattacharya, Vidhushekhara 186R
Biallas, Franz Xaver 50L, 74R
Bidens 68R
Bieg, Lutz 50L
Bielefeldt, Carl 193R, 217R
Bielenstein, Hans 38L, 127R
Bigelow, William Sturgis 190L, 214R
Bilsky, Lester James 19R, 74R
Binyon, Laurence 233R
Birch, Cyril 25R, 139R
Birnbaum, Raoul 186R, 201R, 254L, 257R, 266L
Biroen, H. 100L
Bischoff, Friedrich A. 137R, 186R, 254L
Bishop, Carl W. 20L, 50L, 125R
Bishop, D.F. 247R
Bishop, Donald H. 150L, 175L
Bisson, T.A. 84L
Biswas, D.K. 198R
Bitton, W. Nelson 117R
Black, W.H. 131R
Blacker, Carmen 23R, 46R, 225R
Blake, Brian 161L
Blake, C. Fred 117R, 160R
Blake, Lady 143L

Blanchard, Rafael 131R
Blanchet, C. 259L
Bleeker, C.J. 13R
Bleichsteiner, R. 226L
Bliss, Edwin Munsell 51R, 83L
Block, Marguerite 79L
Blodget, Henry 68R, 74R, 112R
Blofeld, John C. (see also Chu Ch'an) 79L, 100L, 105L, 112R, 187R, 205L, 213R, 217R, 218L, 219L, 226L, 231R, 250L, 254L, 259L, 262R, 266L
Bloom, Alfred 5R, 201R, 205L, 213R
Blyth, R.H. 218L
Blythe, Wilfrid 143L, 160R
Boardman, Eugene P. 38L
Bock, Carl 250L
Bocking, Brian 62L, I65L
Bodde, Derk 5R, 10R, 20L, 25R, 42L, 42R, 84L, 85L, 108L, 110R, 117R, 131R, 138L, 183L, 201R, 202L, 220L
Boehmer, Thomas 100L
Boerschmann, Ernst 5R, 29L, 68R, 73L, 236R, 237L, 238L, 238R, 239L, 249L, 250L
Bohlin, B. 251L
Boin, Sara A. 193R, 201R
Boltz, William G. 20L, 117R
Bone, Charles 105R, 108L, 117R
Bonin, Charles-Eudes 249L, 251L
Bonmarchand, G. 100L
Bönner, Theodor 5R
Bonsall, Bramwell S. 50L, 79L
Boodc, P. 247R
Boone, William J. I8L, I9L
Borch, A. von 74R
Borel, Henri 84L, 254R
Borsig, Tet 241R
Bose, Phanindra Nath 205L
Böttger, Walter 29L, 131R, 243L
Bouchot, J. 238L
Bouillard, Georges 74R, 75L, 108L, 117R, 121R, 122L, 234R, 236L
Bouïnais, Lt-Col Albert M.A. 5R, 68R, 165L
Boulting, William 228R
Bourgeois 11L
Bourne, Frederick S.A. 75L, 99L, 122L
Bowen, A.J. 238L
Bowers, John Z. 133R
Bowker, John 150L
Bownas, Geoffrey 55R
Bowring, John 18L, 194R
Box, Ernest 108L

Gundry, R.S. 250R
Gurij, P. 202L
Gützlaff, Charles (see also Philosinensis, pseud)
8R, 97R, 109R, 114L, 123L, 139R, 144R, 18OR,
183R, 250R, 259R
Gynz-Rekowski, George v. 32L, 44R

H

H. 250R
E.M.H. 53L
Haar, Hans 3L, 167L
Haas, Hans 54L, 85R, 195L, 208L, 215R
Hackenbroich, H. 76L
Hackin, J. 27R, 106R, 115L, 233R
Hackmann, Heinrich F. 8R, 44R, 80R, 95L, 99L,
134R, 18OR, 183R, 188L, 202L, 214L, 215R,
226R, 227L, 256L, 259R, 264R
Haden, R.A. 139R
Hadl, Richard 244R, 251R
Haenisch, Erich 65L, 208L
Hager, Joseph 21R, 112L, 167L
Hail, William J. 8OR
Haimes, Norma 3L, 134R, 220R
Hakayama, Noriaki 195L
Hakeda, Yoshito S. 54R, 101R, 187R, 188L, 202R,
214L, 215R
Halwachs, Maurice 21R
Hales, Dell R. 139R
Hall, Ardelia R. 32L
Hall, David A. 214L
Hall, David L. 91R
Hall, Isaac 6R, 79R
Hall, Manly P. 97R, 134R, 266R
Hallade, Mlle M. 252R
Hamilton, Clarence H. 3L, 148L, 183R, 188R,
195L, 202R, 215R, 259R
Hanayama, Shinsho 3L
Hand, Wayland D. 108R
Haneda, A. 208L
Haneda, T. 181L
Hang, Thaddeus T'ui-chieh 65L, 157L
Hankey, Rosalie 109R, 130R, 139R, 161L
Hannay, Alastair 52L, 64R
Hansen, Chad 54R, 65L
Hansford, S. Howard 32L, 248L
Happel, Julius 8R, 76L
Happer, A.P. (see also Inquirer, pseud) 76L, 76R,
123L
Harding, D.E. 8R
Harding, H.L. 105R, 11OL, 128L
Hardon, John A. 54R, 80R, 167L

Hardwick, Charles 8R, 54R, 80R, 183R
Hardy, Jacques 70L, 227L
Hardy, Spence 186R
Hare, William L. 8R, 81L, 95R
Harlez, Charles de 8R, 12R, 21R, 26R, 39R, 44R,
76R, 85R, 89L, 89R, 128L, 134R, 148L, 167L,
183R, 188R, 192R, 195R, 202R, 205R, 214L,
215R, 227L, 229R
Harper, Donald J. 21R, 44R, 128L
Harrassowitz, Otto (publishers) 3L
Harrell, C. Stevan 44R, 70L, 106R, 112L, 157L
Harrison, James P. 39R, 151R
Hart, Henry H. 114L
Hart, Virgil C. 54R, 80R, 95L, 249R
Hartman, Joan M. 32L
Hartman, L.O. 9L
Hartman, Sven S. 24R, 173R
Hartner, Willy 32L, 134R
Harvey, E.D. 106R, 130R
Harvey, Pharis 154L, 171R, 177L
Hashimoto, Hokei 195R, 258L
Hasumi, Toshimitsu 220R
Hattori, U. 54R
Havret, Henri 18R, 195R, 208L, 243R
Hawkes, David 139R
Hawkridge, Emma 9L
Hay, Eldon R. 45L
Haydon, A. Eustace 112L, 183R, 258L
Hayes, Helen M. 256L
Hayes James W. 70R, 73R, 123L, 124R, 144R,
161L, 161R, 162L, 164L
Hayes, L. Newton 32L, 112L, 249R
Hazai, Georg 188R, 195R
Headland, Isaac T. 9L, 70L, 106R, 11OL, 126L
Hébert-Stevens, François 78L, 234R, 242R, 247R
Hecken, Joseph van 227L
Heckethorn, Charles W. 144R
Hée, Louis van 208L, 235L
Hefter Jonny 78R, 106R
Hegel, Robert E. 99L, 114L, 119L, 120R, 130R,
157L, 159L
Heidenreich, Robert 32L, 76R
Heifetz, Harold 220R
Heigl, Ferdinand 76R
Heiler, F. S9L 85R, 167L
Heine-Geldern 35R
Hejzlar, Josef 251R
Held, AxeI 215R
Held, Mans Ludwig 3L
Hell, H. (E. de T.) 119L
Helm, B. 18R

Ju, I-hsiung 22R, 45R
Julien, Stanislas 85L, 87L, 89R, 96L 132R 140L, 141L, 181L, 214L, 216L, 229L, 229R, 231R, 256R, 265R
Jundt, Pierre 8L
Jung, C.G. 91L, 100L, 102L, 105L, 165R
Jung, Hwa Yol 65R
Jung, Moses 60L, 171R
Jurji, Edward J. 9R, 38R, 54R, 55R, 8OR, 81L, 175L

K

K. 77L
Kadowaki, J.K. 221R, 264R
Kagan, Richard C. 130R
Kahlenbach, Gerhard 86L, 88L
Kaizuka, Shigeki 55R
Kaler, Grace 33L
Kalff, L. 70L
Kaltenmark, Maxime 9R, 10R, 18R, 22R, 27L, 33L, 39R, 55R, 8OL, 81L, 81R, 86L, 89R, 92L, 93L, 95L, 97R, 102L, 106R, 126L, 132R, 135L, 176L
Kaltcnmark, Odile 9R
Kalupahana, David J. 202R, 221R
Kalvodová, Dana 140L
Kamiya, Joe 4R, 224R
Kamm, John Thomas 74L, 161R
Kamstra, J.H. 209L
Kran, Arthur 97L, 112L
Kanaoka, Shoko 196L, 252L
Kanaoka, Shuyu 235L
Kandel, Barbara 39R, 81L, 89R, 152L
Kanellakos, Demetri P. 4R, 224R
Kang, Thomas H. 3L, 55R
K'ang Yu-wei 64L, 148R
Kao, Chü-hsün 40L, 114R
Kao, Frederick F. 65R, 135L
Kao, John J. 65R, 102R, 135L
Kao, Lu 152L
Karetzky, Patricia Eichenbaum 244R
Karlgren, Bernhard 22R, 31L, 33L, 86L, 133L, 196L
Karmay, Heather 246R, 264R
Karpinski, Leszek M. 3L
Karutz, Richard 232R, 254R
Kasugai, Shinya 209L
Kasulis, Thomas P. 221R
Kato, Bunno 189L
Kato, Joken 45R
Katschen, Leopold 144R

Katsumata, Shunkyo 202R
Kaufman, Walter 9R
Kaul, T.N. 248L
Kawamura, Leslie S. 184L
Kawase, Kozyun 188L
Kaye, Lincoln 121L, 126L, 157R, 160L
Keeble, F.H.G. 240R
Keep, Ann E. 234L
Keightley, David N. 22R, 23L, 128R
Kelen, Betty 55R
Kellett, E.E. 55R
Kelley, Charles F. 240R, 244R
Kemp, Craig Charles 240R, 254R
Kemp, E.G. 55R, 123R, 249R
Kendall, Carlton 135L
Kendall, Elizabeth 249R
Kennedy, J. 209L
Kennelly, M. 7L, 106L
Kenney, Edward H. (see Herbert, Edward, pseud)
Kenny, P.D. 9R
Kermadec, H. de 106R
Kern, Maximilian 9R, 55R, 81L
Kershaw, F.S. 246R
Kervyn, Joseph 135L
Kesson, John 9R, 145L
Keupers, John 93L, 157R
Kiang, Alfred 227L, 261R
Kiang, Chao-yuan 23L, 132R
Kiang, Kang-hu 9R, 65R
Kidd, Samuel 9R
Kielhorn, F. 196L
Kierman, Frank A. jr 23R
Kim, Chewon 22L, 27L, 167L
Kim, Ha Tai 45R, 55R, 62R
Kim, Won-yong 240R
Kim, Young Oon 9R, 55R, 81L, 184L
Kimm, Chung Se 196L
Kimura, Eiichi 40L, 45R, 55R, 81L, 86L, 95L
Kimura, Mitsutaka 196L
Kimura, Ryukan 209L
King, Frank H.H. 155L
King, Gordon 248L, 253R
King, Winston L. 81L, 168L, 184L, 214L, 264R
King, Yung-hua 252L
Kingman, S. 240R
Kingsmill, Thomas W. 27L, 86L
Kishi, Masakatsu 248R
Kitagawa, Joseph M. 9R, 147R, 15OR, 152L, 193L, 209L, 262L
Kiyota, Minoru 184L, 196L
Klaproth, Julius H. 81L, 82L, 95L, 126L, 184L,

256

Parry, D. 98L
Parsons, James B. 41L, 203L, 209R
Partington, J.R. 103R
Pas, Julian 93R, 158L, 169R, 174R, 198R, 214R
Pasternak, Burton 71R, 158L, 173R
Patai, R. 12L, 169R
Paton, William 12L
Paul, Diana 41L, 190R, 198R, 211L, 216R, 267L
Paulus, A. 165L
Pauthier, Georges 46R, 82L, 87L, 95L, 96L, 169R, 265R
Pauthier, M. 96L
Pavie, Théodore 12L, 98L, 141L, 257L
Payne, Henry 250L
Payne, Jessie E. 249R
Peachey, Paul 219R
Peake, Cyrus H. 58L, 149L
Peat, Wilbur D. 243R
Peeters, Hermes 12L, 58L, 82L, 107L, 185L
Peeters, Jan 41L
Peisson, J. 12L
Peisson, Z. 58L
Pelerzi, E. 249L
Pelliot Paul 8R, 27L, 32R, 34R, 37R, 47L, 75L, 87L, 89L, 90L, 96L, 103R, 146L, 168L, 176R, 18OL, 181L, 181R, 187R, 188L, 190R, 198R, 201L, 205R, 211L, 228R, 230R, 233R, 241R, 245L, 246L, 247L, 251R, 252L, 252R, 253L, 255L
P'eng, Tso-chih 74L, 77R
Pennick, Nigel 74L
Penniman, T.K. 34R
Peri, Noël 227R, 250R, 255L
Pernitzsch, Max G. 12L
Perrault, J. 241R
Perrot, Albert 58L, 77R, 149L
Perry, Elizabeth J. 41L, 146L
Perry, John 29L
Perry, John W. 28L, 77R
Perzynski, Friedrich 12L, 34R, 112L, 247R
Petech, Luciano 230R
Peterson, Mark A. 74L
Petit, J.A. 12L
Petrie, James B. 115R, 158L
Petrucci, Raphael 234L, 245L, 247R, 252L
Petterson, Richard 34R, 158L
Petty, Orville A. 147R
Petzold, Bruno 198R, 203R, 214R, 222R
Peyraube, Alain 82L, 107L, 176R
Pfizmaier, August 90L, 98L, 103R, 115R, 126R
Pfleiderer, Otto 12L

Pham-Quynh 58L
Phelps, Dryden Linsley 249R
Philastre, P.L.F. 90L
Phillips, Catherine A. 233R
Phillips, Edith C. 12L
Philo 19L
Philosinensis (pseud of Charles Gützlaff, q.v.) 250R
Pichon, Jean-Charles 24L, 34R
Pickering, W.A. 146L
Pike, E. Royston 66L
Pillai, A. Balakrishna 211L
Pimpaneau, Jacques 131L, 141L
Pinto, Justine 4R
Pitcher, P.W. 71R
Piton, Charles 185L, 211L
Plaks, Andrew H. 28L, 141L
Planchat, Edmond 58L
Plath, J.H. 24L
Playfair, G.M.H. 77R, 146L
Plopper, Clifford H. 141L
Plumer, James M. 35L, 241R, 252L, 254L
Png, P'oh-seng 162R
Podgorski, Frank 46R, 58L, 87L, 9OL
Pohlman, W.J. 66L, 255L
Poirot 11L
Pokora, Timoteus 103R, 211R
Politella, Joseph 58L, 82L
Polonyi, P. 247L
Pommeranz-Liedtke, Gerhard 35L, 107L, 245L
Pomonti, M. 31R
Pompignan, R.H. Assier de 184R
Pönisch-Schoenwerth, Ch. 221L, 234L
Pontynen, Arthur 35L, 87R, 169R, 241R, 265R
Poon, Eddie K.K. 2L
Poon, Walter 248R
Poor, Robert 241R, 255L
Poore, Major R. 71R, 169R, 170R
Pope, John A. 247L
Popenoe, Cris 3R
Porkert, Manfred 12L, 35L, 98L, 136L, 141L
Porter, Henry D. 11OR, 146L, 149L
Porter, Lucius C. 74L, 149L
Poseck, Helena von 71R, 141R
Pott, William S.A. 46R, 58L, 66L
Potter, Charles Francis 58L, 87R
Potter, Jack M. 71R, 74L, 111L, 131L
Pourvoirville, Albert de (see also Matgioï, pseud) 146L
Power, Eileen 115R
Pratt, James Bissett 185L, 203R, 260L

Index of Publications 1981 through 1990

Dove, Victor 89
Dragan, Raymond 2
Drake, F. S. 105
Drège, Jean-Pierre 93, 184, 191
Duan, Wenjie 188
Duara, Prasenjit 86
Dubs, Homer H. 31, 41, 60, 96
Dudbridge, Glen 8, 85, 86, 99
Dumoulin, Heinrich 160
Duquenne, Robert 174
Durrant, Stephen W. 35
Durt, Hubert 2, 14, 134, 177
Düssel, Reinhard 41, 122
Dutt, S 152
Dy, Manuel B. 41, 122
Dzo, Ching-chuan 184

E

Eastman, A. C. 8
Eastman, Lloyd E. 84
Eastman, K. W. 167, 187
Eber, Irene 41, 59
Eberhard, Wolfram 14, 26, 53
Ebert, Jorinde 26, 67, 77, 110
Ebrey, Patricia 17, 41, 53, 91
Ecsedy, I. 95
Edde, Gérard 59
Edkins, Joseph 31, 168
Edsman, Carl-Martin 5, 106
Edwards, Richard 175, 178, 181
Eichhorn, W. 60
Eide, Elling O. 60
Eilert, Hakan 157
Eisenstadt, Shmuel N. 129
Eitel, Ernest J. 8, 59, 134
Elder, Gove 53, 116, 122
Eliade, Mircea 17, 20
Eliasberg, Danielle 14, 174, 184
Elisabeth, Anna Gronvald 178
Elisséev, M. S. 175
Elliott, Alan J. A. 116
Elvin, Mark 31, 35, 41
Emmons, Charles F. 83
Endres, Günther 73, 99
Engelhardt, Ute 79, 97
Eno, Robert 20, 41, 86
Enomoto, Fumio 139, 147
Eoyang, Eugene 143
Epping, Franz M. 160
Eracle, J. 157

Erkes, Eduard 8, 54
Eskildsen, Steve 77, 79
Etiemble, René 41, 196
Evans, John Karl 54, 122
Ewing, W. Carroll jr. 106
Exner, Walter 2
Eynon, Matthew 122, 131

F

Fabian, Ludwig 136, 160
Fairbank, Wilma 27
Falkenhausen, Lothar von 54, 60
Fang, Li-t'ien 168
Fang, Litian 135
Faure, Bernard 143, 147, 160, 161
Faure, David 89, 103, 116
Favre, Benoit 103
Fei, He 183
Feibleman, James K. 106
Fellows, Ward J. 5, 41, 62
Feng, Youlan 41, 161
Fengère, Laure 188
Ferguson, John 131
Ferrar, Anne 190
Feuchtwang, Stephen 14, 84, 106
Fielde, Adele M. 8
Fischer-Schreiber, Ingrid 62
Fisher, John F. 161
Fisher, Tom 8
Fitch, R. F. 54
Flinn, Frank K. 15
Foh, Chang Pat 88, 116
Fong, Lo Yik 59, 116
Fong, Mak Lau 103, 116
Fong, Mary H. 54, 86
Fong, Peng-Khuan 54, 89
Fong, Pong-khuan 116
Fong, Wen 176, 188
Fontein, Jon 26
Forte, Antonino 31, 35, 136, 141, 147, 155, 184, 186
Fossati, Gildo 175
Fourcade, Francois 188
Fowler, K. 21
Fowler, Vernon K. 96
Fracasso, Riccardo 8, 23, 93
Franck, Frederick 161
Franke, Herbert 122, 139, 147, 169
Franke, Wolfgang 41, 62, 116
Franz, Rainer von 31, 148

G

H

278

M

X

Y

Z

MONOGRAPHS OF THE ASSOCIATION FOR ASIAN STUDIES

   *   Indicates publication is available.